Social Studies

my World

INTERACTIVE

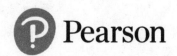 Pearson

Boston, Massachusetts   Chandler, Arizona
Glenview, Illinois   New York, New York

Pearson would like to extend a special thank you to all of the teachers who helped guide the development of this program. We gratefully acknowledge your efforts to realize the possibilities of elementary Social Studies teaching and learning. Together, we will prepare students for college, careers, and civic life.

Cover: Hill Street Studios/Eric Raptosh/Getty Images

Credits appear on pages R79–R81, which constitute an extension of this copyright page.

ISBN-13: 978-0-328-97311-8
ISBN-10: 0-328-97311-4

5 19

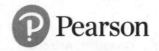

Program Authors

Dr. Linda B. Bennett
Faculty, Social Studies Education
College of Education
University of Missouri
Columbia, MO

Dr. James B. Kracht
Professor Emeritus
Departments of Geography and
 Teaching, Learning, and Culture
Texas A&M University
College Station, TX

Reviewers and Consultants

Program Consultants

ELL Consultant
Jim Cummins Ph.D.

Professor Emeritus,
Department of
 Curriculum, Teaching,
 and Learning
University of Toronto
Toronto, Canada

**Differentiated Instruction
Consultant**

Kathy Tuchman Glass
President of Glass
 Educational Consulting
Woodside, CA

Reading Consultant
Elfrieda H. Hiebert Ph.D.

Founder, President and
 CEO, TextProject, Inc.
University of California
 Santa Cruz

Inquiry and C3 Consultant

Dr. Kathy Swan
Professor of Curriculum
 and Instruction
University of Kentucky
Lexington, KY

Academic Reviewers

Paul Apodaca, Ph.D.

Associate Professor,
 American Studies
Chapman University
Orange, CA

Warren J. Blumenfeld, Ed.D.

Former Associate
 Professor, Iowa State
 University, School
 of Education
South Hadley, MA

Dr. Albert M. Camarillo

Professor of History,
 Emeritus
Stanford University
Palo Alto, CA

Dr. Shirley A. James Hanshaw

Professor, Department
 of English
Mississippi State
 University
Mississippi State, MS

Xiaojian Zhao

Professor, Department
 of Asian American
 Studies
University of California,
 Santa Barbara
Santa Barbara, CA

Teacher Reviewers

Mercedes Kirk
First grade teacher
Folsom Cordova USD
Folsom, CA

Julie Martire
Teacher, Grade 5
Flocktown Elementary School
Long Valley, NJ

Kristy H. Spears
K-5 Reading Specialist
Pleasant Knoll Elementary School
Fort Mill, SC

Kristin Sullens
Teacher, Grade 4
Chula Vista ESD
San Diego, CA

Program Partner

Campaign for the Civic Mission of Schools is a coalition of
over 70 national civic learning, education, civic engagement,
and business groups committed to improving the quality and
quantity of civic learning in American schools.

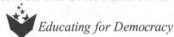

CAMPAIGN FOR THE CIVIC MISSION OF SCHOOLS
Educating for Democracy

🌐 Geography Skills Handbook

✏️ Writing Workshop

🔍 Using Primary and Secondary Sources

GO ONLINE FOR
DIGITAL RESOURCES

 eTEXT

 VIDEO

- **Field Trip Video**
  Redwood National
  and State Parks:
  Giants in the Mist

- **Digital Skill
  Practice**
  Read Inset Maps
  Summarize

 AUDIO

Rap About It lyrics
and music

 INTERACTIVITY

- **Big Question
  Activity**
  How does
  geography affect
  the way we live?

- **Quest
  Interactivities**
  Quest Kick Off
  Quest Connections
  Quest Findings

- **Lesson
  Interactivities**
  Lesson Introduction
  Lesson Review

GAMES

Vocabulary Practice

ASSESSMENT

Lesson Quizzes and
Chapter Tests

The BIG Question How does geography affect the way we live?

Chapter 2

Americans and Their History

GO ONLINE FOR DIGITAL RESOURCES

 eTEXT

 VIDEO

- **Field Trip Video** Our History
- **Digital Skill Practice** Compare and Contrast Interpret Timelines

 AUDIO

Rap About It lyrics and music

INTERACTIVITY

- **Big Question Activity** How have people stayed the same or changed during our history?
- **Quest Interactivities** Quest Kick Off Quest Connections Quest Findings
- **Lesson Interactivities** Lesson Introduction Lesson Review

GAMES

Vocabulary Practice

ASSESSMENT

Lesson Quizzes and Chapter Tests

The BIG Question How have we stayed the same or changed during our history?

GO ONLINE FOR
DIGITAL RESOURCES

eTEXT

VIDEO

- **Field Trip Video**
Redwood National
and State Parks:
Giants in the Mist

- **Digital Skill
Practice**
Read Inset Maps
Summarize

AUDIO

Rap About It lyrics
and music

INTERACTIVITY

- **Big Question
Activity**
How does
geography affect
the way we live?

- **Quest
Interactivities**
Quest Kick Off
Quest Connections
Quest Findings

- **Lesson
Interactivities**
Lesson Introduction
Lesson Review

GAMES

Vocabulary Practice

ASSESSMENT

Lesson Quizzes and
Chapter Tests

The BIG Question How does geography affect the way we live?

GO ONLINE FOR
DIGITAL RESOURCES

 eTEXT

VIDEO

- **Field Trip Video**
  Our History
- **Digital Skill Practice**
  Compare and Contrast
  Interpret Timelines

 AUDIO

Rap About It lyrics
and music

INTERACTIVITY

- **Big Question Activity**
  How have people stayed the same or changed during our history?
- **Quest Interactivities**
  Quest Kick Off
  Quest Connections
  Quest Findings
- **Lesson Interactivities**
  Lesson Introduction
  Lesson Review

GAMES

Vocabulary Practice

ASSESSMENT

Lesson Quizzes and
Chapter Tests

The **BIG** Question How have we stayed the same or changed during our history?

GO ONLINE FOR
DIGITAL RESOURCES

 eTEXT

 VIDEO

- **Field Trip Video**
  New Jersey Today
- **Digital Skill
  Practice**
  Categorize
  Compare Points
  of View

 AUDIO

Rap About It lyrics
and music

 INTERACTIVITY

- **Big Question
  Activity**
  What is special
  about American
  government?
- **Quest
  Interactivities**
  Quest Kick Off
  Quest Connections
  Quest Findings
- **Lesson
  Interactivities**
  Lesson Introduction
  Lesson Review

 GAMES

Vocabulary Practice

ASSESSMENT

Lesson Quizzes and
Chapter Tests

The BIG Question What is special about American government?

Chapter 4

The Nation's Economy

The **BIG** Question How does the economy meet our needs and wants?

Chapter 5
Regions: The Northeast

GO ONLINE FOR
DIGITAL RESOURCES

📖 **eTEXT**

▶ **VIDEO**

- **Field Trip Video**
  New York City: A
  City of Sights and
  Variety
- **Digital Skill
  Practice**
  Cause and Effect
  Work in Teams

🔊 **AUDIO**

Rap About It lyrics
and music

👆 **INTERACTIVITY**

- **Big Question
  Activity**
  How does where
  we live affect who
  we are?
- **Quest
  Interactivities**
  Quest Kick Off
  Quest Connections
  Quest Findings
- **Lesson
  Interactivities**
  Lesson Introduction
  Lesson Review

 GAMES

Vocabulary Practice

 **ASSESSMENT**

Lesson Quizzes and
Chapter Tests

The BIG Question How does where we live affect who we are?

Chapter 6 Regions: The Southeast

GO ONLINE FOR DIGITAL RESOURCES

 eTEXT

 VIDEO

- **Field Trip Video**
  Mobile Bay: A Busy Port with Natural Beauty
- **Digital Skill Practice**
  Use a Road Map and Scale
  Distinguish Fact From Opinion

 AUDIO

Rap About It lyrics and music

👆 INTERACTIVITY

- **Big Question Activity**
  How does where we live affect who we are?
- **Quest Interactivities**
  Quest Kick Off
  Quest Connections
  Quest Findings
- **Lesson Interactivities**
  Lesson Introduction
  Lesson Review

🎮 GAMES

Vocabulary Practice

☑ ASSESSMENT

Lesson Quizzes and Chapter Tests

The BIG Question How does where we live affect who we are?

Rap About It! Down in the Southeast 217

Quest Save the Southeast Coast! 220

GO ONLINE FOR DIGITAL RESOURCES

 eTEXT

▶ VIDEO

- **Field Trip Video**
  Nebraska: Great Land for Farming
- **Digital Skill Practice**
  Give an Effective Presentation
  Identify Main Idea and Details

◀)) AUDIO

Rap About It lyrics and music

👆 INTERACTIVITY

- **Big Question Activity**
  How does where we live affect who we are?
- **Quest Interactivities**
  Quest Kick Off
  Quest Connections
  Quest Findings
- **Lesson Interactivities**
  Lesson Introduction
  Lesson Review

🎮 GAMES

Vocabulary Practice

☑ ASSESSMENT

Lesson Quizzes and Chapter Tests

The BIG Question How does where we live affect who we are?

GO ONLINE FOR DIGITAL RESOURCES

 eTEXT

 VIDEO

- **Field Trip Video**
  Arizona: A Sunny Wonderland
- **Digital Skill Practice**
  Latitude and Longitude
  Draw Inferences

🔊 AUDIO

Rap About It lyrics and music

👆 INTERACTIVITY

- **Big Question Activity**
  How does where we live affect who we are?
- **Quest Interactivities**
  Quest Kick Off
  Quest Connections
  Quest Findings
- **Lesson Interactivities**
  Lesson Introduction
  Lesson Review

🎮 GAMES

Vocabulary Practice

☑ ASSESSMENT

Lesson Quizzes and Chapter Tests

The **BIG** Question

How does where we live affect who we are?

Chapter 9 Regions: The West

GO ONLINE FOR DIGITAL RESOURCES

eTEXT

VIDEO

- **Field Trip Video**
  San Diego: The City by the Sea
- **Digital Skill Practice**
  Make Generalizations
  Analyze Images

AUDIO

Rap About It lyrics and music

INTERACTIVITY

- **Big Question Activity**
  How does where we live affect who we are?
- **Quest Interactivities**
  Quest Kick Off
  Quest Connections
  Quest Findings
- **Lesson Interactivities**
  Lesson Introduction
  Lesson Review

GAMES

Vocabulary Practice

ASSESSMENT

Lesson Quizzes and Chapter Tests

The BIG Question How does where we live affect who we are?

Quests

Ask questions, explore sources, and cite evidence to support your view!

Maps

Where did this happen? Find out on these maps in your text.

Maps continued

Maps continued

Graphs and Charts

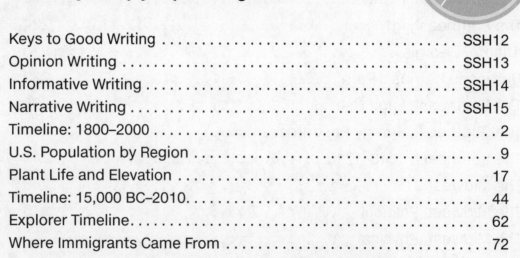

Find these charts, graphs, and tables in your text. They'll help you pull it together.

Graphs and Charts continued

Primary Sources

Read primary sources to hear voices from the time.

Primary Sources continued

Primary Sources continued

People to Know

Read about the people who made history.

Citizenship

Biographies Online

Abigail Adams

John Adams

Samuel Adams

Elsie Allen

James Armistead

Benedict Arnold

Clara Barton

Delilah Beasley

James Beckwourth

William Bradford

Chaz Bono

Sergey Brin

Jerry Brown

Edmund Burke

Juan Rodriguez Cabrillo

Tani Gorre Cantil-Sakauye

Christopher "Kit" Carson

César Chávez

Louise Clappe

Thomas Clifford

Christopher Columbus

Hernán Cortés

Juan Crespi

Charles Crocker

Hallie M. Daggett

Juan Bautista de Anza

Pedro Menéndez de Avilés

Samuel de Champlain

Gaspar de Portolá

Antonio Lopez de Santa Anna

María Angustias de la Guerra

Bartolomeu Dias

John Dickinson

Walt Disney

Frederick Douglass

Ralph Waldo Emerson

William Fargo

First Lady Pat Nixon

Wong Chin Foo

Benjamin Franklin

John C. Fremont

Eric Garcetti

John Gast

Nathan Hale

Alexander Hamilton

John Hancock

Kamala D. Harris

Mary Ludwig Hays

Patrick Henry

Mark Hopkins

Henry Hudson

Dolores Huerta

Collis P. Huntington

Anne Hutchinson

Daniel Inouye

Joseph James

Thomas Jefferson

Hiram Johnson

Billie Jean King

Martin Luther King, Jr.

King Charles III

King George III

Dorothea Lange

Lewis and Clark

Abraham Lincoln

Henry Wadsworth Longfellow

Lord Dunmore

Ferdinand Magellan

Wilma Mankiller

James Wilson Marshall	José Julio Sarria
John Marshall	Dalip Singh Saund
Biddy Mason	Junípero Serra
Louis B. Mayer	Roger Sherman
Sylvia Mendez	Sir Francis Drake
Metacom	John Drake Sloat
Harvey Milk	Jedediah Smith
James Monroe	John Smith
Samuel Morse	Leland Stanford
John Muir	John Steinbeck
Nicolás José	Levi Strauss
Thomas Paine	John A. Sutter
Charley Parkhurst	Mary Tape
William Penn	Archie Thompson
William Pitt	Tisquantum
James K. Polk	Harriet Tubman
Prince Henry the Navigator	Mariano Guadalupe Vallejo
Edmund Randolph	Earl Warren
Ronald Reagan	Mercy Otis Warren
Paul Revere	George Washington
Sally Ride	Henry Wells
Jackie Robinson	Phillis Wheatley
Eleanor Roosevelt	Narcissa Whitman
Sarah Royce	Mary Williams
Bernarda Ruiz	Roger Williams
Sacagawea	Sarah Winnemucca
Haym Salomon	John Winthrop
Deborah Sampson	Jerry Yang

Skills

Practice key skills in these skills lessons.

Powers of State Government | Shared Powers | Powers of National Government

Literacy Skills

Critical Thinking Skills

Map and Graph Skills

Skills continued

Skills Online

Gold found at Sutter's Mill. Calif beco

:48 1849 1850

Analyze Cause and Effect

Analyze Costs and Benefits

Analyze Images

Ask and Answer Questions

Classify and Categorize

Compare and Contrast

Compare Viewpoints

Conduct Research

Create Charts

Deliver an Effective Presentation

Distinguish Fact and Opinion

Distinguish Fact from Fiction

Draw Conclusions

Draw Inferences

Evaluate Media Content

Generalize

Generate New Ideas

Identify Bias

Identify Main Idea and Details

Interpret Cultural Data on Maps

Interpret Economic Data on Maps

Interpret Graphs

Interpret Physical Maps

Interpret Timelines

Make Decisions

Predict Consequences

Resolve Conflict

Sequence

Solve Problems

Summarize

Use and Interpret Evidence

Use Latitude and Longitude

Use Primary and Secondary Sources

Use the Internet Safely

Work in Cooperative Teams

Welcome to Your Book!

Your Worktext is made up of chapters and lessons.
Each lesson starts with pages like this.

> **Look for these words as you read.**

> **Words with yellow highlight are important social studies words. The sentence with the word will help you understand what the word means.**

Lesson 1 — America and Europe

INTERACTIVITY

Participate in a class discussion to preview the content of this lesson.

Vocabulary

archeologist
artifact
hunter-gatherer
agriculture
culture
colony
enslaved
tradition

Academic Vocabulary

claim
create

Primary Source

W. Langdon Kihn traveled North America and painted American Indians during the early 1900s.

Unlock The BIG Question

I will know that when Europeans and American Indians met, their cultures changed forever.

Jumpstart Activity

Divide into teams and imagine you are planning a trip to Mars. You know it is in space, but you don't know anything about its environment. Figure out what you would take with you and why. Discuss how you feel about going to an unknown place so far away.

People have lived in the Americas for thousands of years. To learn more about them, we read the work of historians. Historians are people who study the past. They want to learn about how people have changed and how people have stayed the same.

The First Americans

Historians work with archeologists to learn about the distant past. An **archeologist** (ar kee AHL uh jihst) studies artifacts and sites to learn about ancient people. An **artifact** is an object made by humans. Artifacts can tell a lot about the history of a place and its people.

Most historians and archeologists believe the first Americans came from Asia. Thousands of years ago, land connected Asia and the Americas. Small groups of hunters crossed over from Asia. Others may have come by water. They were **hunter-gatherers**. They hunted animals and gathered plants for food. Over a very long time, these early people spread across North and South America.

From the far north to the tip of South America, from the Pacific to the Atlantic, many different American Indian groups lived on the land. Then agriculture changed the way many of these people lived. **Agriculture** is the planting and growing of crops for food. Once people learned how to farm, they could stay in one place.

The environment affected the cultures they developed. A **culture** is the way of life of a group of people. In some places, American Indians farmed and lived in small villages or large communities. In others, groups moved from place to place. They followed the animals they hunted. Across the Americas, American Indians created a wide range of cultures. Today, their descendents value those ancient traditions.

1. ☑ **Reading Check** **Identify** and circle the place on the map that allowed people to cross from Asia to North America. How do you know by looking at the map?

_____

_____

Word Wise

Suffixes The suffix *–er* can mean someone who does something: *make, maker; write, writer.* Circle a word on this page that ends with *–er* and means someone who does something.

Routes of First Americans

ASIA
Beringia Land Bridge
Bering Strait
NORTH AMERICA
PACIFIC OCEAN
ATLANTIC OCEAN
SOUTH AMERICA

0   2,000 mi
0   2,000 km

LEGEND
☐ Dry land in the past
☐ Glacier in the past
→ Route of first people

> **Reading Checks will help you make sure you understood what you read.**

Your Turn!

Flip through your book with a partner.

1. Find the start of another lesson.
   What do you see on the page?

This book will give you a lot of chances to figure things out. Then you can show what you have figured out and give your reasons.

The Quest Kick Off will tell you the goal of the Quest.

Watch for Quest Connections all through the chapter.

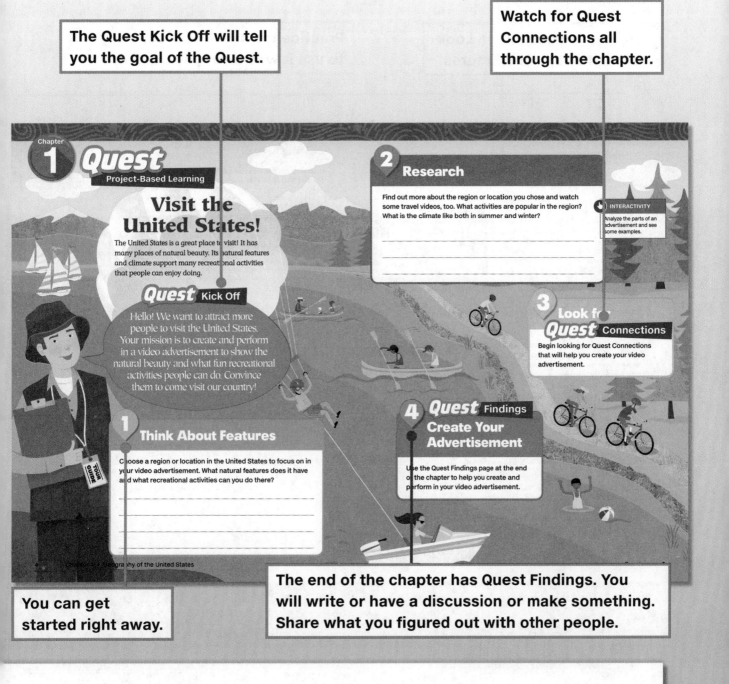

Chapter 1

Quest
Project-Based Learning

Visit the United States!

The United States is a great place to visit! It has many places of natural beauty. Its natural features and climate support many recreational activities that people can enjoy doing.

Quest Kick Off

Hello! We want to attract more people to visit the United States. Your mission is to create and perform in a video advertisement to show the natural beauty and what fun recreational activities people can do. Convince them to come visit our country!

1
Think About Features

Choose a region or location in the United States to focus on in your video advertisement. What natural features does it have and what recreational activities can you do there?

2
Research

Find out more about the region or location you chose and watch some travel videos, too. What activities are popular in the region? What is the climate like both in summer and winter?

INTERACTIVITY

Analyze the parts of an advertisement and see some examples.

3
Look for *Quest* Connections

Begin looking for Quest Connections that will help you create your video advertisement.

4
Quest Findings
Create Your Advertisement

Use the Quest Findings page at the end of the chapter to help you create and perform in your video advertisement.

4 Chapter 1 · Geography of the United States

You can get started right away.

The end of the chapter has Quest Findings. You will write or have a discussion or make something. Share what you figured out with other people.

2. Find two words with yellow highlight. What page are they on?

3. Find another Reading Check. What does it ask you to do?

4. Find another Quest. What is it called?

Learn to use important skills.

Read the explanation. Look at all the text and pictures.

Practice the skill. You'll be ready to use it whenever you need it.

Critical Thinking Skills

Give an Effective Presentation

Suppose everyone in your class had to give a social studies presentation. Some of the presentations would be interesting. Others might not be. What is the difference between an effective, interesting presentation and a weaker one? You might guess it is the subject matter. Think again. You can make anything interesting if you know how to prepare. To give an effective and interesting presentation, follow the steps below:

1. **Know your audience.** It is always important to keep in mind the people to whom you'll be speaking. How much do they already know?

2. **Identify your main idea and state it at the beginning and the end.** Your audience needs to know right away what your presentation is about. Otherwise, they may lose interest. It is also good to remind people of your main idea before you close.

▶ **VIDEO**
Watch a video about how to give an effective presentation.

3. **Choose your details carefully.** Your audience does not need to know every single detail you found in your research. Choose only the most interesting details that support your main point.

4. **Speak clearly and loudly.** A presenter who mumbles or whispers will quickly frustrate his or her listeners. Audiences lose interest when they cannot hear clearly. Also make sure you look up at your audience from time to time when you make a presentation.

5. **Use visuals.** A visual, such as a map or picture, gives the audience something else to focus on. Using visuals is also a great way to illustrate your point.

6. **Practice before you present.** Effective presenters practice their presentations so that they feel comfortable with their material.

Your Turn!

Analyze this student's notes for a presentation about the Great Lakes. Then answer the questions.

> **Great Lakes Presentation**
>
> I am doing a presentation about the Great Lakes. My main idea is that the Great Lakes are important to the states that border them, especially Illinois, and to the port of Chicago. I will speak clearly and loudly when I present.

1. Review the steps to an effective presentation. **Identify** three things that the student is missing.

2. What do you think is the most important step to an effective presentation? **Explain** your answer.

3. Plan a presentation **explaining** something you find interesting about the Midwest. Write your notes for the presentation in the space provided. Remember to include all the steps for giving an effective presentation.

   Topic:

   Notes:

Your Turn!

Work with a partner.

1. Find another skill lesson. What skill will you learn? Talk about another time you might need that skill.

Every chapter has primary source pages. You can read or look at these sources to learn right from people who were there.

Find out what this source is about and who made it.

These questions help you think about the source.

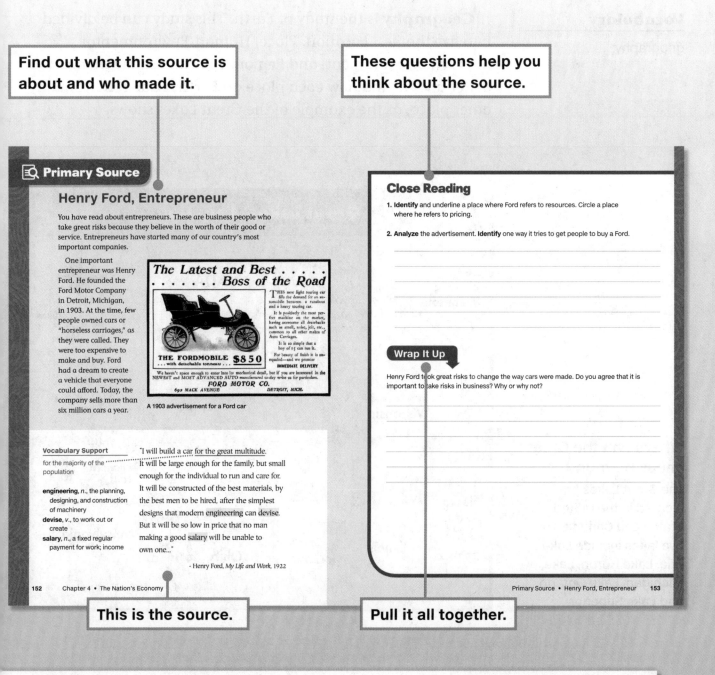

Primary Source

Henry Ford, Entrepreneur

You have read about entrepreneurs. These are business people who take great risks because they believe in the worth of their good or service. Entrepreneurs have started many of our country's most important companies.

One important entrepreneur was Henry Ford. He founded the Ford Motor Company in Detroit, Michigan, in 1903. At the time, few people owned cars or "horseless carriages," as they were called. They were too expensive to make and buy. Ford had a dream to create a vehicle that everyone could afford. Today, the company sells more than six million cars a year.

The Latest and Best . . . . Boss of the Road

THE FORDMOBILE $850
. . . with detachable tonneau . . .

FORD MOTOR CO.
692 MACK AVENUE   DETROIT, MICH.

A 1903 advertisement for a Ford car

Vocabulary Support

for the majority of the population

engineering, *n.*, the planning, designing, and construction of machinery

devise, *v.*, to work out or create

salary, *n.*, a fixed regular payment for work; income

"I will build a car for the great multitude. It will be large enough for the family, but small enough for the individual to run and care for. It will be constructed of the best materials, by the best men to be hired, after the simplest designs that modern engineering can devise. But it will be so low in price that no man making a good salary will be unable to own one..."

- Henry Ford, *My Life and Work*, 1922

152   Chapter 4 • The Nation's Economy

Close Reading

1. **Identify** and underline a place where Ford refers to resources. Circle a place where he refers to pricing.

2. **Analyze** the advertisement. **Identify** one way it tries to get people to buy a Ford.

Wrap It Up

Henry Ford took great risks to change the way cars were made. Do you agree that it is important to take risks in business? Why or why not?

Primary Source • Henry Ford, Entrepreneur   153

This is the source.

Pull it all together.

2. Find another primary source lesson in your book. What is the source about?

Geography Skills Handbook

Five Themes of Geography

Vocabulary

geography

Geography is the study of Earth. This study can be divided into five themes: Location, Place, Human/Environmental Interaction, Movement, and Region. You can use the themes to better understand how each place on Earth is different from any other place, as the example of the Great Lakes shows.

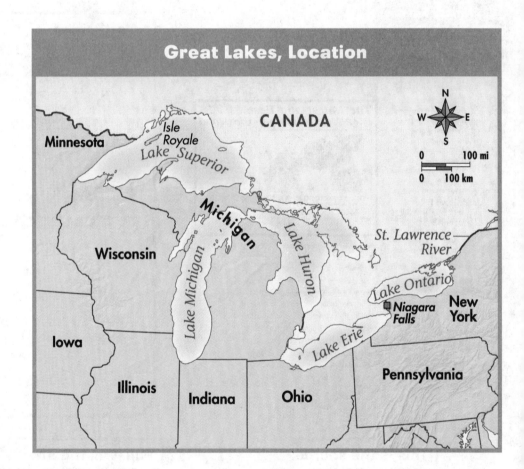

Great Lakes, Location

Where can the Great Lakes be found?

The Great Lakes are located in the United States and Canada. The five lakes include Lake Erie, Lake Huron, Lake Michigan, Lake Ontario, and Lake Superior.

Place

How is this place different from others?

The Great Lakes have 35,000 islands. The islands in Lake Superior, which is the largest of the five lakes, include Isle Royale and the Apostle Islands.

Human/Environment Interaction

How have people changed a place?

Canals are human-made waterways that are dug across land. Canals around the Great Lakes connect these lakes to other lakes and to rivers in the area. In Illinois, for example, a canal connects Lake Michigan to the Illinois River.

Movement

How has movement changed a place?

Since the Great Lakes connect to the Atlantic Ocean by the St. Lawrence Seaway, shipping is a major industry here.

Region

What is special about the region that includes the Great Lakes?

There are many natural areas where birds can nest or take shelter.

North America

Atlantic Ocean

Pacific Ocean

South America

Reading Globes

This is an image of Earth. It shows some of Earth's large landforms, called continents. It also shows Earth's large bodies of water, called oceans.

1. ☑ **Reading Check** **Identify** the two continents and the two oceans shown in this photo of Earth.

north America south America, Atlantic ocean Pacific ocean

This is a **globe**, a round model of Earth. Some globes are small enough to hold in your hands. It shows the true shapes and locations of Earth's continents and oceans.

A globe often shows two lines that divide Earth into halves. These two lines are called the prime meridian and the equator. You can see the equator on this globe.

Vocabulary

globe
hemisphere
prime meridian
equator

Earth's Hemispheres

The equator and the prime meridian divide Earth into halves called **hemispheres**. The **prime meridian** is a line drawn from the North Pole to the South Pole that passes through Europe and Africa. That line divides Earth into the Western Hemisphere and the Eastern Hemisphere.

The **equator** is a line drawn around Earth halfway between the North Pole and the South Pole. It divides Earth into the Northern and Southern Hemispheres.

Because Earth is divided two ways, it has four hemispheres.

Western Hemisphere

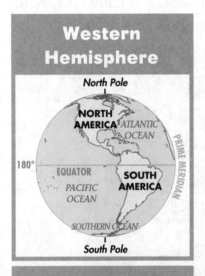

Eastern Hemisphere

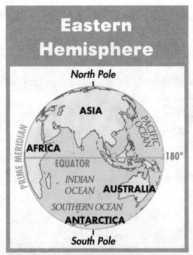

Northern Hemisphere

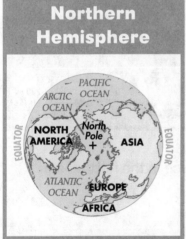

Southern Hemisphere

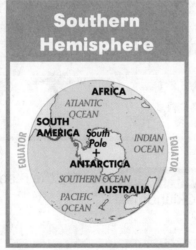

2. ☑ **Reading Check** **Identify** the two hemispheres that North America is located in.

northren and westren

3. **Identify** whether Asia is north or south of the equator.

north

Maps Show Direction

Vocabulary

compass rose
cardinal direction
intermediate direction
map scale

Maps show real directions. A **compass rose** is a symbol that shows directions on a map. There are four **cardinal directions**—north, south, east, and west. North points toward the North Pole and is marked with an *N*. South points to the South Pole and is marked with an *S*.

Look at the compass rose on the map below. In addition to showing the cardinal directions, it shows directions that are midway between them. These are the **intermediate directions**. They are northeast, southeast, southwest, and northwest.

This map shows land use in the Southwest. It is called a special purpose map and has a compass rose to show direction.

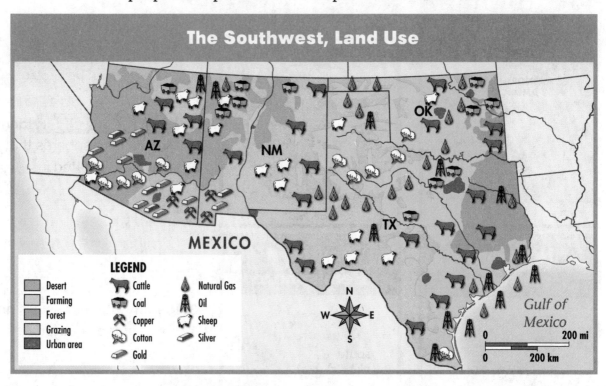

The Southwest, Land Use

LEGEND
- Desert
- Farming
- Forest
- Grazing
- Urban area
- Cattle
- Coal
- Copper
- Cotton
- Gold
- Natural Gas
- Oil
- Sheep
- Silver

MEXICO

Gulf of Mexico

0   200 mi
0   200 km

4. ☑ Reading Check **Identify** the resource in the northeast corner of Oklahoma.

It shows were everything is.

5. **Identify** the body of water that is southeast of Texas.

Gulf of Mexico.

Maps Show Distance

A map is a very small drawing of a large place. However, you can find real distances in miles or kilometers from one point to another on Earth by using a map scale. A **map scale** shows the relationship between distance on the map and distance on Earth. One way to use the scale is to hold the edge of a piece of paper under the scale and copy it. Then place your copy of the scale on the map to measure the distance between two points.

The map below shows the path of Hurricane Sandy. You can use the scale to track the miles the storm traveled.

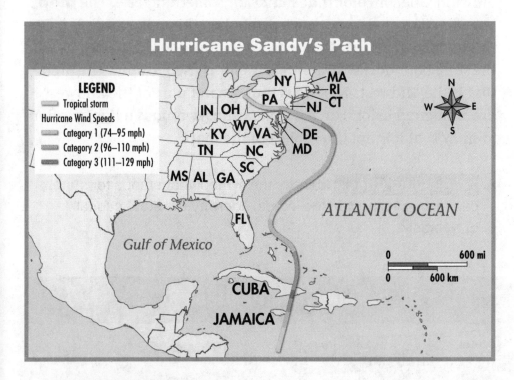

6. ☑ **Reading Check** **Identify** the country where Hurricane Sandy became a Category 3 hurricane.

Cuba

7. **Identify** about how many miles Hurricane Sandy traveled as a tropical storm, after it made landfall.

300 miles

Political Maps

Vocabulary

political map
symbol
map legend
physical map
atlas

A map is a flat drawing of all or part of Earth. It shows a place from above.

Different kinds of maps show different information. A map that shows boundaries for counties, states, or nations, as well as capital cities, is called a **political map**. This kind of map often shows major landforms and bodies of water to help locate places.

Each map has a title. The title tells you what the map is about. Maps use symbols to show information. A **symbol** is a small drawing, line, or color that stands for something else. The **map legend** or key tells what each symbol on the map stands for. On this political map, a star stands for the state capital. Lines show the state boundaries, or borders. Color is used to show the area that is the Midwest. The areas that are not part of the Midwest are a different color. For example, Pennsylvania is a lighter color to show that it is not the subject of the map.

8. ☑ Reading Check **Identify** the symbol that stands for state capital by circling it in the legend. **Identify** the state capital of Nebraska.

The Midwest, Political

Physical Maps

A **physical map** shows landforms, such as mountains, plains, and deserts. It also shows bodies of water, such as oceans, lakes, and rivers. Physical maps often show borders between states and countries to help locate these landforms. A good place to look for political and physical maps is an atlas. An **atlas** is a collection or book of maps.

The physical map of the Northeast includes labels for islands, or land that is completely surrounded by water. It also has labels for bays and capes. A bay is a body of water that is partly surrounded by land. A cape is an area of land that sticks out from the coastline into an ocean, sea, or lake. This physical map not only identifies mountains of the Northeast, it also tells you how high these mountains are.

9. ☑ Reading Check **Identify** the tallest mountain in the Northeast. **Identify** the bay that is southeast of Washington, D.C.

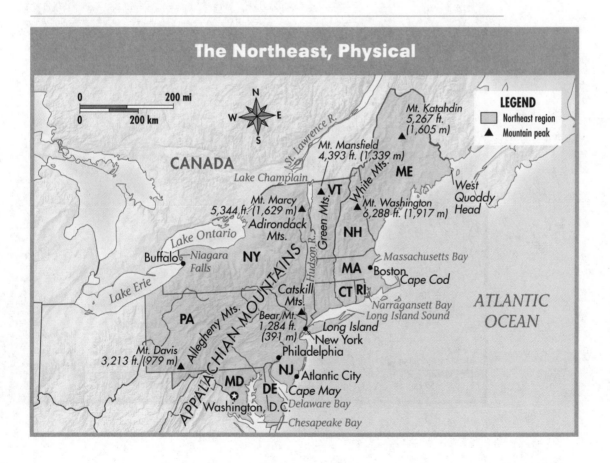

The Northeast, Physical

LEGEND
☐ Northeast region
▲ Mountain peak

Mt. Katahdin 5,267 ft. (1,605 m) ▲

St. Lawrence R.

CANADA

Mt. Mansfield 4,393 ft. (1,339 m)

Lake Champlain

White Mts.

ME

West Quoddy Head

Mt. Marcy 5,344 ft. (1,629 m) ▲

Green Mts.

VT

Mt. Washington 6,288 ft. (1,917 m) ▲

Adirondack Mts.

NH

Lake Ontario

Hudson R.

Buffalo Niagara Falls

NY

MA Boston

Massachusetts Bay

Lake Erie

APPALACHIAN MOUNTAINS

Catskill Mts.

CT RI

Cape Cod

Narragansett Bay

Long Island Sound

ATLANTIC OCEAN

Allegheny Mts.

PA

Bear Mt. 1,284 ft. (391 m) ▲

Long Island

New York

Mt. Davis 3,213 ft. (979 m) ▲

Philadelphia

NJ Atlantic City

MD

DE Cape May

Washington, D.C.

Delaware Bay

Chesapeake Bay

0 | 200 mi
0 | 200 km

N W E S

Elevation Maps

Vocabulary

elevation
grid

An elevation map shows you how high the land is. **Elevation** is height above sea level. A place that is at sea level is at the same height as the surface of the ocean's water.

Elevation maps use color to show elevation. To read this kind of map, first look at the map legend. Note that there are numbers next to each color on the map legend. The numbers show the range of elevations that each color represents. On this Pennsylvania map, dark green represents the lowest elevations. The range for dark green is between 0 and 500 feet above sea level.

10. ☑ **Reading Check** **Identify** the elevation range of the Allegheny Plateau.

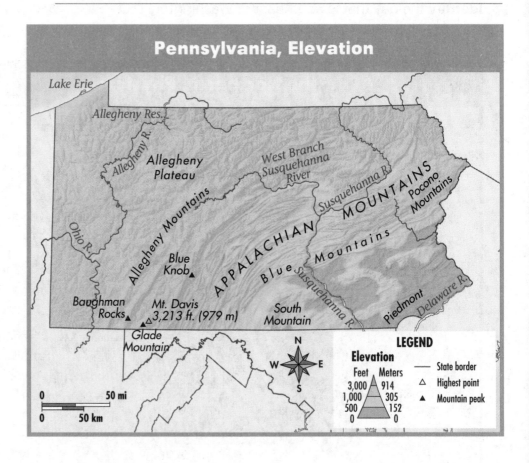

Pennsylvania, Elevation

Use a Grid

A city map shows the streets of a city. It might also show points of interest and natural features. To help locate places more easily, this city map has a grid. A **grid** is a system of lines that cross each other forming a pattern of squares. The lines are labeled with letters and numbers. These squares give every place on the map a location.

To find a specific location, the map has an index. An index is an alphabetical listing of places. The index gives the letter and number of the square where the place is located.

11. ☑ **Reading Check** **Identify** the number and letter set for Forest Park and add it to the index.

Index	
Lilburn	A4
Stone Mountain Park	B4
Forest Park	

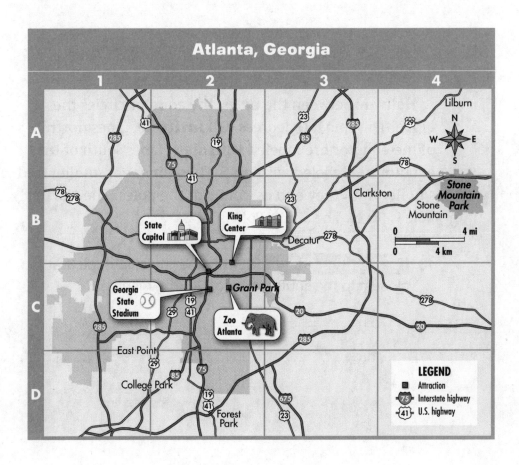

Vocabulary

degree
longitude
latitude

Use Latitude and Longitude for Exact Location

Long ago, mapmakers made a system for locating exact places on Earth. The system uses two sets of lines that form a grid around the globe. These lines are numbered in units called **degrees**.

One set of lines runs from the North Pole to the South Pole. These are lines of **longitude**. The prime meridian is labeled 0 degrees (0°) longitude. Lines of longitude are labeled from 0° to 180°. Lines east of the prime meridian are labeled with an *E*. Lines west of it are labeled with a *W*.

Longitude

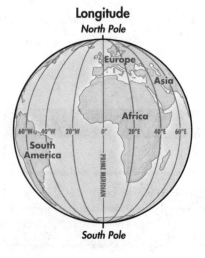

12. ☑ **Reading Check** **Identify** about how many degrees east the center of Africa is from the prime meridian.

_____

_____

Halfway between the poles, the equator circles the globe. This line is 0 degrees (0°) **latitude**. Lines north of the equator are labeled with an *N*. Lines south of the equator are labeled with an *S*. These lines get smaller and smaller until they end as points at the poles. The North Pole is 90°N. The South Pole is 90°S.

Latitude

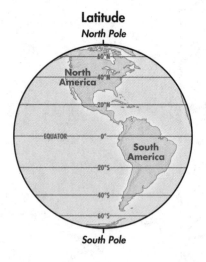

13. ☑ **Reading Check** **Identify** the line of latitude that is closest to the southern tip of South America.

_____

_____

Maps Show Events

Maps can also show events. These might be current events, such as a map of battles that are being fought between different countries, or a weather map that shows the path of a severe storm. Another example of an events map is a map of special activities at a fairground or festival.

Maps can also show events from the past, or historic events. You can use the lines of longitude and latitude on the map of explorers in the Americas to locate and compare events that happened long ago.

14. ☑ **Reading Check** **Locate** and circle the island that was explored at 80°W.

15. **Identify** and circle the explorer who traveled above 50°N.

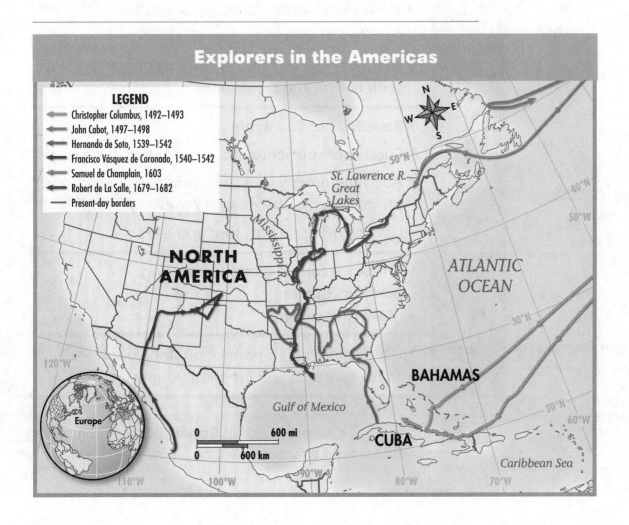

Explorers in the Americas

LEGEND
- Christopher Columbus, 1492–1493
- John Cabot, 1497–1498
- Hernando de Soto, 1539–1542
- Francisco Vásquez de Coronado, 1540–1542
- Samuel de Champlain, 1603
- Robert de La Salle, 1679–1682
- Present-day borders

NORTH AMERICA

St. Lawrence R.
Great Lakes
Mississippi R.

ATLANTIC OCEAN

Gulf of Mexico

BAHAMAS

CUBA

Caribbean Sea

Europe

0   600 mi
0   600 km

120°W 110°W 100°W 90°W 80°W 70°W 60°W 50°W
50°N 40°N 30°N 20°N

Writing Workshop

Keys to Good Writing

Good writers follow five steps when they write.

Plan	• Brainstorm to choose a topic. • Find details about the topic. • Take notes from sources. • Write down your sources. • Plan how to use the details.
Draft	• Write down all of your ideas. • Think about which ideas go together. • Put ideas that go together in groups. • Write a sentence for the introduction and write a sentence for the conclusion.
Revise	• Review what you wrote. • Check that your ideas and organization make sense. • Add time-order words and transitions (words and phrases such as *because* or *for example*). • List any more sources that you used.
Edit	• Check for correct grammar, spelling, and punctuation. • Make a final copy.
Share	• Use technology to print or publish your work. • Make sure that you list all of your sources.

1. ☑ **Reading Check Cause and Effect Explain** how not completing one of these steps might affect your writing piece.

_____

_____

_____

There are three main writing genres. They are opinion, informative, and narrative writing. They all have a different purpose.

Opinion Writing

When you write an opinion piece, you share your point of view on a topic. Your goal should be to make your point of view clear. You also need to support your point of view with evidence. Read the steps and sample sentences below to see how to write effective opinion pieces.

CityCenter in Las Vegas, Nevada, is made up of "green" buildings.

1	**Introduce the topic.** *Today, many businesses are building so-called "green" buildings that are better for the environment.*
2	**State your opinion.** *It is a good idea to build more "green" buildings, because they help conserve natural resources.*
3	**Support it with reasons, including facts and details.** *A group of new "green" buildings in Las Vegas, Nevada, were designed to save more than 50 billion gallons of water each year.*
4	**Make sure that your ideas are clear and organized to support your purpose.**
5	**Support your opinion statement with a conclusion.** *"Green" buildings will help conserve important natural resources such as water.*

2. ✓ **Reading Check** **Explain** how you support your point of view.

The cotton gin was invented by Eli Whitney in 1793.

Informative Writing

Informative writing is also called explanatory writing, because you are writing to inform, or teach, and explain a topic to your reader. Credible, or reliable, sources are very important to use in this kind of writing. Make sure to avoid plagiarism. This means using someone else's words without giving that person credit. Take notes on your sources, including what they say and where you found them. Keep in mind that a reader may know nothing about your topic. You must be the expert and be clear in what you write. Read the steps and sample sentences below.

1 | **Introduce the topic.**
The invention of the cotton gin in 1793 boosted the economy of states in the Southeast region.

2 | **Develop the topic with facts, definitions, and concrete details.**
Before the cotton gin, seeds found in cotton had to be picked out by hand. This was difficult and time-consuming labor. After the cotton gin was invented, cotton production became much faster. As a result, cotton production increased and the economy of the Southeast, which depended on cotton, expanded.

3 | **Link an example with words, phrases, or clauses.**
In 1800, cotton production in the southeastern state of Mississippi was practically nothing. In 1860, Mississippi produced about 500,000 bales of cotton.

4 | **Use precise language and content words.**
A bale is about 500 pounds of cotton bundled together.

5 | **Write a conclusion that supports your introduction.**
The invention of the cotton gin had a significant effect on the economy of the Southeast.

3. ☑ **Reading Check Draw Conclusions Discuss** with a partner why it is important to use concrete details and precise language in your writing.

Narrative Writing

When you write a narrative piece, you are telling a story. The story can be about a real or made-up event or experience. Use sensory words to show, rather than tell, the reader what happened. Sensory words describe what a person sees, hears, touches, tastes, or smells. You want the reader to be able to visualize, or see, what you are describing. The events in your narrative should be clear and connect to each other. Read the steps and sample sentences below.

1	**Introduce the story and characters.** *Javier wanted to warm up before his game, and he needed a catcher. His father had promised to help him warm up, but he was busy at work picking almonds. It was harvest time.*
2	**Use dialogue and descriptive words.** *"Dad, when will you be finished? I have to be at the field in less than an hour!" Javier yelled over the huge pile of almonds. Javier had been practicing his fastball all week because it was the championship, and he was going to pitch.*
3	**Use details to develop your writing.** *Javier's eyes lit up when he saw his father shake the last almond tree in the row and grab his mitt from the ground. They hurried to the championship game and had time for a couple practice pitches.*
4	**Strengthen your writing with sensory words.** *During the last pitch of the big game, Javier rubbed the baseball against his sleeve, noticing the strong scent of the leather from his glove. He could almost taste victory.*
5	**Write a strong conclusion to close the narrative.** *After Javier received the championship trophy, he handed it to his father. He felt he would not have won without his father's help, love, and support.*

4. ☑ **Reading Check** **Draw Conclusions Analyze** this question with a partner: Do you think the conclusion is strong and wraps up the story?

Researching on the Internet

There are many Web sites on the Internet, but not all of them can be used for research. Look for Web sites with .org, .edu, or .gov, which have reliable content. Content from sites that end in .com cannot necessarily be trusted. If you do use them, check one or two other sources from reliable sites. Also check to see who published the information and how old it is. Is there an author's name listed? Is there a date?

Using a Library Media Center to Write a Research Paper

When you are writing a research paper, it is helpful to use the resources available in your Library Media Center. To use them effectively, make sure that you:

- Use different kinds of print and digital sources and make sure they are reliable.
- Compare the information you find in sources.
- Take notes by paraphrasing or categorizing content from your sources.
- Ask a librarian for help if you are unsure what sources to use for your topic.

Follow these steps to write a research paper:

1. Write down two or three questions to guide your research.
2. Use reliable sources to do your research and answer the questions. Revise the questions if needed.
3. Based on the answers to your questions, organize your topic so that details for each part of your topic are together.
4. Write a statement about your topic based on your research and evidence. This will become your introduction.
5. Use evidence in the form of details, examples, and quotes to support your statement.
6. Use transitions and clauses to connect your ideas.
7. Write a strong conclusion that goes back to what you stated in the introduction.
8. Make a list of your sources.

5. ☑ **Reading Check** **Draw Conclusions Explain** why it is important to check more than one source when you are researching a topic.

_____

_____

_____

Using Primary and Secondary Sources

Primary and Secondary Sources

A **primary source** is one made or written by a person who witnessed an event firsthand. Primary sources can include diaries, letters, historical documents, photographs, videos, newspaper articles, and interviews. Artifacts, or objects made or used by people, are also a primary source. So are buildings and their architecture, or design. Sources can be written down, like a letter. They can also be **oral**, or spoken, like a recording of a speech or an interview.

A **secondary source** is a source written or created by someone who did not witness an event. The writer of a secondary source did not experience events he or she writes about firsthand. Most books about history are secondary sources even though their writers do much of their research using primary sources. This textbook, for example, is a secondary source. Reference books like atlases and encyclopedias are secondary sources. **Biographies**, or books about people's lives, are also secondary sources.

1. ☑ **Reading Check** **Identify** two examples of primary sources.

_____

_____

2. **Identify** and underline in the text examples of secondary sources.

primary source
oral
secondary source
biography

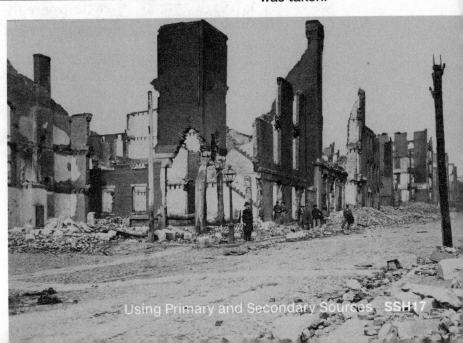

This photo of the city of Richmond, Virginia, after the Civil War is an example of a primary source since the photographer was at the event when the picture was taken.

Comparing Primary and Secondary Sources

Read these two sources of information about the San Francisco Earthquake of 1906. Then answer the question below.

Primary Source

Zellerbach: I don't think I've told you about the earthquake and fire.

Nathan: No. I'd like to hear about that.

Zellerbach: . . . I was asleep when it started to shake. I buried my head in the pillow; it felt like this was the end of the world. . . . When it finally settled down the side of the house had gone out, right alongside of my room. It opened up the side of the house, and here I was, looking up in the sky. . . . The fire was moving up . . . So our house burned down.

–Interview with Harold Zellerbach, Regional History Office, University of California Berkeley, 1971

Secondary Source

On the morning of April 18, 1906, a massive earthquake shook San Francisco, California. Though the quake lasted less than a minute, its immediate impact was disastrous. The earthquake also ignited several fires around the city that burned for three days and destroyed nearly 500 city blocks.

–National Archives, "San Francisco Earthquake, 1906"

3. ☑ Reading Check **Compare** the primary source and secondary source. How are they similar? How are they different?

_____

_____

_____

_____

How to Interpret an Artifact

The Mississippians were an American Indian group who lived in the Southeast region from about the year 700 to the year 1600. This piece of pottery was discovered by archeologists at the Etowah Indian Mounds Historic Site in Georgia. The pottery is an artifact. One way to interpret or understand an artifact is to study the object and then ask questions. Asking questions helps you understand what type of source you are looking at and what it can teach you.

Study the artifact. Then answer the questions to help you interpret it.

This artifact was found at the Etowah Indian Mounds Historic Site in northwestern Georgia.

4. ☑ Reading Check Interpret the artifact. What do you think it was used for? Describe what you see. Write two questions you have about the artifact.

_____

_____

_____

_____

5. What can you learn about the Mississippians from the artifact? Explain why the artifact is a primary source and not a secondary source.

_____

_____

_____

_____

How to Interpret a Historical Document

Just like artifacts, you can interpret historical documents by studying them and asking and answering questions. The United States Constitution is a historical document and a primary source. The constitution provides a plan for the country's government and outlines the basic rights of all American citizens. Study Article I of the United States Constitution and use it to answer the questions.

Primary Source

UNITED STATES CONSTITUTION

ARTICLE I.

SECTION 1. All legislative Powers herein granted shall be vested in a Congress of the United States, which shall consist of a Senate and House of Representatives.

SECTION 2. The House of Representatives shall be composed of Members chosen every second Year by the People of the several States ...

SECTION 3. The Senate of the United States shall be composed of two Senators from each State ... for six Years ...

—The United States Constitution, Article I, Section 1, Section 2, and Section 3, September 17, 1787

6. **Reading Check** **Identify** some questions that you have about this document.

_____

_____

_____

7. **Synthesize Identify** a secondary source connected to the Constitution.

_____

_____

_____

How to Interpret Secondary Sources

This textbook will teach you about the different regions of the United States. But it was not written by someone who was there at the time. The authors did not see or live through the events that are described. They learned by reading other people's writing and looking at primary sources, such as photographs, diaries, and letters. We can ask and answer questions to interpret secondary sources just like primary sources. Read the passage below and answer the questions that follow.

Secondary Source

Southeastern states are the leading producers of some crops. Georgia raises more peanuts, peaches, and pecans than any other state. Other main crops include fruits, corn, and soybeans. Soybeans are used to make food for livestock, vegetable oil, and other foods.

Peanuts and soybeans have not always been major Southeastern crops. In the 1700s and 1800s, the region mostly grew cotton. However, growing cotton damaged the soil. An agricultural scientist named George Washington Carver helped farmers with this problem. Carver was an expert in growing crops. While working in Alabama in the 1880s, he discovered that growing peanuts and soybeans restored the soil.

8. ☑ **Reading Check** **Explain** how peanuts and soybeans became major crops in the Southeast.

_____

_____

_____

9. Turn to a partner and **identify** one benefit to reading secondary sources about unfamiliar topics.

George Washington Carver's discoveries helped the economy of the Southeast change from growing mostly cotton to growing peanuts and soybeans.

Chapter 1

Geography of the United States

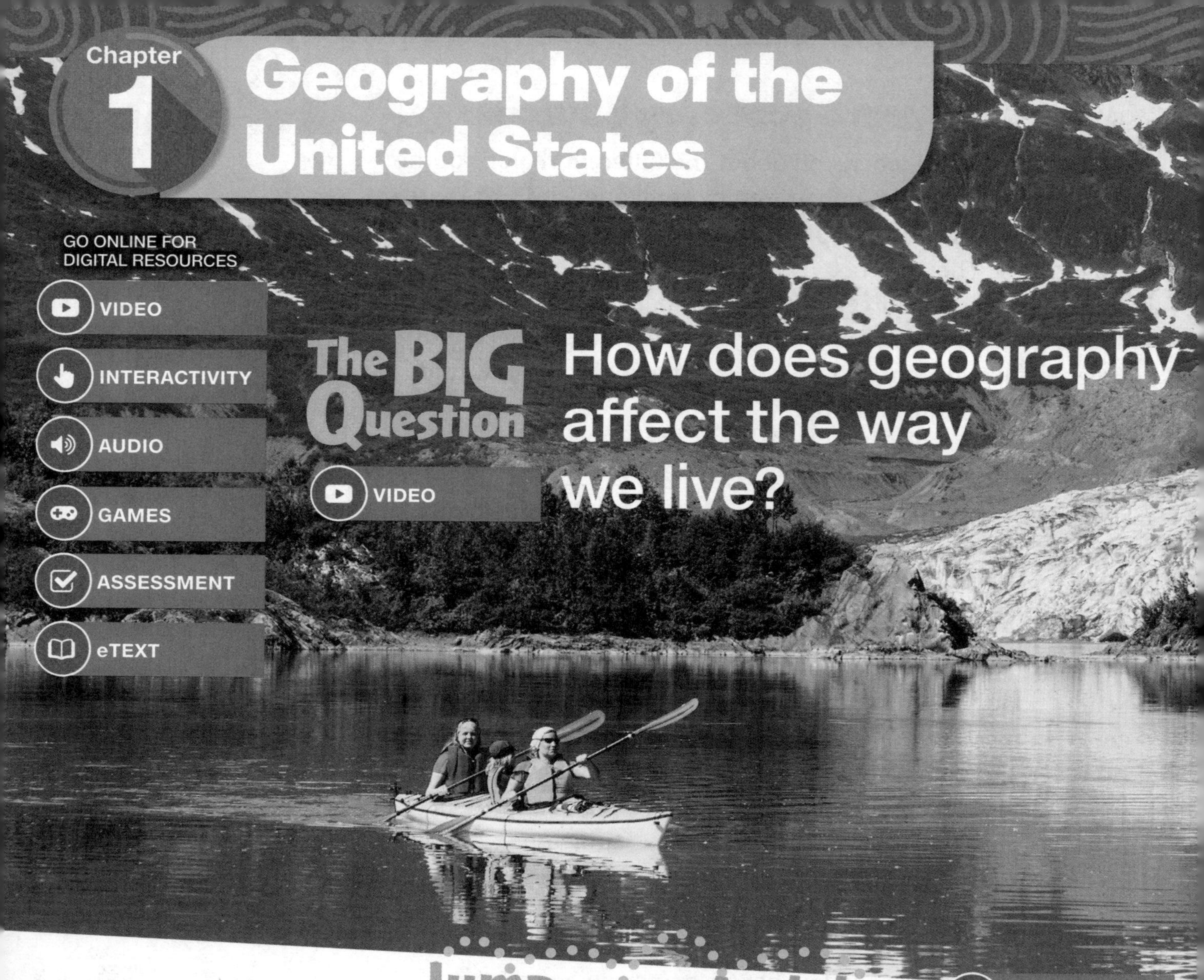

GO ONLINE FOR DIGITAL RESOURCES

- VIDEO
- INTERACTIVITY
- AUDIO
- GAMES
- ASSESSMENT
- eTEXT

The BIG Question

How does geography affect the way we live?

VIDEO

Lesson 1
Land and Regions in the United States

Lesson 2
Weather and Climate

Lesson 3
Regions and Resources

Lesson 4
People and the Land

Jumpstart Activity

INTERACTIVITY

With your teacher's help, decide on a name for five areas of your classroom. Each area should be named for one of the regions of the United States. Walk around to each area and choose the one that you think would be best to live in. Once you have made a choice, write why you picked this region.

____

____

____

____

____

Geography of Our Country

Preview the chapter **vocabulary** as you sing the rap.

Let's check out the geography of the United States,
There's **landforms** all around us - hills, mountains, plains,
The U.S. is divided into five **regions**
With states sharing similar characteristics, or features.

The Northeast, Midwest, Southeast, Southwest, and West.
You'll find mesas, deserts, canyons, cliffs.
In each region you can find **natural resources**,
In the Northeast they have fertile soil and forests.

In the Midwest you can find rivers and lakes
That help define **boundaries** that divide areas and states.
The Southeast has mountains, and a low coastal plain,
In the Southwest there are **deserts** that get very little rain.

The West is the most varied region,
With mountains, plains, and a long coast to see.

Geography of the United States

PACIFIC
OCEAN

West

Midwest

Northeast

Southwest

Southeast

ATLANTIC
OCEAN

Where is the United States?

The United States is located in the Western Hemisphere on the continent of North America. It is composed of fifty states. The states can be grouped into five geographic regions: the Northeast, the Southeast, the Midwest, the Southwest, and the West. Find the region where you live.

What happened and When?

Read and interpret the timeline to find out about how the population of the United States has changed over time.

1800

1900

1790
3.9 million people live in the United States.

1890
62.9 million people live in the United States.

TODAY
The population of the United States is more than 325 million people.

The Regions of the United States

West Region

Midwest Region

Northeast Region

Southwest Region

Southeast Region

2000

1990
248.7 million people live in the United States.

2010
308.7 million people live in the United States.

TODAY
The United States is the third largest country in size in the world and nearly the third largest in terms of population.

2000
281.4 million people live in the United States.

Quest
Project-Based Learning

Visit the United States!

The United States is a great place to visit! It has many places of natural beauty. Its natural features and climate support many recreational activities that people can enjoy doing.

Quest Kick Off

Hello! We want to attract more people to visit the United States. Your mission is to create and perform in a video advertisement to show the natural beauty and what fun recreational activities people can do. Convince them to come visit our country!

1 Think About Features

Choose a region or location in the United States to focus on in your video advertisement. What natural features does it have and what recreational activities can you do there?

....

....

....

....

TOUR GUIDE

2 Research

Find out more about the region or location you chose and watch some travel videos, too. What activities are popular in the region? What is the climate like both in summer and winter?

 INTERACTIVITY

Analyze the parts of an advertisement and see some examples.

....

....

....

3 Look for *Quest* Connections

Begin looking for Quest Connections that will help you create your video advertisement.

4 *Quest* Findings
Create Your Advertisement

Use the Quest Findings page at the end of the chapter to help you create and perform in your video advertisement.

Land and Regions in the United States

INTERACTIVITY

Participate in a class discussion to preview the content of this lesson.

Vocabulary

landform
mesa
plateau
canyon
flood plain
region
desert
boundary

Academic Vocabulary

feature
varied

Unlock
The **BIG**
Question

I will know that the United States is divided into five regions, each with unique landforms.

JumpStart Activity

Look out the window. Are there mountains, or is the land flat? Do you see a forest, or is there water nearby? Discuss what you see with a partner. Then draw what you see on a separate piece of paper.

No matter where you live in the world, you are near landforms. A **landform** is a natural feature of Earth's surface, such as a hill, a cliff, or even an island. The United States is a large country. A country this large has many different landforms.

Landforms and Bodies of Water

Mountain Peak

Plateau

Canyon

Flood Plain

River

Landforms and Bodies of Water

One of the many landforms in the United States is a mountain. Mountains rise high above the land around them. They can have steep sides, rocky cliffs, and towering peaks. Some mountains form in large chains or groups called mountain ranges.

Primary Source

Mountains are earth's undecaying monuments.

–Nathaniel Hawthorne, *Mosses from an Old Manse*, 1846

Hills are also raised landforms. They are not as high as mountains. A **mesa** is like a hill, but its top is flat.

Other landforms include plains, plateaus, and canyons. Plains may be large or small and are often covered with grasses. **Plateaus** are large, flat, raised areas of land. A **canyon** is a deep, narrow valley with steep, rocky sides.

The United States also has many different lakes, rivers, bays, and oceans. Most lakes are made up of water that is fresh, not salty as the ocean is. The land along many rivers is called a **flood plain**, which is formed after a river has overflowed. Landforms along the coast include beaches, dunes, and cliffs.

Quest Connection

Underline all of the landforms and bodies of water that would attract visitors to the United States.

INTERACTIVITY

Explore more landforms and bodies of water that attract visitors to the United States.

Mountain Range

Hill

Plain

Bay

Lake

Ocean

Island

Coast

Cliff

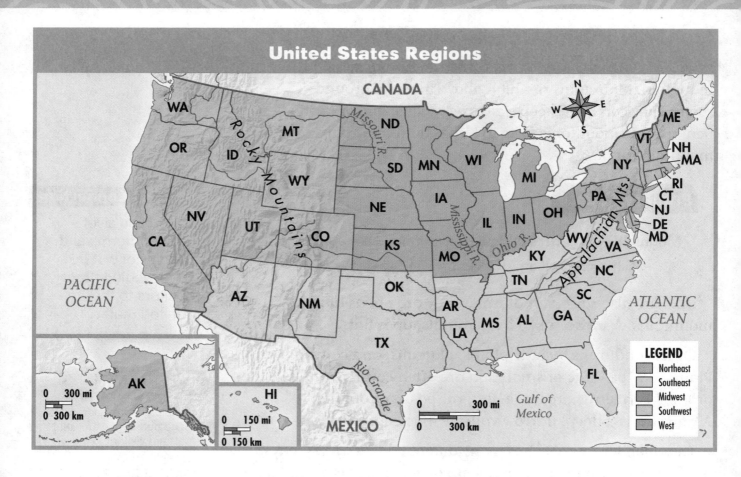

United States Regions

Regions in the United States

1. **☑ Reading Check**
Identify your state on the map. Mark it with an X. Write the name of the region where you live.

_____

_____

_____

_____

To study the United States, geographers and others divide it into smaller areas called regions. A **region** is an area in which places share similar characteristics. This map shows the five regions in the United States: the Northeast, the Southeast, the Midwest, the Southwest, and the West. These regions are organized based on the location of the states.

In the Northeast region, along the northern coast, there are forests and hills. The soil is rocky. Farther south and west, the soil is good for farming. The Appalachian Mountains run through the region.

The Appalachians also run through the Southeast region. The Southeast has a low coastal plain along the Atlantic Coast and Gulf of Mexico Coast. The Mississippi River flows through the region.

The Midwest region is known for its broad grassy plains, but it also has forests and rolling hills. Major rivers such as the Missouri, Mississippi, and Ohio flow through the Midwest.

The land of the Southwest is very different from the land of the Midwest. Here there are low coastal areas, dry plains, canyons, and deserts. A **desert** is a dry area that gets little rain. One of the region's best-known landforms is the Grand Canyon. Formed by the Colorado River over millions of years, it cuts through the Colorado Plateau.

The West is the nation's largest, most **varied** region. There are forests, rich soil for farming, and a long coast. Its landforms also include plains and mountains. Both the nation's highest and lowest points are found in this region. Alaska's Mount McKinley (Denali) is the highest point, and Death Valley, in California, is the lowest point.

Academic Vocabulary

varied • *adj.*, different or changed

Where People Live

In each region there are large cities where many people live and work. Our country's three largest cities are New York, New York; Los Angeles, California; and Chicago, Illinois. These cities have large populations, and people often live close to each other.

Each region also has areas where people live farther apart than in cities. On the plains of Texas, some people raise animals, such as cows and sheep. They live far from their neighbors because they use a large area of land to grow grasses for their animals to eat.

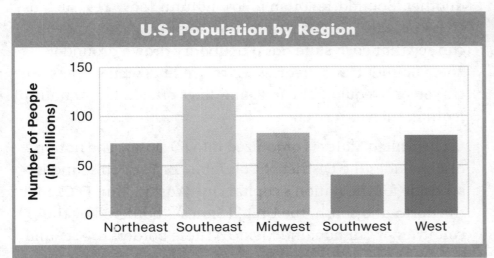

U.S. Population by Region

Source: Census Bureau, 2016

2. ☑ **Reading Check**
Identify the name of the region with the smallest population by circling it.

The Great Lakes Region

LEGEND
National border
State border
State capital

CANADA

Minnesota

Lake Superior

St. Paul

Wisconsin

Michigan

Lake Huron

0 100 mi
0 100 km

Lake Ontario

Madison

Iowa

UNITED STATES

Lake Michigan

Lansing

New York

Illinois

Indiana

Ohio

Lake Erie

Pennsylvania

map area

Boundaries and Borders

Academic Vocabulary

feature • *n.*, a part or characteristic

3. ☑ **Reading Check**
With a partner, **compare** the border between Michigan and Wisconsin with the border between New York and Pennsylvania. **Discuss** how they are different.

When you look at a political map of the United States, one of the first things you can see are lines that show boundaries. A **boundary** is a line that divides one area or state from another. Boundaries often follow natural **features**, such as rivers or lakes. On the map of the Great Lakes region, you can see that each state has a boundary drawn around it. Some boundaries appear as a straight line, while others are curved or irregular. The irregular lines often follow a natural feature, such as a river.

The United States is organized into 50 states. The nation also includes the District of Columbia, or D.C. This land is set aside for the nation's capital city, Washington, D.C. To the north and south, the United States is bordered by the countries of Canada and Mexico. These borders are set and agreed to by the governments of each nation involved.

Regional boundaries are different from city, state, or national borders, since they are not set by laws. In fact, regions can be based on many other characteristics. Regions can be based on major landforms found in a given area. Regions can also be based on what the people there do for a living or on what language is spoken there. Unlike cities, states, and nations, most regions are not marked with signs.

The Four Corners is where New Mexico, Arizona, Utah, and Colorado meet. Since this is a unique area, people have marked the borders on the ground.

INTERACTIVITY

Check your understanding of the key ideas of this lesson.

☑ Lesson 1 Check

4. **Cause and Effect Explain** what can cause people to live far from each other.

_____

_____

_____

5. **Describe** how the landforms in your region affect activities you do.

_____

_____

_____

6. **Understand the Quest Connections Explain** why you think people would want to visit the United States to see its landforms and bodies of water.

_____

_____

Lewis and Clark Expedition

Meriwether Lewis and William Clark went on an expedition that would last nearly two years. President Thomas Jefferson asked them to explore the new lands gained from the Louisiana Purchase. He hoped they would find a water route that would link the Mississippi River with the Pacific Ocean. Jefferson also asked them to learn about American Indians and to bring back information about the land that they explored. In this primary source excerpt from the *Original Journals of the Lewis and Clark Expedition*, Lewis describes what he saw.

Vocabulary Support

The rocks are completely dark.

remarkable, *adj.*, surprising

perpendicularly, *adv.*, rising straight up or to the side at a 90-degree angle from another surface

projecting, *adj.*, sticking out

". . . this evening we entered much the most remarkable clifts that we have yet seen. these clifts rise from the waters edge on either side perpendicularly to the hight of 1200 feet. every object here wears a dark and gloomy aspect. the tow[er]ing and projecting rocks in many places seem ready to tumble on us."

–Meriwether Lewis, *Original Journals of the Lewis and Clark Expedition*, July 19, 1805

Gates of the Mountain, Montana

Fun Fact
The expedition discovered 122 new animals and 178 new plants and had to face tons of mosquitoes!

Close Reading

1. **Identify** and circle words that describe the rocks in the area that Lewis and Clark were exploring. How does Lewis describe what he sees?

_____

_____

_____

_____

2. Do you think that Lewis was fearful in this place, or was he more in awe of what he saw?

_____

_____

_____

Wrap It Up

What area or region of the United States do you think Lewis is describing? **Draw an inference** based on what you know already about the regions of the United States and the area that Lewis and Clark explored.

_____

_____

_____

_____

Lesson 2 Weather and Climate

INTERACTIVITY

Participate in a class discussion to preview the content of this lesson.

Vocabulary

weather
climate
temperature
precipitation
humidity
elevation

Academic Vocabulary

contribute
factor

Unlock The BIG Question

I will know that weather and climate vary across the regions of the United States.

JumpStart Activity

Different regions of the country have different climates. In a small group, act out what clothing you would wear and activities you would do for different climates of the United States. Members of your group will guess and write down what clothes you are acting out and what activity you are performing. When everyone has had a turn, share and compare notes.

In most parts of the country, the weather changes with the seasons. Seasonal changes are part of the climate of a place.

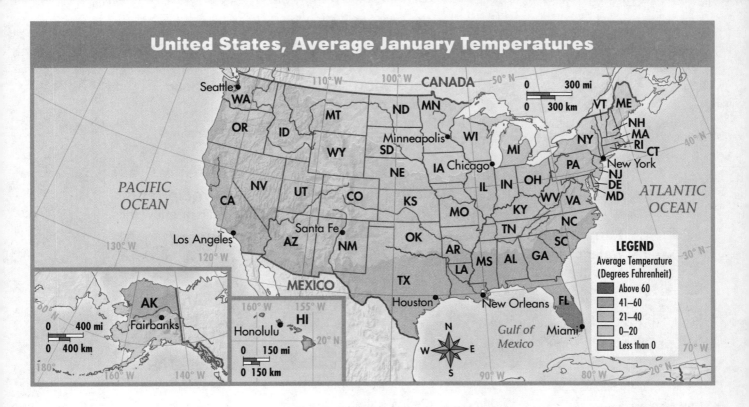

United States, Average January Temperatures

LEGEND
Average Temperature
(Degrees Fahrenheit)
Above 60
41–60
21–40
0–20
Less than 0

No matter where you live, weather affects you. **Weather** is the condition of the air at a certain time and place. The weather can affect what you wear and the activities you do. When it is warm outside, you may want to go swim. If it is raining, you may stay inside.

Weather and Climate

The weather can be hot, cold, rainy, or windy. It changes from day to day. **Climate** is the pattern of weather in a place over a period of time. For example, changes in weather that come with the seasons year after year are part of the climate of a place.

Two major factors of weather and climate are temperature and precipitation. **Temperature** is how hot or cold a place is. The **precipitation** of a place is the amount of rain or snow that falls there.

The United States includes places with a wide variety of weather and climates. On a winter day, it might be far below freezing in Minnesota. On the same day, it might be over 50 degrees in southern Louisiana. The Average January Temperatures map shows that the temperature varies across regions.

1. ☑ **Reading Check**
Locate the area where you live. Circle the average temperature on the map legend.

The Water Cycle

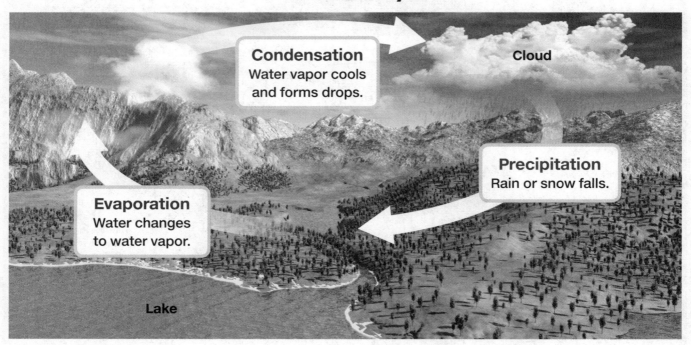

Condensation
Water vapor cools and forms drops.

Cloud

Precipitation
Rain or snow falls.

Evaporation
Water changes to water vapor.

Lake

Word Wise

Suffixes The suffix *-tion* means "the action of." How does knowing the meaning of this suffix help you to better understand the meaning of *condensation*, *evaporation*, and *precipitation*?

Water and Climate

Another important feature of weather and climate is humidity. **Humidity** is the amount of water in the air. You cannot see this water, but sometimes you can feel it. When humidity is high, the air feels damp.

Water gets into the air by evaporation. In this process, the sun heats the oceans, lakes, and rivers. Heat changes some of the water into a gas called water vapor. This vapor rises into the air.

High in the air, water vapor cools and forms small drops. This process is called condensation. The drops gather together to form clouds. Inside the clouds, small drops combine to form bigger drops. Finally, the drops fall to the ground as precipitation. The drops fall as rain, snow, or sleet, depending on the temperature of the air.

Much precipitation falls on water, since most of Earth is covered by water. Rain that falls on land soaks into the ground. It also runs into streams and rivers, which flow into lakes or back to seas or oceans. Then the cycle begins all over again.

2. ☑ **Reading Check** **Cause and Effect** Work with a partner and **explain** what causes evaporation.

Other Climate Factors

What other **factors** affect the climate of a place? One factor is location. Places near the equator receive the most direct sunlight. The equator is an imaginary line that circles Earth halfway between the North Pole and South Pole. As you move away from the equator, the climate gets cooler.

Academic Vocabulary

factor • *n.*, a cause

Primary Source

As you stand at this point on the 45th parallel you are half way between the Equator and the North Pole.

—Historical Marker at Stewartstown, New Hampshire

Lakes and oceans also shape the climate of a place. They affect the amount of precipitation that falls. They also can affect the temperature. In the winter, water is often warmer than the land. Winds from the water warm the air nearby. In summer, breezes blow from the water and cool the nearby air.

The climate of a place is also affected by **elevation**, or how high the land is above sea level. Places at high elevations are generally colder than lower areas.

Wind also **contributes** to climate and weather. Winds bring air of varying temperature and humidity from one place to another.

3. **☑ Reading Check**
Analyze the chart. Work with a partner and **discuss** why different plants grow at different elevations.

Academic Vocabulary

contribute • *v.*, to give to

Plant Life and Elevation

elevation (in feet)	
12,000	
10,000	Alpine
8,000	Conifer Forest
6,000	Aspen
4,000	Ponderosa Pine
2,000	Sage Brush
sea level	Mesquite

 Connection

Circle places that have a warm climate. Underline places that are cooler. These details will help you when you make your advertisement, as some visitors may want to know where warmer places are while others want cooler places.

INTERACTIVITY

Explore how the climate affects the activities that people do.

Climate Regions

The climate map shows the different climate regions in the United States. Arctic or polar climates are the coldest. Places near the North Pole have arctic climates. The only place in the United States with this climate is northern Alaska. Here the summers are short and the winters are very cold.

Tropical climates are warm or hot all year. Places with tropical climates are located near the equator. South Florida has a tropical climate. In the winter, the temperature is often warmer than in other parts of the country. The summers can be hot with high humidity.

Most of the United States has a temperate climate. Places with temperate climates are not as cold as the arctic regions nor as hot as the tropical ones. For example, the Northeast has cold winters, but not nearly as cold as northern Alaska. Precipitation in the Northeast is moderate, which means it is neither extremely wet nor extremely dry.

To the west, however, less rain falls. Parts of Arizona and New Mexico are very dry. Summer days there are hot, but winters are cold in the Southwestern mountains.

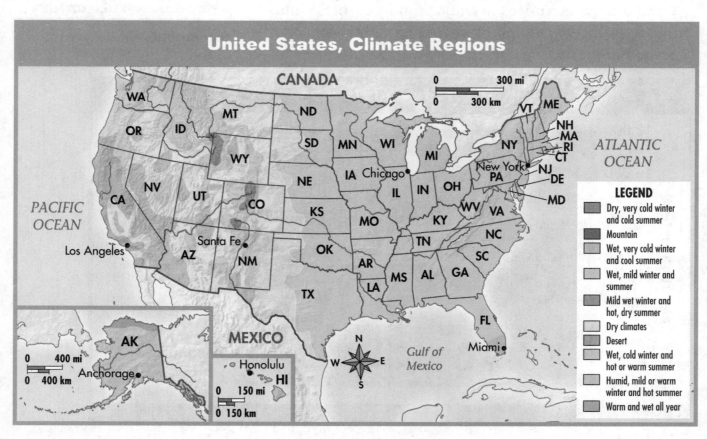

United States, Climate Regions

LEGEND
- Dry, very cold winter and cold summer
- Mountain
- Wet, very cold winter and cool summer
- Wet, mild winter and summer
- Mild wet winter and hot, dry summer
- Dry climates
- Desert
- Wet, cold winter and hot or warm summer
- Humid, mild or warm winter and hot summer
- Warm and wet all year

4. ☑ **Reading Check** **Compare and Contrast** Fill in the chart to **explain** how the climate of your region and one other region are alike or different.

Compare Climates

Another beautiful winter day—70 degrees!

Other Region	My Region
_____	_____
_____	_____
_____	_____
_____	_____
_____	_____
_____	_____

☑ **Lesson 2 Check**

INTERACTIVITY

Check your understanding of the key ideas of this lesson.

5. **Cause and Effect Describe** how elevation affects climate.

_____

_____

_____

6. **Describe** how the changing seasons affect what you do outdoors.

_____

_____

7. **Understand the** *Quest* **Connections** **Explain** how the climate affects the activities that people do in the United States.

_____

_____

Read Inset Maps

Notice that there are one large, main map and two smaller, separate maps on this page. Small maps that are related to a main map are called inset maps.

Inset maps give details that can't be shown on a main map. The places shown on the inset map may be too large, too small, or too far away to be included on the main map. Suppose you want to show a map of the United States. In order to include Alaska and Hawaii you would need to include Canada and a large area of the Pacific Ocean. The United States would be shown smaller with less room for details. If you use inset maps to show both Alaska and Hawaii, you can show more details of all of the states and less of the surrounding areas.

▶ VIDEO

Watch a video about maps.

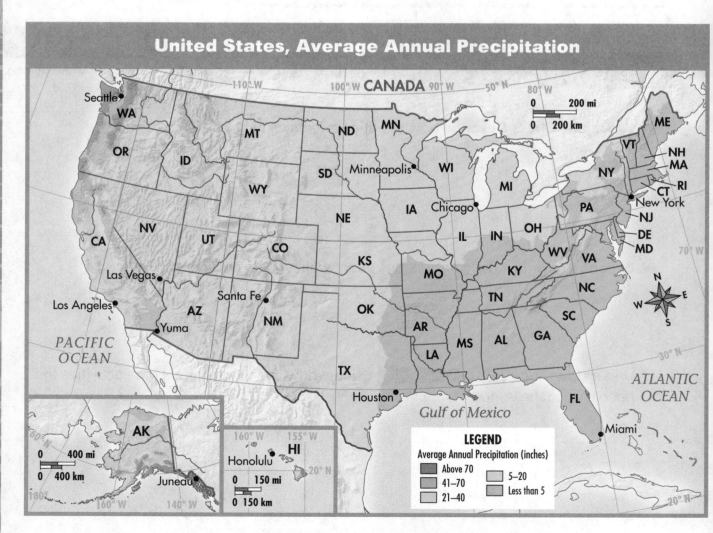

United States, Average Annual Precipitation

LEGEND
Average Annual Precipitation (inches)
- Above 70
- 41–70
- 21–40
- 5–20
- Less than 5

To read an inset map, first study the main map. Look at the title and scale. Then examine the inset maps. Ask yourself how they relate to the main map. What do the inset maps show that the main map does not?

1. **Describe** what the main map shows.

   _____

   _____

2. **Identify** what the inset maps show.

   _____

   _____

3. **Explain** how the inset maps relate to the main map.

   _____

   _____

4. **Analyze** why the mapmaker used inset maps rather than one map to show precipitation in the United States.

   _____

   _____

   _____

   _____

   _____

Lesson 3 Regions and Resources

INTERACTIVITY

Participate in a class discussion to preview the content of this lesson.

Unlock The BIG Question

I will know that each region has natural resources that are used to make products.

Vocabulary

natural resource
economy
product
capital resource
human resource
nonrenewable
conserve
renewable

Academic Vocabulary

produce
process

JumpStart Activity

Make a list of natural resources you are familiar with. Then walk around the classroom and write different objects you see that are made of the natural resources you listed. Share your list and talk about it with a partner.

The United States is a nation that is rich in natural resources. A **natural resource** is something in the environment that people can use. Soil, water, and trees are all examples of natural resources.

Fish and shellfish are brought to shore in the Northeast.

Natural Resources in the United States

Each region of the country has many different natural resources. The Northeast has forests and fertile soil. It also has rivers and a long coast that make fishing possible. Coal, found in Pennsylvania, is another natural resource in the Northeast.

In the Southeast, fertile soil is an important resource. The soil and the warm climate make farming a leading activity. Farmers grow cotton, rice, citrus fruits, peanuts, and other crops. The Southeast also **produces** oil, coal, and lumber.

Farming is a large part of the economy of the Midwest. An **economy** is the use of the wealth and resources in a place. The region's fertile soil is ideal for growing soybeans and corn. Farmers also raise hogs and cows. Cows' milk is used to make dairy products such as butter and cheese. **Products** are items people make or grow to sell. Coal, oil, and iron ore are also natural resources in the region. Iron ore is used to make iron and steel.

The plains of the Southwest are a major center for raising cattle and sheep. Cotton is the region's leading crop. Oil is a valuable resource found in Oklahoma and Texas. Copper is mined in Arizona and New Mexico.

The West is known for cattle ranching and copper, silver, and gold mining. In the warm valleys near the Pacific Coast, farmers raise fruits, nuts, and vegetables. Oil, lumber, and fish are also found in the West.

1. ☑ **Reading Check** **Identify** the natural resource in this picture by labeling it.

Farmers plow the soil before planting.

Using Resources

Natural resources are used to make the things we use every day. Your clothes, your books, your desk in school, what you eat for lunch, all come from natural resources. For example, trees are a natural resource. After trees are cut down, the wood is made into lumber. The lumber can be used to build houses or for other products. Wood, when it is shredded and softened, is also made into paper.

People also use capital resources to make products. **Capital resources** are the human-made things that we use to grow or make other things. Tools, machines, and buildings are examples of capital resources. A lumber company's capital resources might include the mills where trees are cut into lumber.

A third type of resource is also needed to make products. Can you guess what it is? It's people! **Human resources** include people and their skills, ideas, and hard work. Without human resources, nothing could be produced.

Some businesses in the Southeast and the Southwest drill for oil. The oil that is pumped from underground is not ready to be used. The oil is **processed** and made into gasoline or other products for people to use.

2. ☑ **Reading Check** These pictures show the resources that are used to make oil into gasoline. **Classify** the types of resources being used by labeling the pictures.

Academic Vocabulary

process • v., to use a series of actions to make something

Regional Industries

The natural resources in a region shape the economy and the businesses that are found there. A region with large deposits of iron ore will likely have steel factories. It may also have a port so that iron ore and steel can be easily shipped. For farms to thrive, a region must have rich soil and the right climate.

Similar businesses can vary from region to region. People across the country farm. However, what they grow differs from one place to another. In one part of the Southeast, the soil and warm climate are good for growing citrus trees. Here the trees grow through much of the year, and the winters are not too cold. In the Midwest region, however, the soil and climate are better for growing crops such as corn and soybeans.

3. ☑ **Reading Check** **Explain** why farmers in different regions might grow different crops.

_____

_____

_____

_____

Once oil is made into gasoline, people use it to fill their cars.

4. ☑ **Reading Check**
Draw Conclusions
Discuss with a partner why it is important to conserve resources.

Protecting Resources

Some of the resources that people depend on most are **nonrenewable**. This means the resources cannot be replaced or would take a long time to form again. These resources exist in large but limited amounts. When they are used up, they are gone for a long time.

Primary Source

The wealth of the nation is its air, water, soil, forests, minerals, rivers, lakes, oceans, scenic beauty, wildlife habitats and biodiversity. Take this resource base away and all that is left is a wasteland.

–Gaylord Nelson, Speech given on the Silver Anniversary of Earth Day, 1995

Coal, oil, and natural gas are nonrenewable resources. People use these fuels to heat their homes, cook food, and run their cars. People also use them to make electricity to power lights and machines.

Since these resources cannot be replaced easily, it is important to conserve them. To **conserve** means to save or protect them. There are many ways to do this. People conserve electricity when they turn off lights that are not being used. People can walk or ride their bikes instead of driving a car. In winter, some people limit how warm they keep their homes.

Some natural resources are **renewable**. This means they can be replaced. For example, when trees are cut down for lumber to make furniture, new trees are planted. However, trees take years to grow. Therefore, it is still important to conserve them.

Replanting trees and recycling paper are good ways to care for our forests.

Soil and water are also renewable resources. Soil can be used year after year if it is nourished and taken care of. Water is renewed through the water cycle. However, pollution can dirty the water and damage the soil. It can also harm plants and animals. Many people work to limit the amount of pollution released into the environment.

Another way people care for natural resources is by recycling. To recycle means to reuse the things we often throw away. People recycle many items, including glass, metal, plastic, and paper. These materials are processed and used again.

5. ☑ **Reading Check** **Categorize** the following resources by writing them in the correct column: water, fish, coal, soil, trees, natural gas, wheat, oil.

Categorize Resources

Renewable	Nonrenewable

INTERACTIVITY

Check your understanding of the key ideas of this lesson.

☑ Lesson 3 Check

6. **Summarize** **Explain** the ways people conserve natural resources.

_____

_____

7. Think of a business near you. **Describe** the types of resources that it uses to provide its product or service.

_____

_____

_____

_____

_____

8. **Identify** natural resources that the Northeast offers to tourists.

_____

Lesson 4 | People and the Land

INTERACTIVITY

Participate in a class discussion to preview the content of this lesson.

Unlock The BIG Question

I will know that people adapt to and change the environment to meet their needs.

Vocabulary

adapt
technology
irrigation
aquifer

Academic Vocabulary

depend
monitor

JumPstart Activity

Imagine that you and your family are moving somewhere that has a different environment from the place where you live now. Work with a partner to decide what new things you might encounter. What activities might be different? Write two of your answers on the board to share with the class.

Academic Vocabulary

depend • *v.*, to rely on

What physical features are in your community? Are there plains, mountains, or a beach? Each of these features can affect the way people live. Some people live near the ocean because they enjoy the climate of areas along the coast. Others live near natural resources. These people might work in businesses that use the resources or have jobs that **depend** on those businesses. For example, since the late 1800s, miners have lived near the coal mines of Illinois.

The environment affects where people live. This home was built on open land on the side of a mountain.

People Adapt to the Environment

Wherever people live, they adapt to their environment. To **adapt** means to change to fit a new set of conditions. Suppose you moved from Florida to Wisconsin. The climates and landforms of these two states are different. How would you adapt to the land and climate of Wisconsin?

To begin with, you would wear different clothes. Instead of wearing lightweight clothes in winter, you would bundle up against the cold. You would also use more heat to warm your house. You may use less air conditioning in summer than you did in Florida.

Your activities would change, too. In Florida, you might have gone to the beach often to swim and surf in the ocean. Wisconsin has no ocean beaches. Instead, in summer you could swim in a freshwater lake. In winter, you could ski down snow-covered hills. That is not possible in Florida.

People don't just adapt themselves to the environment. They also adapt how and what they build. In regions with lots of rain or snow, some people build houses with steep, sloped roofs. A slope keeps rain and snow from collecting on top. People may also build tunnels. In Minneapolis, Minnesota, people have built a system of glass tunnels that connect buildings. These tunnels link about 80 city blocks! The tunnels allow people to get around in the city without going outside during the cold, snowy winter.

In towns along the coast in North Carolina, beach houses might be raised to keep them from flooding when water levels rise. Along the coast, people also build their homes to withstand strong winds and heavy rainfall, since large and dangerous storms sometimes strike the area.

Quest Connection

Circle the ways that people enjoy the environment in the United States.

INTERACTIVITY

Take a closer look at ways people enjoy the environment.

1. ☑ **Reading Check**
Identify one way people in Minnesota have adapted to the environment. Underline it in the text.

Stilts keep rising water from flooding buildings.

Workers today can easily clear land with heavy machines.

People Change the Environment

Long before the first explorers arrived, American Indians changed the land by burning prairies and forests. They did this to clear land, to make rich soil, and to create better grazing areas for animals. Early settlers in the Northeast also changed the land. They cut down forests to clear fields for planting. Today, people continue to change the environment. Land is cleared to build homes, shopping centers, and farms.

Over time, people have been able to make greater changes to the land. This is possible due to technology. **Technology** is the use of tools and scientific knowledge to do work. In the late 1800s, people cut trees down by hand with saws and axes. Today, however, large machines are used to cut trees. People can clear a larger area much more quickly.

Primary Source

Any sufficiently advanced technology is indistinguishable from magic.

—Arthur C. Clarke, "Hazards of Prophecy: The Failure of Imagination," 1973

People today can more easily build large structures, too. People make roads on mountains, complex highway systems, and bridges that connect places that were once separated by wide rivers or streams. People also use new technologies to build dams to hold back rivers.

Word Wise

Context Clues You can use context clues to figure out the meaning of unfamiliar words. You can look at words and phrases before or after the sentence in which it appears to help you. Using this strategy, what do you think *complex* means?

People use new technologies for irrigation, too. **Irrigation** is the use of technology to bring water to crops. In some states, farms are not located near a water source. People irrigate their crops with water brought in through pipes from lakes, streams, and rivers. In other states, people irrigate their crops with water from an aquifer. An **aquifer** is an underground layer of porous rock that holds water.

The Ogallala Aquifer (oh ga LAH la AH kwuh fur) is a large aquifer near the center of the United States. In fact, it lies beneath parts of eight different states in the Midwest, the West, and the Southwest. The aquifer is used to irrigate millions of acres, or large land areas, of wheat, corn, and other crops. People use many different machines to use and **monitor** the aquifer. Large pumps and tunnel systems bring the water up from underground and pump it to farms. Computers measure the amount of water that is drawn from the aquifer. They also track where the water is sent and how much water is left in the aquifer.

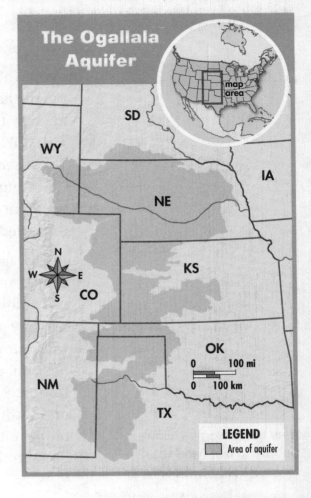

The Ogallala Aquifer

2. ✓ **Reading Check** **Cause and Effect** **Explain** why the Ogallala Aquifer is important to farming.

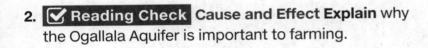

_____

_____

Academic Vocabulary

monitor • *v.*, to control

Nearly all the water drawn from the Ogallala Aquifer is used for irrigation.

Saving Resources with Technology

Just as people use new technologies to change the land, people also use new technologies to conserve resources. When people first used the Ogallala Aquifer, they dug large ditches to carry the water to farms. Soon people realized that they were taking out water faster than it was replaced by rainfall. To conserve the aquifer, people used large machines to dig and connect underground tunnels to carry the water so it would not be lost through evaporation. They also created improved irrigation systems that wasted less water.

New technology allows factories to better conserve and protect other resources as well. Today, factories can reduce the amount of pollution they release by sending the polluted air they produce through a scrubber. In the scrubber, water or chemicals are used to reduce the amount of harmful particles in the air. New technologies protect water resources, too. Some water treatment plants provide homes and businesses with clean, drinkable water. Other treatment plants filter wastewater and treat it with chemicals before it flows into rivers and other bodies of water.

New technologies allow people to use wind to make electricity cleanly.

New technologies also allow people to use other renewable sources of energy. These sources include wind, sunlight, and ocean waves. Solar panels, for example, change energy from the sun into electricity. Sunlight, wind, and waves are all resources that can be used over and over. Many of the resources people use for fuel, such as oil, are nonrenewable and limited. Other sources of energy allow people to conserve oil and other fuels.

3. ☑ **Reading Check** **Main Idea and Details** Fill in the chart to **identify** details about conserving resources.

Technology at Work

Use of Technology to Conserve Resources

↑ ↑ ↑ ↑

🖱 **INTERACTIVITY**

Check your understanding of the key ideas of this lesson.

☑ Lesson 4 Check

4. **Cause and Effect Explain** why people might settle near certain natural resources.

_____

_____

5. **Describe** how you adapt to your physical environment.

_____

_____

_____

6. **Understand the** *Quest* **Connections** **Identify** some activities people do outside that visitors to the United States would also want to do.

_____

Summarize

When you **summarize** something you read, you retell it in your own words. Summaries help you check your understanding of what you read. Summaries are short, usually no longer than a few sentences.

 VIDEO

Watch a video about summarizing.

To summarize, find the main idea and the important details of what you are reading. Then put the main idea and details in your own words. Read the paragraphs here and look for the main idea and details.

The United States is located in the continent of North America. It is surrounded by both land and water. The Pacific Ocean is to the west and the Atlantic Ocean is to the east. Mexico and the Gulf of Mexico are to the south, and Canada and the Great Lakes are to the north. The United States is more than 3.5 million square miles in land area. It would take more than two days and nights of nonstop driving to cross the country coast to coast.

Across the regions of the United States, landforms can be very different. Farmlands stretch through the Midwest. Warm, sandy beaches line the Southeast, and tall, jagged mountains rise in the West. Climates range from freezing cold to dangerously hot. Even within each region, the climate can be different. For example, in the West are the hottest and coldest areas of the continental United States.

Your Turn!

1. Fill in the graphic organizer showing the main idea and details of the selection you just read. Then use the summary box to write one or two sentences that summarize the paragraphs.

MAIN IDEA

_____

_____

_____

_____

_____

DETAILS

_____

_____

_____

_____

_____

SUMMARY

_____

_____

_____

_____

2. Read the last paragraph of Lesson 4 under the heading "Saving Resources with Technology." Write one sentence that summarizes the paragraph.

_____

_____

_____

_____

Quality:

Determination

Marjory Stoneman Douglas visited the Everglades in the 1920s.

Marjory Stoneman Douglas (1890–1998)
Rescuer of the Everglades

Some people really do change the world! Marjory Stoneman Douglas proved that. Douglas was a journalist and writer. In 1915, she moved from Massachusetts to Miami, Florida, to work for a newspaper.

Soon after Douglas arrived in Florida, she discovered how much her new state had to offer. She wrote about the people and different places in the state. Some of those stories were about the Everglades, a marshy area in southern Florida. Douglas found that the Everglades have a truly remarkable environment. Alligators, turtles, and panthers roam this watery world. Deer, gray foxes, and even marsh rabbits call the Everglades home. Countless birds and butterflies also live here.

She wrote a book about the Everglades that helped to make them a national park. But the Everglades were not exactly safe. Some people wanted to build an airport next to them. Her determination to preserve and protect the Everglades became even more evident when in 1969, she started the organization Friends of the Everglades to work to look after this special place.

Find Out More

1. Explain why Douglas was determined to help the Everglades.

_____

_____

_____

2. Today, people still work hard to preserve the environment. Work with a partner to find a local group that helps preserve the environment. What do they do?

_____

_____

_____

Visual Review

Use these graphics to review some of the vocabulary, people, and ideas from this chapter.

Land and Regions in the United States

- The United States is divided into five regions: the Northeast, the Southeast, the Midwest, the Southwest, and the West.
- Each region has landforms and bodies of water that make it special.
- Every region has cities as well as areas where fewer people live.

Weather and Climate

- Weather can change daily, while climate is a pattern over time.
- Key features of climate are temperature, precipitation, and humidity.
- Climates vary across the five regions of the United States. Location, elevation, wind, and oceans contribute to climate differences.

Regions and Resources

- Each of the five regions is rich in natural resources.
- Resources and products vary from region to region.
- Natural, capital, and human resources make products.
- Natural resources are either renewable or nonrenewable.

People and the Land

- People live where they do for different reasons.
- People adapt to and change the environment in many ways.
- People have found ways to conserve resources. Technology is used to help protect the environment.

☑ Assessment

 GAMES

Play the vocabulary game.

Vocabulary and Key Ideas

1. **Identify** each word by matching it to its definition.

   flood plain   hill with a flat top

   mesa   flat, raised land

   canyon   a plain along a river that floods

   plateau   deep, rocky valley

2. **Explain** how regions and landforms can be related.

   _____

   _____

3. **Identify** the region for each state.

   Georgia _____

   Montana _____

   New York _____

   Illinois _____

   Oklahoma _____

4. **Compare** weather and climate. How are they different?

   _____

   _____

   _____

5. **Identify** and label the missing part of the water cycle.

Condensation

Evaporation

Critical Thinking and Writing

6. **Describe** natural, human, and capital resources. Give an example of each.

_____

_____

_____

_____

7. **Explain** why water is a renewable resource.

_____

8. **Explain** why the Northeast has a colder climate than the Southeast.

_____

_____

9. **Revisit the Big Question** Tell how the geography of where you live affects your daily life. Support your answer with examples.

_____

_____

_____

10. **Writing Workshop: Write Informative Text:** On a separate sheet of paper, write two short paragraphs comparing the region of the United States where you live with another region. Think about how the different resources, climate, landforms, and bodies of water in each region make them unique.

Analyze Primary Sources

"There are no other Everglades in the world. They are, they always have been, one of the unique regions of earth, remote, never wholly known."

—Marjory Stoneman Douglas, *The Everglades: River of Grass*, 1947

11. **Explain** why you think Douglas described the Everglades as a unique region. Use what you learned in this chapter about Marjory Douglas to support your answer.

_____

_____

_____

_____

_____

_____

Summarize

12. Write a summary about the differences in the climate across the regions of the United States.

_____

_____

_____

_____

_____

_____

Quest Findings

Create Your Video Advertisement

You've read the lessons in this chapter and now you're ready to create and perform in your video advertisement. Remember that the goal of your advertisement is to attract people to come to the region or location that you chose.

INTERACTIVITY

Use this activity to help you prepare to create your video advertisement.

1 Prepare to Write

Write down the name of the region or location in the United States that you want to attract visitors to. Then, use a Web graphic organizer to write details about it such as natural features, climate, and recreational activities.

2 Write a Script

Use your graphic organizer and the answers from your Quest Connections to write the script for your advertisement. This will be the audio part of your ad that you will read.

3 Share With a Partner

Show your script to a partner. Make any corrections or revisions as needed. When it is your turn, politely do the same.

4 Create Your Video Advertisement

Work with a group to use video equipment to shoot your ad. Add pictures or graphics you find or draw to make your advertisement more appealing.

Americans and Their History

GO ONLINE FOR
DIGITAL RESOURCES

▶ VIDEO

👆 INTERACTIVITY

🔊 AUDIO

🎮 GAMES

☑ ASSESSMENT

📖 eTEXT

The **BIG** Question

How have we stayed the same or changed during our history?

▶ VIDEO

JumPstart Activity

 INTERACTIVITY

Talk with a classmate about skills and school rules you learned while in kindergarten and first grade. Then, discuss what fourth grade would be like if you had never learned those things. How does what you learned in the past help you in the present? Write down your thoughts.

_____

_____

_____

Moving Through Time

Preview the chapter **vocabulary** as you sing the rap.

Colonists wanted their own laws, and started
  a **tradition**

Of self-government which helped lead to **independence**.

Colonists were taxed and felt they were losing rights.

They declared that they were free and organized
  to fight.

They won the war, the American Revolution,

And planned their government with the **constitution**.

The nation grew and continued to expand,

Territories were set up in much of this new land.

Immigrants came from other countries,

And helped build the nation's growing **industry**.

By the mid-1800s tensions grew and

The South decided to **secede**, or leave the Union.

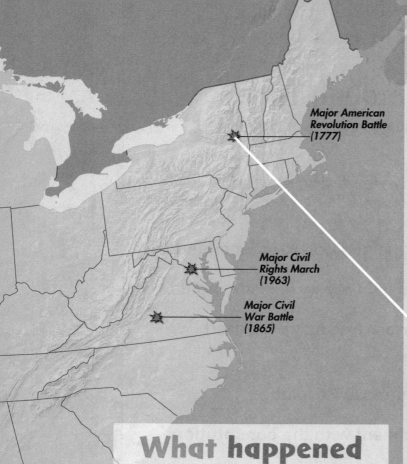

Major American
Revolution Battle
(1777)

Major Civil
Rights March
(1963)

Major Civil
War Battle
(1865)

Where have Americans fought for a cause important to them?

On the East Coast of present-day United States, Americans fought for freedom from the British. This map shows a few places where Americans have fought for freedom, states' rights, and civil rights.

Battle of Saratoga, New York, 1777

What happened and When?

Read the timeline to find out about the first Americans and key events in our history.

15,000 BC   **1400**   **1800**

15,000 BC
First inhabitants migrate to the United States.

1492
Columbus reaches the Americas.

1803
Louisiana Purchase doubles the size of the United States.

TODAY
You can visit the Jefferson National Expansion Memorial in St. Louis.

Who will you meet?

James Madison was the fourth president of the United States (1809–1817) who helped write the Constitution.

Abraham Lincoln was the sixteenth president of the United States (1861–1865) who fought against slavery.

Chief Joseph was a Nez Percé leader who fought to protect his people's land.

Rosa Parks was a civil rights leader who fought against discrimination.

 INTERACTIVITY

Complete the interactive digital activity.

1840

1950

2010

1861–1865
Civil War

1939–1945
World War II

2001
Terrorists attack the United States.

TODAY

The National Civil War Museum, located in Harrisburg, Pennsylvania, is near the famous Gettysburg and Vicksburg battlegrounds. It has a collection of nearly 25,000 Civil War items.

Quest
Project-Based Learning

Shaping Our Nation: Important Americans

My name is Tia Williams, and I am dressed as Harriet Tubman. My class is creating a living wax museum of important Americans. Harriet Tubman shaped our nation. She helped enslaved African Americans escape slavery during the late 1800s.

Quest Kick Off

Your job is to make a presentation about an important American who shaped our nation. Research a person from American history. Learn how he or she helped to shape America. Dress up and present your findings to your school community.

1 Think and Plan

Think about certain Americans from history who have made a positive contribution to our country. Choose someone and write why you think he or she shaped history.

....

....

....

....

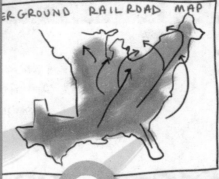

 INTERACTIVITY

Complete the digital activities to get started on your presentation.

3 Look for Quest Connections

Begin looking for Quest Connections that will help you present information on your important American.

2 Research

Find key facts about your chosen individual in books and on trusted Web sites. How can you tell how he or she changed history?

....

....

....

....

....

....

4 Quest Findings

Present at the Wax Museum

Use the Quest Findings page at the end of the chapter to help present the American from history who helped to shape our nation.

America and Europe

INTERACTIVITY

Participate in a class discussion to preview the content of this lesson.

Unlock The BIG Question

I will know that when Europeans and American Indians met, their cultures changed forever.

Vocabulary

archeologist
artifact
hunter-gatherer
agriculture
culture
colony
enslaved
tradition

Academic Vocabulary

claim
create

JumPstart Activity

Divide into teams and imagine you are planning a trip to Mars. You know it is in space, but you don't know anything about its environment. Figure out what you would take with you and why. Discuss how you feel about going to an unknown place so far away.

People have lived in the Americas for thousands of years. To learn more about them, we read the work of historians. Historians are people who study the past. They want to learn about how people have changed and how people have stayed the same.

Primary Source

W. Langdon Kihn traveled North America and painted American Indians during the early 1900s.

The First Americans

Historians work with archeologists to learn about the distant past. An **archeologist** (ar kee AHL uh jihst) studies artifacts and sites to learn about ancient people. An **artifact** is an object made by humans. Artifacts can tell a lot about the history of a place and its people.

Most historians and archeologists believe the first Americans came from Asia. Thousands of years ago, land connected Asia and the Americas. Small groups of hunters crossed over from Asia. Others may have come by water. They were **hunter-gatherers**. They hunted animals and gathered plants for food. Over a very long time, these early people spread across North and South America.

From the far north to the tip of South America, from the Pacific to the Atlantic, many different American Indian groups lived on the land. Then agriculture changed the way many of these people lived. **Agriculture** is the planting and growing of crops for food. Once people learned how to farm, they could stay in one place.

The environment affected the cultures they developed. A **culture** is the way of life of a group of people. In some places, American Indians farmed and lived in small villages or large communities. In others, groups moved from place to place. They followed the animals they hunted. Across the Americas, American Indians created a wide range of cultures. Today, their descendents value those ancient traditions.

1. ☑ **Reading Check** **Identify** and circle the place on the map that allowed people to cross from Asia to North America. How do you know by looking at the map?

_____

_____

Word Wise

Suffixes The suffix *–er* can mean someone who does something: *make, maker; write, writer*. Circle a word on this page that ends with *–er* and means someone who does something.

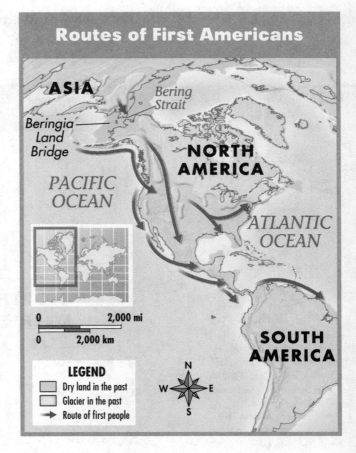

Routes of First Americans

ASIA

Bering Strait

Beringia Land Bridge

NORTH AMERICA

PACIFIC OCEAN

ATLANTIC OCEAN

SOUTH AMERICA

| 0 | 2,000 mi |
| 0 | 2,000 km |

N
W   E
S

LEGEND
☐ Dry land in the past
☐ Glacier in the past
➜ Route of first people

Europeans Explore

On a warm Friday morning in October 1492, three Spanish ships approached a small island off the coast of North America. Their leader was an explorer named Christopher Columbus. Like others in Europe, Columbus wanted to find a direct route to Asia. Europeans traded in Asia for spices and other goods but only knew long, dangerous routes to get there.

Columbus had no idea that North America even existed. Seeing land, he believed that he had reached the Indies. The Indies were islands near Asia. When he saw the people who lived on the island, he called them "Indians."

On that morning, Columbus **claimed** the land he found for Spain. He also claimed the people. For about 200 years, explorers would come to North and South America from Spain, France, Portugal, the Netherlands, and England.

Most explorers who came to North America were like Columbus. They were looking for a shorter route to the riches of Asia. Like Columbus, they would also claim the land of North America. The encounters, or meetings, between the two groups would change the lives of Europeans and American Indians forever.

Academic Vocabulary

claim • *n.*, the official declaration of owning something, such as an area of land

2. ☑ **Reading Check**
Sequence Analyze the map. Which explorer came to the Americas first? Which explorer came 110 years later? **Discuss** with a partner.

Explorers in the Americas

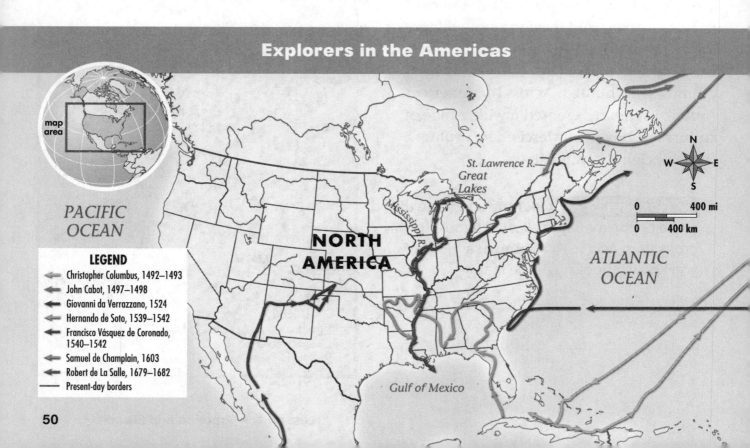

map area

PACIFIC OCEAN

NORTH AMERICA

St. Lawrence R.
Great Lakes

Mississippi R.

ATLANTIC OCEAN

Gulf of Mexico

N W E S

0   400 mi
0   400 km

LEGEND
← Christopher Columbus, 1492–1493
← John Cabot, 1497–1498
← Giovanni da Verrazzano, 1524
← Hernando de Soto, 1539–1542
← Francisco Vásquez de Coronado, 1540–1542
← Samuel de Champlain, 1603
← Robert de La Salle, 1679–1682
— Present-day borders

50

European Colonies

In the 1500s, Europeans began to settle the Americas. Countries like Spain, England, Portugal, the Netherlands, and France founded colonies. A **colony** is a settlement ruled by another country.

Europeans often built forts. A fort is a military settlement surrounded by walls. In 1565, Spaniards settled St. Augustine in what is now Florida. Later, English colonists came. Colonists are the people who settle a colony. Their first lasting colony was at Jamestown. It was formed in 1607. They named the surrounding land Virginia. In 1620, another group of English colonists called Pilgrims settled north of Virginia. They were looking for religious freedom. They named their community Plymouth in what is now Massachusetts.

For more than 200 years, Europeans colonized America. The French settled Canada and called it New France. Spanish explorers claimed much of the Southwest region. And by the early 1700s, thirteen English colonies stretched along the Atlantic coast.

In this recent photograph, a historical performer recreates daily life at Jamestown in the early seventeenth century. Today, many African Americans are descendants of the enslaved men and women from the colonies.

Starting in 1619, another group of people arrived in America. European traders brought men and women from Africa to work. Gradually, farmers depended on the labor of enslaved Africans. A person who is **enslaved** is not free.

In 1492, America belonged to the American Indians. Three hundred years later, Americans were a diverse people. Some had European backgrounds. Others were from Africa. Some were American Indians. By 1790, almost 4 million colonists and enslaved Africans lived in North America along with the American Indians.

The Columbian Exchange

What did you have for breakfast this morning? Perhaps you had a glass of milk, a piece of toast, and maybe some applesauce. You probably did not thank Christopher Columbus, but you should have. Before 1492, there were no cows, no wheat, and no apples in the Americas!

For hundreds of years, the Americas, which are in the Western Hemisphere, were isolated from the Eastern Hemisphere. That all changed in 1492. Columbus and other explorers brought plants, animals, and more to the Americas. From American Indians, Europe got corn, potatoes, vast amounts of gold, and other resources. When Columbus returned to Europe from his travels, he brought plants that grew pineapples. He may also have brought tobacco. This was just the beginning of a giant exchange called the Columbian Exchange.

The Columbian Exchange was helpful in many ways. Corn and potatoes helped feed people in Europe. They helped the population grow. Wheat and rice did the same thing in the Americas. Horses improved work and transportation for everyone in the Americas.

Not all of the exchanges were good, however. Europeans brought germs that were deadly to the American Indians. The results were terrible. American Indians had no protection against the germs. Many thousands of American Indians died of smallpox. American Indians would continue to die from deadly germs.

American Indians shared plants and animals that were new to Europeans.

Europeans brought many plants and animals that were new to the Americas.

3. ☑ **Reading Check** **Categorize** **Analyze** the pictures. Then **think** about the food you ate recently. **Identify** some ingredients that came from Europe to the Americas. Then **identify** some that went to Europe from the Americas.

_____

_____

_____

Government in the English Colonies

The English colonists who lived on the Atlantic coast brought an important tradition with them. A **tradition** is a belief or custom handed down through generations. For many years, English people had played a role in their government. The new colonists expected to do the same. They wanted to make their own laws.

In 1619, the colonists of Virginia were allowed to **create** the House of Burgesses. Communities elected representatives to make laws for the colony. Representatives act on behalf of a group of people. The House of Burgesses started our tradition of self-government.

Academic Vocabulary

create • *v.*, to cause something to happen as a result of action

4.  **Reading Check** **Explain** how the idea of self-government might have led the English colonists to want freedom from the King of England.

_____

_____

 **INTERACTIVITY**

Check your understanding of the key ideas of this lesson.

Lesson 1 Check

5. **Sequence Identify** the order in which the following events happened by labeling them with the numbers 1, 2, and 3.

_____ House of Burgesses meets in Virginia.

_____ Christopher Columbus reaches the Americas.

_____ English people set up first colonies on the Atlantic coast.

6. **Describe** one building or place that tells something about the history of your community. How has it changed over time?

_____

_____

7. **Summarize** the ways that Europeans changed the culture of American Indians forever.

_____

_____

_____

Compare and Contrast

How are things alike? How are things different? These two questions will help you compare and contrast. To compare means to tell ways in which things are alike. To contrast means to tell ways in which things are different.

Writers often use comparisons and contrasts to make information clearer. They use clue words.

- *Like, both, similar to, as, in common,* and *also* show comparisons.
- *Unlike, different, yet, however, instead,* and *but* show contrasts.

Sometimes writers let readers make comparisons for themselves.

You can use a Venn diagram to analyze and sort out information to see how things are alike and different. Read the paragraph below about animals of the Ice Age and then look at the diagram.

Ancient American Indian groups in North America might have seen woolly mammoths and saber-toothed cats in their travels. The mammoths looked a bit like elephants but had thick hairy coats. Their tusks were curved. The saber-toothed cats also had thick coats, but they looked something like tigers. Their saber-like teeth were also curved. Mammoths ate grasses, but saber-toothed cats ate ancient horses.

Woolly mammoths   **Saber-toothed cats**

Both

- Looked like elephants
- Had tusks
- Ate grass

- Hairy coats
- Curved tusks or teeth

- Looked like tigers
- Had teeth
- Ate ancient horses

Read about the lives of ancient American Indian groups. Then answer the questions.

▶ VIDEO

Watch a video about comparing and contrasting.

During the last Ice Age, hunter-gatherers appeared in North America. Some say they followed great herds of giant beasts over a land bridge from Asia. Others say they came by boat or crossed the ice fields from Europe. They spread across the land, hunting woolly mammoths and giant bison for food.

Then the Ice Age ended. The glaciers retreated. The giant beasts died out. Smaller animals, such as elk, buffalo, bear, and deer flourished. The hunter-gatherers had to adapt to a different way of life. Instead of following great mammoths, they hunted the smaller animals and gathered more plants for food than before. They learned to save the seeds and plant them to grow crops for food. Agriculture became important. Instead of traveling all the time, people settled into small villages near their fields. But they still hunted game for meat and gathered wild plants, just like the earliest people.

1. **Analyze** the information. Then circle the clue words in the paragraphs above that show contrast.

2. **Analyze** the information by **comparing** in what ways the lives of the first hunter-gatherers were similar to the lives of the people who learned to farm.

_____

_____

3. On a separate sheet of paper, **create** a Venn diagram to **compare** and **contrast** what you had for breakfast this morning with what you had for dinner last night.

INTERACTIVITY

Participate in a class discussion to preview the content of this lesson.

Vocabulary

independence
confederation
congress
constitution
delegate
ratify
amendment
territory

Academic Vocabulary

organize
compromise

Unlock The BIG Question

I will know that the United States grew out of the English colonies and became an independent nation.

JumpStart Activity

Your teacher probably has rules about what is allowed in class. George Washington helped make rules for America. Why do you think both schools and countries need rules? Write a list of some reasons.

It was July 1776. In Philadelphia, Pennsylvania, more than 50 men came together and said, "We . . . declare that these united colonies are . . . free and independent states." Each of the 13 colonies was governed by Britain. This made the colonists British subjects. Why were they declaring independence? **Independence** is freedom from rule by others.

George Washington was a strong leader. He led the Americans to victory against the British army.

The American Revolution

In 1763, the British won an expensive war against France in North America. The British wanted to tax the colonists to help pay for it. They passed tax laws such as the Stamp Act and the Townshend Acts. The colonists were very angry. Patrick Henry, a member of the Virginia House of Burgesses, gave a speech opposing the Stamp Act.

The British ruler, King George III, did something else that angered colonists. The Proclamation of 1763 drew an imaginary line along the Appalachian Mountains. He said no colonists could live west of the line. Since colonies were expanding, colonists wanted to be able to move west to find new land.

Many colonists feared that they were losing their right to self-government. So, in 1776, leaders from the different colonies met in Philadelphia and asked Thomas Jefferson to write the Declaration of Independence. The Declaration marks the time when the colonies broke free from British rule and became independent. However, some Americans and most British disagreed and wanted the colonies to remain under Britain's government.

The colonists began **organizing** and planning to fight for independence. When the war started in 1775, they formed the Continental Army. Its leader was General George Washington of Virginia. King George III was furious. He sent soldiers to the colonies. Their job was to stop the independence movement.

Academic Vocabulary

organize • *v.*, to form a group

The colonists were successful in small, early battles. But they faced a strong British army and navy. Soon it looked as if the colonists might lose. After a defeat in New York, Washington won a battle at Trenton, New Jersey.

In 1777, the Continental Army won an important battle. They defeated the British at Saratoga, New York. Seeing that the Americans could win, France agreed to help the colonists.

Across the colonies, more people became involved. About 5,000 black colonists joined the Continental Army. Women worked at home to help. Some fought on the battlefield. In 1781, George Washington led his soldiers to victory at Yorktown, Virginia. By 1783, the long war would finally be over.

Many of the farmers in Shays' Rebellion had fought in the Revolution. They were disappointed in the government formed under the Articles of Confederation.

A Hard Job

After winning independence, the Americans had to build a nation. The 13 new states called themselves the United States of America, but the country was not united in the way it is today. Each state felt independent. They were not used to working together. In 1781, the states signed the Articles of Confederation to govern the country. A **confederation** is a union of states that agree to cooperate.

Leaders from the states met in a congress. A **congress** is a group of people who are responsible for making a country's laws. But soon they were arguing. They disagreed about money, so soon each state was printing its own money. They also disagreed about who owned land in the west.

The new Congress of the Confederation did make some important decisions. It set up a way for new states to join the United States, for example. However, money problems continued. Taxes went up, and the economy slowed down. Many people felt desperate in the bad times. In 1786, a farmer organized a revolt. Daniel Shays and about 1,200 Massachusetts farmers attacked government buildings. It was time for change.

A New Constitution

Once again, leaders felt the need to meet and discuss the country's future. They planned to revise the Articles of Confederation. Instead, they created an entirely new government. The plan they created is still the plan of government for our nation today. The planners held a Constitutional Convention. A **constitution** is a plan of government. In May 1787, 55 delegates met in Philadelphia. A **delegate** is someone who represents a group of people. These delegates represented their states.

1. ☑ **Reading Check** **Cause and Effect** Talk with a partner and **explain** how the Articles of Confederation led to the Constitution.

The road to a new government was not smooth. The first problem was size. Some states had large populations. Other states were smaller. But every state wanted the same amount of power. The delegates argued for weeks. Eventually, they made a **compromise**. There would be a Senate, where each state would have two members. There would also be a House of Representatives. There, each state would send representatives based on the state's population.

The second argument was over how much power the government should have. Many people wanted a central government that was strong enough to solve the country's problems. Others wanted states to have more power. They worried that the leader of a strong national government might act like another king. The new constitution had to balance these concerns.

Finally, in September, the delegates were ready to sign the new Constitution. Then they faced a new challenge. They had to convince the people that the new Constitution could help save the nation.

One by one, each state ratified the new Constitution. To **ratify** means to approve. Some people said the new Constitution did not protect the rights of the people. So amendments were written. An **amendment** is a change or addition. These first ten amendments are called the Bill of Rights. The Senate and the House of Representatives urged the states to ratify, or adopt, these amendments.

The new nation needed a president. On April 30, 1789, George Washington took an oath. He promised to "preserve, protect and defend the Constitution."

Academic Vocabulary

compromise • *n.*, an agreement

James Madison played an important role at the Constitutional Convention. Sometimes he is called the Father of the Constitution.

The First Amendment

The First Amendment protects freedom of religion, speech, and the press.

It guarantees that people can assemble, or gather, peacefully.

It guarantees that people can petition, or ask, the government to make changes.

2. ☑ Reading Check **Analyze** the summary of the First Amendment. Then **explain** why you think it is important.

_____

_____

_____

The New Nation Grows

After independence, the new nation stretched from the Atlantic Ocean to the Mississippi River. Only some of that land was organized into the 13 states. Soon people living in other parts of the United States wanted to become states, too.

The government set up territories first. A **territory** is an area that is governed by a country but is not a state. The Northwest Territory was organized under the Articles of Confederation. Eventually its land became the states of Ohio, Indiana, Illinois, Michigan, and Wisconsin. Other states were formed, too. The area between New York and New Hampshire became Vermont, for example.

A big change came in 1803. Thomas Jefferson was president then. The leader of France was a man named Napoleon. He offered to sell the United States land that would double its size for less than three cents an acre. For $15 million, Jefferson purchased the Louisiana Territory. It was an area of 828,000 square miles. Eventually it would become all or part of 15 new states.

3. ☑ **Reading Check**
Compare and Contrast
Analyze the map. How did the size of the country change after the Louisiana Purchase? Tell a partner.

The United States, 1804

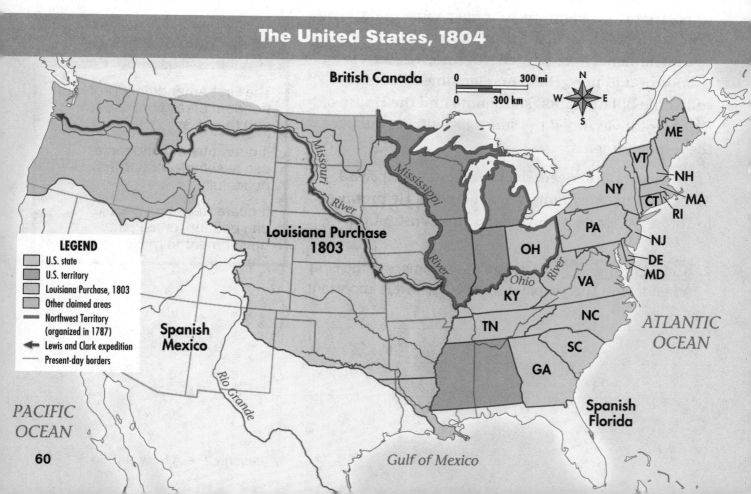

British Canada

0 ———— 300 mi
0 ———— 300 km

N W E S

ME
VT
NH
NY
CT MA
RI

Missouri River

Mississippi River

Louisiana Purchase 1803

PA
OH
NJ
DE
MD

Ohio River

VA

KY

LEGEND
- U.S. state
- U.S. territory
- Louisiana Purchase, 1803
- Other claimed areas
- ▬▬ Northwest Territory (organized in 1787)
- ◀— Lewis and Clark expedition
- — Present-day borders

Spanish Mexico

TN

NC

SC

GA

ATLANTIC OCEAN

Rio Grande

Spanish Florida

PACIFIC OCEAN

60

Gulf of Mexico

Lewis and Clark Explore the West

Quest Connection

Identify how each of the key historical figures from the lesson shaped America.

Thomas Jefferson knew that the rivers of the United States were important. The Louisiana Purchase gave Americans control of the Mississippi River. Now Jefferson wanted to find a river route to the Pacific Ocean. He hoped the Missouri River could be part of that route. He also wanted to make contact with the American Indians in the region. So he sent an expedition west. An expedition is a journey made for a special purpose.

INTERACTIVITY

Explore important Americans.

Meriwether Lewis and William Clark led the expedition. They took about 50 men with them. Sacagawea, an American Indian, helped Lewis and Clark. She was a valuable guide. They explored the rivers. The round trip was almost 8,000 miles long. It took more than two years. There was no river route to the Pacific, but they brought back important information about the land and people of the west.

INTERACTIVITY

Check your understanding of the key ideas of this lesson.

☑ Lesson 2 Check

4. **Summarize Write** a summary to **explain** Thomas Jefferson's contributions to the early history of the United States.

_____

_____

_____

5. **Analyze** the history of your state. How has it changed over time? In 1804, was it a state, a territory, or something else?

_____

_____

6. **Understand the** **Quest** **Connections** **Describe** one event that happened during the late 1700s or early 1800s that changed America. Who was involved with that event and why?

_____

_____

_____

Interpret Timelines

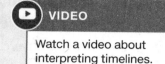 **VIDEO**

Watch a video about interpreting timelines.

Knowing the order of events is important when you study history. A timeline can help you understand sequence. Sequence means the order of events. A timeline is a kind of chart. It shows events and the dates they occurred. The events are placed in the order in which they happened. This can help you understand connections between events.

This timeline shows important events in colonial American history. The events are about Spanish exploration and settlement. Look at the timeline. You read it from left to right, like a book. The earliest date on the timeline is on the left. The most recent date is on the right. A timeline is divided into equal units of time. On this timeline, each unit equals 20 years.

Timelines can also help you understand different periods of time. A timeline may be divided into years, decades, or even centuries. A decade is a period of ten years. A century is one hundred years.

By 1673, Spaniards in St. Augustine had built a strong fort called Castillo de San Marcos. The fort protected the settlement. Today, visitors can see what the fort looked like nearly 350 years ago.

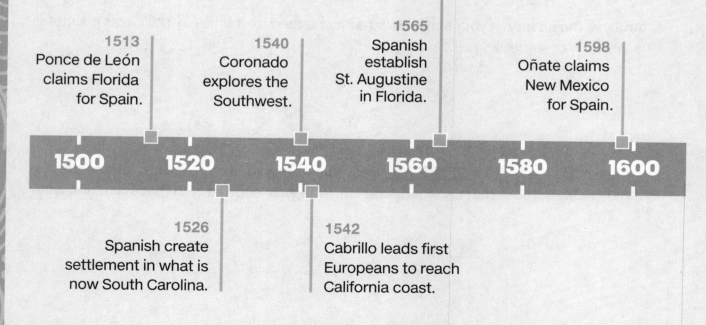

1513 Ponce de León claims Florida for Spain.

1540 Coronado explores the Southwest.

1565 Spanish establish St. Augustine in Florida.

1598 Oñate claims New Mexico for Spain.

1500　1520　1540　1560　1580　1600

1526 Spanish create settlement in what is now South Carolina.

1542 Cabrillo leads first Europeans to reach California coast.

Use the timeline to answer the following questions.

1. **Analyze** the timeline. Does it cover a period of one decade or one century?

   _____

2. **Explain** how the timeline is divided.

   _____

3. **Sequence** these Spanish claims. Did Spain claim New Mexico or Florida first?

   _____

4. **Identify** the year when St. Augustine was established.

   _____

5. **Apply** Complete a timeline to **sequence** events in your own life. **Write** three important events in your life that have already happened. **Draw** lines that connect the events to their correct place on the timeline. Then **write** one event that you're looking forward to.

```
┌─────────────────┐                              ┌─────────────────┐
│                 │                              │                 │
│  _____  │                              │  _____  │
│                 │                              │                 │
│  _____  │                              │  _____  │
│                 │                              │                 │
│  _____  │                              │  _____  │
└─────────────────┘                              └─────────────────┘
```

| **2005** | **2010** | **2015** | **2020** | **2025** |

```
            ┌─────────────────┐        ┌─────────────────┐
            │                 │        │                 │
            │  _____  │        │  _____  │
            │                 │        │                 │
            │  _____  │        │  _____  │
            │                 │        │                 │
            │  _____  │        │  _____  │
            └─────────────────┘        └─────────────────┘
```

3 Growth and Civil War

INTERACTIVITY

Participate in a class discussion to preview the content of this lesson.

Vocabulary

immigrant
industry
states' rights
abolitionist
secede
Reconstruction
segregation
reservation

Academic Vocabulary

productive
pursue

Unlock The BIG Question

I will know that the growing nation had deep divisions that led to the Civil War.

Jumpstart Activity

Talk with a partner about a time you spoke out when you saw something wrong. Who or what did you stand up for and why?

In 1847, San Francisco, California, was a tiny town. After gold was found nearby in 1848, about 25,000 people lived there by the end of 1849. Other western towns were growing, too. Americans were on the move!

San Francisco grew rapidly during the Gold Rush. It was a busy, bustling city by 1849.

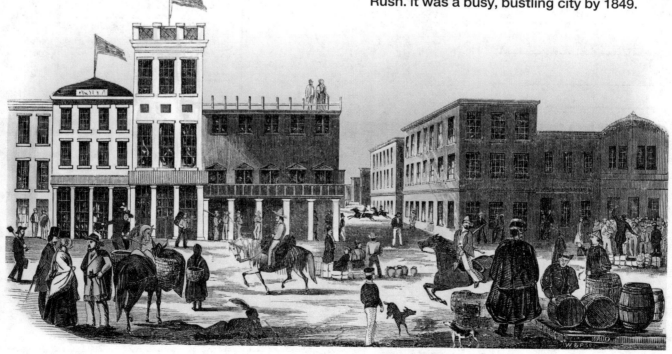

Manifest Destiny

The Louisiana Purchase doubled the size of the nation. There was more territory to the west as well. Great Britain controlled much of Oregon. Spain, and later Mexico, controlled the Southwest.

Americans in the East began moving west to find land, gold, or furs. People spoke of Manifest Destiny. If something is considered to be manifest, it means something is clear or obvious. Destiny is what must happen. In other words, some believed it was Americans' "clear duty" to expand the nation from coast to coast. However, American Indians lived in these areas. The two groups were going to have to fight for control of the land.

The United States and Mexico also fought a war for control of land in the Southwest. The Treaty of Guadalupe-Hidalgo ended the war in 1848. The nation finally stretched from the Atlantic to the Pacific.

New Industries

The United States was growing in other ways, too. In the 1840s, many European immigrants arrived. An **immigrant** is a person who comes to live in a new land. These immigrants helped build the nation's growing industry. **Industry** is the part of the economy in which machines are used to do the work.

This period of change is called the Industrial Revolution. During this time, more and more goods were produced by machines in large factories. Later, farmers used machines to do work they once did by hand or with animal power. These changes made the economy very **productive**.

Inventions changed more than just farm and factory work. There were big changes in transportation, too. Railroads let people travel faster and easier. Better roads and the new Erie Canal helped Americans go west. The telegraph helped them communicate, or keep in touch. Inventions such as these played an important role in the nation's growth.

This is an advertisement for the Pony Express, which was a service that carried mail to California from 1860 to 1861.

Academic Vocabulary

productive • *adj.*, able to make large amounts of goods

Frederick Douglass was an abolitionist and a newspaper publisher.

Harriet Tubman was an abolitionist. She helped people escape slavery.

Quest Connection

Underline two sentences that describe Lincoln's beliefs.

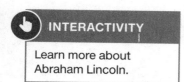

INTERACTIVITY

Learn more about Abraham Lincoln.

The North and the South

The North and the South had different ways of life. The North had more people, cities, and factories. The South was largely a farming region. At the heart of all of the differences was slavery. The South depended on enslaved Africans to work in cotton fields. Northern factories needed cotton to make cloth. As a result, Southern growers relied more on enslaved workers.

Southern states argued for **states' rights**. This was a belief that each state should solve its own problems. It also meant that new states could allow slavery if they wanted. Many Northerners, however, did not want slavery in new states. They believed in free labor. Many were abolitionists. An **abolitionist** is someone who wants to abolish, or end, slavery completely.

Black and white abolitionists worked together to help men, women, and children escape from slavery. Abolitionists published newspapers and spoke out at public meetings. They protected enslaved people who had run away. They told about the horrors of slavery.

By the mid-1800s, the nation was growing more divided and angry. In 1860, Abraham Lincoln was elected president. Southerners were furious after his election. Lincoln wanted to stop the spread of slavery. Southern states threatened to leave the Union. Many said Lincoln's election could lead to war. Sadly, it did.

The Civil War

After the election, South Carolina seceded from the Union. To **secede** means to break away from or officially withdraw. Soon after, ten more Southern states seceded. They called themselves the Confederate States of America and elected a president: Jefferson Davis. The United States had become two nations. Southerners said they had a right to do this. President Lincoln said they did not.

The Civil War began in April 1861. It started with a battle over Fort Sumter. This fort belonged to the United States, but it was in South Carolina, a Confederate state.

Soon the president called for 75,000 volunteers to fight for the Union. People believed the war would be over soon. They were wrong. It would go on for four years. More than 2.3 million soldiers fought in the war. More than 1 million of them died or were wounded.

The North and South fought on land and at sea. They fought along the Mississippi River and as far west as New Mexico. Each side had strong leaders. Robert E. Lee of Virginia was a Confederate general. Ulysses S. Grant of Ohio was a Union general.

Finally, the Union defeated the Confederacy. On April 9, 1865, General Lee surrendered. The terrible war was over. Now the job of healing the nation began.

President Lincoln was shot and killed just five days after General Lee surrendered to General Grant. The nation lost a strong leader.

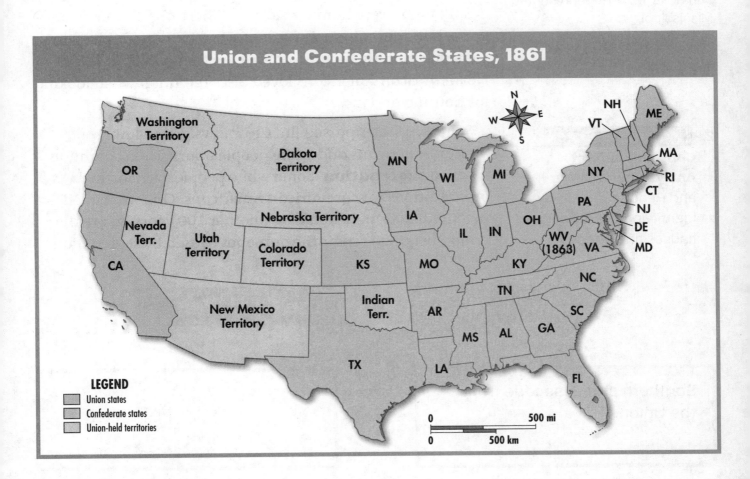

Union and Confederate States, 1861

LEGEND
- Union states
- Confederate states
- Union-held territories

0   500 mi
0   500 km

1. ✓ **Reading Check** Analyze the map. Which has more land, the Union States or the Confederate States?

_____

During Reconstruction, the first African Americans were elected to Congress. Blanche Bruce was elected to the Senate in 1874. He represented Mississippi.

Rebuilding the Nation

President Lincoln had wanted to heal the nation after the war but was killed before he could try. After his death, Congress controlled **Reconstruction**. Reconstruction was the period of time when the South was rebuilt. Congress made rules for the Southern states to follow to help newly freed African Americans in the South.

Three amendments to the Constitution helped African Americans. The Thirteenth Amendment made slavery against the law. The Fourteenth Amendment gave equal rights to former slaves. The Fifteenth Amendment granted African American men the right to vote. The amendments helped make the nation stronger and freer.

Still, times were hard for African Americans. Slavery was gone, but discrimination was not. Discrimination is treating someone unfairly because of race or other qualities. In the North, African Americans faced discrimination when looking for housing and jobs.

Southern states passed Jim Crow laws. These laws kept African Americans and white people apart. This separation is called **segregation**. Some white people even formed organizations to scare African Americans. One was called the Ku Klux Klan. It would be another 100 years before the nation began to repair the damages caused by segregation.

2. ☑ **Reading Check**
Cause and Effect
Analyze the Civil War and Reconstruction by identifying the missing causes and effects.

Causes and Effects of the Civil War

Causes	Effects
Southern states secede from the Union.	_____ _____
_____ _____	Reconstruction begins.

Changes for American Indians

In the 1860s, many Americans were moving west. They settled in the Plains. Many American Indian groups, including the Cheyenne, the Lakota, the Comanche, and the Nez Percé already lived there, however. The cultures of these American Indian groups were very different from the cultures of the white settlers. The two peoples fought constantly over land.

During the next 30 years, the government forced American Indians to move. The government set up reservations. A **reservation** was an area set aside for American Indians. American Indians did not want to move. To avoid going to the reservation, Nez Percé leader Chief Joseph led his people from their home in Oregon across many miles to Montana. United States troops **pursued**. Finally, the Nez Percé gave up. Chief Joseph said, ". . . I will fight no more forever."

When white settlers wanted to take their land, Chief Joseph and his people resisted.

Academic Vocabulary

pursue • *v.*, to chase

INTERACTIVITY

Check your understanding of the key ideas of this lesson.

 **Lesson 3 Check**

3. **Main Idea and Details** Jim Crow laws show conflict between white Americans and African Americans. **Identify** an example of cooperation between them from the 1800s.

_____

_____

4. Many Americans moved west in the 1800s. **Describe** how your family or a family you know has been shaped by moving or relocating.

_____

_____

_____

5. **Understand the** Quest **Connections** **Identify** the issues that people in the North and South viewed differently. Choose one issue and **explain** to a partner how it led to war.

The United States Becomes a World Power

 INTERACTIVITY

Participate in a class discussion to preview the content of this lesson.

Vocabulary

transcontinental
manufacturing
entrepreneur
diverse
depression
fascism

Academic Vocabulary

influence
limit

Today, visitors can see restored trains at the Golden Spike National Historic Site in Utah.

Unlock The BIG Question

I will know that the United States became one of the world's most powerful nations after the Civil War.

Jumpstart Activity

Talk with a partner about a time when a big event in the country or the world happened. Discuss how you felt about the event. How did it affect your life, or your family and friends?

The railroad owner lifted his hammer and hit a golden spike. The news went out across the nation. "DONE," the telegraph said. It was May 10, 1869. The transcontinental railroad linked the East Coast and the West Coast.

Transcontinental means "crossing a continent," such as North America. Now, a traveler could cross the country in a week. Before, such a trip would take about six months. The new railroad changed more than travel time. It was a key part of an even larger change in the nation.

An Industrial Nation

Between the Civil War and 1900, the United States became the world's leader in manufacturing. **Manufacturing** is making goods by machines, usually in factories. These factories depended on railroads. Trains carried resources to factories where certain goods were produced. Those goods could then be carried all across the country by railroad for sale. Railroads helped American businesses of all kinds to grow.

Just as businesses and factories were growing, so were cities. Cities were the home to many big businesses, which provided jobs for people. By 1900, four out of every ten Americans lived in a city. The nation was changing.

Inventions Bring Change

Inventions of the late 1800s changed people's lives. We use them all the time today: electric lights, elevators, telephones, automobiles, and more. Thomas Edison was one of the most important inventors. In 1879, he invented an electric light bulb that stayed lit for a long time. Edison worked on more than 1,000 inventions. Most were related to electricity.

Edison was not the only inventor to **influence** American life. Alexander Graham Bell invented the telephone in 1876. Later, Henry Ford made a successful automobile with a gasoline engine. The first typewriters changed the way businesses worked. The first sewing machines changed the way that clothes were made. With the invention of elevators, tall buildings were more practical.

American entrepreneurs built many big businesses. An **entrepreneur** risks money to start a new business. Some entrepreneurs became very rich. Big business was part of the reason why the nation was growing.

1. **☑ Reading Check** Turn to a partner. **Explain** how the growth of railroads affected where people lived and settled.

Academic Vocabulary

influence • *v.*, to have an effect or impact

A Diverse Nation

The growing United States was a "land of opportunity" for people living in other countries. A large group of immigrants arrived in the 1840s. Later, many more came. There were 9 million newcomers from 1880 to 1900 alone. The nation was becoming more **diverse**, or varied, as people came to the United States from different places.

Industries needed workers. Many immigrants found jobs in the nation's cities. As a result, the populations of cities grew. Chicago grew more than five times bigger between 1870 and 1900. Other newcomers worked to build railroads. Still others started farms on the inexpensive farmland west of the Mississippi River.

Some "old" Americans were afraid that these "new" Americans would steal their jobs. They were nervous about people whose religion or culture was different. Immigrants faced discrimination. During this period the United States passed laws to **limit** the number of immigrants.

Many new immigrants were families with children.

Academic Vocabulary

limit • *v.*, to control

2. ☑ **Reading Check** **Compare and Contrast** **Analyze** the two graphs and **compare** them. **Circle** the region that had the biggest increase in immigrants between 1840 and 1900.

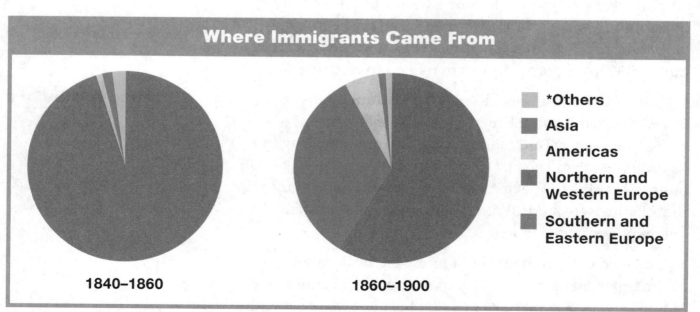

Where Immigrants Came From

1840–1860

1860–1900

- *Others
- Asia
- Americas
- Northern and Western Europe
- Southern and Eastern Europe

*Includes Southern and Eastern Europe

Source: Historical Statistics of the United States.

Depression and the New Deal

In the early 1900s, America's economy grew rapidly, and by the 1920s, the economy was booming. Businesses were expanding. People were making and spending a lot of money. Things were going so well that people called the period "the Roaring Twenties."

Then all of a sudden, in 1929, the Roaring Twenties came to a halt. As people began to lose money, they panicked. Banks closed and businesses failed. People lost their jobs. The economy slowed down so much that it went into a depression. In a **depression**, the economy goes into a deep and serious slowdown. Jobs are very hard to find in such a period. This depression was so bad that it is called the Great Depression.

The United States elected a new president in 1932. His name was Franklin D. Roosevelt. He offered America a "New Deal." An important goal was to give people jobs. After his election, President Roosevelt and Congress created programs to make the economy stronger.

One program was the Civilian Conservation Corps (CCC). Several million people were paid to help care for the environment. The Works Progress Administration (WPA) put artists to work creating art for the public. For example, artists painted murals, or large paintings, on the walls of public buildings.

Some New Deal programs still exist today. Social Security is one of them. Social Security helps support people when they cannot work or are retired.

By the end of the 1930s, the economy was stronger. Still, the Great Depression did not end until 1942. By then, the world was at war.

Word Wise

Context Clues When you read a word that you do not understand, look for other words or phrases that might give clues to its meaning. Sometimes nearby sentences have words that provide the meaning. What do you think *slowdown* means?

3. **☑ Reading Check** **Sequence** **Identify** and underline the dates when the following events happened: the Great Depression began; Roosevelt elected president; the Great Depression ended.

Working Together to Win World War II

African Americans served in units like the Naval Construction Battalions.

More than 400,000 women were in the military.

Children collected scrap metal that was used to build guns and bullets.

More than 16 million Americans served in the war.

Two World Wars

In 1914, the nations of Europe went to war with each other. The conflict was called World War I. By its end, more than 37 million people were dead or wounded. Many people in the United States wanted to stay out of the war. For several years, it did. But the United States had become a world power. When American ships were sunk, the nation declared war against Germany.

Germany lost the war. Afterward, many Germans were angry. Some followed a leader named Adolf Hitler, who led the Nazi Party. In the 1930s the Nazis gained control in Germany. Soon they were invading other European countries. By 1939, Europe was at war again.

At first, the United States stayed out of the new war. But on December 7, 1941, Japanese planes attacked Pearl Harbor, an American naval base in Hawaii. Japan was on Germany's side. The next day, the United States entered World War II.

World War II was fought by millions of American men and women in Europe, Africa, Asia, and the Pacific. It was a horrible conflict. More people were killed in World War II than in any other war. Many cities in Europe and Asia were bombed and destroyed.

4. ☑ Reading Check **Classify** different ways in which Americans worked to win World War II. **Write** *H* on a picture of people helping at home. **Write** *M* on a picture of people in the military.

Germany was run by a fascist government. Under **fascism** (FASH iz um), a leader like Hitler has complete power over a country. One of Hitler's most horrible acts was his attack on Jewish people. Jewish people were taken from their homes and killed. About 6 million Jewish people died in what is called the Holocaust. Several other groups were targeted and killed because of their beliefs, race, and physical features. Historians estimate the total loss of lives during the Holocaust to be between 11 million and 18 million people.

The war came to an end when two powerful atomic bombs were dropped on Japan in 1945. The cities of Hiroshima (heer uh SHEE muh) and Nagasaki (nah guh SAH kee) were destroyed. The worst war in human history was finally over.

Primary Source

People celebrated when Japan surrendered.

INTERACTIVITY

Check your understanding of the key ideas of this lesson.

☑ Lesson 4 Check

5. **Cause and Effect Explain** how immigration affected the United States in the late 1800s.

6. **Write** about an invention described in this lesson. **Describe** how your family's life would have been different if it had not been invented.

7. **Sequence Identify** a sequence of at least two events that happened during the late 1800s and early 1900s. Then, **write** how they affected life in the United States.

"The New Colossus"

As you have read, large waves of immigrants came to the United States from the mid-1800s to the early 1900s. For most of these new arrivals, the first American landmark they saw was the Statue of Liberty in New York Harbor. The Statue of Liberty was a present from the people of France. This poem by Emma Lazarus is displayed on its pedestal. Emma Lazarus was a descendant of a Jewish immigrant family.

Vocabulary Support

Colossus, a giant statue from Greek mythology

Do not talk about victories of the past

The immigrants who continuously arrive

astride *adv.*, with a leg on either side

Exiles *n.*, persons living away from their country

huddled *v.*, to be crowded close together

tempest-tost *adj.*, misfortunate

Not like the brazen giant of Greek fame,
With conquering limbs astride from land to land;
Here at our sea-washed, sunset gates shall stand
A mighty woman with a torch, whose flame
Is the imprisoned lightning, and her name
Mother of Exiles. From her beacon-hand
Glows world-wide welcome; her mild eyes command
The air-bridged harbor that twin cities frame.

"Keep ancient lands, your storied pomp!" cries she
With silent lips. "Give me your tired, your poor,
Your huddled masses yearning to breathe free,
The wretched refuse of your teeming shore.
Send these, the homeless, tempest-tost to me,
I lift my lamp beside the golden door!"

– Emma Lazarus, November 2, 1883

Fun Fact

Money nearly ran out before the pedestal was finished. Emma Lazarus wrote her poem to help raise money for its completion.

Close Reading

1. **Identify** and circle words in the poem that describe the condition of immigrants arriving to the United States.

2. Emma Lazarus calls the Statue of Liberty the "Mother of Exiles." Do you think this is a good name for the statue? **Explain** your answer.

_____

_____

_____

_____

Wrap It Up

Did the immigrants coming to America from the mid-1800s to the early 1900s have a good chance for a better life in the United States? Support your answer with information from the chapter.

_____

_____

_____

_____

_____

_____

_____

_____

The United States Since World War II

INTERACTIVITY

Participate in a class discussion to preview the content of this lesson.

Unlock
The **BIG** Question

I will know that the United States faces continuity and change in the twenty-first century.

Vocabulary

Cold War
communism
high-tech
civil rights
boycott
terrorist
interdependent

Academic Vocabulary

rivalry
cooperate

Jumpstart Activity

Work in a small group and talk about any changes you would like to see in your school or community. For example, do you feel safe crossing the streets near your school? Do you think your school cafeteria serves healthy food?

The end of World War II was a turning point for the United States. The country was a "superpower," which meant it had a strong economy and military. It also had exploded an atomic bomb. The Soviet Union was also a superpower, however. The decades after World War II were years of tension and conflict between these two nations.

Two veterans look for the name of a fallen soldier at the Vietnam Veterans Memorial in Washington, D.C. The Vietnam War lasted from 1954 to 1975.

Cold War Conflicts

The **rivalry** between the United States and the Soviet Union was called the **Cold War**. No one wanted to risk a "hot war" that would involve atomic bombs. But people were still afraid. The Cold War lasted for more than 40 years.

The leaders of the Soviet Union believed in **communism**. In a communist country, the government controls the economic and political systems. The Soviet Union wanted to expand communism to other countries. The United States, however, did not want communism to spread. Wars were fought in two Asian countries, Korea and Vietnam, over this issue.

Then in 1962, the Soviets put missiles in Cuba. Cuba is very close to Florida. The United States demanded that the missiles be removed. This conflict was called the Cuban Missile Crisis. Because of diplomacy, it ended peacefully. Diplomacy is when nations solve their problems without going to war.

The United Nations, or UN, also helps countries avoid war. The UN is dedicated to preventing another world war. The United States helped create the United Nations.

Academic Vocabulary

rivalry • *n.*, a competition for superiority

Technology Takes Off

The Cold War was also fought over science and technology. The United States was a leader in these areas in many ways. For example, the nation produced some of the world's most **high-tech**, or advanced, computers.

Americans led the way with another high-tech invention: television. In 1950, about 4 million American families had the new devices. Just ten years later, more than 50 million families had TVs. American technology, such as computers and televisions, was helping to change the world.

The Soviet Union was leading the way in the race into outer space, however. The Soviets put a person into space before the Americans did. The next goal was to put a person on the moon. America won that race. In 1969, two American astronauts walked on the moon.

1. ☑ **Reading Check**
Identify how technology played a role in the Cold War. **Discuss** with a partner.

The Civil Rights Era

Equality is an American value. The Declaration of Independence says "all men are created equal." But African Americans have not always had equal rights. For example, Jim Crow laws led to segregation in the South.

In 1954, the Supreme Court made a decision. It would lead to huge changes. The decision was called *Brown* v. *Board of Education*. The court said segregation in public schools was against the law. **Civil rights** are the rights to freedom and equality.

In Montgomery, Alabama, Rosa Parks was the cause of a protest. Parks was African American. She refused to give up her seat on a segregated city bus to a white passenger. She was arrested and sent to jail. African Americans in Montgomery called for a **boycott** of city buses. A boycott is when a group of people stops doing something in order to protest. Dr. Martin Luther King, Jr. was a leader of the boycott.

Primary Source

Our mistreatment was just not right, and I was tired of it. … I knew someone had to take the first step.

–Rosa Parks, *Quiet Strength*, 1994

Although many people of all races worked to end segregation, others fought to keep it. The conflict was violent at times. Eventually, the government passed civil rights laws. The Civil Rights Act of 1964 did much to end segregation and guarantee equal rights.

2. ☑ **Reading Check** **Draw Conclusions Analyze** the photo and the text. Then **describe** what life was like for African Americans in segregated places during the 1950s.

_____

_____

_____

_____

Dr. Martin Luther King, Jr. led people in nonviolent, or peaceful, protests. In this photo, Dr. King led a March on Washington, D.C. About 250,000 people came to protest discrimination.

Quest Connection

Who was involved in the civil rights movement? How did they bring change?

INTERACTIVITY

Take a closer look at key people in the civil rights movement.

Working for Rights

Latino Rights
César Chávez organized a union of farmworkers. Most were Mexican American.

American Indian Rights
Wilma Mankiller was the first woman to be chief of the Cherokee Nation.

Women's Rights
Betty Friedan was a writer and leader of the women's movement.

Greater Diversity

The 1960s were a time of great change. Like African Americans, others fought for equality. For example, women struggled for equal rights. A little more than half of all Americans are women, but their opportunities often were more limited than men's. Women often earned less pay than men for the same work. The Civil Rights Act of 1964 said that it was illegal to discriminate based on a person's gender. Gender refers to whether a person identifies as male or female.

The civil rights movement affected immigration, too. After World War I, Congress had limited immigration. Only a certain number of people were allowed to come from certain countries. This was called the quota (KWOH tuh) system. In 1965, Congress changed those laws. They got rid of quotas. That way, no country would be discriminated against.

In the mid-1960s, about 9.5 million immigrants lived in the United States. By 2009, the number was nearly 37 million. Under the new laws, many people from Asia, Africa, and Central and South America came to the United States. This new wave of immigration made the United States more diverse.

3. ☑ **Reading Check**
Main Idea and Details
In the 1960s, life changed for many Americans. Turn and talk to a partner. **Describe** one example of a change from this period.

A New Era

By the end of the twentieth century, the Cold War had ended. The Soviet Union was no longer a communist country. But the United States faced a new threat. On September 11, 2001, terrorists attacked the nation. A **terrorist** is a person who uses violence for political reasons. Terrorists try to make governments do what they want by making people afraid.

On 9/11 (as the event is called), terrorists took over airplanes flying in the United States. Two crashed into and destroyed the World Trade Center towers in New York. Another hit a government building near Washington, D.C. A fourth plane crashed in Pennsylvania. Thousands of people were killed.

Academic Vocabulary

cooperate • *v.*, to work together toward the same end

The terrorists were part of a violent group, al Qaeda, that threatened the United States and other nations. After 9/11, President George W. Bush led the nation into a "war on terror." Many countries **cooperated** in this effort. President Barack Obama continued to make decisions about the conflict.

Continuity and Change

The United States faces challenges in the twenty-first century. As a superpower, it plays a key role in world events. Transportation and communication move faster than ever. Nations are **interdependent**. This means they rely on one another for goods, services, or resources.

The world has changed, but there is also continuity in the basic values of the United States. Continuity is the way things stay the same. For example, the nation believes in the ideas of freedom, equality, and improving conditions for all people.

In 2015, Nepal experienced a horrible earthquake. People from the United States and all over the world cooperated to help with the recovery.

4. ☑ **Reading Check** **Identify** two examples of continuity and two examples of change from Lesson 5.

Continuity and Change Since World War II	
Continuity	**Change**
_____	_____
_____	_____
_____	_____
_____	_____
_____	_____

☑ **Lesson 5 Check**

INTERACTIVITY

Check your understanding of the key ideas of this lesson.

5. **Sequence Analyze** these events and number them from 1 to 4 in the order in which they happened.

	U.S. astronauts on the moon		School segregation outlawed
	Cuban Missile Crisis		The Civil Rights Act became a law

6. **Think** of something that has stayed the same in America during your lifetime. **Explain** why you think that is a good or a bad thing.

_____

_____

7. **Understand the**  **Connections** **Think** about how America changed after the civil rights movement. How did the changes create an opportunity? **Discuss** an example with a partner.

_____

_____

Quality:
Patriotism

Elizabeth Cady Stanton (1815–1902)
American Suffragist

In the 1800s, many jobs were closed to women. Married women could not own property. In time, people realized that women should have the same rights as men.

In July 1848, Elizabeth Cady Stanton and Lucretia Mott organized a meeting to discuss women's rights in Seneca Falls, New York. Nearly 250 men and women attended. At the Seneca Falls Convention, Stanton read a statement based on the Declaration of Independence. It stated that men and women were equal.

This was the beginning of the women's suffrage movement in the United States. Suffrage is the right to vote, and people who worked for women's suffrage were called suffragists. It would take almost 75 years before women gained the right to vote, when the Nineteenth Amendment of the Constitution was ratified in 1920.

A PETITION FOR UNIVERSAL SUFFRAGE.

To the Senate and House of Representatives
The undersigned, Women of the United States, respect
prohibit the several States from disfranchising any of their cit
people—one half the entire population of the country—intelli
stand outside the pale of political recognition.
The Constitution classes us as "free people," and cou
yet are we governed without our consent, compelled to pay t
without choice of judge or juror.
The experience of all ages, the Declarations of the F
revolution through which we have just passed, all prove th
the ballot—the only weapon of self-protection—is not in t
Therefore, as you are now amending the Constitut
new safeguards round the individual rights of four mil
right of Suffrage to Woman—the only remaining class of
obligation "to Guarantee to every State in the Union a
As all partial application of Republican princip
discontented people, we would pray your Honorable B
ensure domestic tranquillity, that you legislate hereafter
For justice and equality your petitioners will ev

NAMES.

Find Out More

1. Identify ways that Elizabeth Cady Stanton showed patriotism for our country.

_____

_____

_____

2. Today, there are ways that you can show patriotism. For example, you can attend a rally about something important you believe in. Ask someone who works for a local organization, or look in the newspaper or online for events. Then talk to a friend or family member about its importance to you. Invite them to join you.

Visual Review

Use these graphics to review some of the vocabulary, people, and ideas from this chapter.

Major U.S. Conflicts

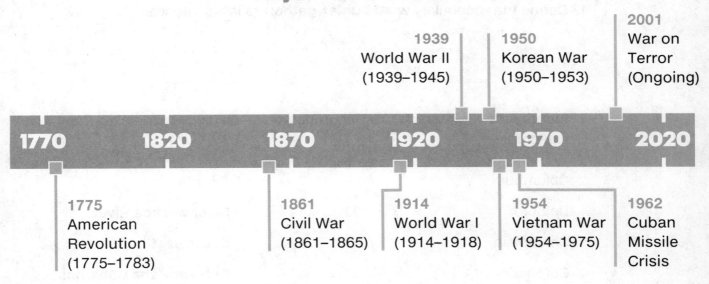

1939
World War II
(1939–1945)

1950
Korean War
(1950–1953)

2001
War on
Terror
(Ongoing)

1770 1820 1870 1920 1970 2020

1775
American
Revolution
(1775–1783)

1861
Civil War
(1861–1865)

1914
World War I
(1914–1918)

1954
Vietnam War
(1954–1975)

1962
Cuban
Missile
Crisis

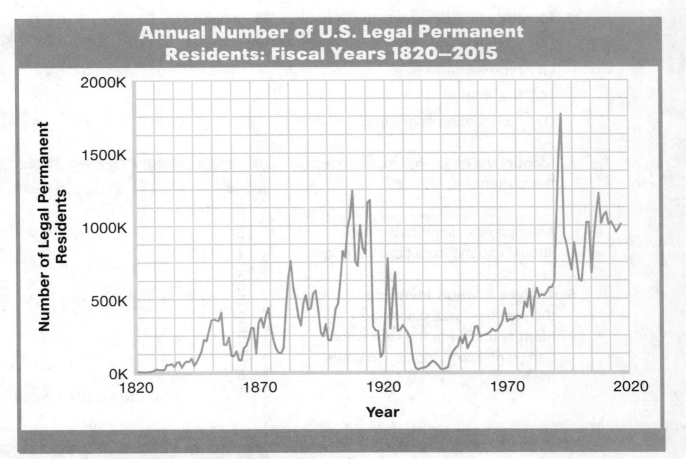

Annual Number of U.S. Legal Permanent Residents: Fiscal Years 1820—2015

Source: U.S. Department of Homeland Security

Vocabulary and Key Ideas

1. **Define** the vocabulary word **hunter-gatherers** in a sentence.

_____

_____

2. **Identify** the explorers by drawing a line from each name to the place he explored.

Columbus	**Florida**
De Soto	**St. Lawrence River**
Champlain	**Southwest**
Coronado	**Cuba and the Bahamas**

3. **Identify** which describes the Columbian Exchange.
   - (A) a settlement
   - (B) representatives
   - (C) the sharing of goods
   - (D) the meeting of groups

4. **Identify** the missing term to complete the sentence.

   _____ was Americans' belief that the nation should expand from coast to coast.

5. **Analyze a Graph Identify** and circle the year gold was discovered. **Identify** and write the year when San Francisco's population grew the most.

   _____

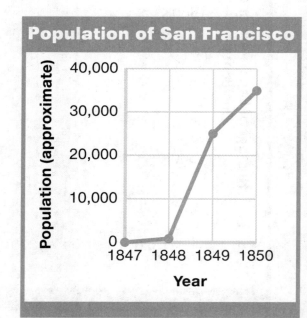

Population of San Francisco

Source: UCSF, U.S. Census

Critical Thinking and Writing

6. **Determine the Cause** Which led directly to the United States entering World War II?

   (A) millions of immigrants arrive

   (B) Pearl Harbor attacked

   (C) banks close and businesses fail

   (D) transcontinental railroad built

7. **Compare and Contrast** How did Abraham Lincoln's beliefs differ from those of Jefferson Davis?

   _____

   _____

   _____

   _____

8. **Explain** how Reconstruction was related to the Civil War.

   _____

   _____

   _____

   _____

9. **Revisit the Big Question** How did Martin Luther King, Jr. shape America?

   _____

   _____

   _____

   _____

10. **Writing Workshop: Write Informative Text** On a separate piece of paper, write two paragraphs that **explain** what the Cold War was and how it affected Americans.

Analyze Primary Sources

"A house divided against itself cannot stand."

—Abraham Lincoln, speech at Republican
State Convention, June 16, 1858

11. Explain what Abraham Lincoln meant by this statement.

_____

_____

_____

Interpret Timelines

12. Analyze the timeline and answer the questions.
In which year did the war begin?

_____

Did the United States write the Declaration of Independence before or after the start of the War for Independence?

_____

Where was the last battle of the war fought? _____

How many years had passed between the signing of the Declaration of Independence and the Battle of Yorktown?

_____

June 1775		December 1776		October 1781
Battle of Bunker Hill		Battle of Trenton		Battle of Yorktown

1774 1775 1776 1777 1778 1779 1780 1781 1782

April 1775	July 1776	October 1777
Fighting at Lexington and Concord	Declaration of Independence	Battle of Saratoga

Quest Findings

Present at the Wax Museum

You have read the lessons in this chapter and now you are ready to present. Remember that the goal of your presentation is to show how your important American shaped history. Follow these steps:

1 Prepare Your Backdrop

You will be standing in front of your backdrop during the presentation, so your backdrop should be colorful. It should include a few key facts about your important American. You will need to research these facts in books or online. Remember to include a button that says, "Push here to learn more about this important American."

2 Write Your Speech

Based on your research, write a short speech about your important American. It should highlight what he or she did to help shape our nation. You can memorize your speech or you can write it down on index cards.

3 Gather Your Props

You will need to dress like your important American. Look at pictures or read descriptions of him or her. Ask friends or family if they can lend you clothing or props, such as glasses or wigs.

4 Present Your Important American

Invite members of the school community to your wax museum. Dress in your costume and stand in front of your backdrop. Enjoy sharing what you have learned about your important American!

GO ONLINE FOR
DIGITAL RESOURCES

 VIDEO

 INTERACTIVITY

 AUDIO

 GAMES

 ASSESSMENT

 eTEXT

The BIG Question

▶ VIDEO

What is special about American government?

Lesson 1

Principles of Our Government

Lesson 2

How Our Government Works

Lesson 3

Our Rights and Responsibilities

JumpStart Activity

 INTERACTIVITY

Your teacher will divide the class into three groups. Your group will think of a new classroom rule and a consequence for not following the rule. Then, each group will present their rule and consequence to the rest of the class. The class will discuss whether the rules and the consequences are fair.

_____

_____

_____

_____

American Government

Preview the chapter **vocabulary** as you sing the rap.

The people decide who ought to lead,

It's what we call a **democracy**.

We believe we have basic rights, nothing less

Than "Life, **Liberty** and the pursuit of Happiness."

The **legislative branch**, called Congress,

Makes laws and has two parts:
   the House and the Senate.

The **executive branch** is led by the president,

Who carries out laws and leads the armed forces.

Let's not forget there's the **judicial branch**, too.

They make sure our laws agree with the Constitution.

These branches divide the power, each plays a role,

Checks and balances keep one branch
   from gaining control.

Government in the United States

Washington, D.C.

- The White House
- Washington Monument
- Jefferson Memorial
- U.S. Supreme Court
- United States Capitol

New York Avenue
Massachusetts Avenue
Pennsylvania Avenue
Constitution Avenue

Where is the White House located?

It is located in our nation's capital, Washington, D.C., as you can see from this map.

On the map, which street would you take to travel from the White House to the U.S. Capitol?

_____

The first president to live in the White House was John Adams. Adams, our second president, moved there in 1800.

What Happened and When?

Read the timeline to learn about key events in the history of the United States government.

1750 **1800** **1850**

1776
The Declaration of Independence is written.

1790
U.S. Constitution is approved by 13 states.

1865
The 13th Amendment abolishes slavery.

TODAY
The U.S. Constitution is the law of the land for 50 states, 1 district (Washington, D.C.), and 5 territories.

Who will you meet?

President Thomas Jefferson wrote the Declaration of Independence and served as the third president of the United States.

Senator Lisa Murkowski is a member of the United States Senate. She is a Republican, representing the state of Alaska.

Associate Justice Sonia Sotomayor is a member of the United States Supreme Court. She was appointed by President Barack Obama in 2009.

Congressman John Lewis serves as a member of the United States House of Representatives. He is a Democrat who represents Georgia's fifth district.

 INTERACTIVITY

Complete the interactive digital activity.

1900

1950

2000

1920
The 19th Amendment gives the vote to women.

1971
The 26th Amendment gives citizens eighteen years and older the right to vote.

TODAY
The United States Constitution has been amended 27 times, most recently in 1992.

Quest
Project-Based Learning

Changing My Community: One Letter at a Time

I'm Lisa and I'm a news reporter in your community. I'm always discovering issues that need to be addressed. When I find a problem, I let local political officials like the mayor know. Will you help me?

Quest Kick Off

Your mission is to identify an issue in the community where you live. Write a letter to convince a local political official to help address the issue. Explain the issue, how you propose to address it, and what type of help you might need.

1 Identify Issues

Think about where you live. What issues can you identify? Write down one issue and why you think it's important to address.

....

....

....

....

2 Think About Solutions

Think about how the issue could be addressed. How might officials within your local government help?

INTERACTIVITY

Explore a local community issue and ways to resolve it.

....

....

....

....

3 Look for *Quest* Connections

Turn to the next page to begin looking for Quest Connections that will help you write your letter.

4 *Quest* Findings
Write Your Letter

Use the Quest Findings page at the end of this chapter to help you write your letter.

Principles of Our Government

Vocabulary

republic
citizen
democracy
sovereignty
self-evident
unalienable
liberty

Academic Vocabulary

purpose
require
establish
define

Unlock The BIG Question

I will know the principles upon which our government is based.

JumpStart Activity

As a class, write a list of classroom rules. Begin by taking turns and giving ideas for rules. After you have ten rules, vote as a class on each rule. Only those rules that are approved by more than half the class go into effect.

The United States has a special type of government. This government serves and protects the people who live here.

On the Fourth of July, we celebrate American independence. This holiday honors the birth of our nation.

What Is Government?

Our government is the system that makes the rules and laws that guide our country. Government includes the people who make the laws and those who make sure the laws are obeyed. We are governed under the rule of law. This means that all people are equal under the law.

Around the world there are different types of governments. In the United States we have a republic. In a **republic**, citizens have the power to elect the leaders who make the country's laws and rules. A **citizen** is an official member of a country.

Our republic is a democracy. In a **democracy**, the power of the government comes from the support of the people. Elected leaders represent the people. If people become unhappy with the government, they can choose new leaders at the next election.

Part of our government's job is to make laws and rules for the common good of the people. These rules and laws create safe conditions for people to work and live. Traffic laws, for example, make our roads safe. Laws against pollution mean we can breathe cleaner air. Without these laws, individuals might feel freer to act in ways that hurt others.

The government also provides public services and goods. These services include mail delivered by a postal worker. When a park employee fixes a swing on a public playground or when your public-school teacher instructs you about history, they are providing government services, too. Government goods include highways, spacecraft, and planes for the military.

Families, clubs, and charities serve people in our country as well. The families in a neighborhood often help each other when one family is in need. A community group might gather signatures to get a traffic light at a busy corner. A local charity might collect money or clothes for people hurt by an earthquake or flood.

Word Wise

Greek and Latin Roots
The word *democracy* comes from the Greek word *dēmokratiā*. That word itself comes from two Greek words: *dēmos*, which means "people," and *kratos*, which means "rule." How do these root words connect to the definition of *democracy* you have learned?

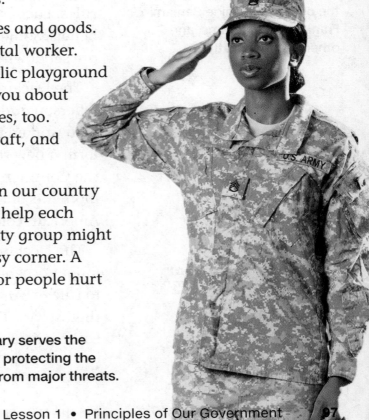

The military serves the nation by protecting the country from major threats.

Thomas Jefferson wrote the Declaration of Independence. The artist painted Jefferson in the center alongside Benjamin Franklin, John Adams, and other Founding Fathers.

The Declaration of Independence

Not all governments are alike. Each one has different rules. Each is based on different principles, or ideas and beliefs. Some of the principles that guide our government are set down in the Declaration of Independence.

The Declaration of Independence was written by Thomas Jefferson and other Founding Fathers. They were the men who worked to gain independence from Great Britain and form a new republic. The approval of the Declaration by the Continental Congress on July 4, 1776, marked the first moments of the United States of America. Before that, the American colonies had been ruled by the British.

The Declaration says that the American colonies no longer accepted Great Britain's **sovereignty**, or right to rule, in America. Instead, Americans would rule themselves. The Declaration explains what the Founding Fathers believed the **purpose** of government should be.

Academic Vocabulary

purpose • *n.*, the reason why something exists

Our Founding Principles

The Declaration of Independence says that "all men are created equal." It says that everyone is born with basic rights that **require** no proof, which means they are **self-evident**. Because no one, including the government, can take away these rights, they are **unalienable**. These rights include "Life, Liberty and the pursuit of Happiness." **Liberty** is the freedom to govern oneself. Protecting these rights is the very reason for government to exist. People consent, or agree, to giving the government power so it can protect these rights. The Declaration suggests that if a government fails to protect these rights, people are free to create a new government.

These ideas are important. They inspired Americans who were fighting for independence from Great Britain. Later they were also used to create a system of government for a new nation, the United States.

Academic Vocabulary

require • v., to need

1. ☑ **Reading Check** **Describe** two ideas that are found in the Declaration of Independence.

_____

_____

_____

_____

_____

_____

John Hancock, the president of the Continental Congress, signed the Declaration first. The delegates then signed the document based on their region. Northern state representatives signed first. Southern state representatives signed last.

The Constitution of the United States

After the American Revolution, American leaders met in 1787 to form a new government. They created the Constitution. This document was the plan and laws for a national government.

The Constitution has an introduction called the preamble. The preamble explains that the Constitution was written to help Americans **establish** and run their government. Its first three words are "We the People." These words state the most important idea about our government. In the United States, we govern ourselves. American citizens determine how the government is run.

The main sections of the Constitution describe how our government works. They explain how the country's leaders will be elected. They **define** and limit the powers of the national government. These powers include things as different as creating post offices, collecting taxes, and declaring war.

Our country was young when the Constitution was written. The Founding Fathers understood that the Constitution might need to change as the nation grew. They came up with a process by which amendments to the Constitution could be made. An amendment is an official change. Amendments must be approved by Congress and the states. Since the Constitution was first written, there have been 27 amendments to the Constitution.

Academic Vocabulary

establish • *v.*, to set up, to organize

define • *v.*, to explain or describe in a specific way

The United States Constitution was signed on September 17, 1787. However, to become the law of the land, it needed the approval of 9 of the 13 original states. There were many debates. By 1790, all 13 states had approved it.

The Bill of Rights

The first ten amendments to the Constitution are called the Bill of Rights. These amendments list the basic rights of every person in the United States. These rights include freedom of speech, freedom of religion, and the right of the press to publish freely. The amendments also set limits on the power of government.

Primary Source

Congress shall make no law ... abridging [taking away from] the freedom of speech, or of the press; or the right of the people peaceably to assemble, and to petition the Government for a redress [correction] of grievances [problems].

–First Amendment to the U.S. Constitution, December 15, 1791

This plan for government has proven to be both strong and flexible. Our Constitution has kept our republic healthy for more than 200 years.

2. ☑ **Reading Check**
Summarize Describe the purpose of the first ten amendments to the Constitution.

_____

_____

_____

_____

_____

_____

 INTERACTIVITY

Check your understanding of the key ideas of this lesson.

☑ Lesson 1 Check

3. **Categorize Identify** three types of workers who provide a government service.

_____

4. **Explain** the purpose of the Declaration of Independence.

_____

_____

_____

5. **Describe** how the principles in the Constitution affect you today.

_____

_____

_____

A Letter From John Adams to Abigail Adams

John Adams was one of our country's Founding Fathers and a leading voice in favor of American independence. In fact, Adams strongly argued for a break from British rule at two separate meetings, or congresses, that took place in 1774 and 1775–1776. During the second of these meetings, the Declaration of Independence was written.

One day before that document was signed, Adams wrote a letter to his wife, Abigail. In it, he described the great importance of what he and his fellow colonial leaders were about to achieve.

Vocabulary Support

to buy and sell goods and services

dissenting, *adj.*, disagreeing
impell'd [impelled], *v.*, to force into taking action
confederation, *n.*, the act of coming together

John and Abigail Adams

Yesterday the greatest Question was decided, which ever was debated in America, and a greater perhaps, never was or will be decided among Men. A Resolution was passed without one dissenting Colony "that these united Colonies, are, and of right ought to be free and independent States, and as such, they have, and of Right ought to have full Power to make War, conclude Peace, establish Commerce, and to do all the other Acts and Things, which other States may rightfully do." You will see in a few days a Declaration setting forth the Causes, which have impell'd Us to this mighty Revolution, and the Reasons which will justify it, in the Sight of God and Man. A Plan of Confederation will be taken up in a few days.

– John Adams, letter to Abigail Adams, July 3, 1776

Close Reading

1. **Identify** the "Acts and Things" that John Adams believed the United States should have a right to do.

_____

_____

2. **Describe** how Adams felt about the issue of American independence. Cite specific language from Adams' letter in your answer.

_____

_____

_____

_____

Wrap It Up

Based on Adams' letter and what you read in Lesson 1, **explain** the importance of the Declaration of Independence.

_____

_____

_____

_____

_____

_____

_____

How Our Government Works

 INTERACTIVITY

Participate in a class discussion to preview the content of this lesson.

Vocabulary

legislative branch
executive branch
judicial branch
checks and balances

Academic Vocabulary

control
enforce
ensure

Lisa Murkowski is a Republican senator from Alaska. There are two major political parties in the United States: Republicans and Democrats.

Unlock The BIG Question

I will know the responsibilities of the three branches of the United States government.

JumpStart Activity

Divide into two groups. One group forms a large outer circle. The other group forms a smaller inner circle. As a class, discuss how you think the outer circle is like the federal government and how the inner circle is like the state government.

The Constitution describes how the federal, or national, government of the United States is set up. The government has three different branches, or parts. They are the legislative branch, the executive branch, and the judicial branch.

The Three Branches and Their Responsibilities

The **legislative branch** of the federal government makes laws, or rules, that Americans must obey. This branch, called Congress, has two parts. One is the House of Representatives, known as the House. The other is the Senate. The House and the Senate work together to create and pass laws.

The nation's citizens elect all members of Congress. Each state elects two representatives, called senators, to the Senate. Each state also elects representatives to the House. The number of House representatives that each state elects depends on the state's population. So California, which has a large population, elects more than 50 representatives to the House. States with a smaller population elect fewer representatives. Alaska, for example, elects one.

Some members of Congress were leaders in other areas of American life before they became Congressmen and Congresswomen. For example, John Lewis, a Congressman from Georgia, was a leader in the struggle for African American civil rights in the 1960s.

The president is the head of the **executive branch**. This branch is in charge of carrying out the laws that are written by Congress. The president is also the head of our country's armed forces. Citizens vote for the president in a national election.

The executive branch includes the vice president and a group of officials called the Cabinet. The Cabinet advises the president on education, health, and the economy. It also gives advice on international issues, such as foreign trade and wars.

The **judicial branch** makes sure that our nation's laws agree with the Constitution. The highest level of the judicial branch is the Supreme Court. Nine justices make up the Supreme Court. Supreme Court justices are not elected. They are appointed by the president and then approved by the Senate. Once they are approved, Supreme Court justices can serve for their entire life.

1. ✅ **Reading Check**
Turn to a partner and **describe** the three branches of government.

The Three Branches of Government

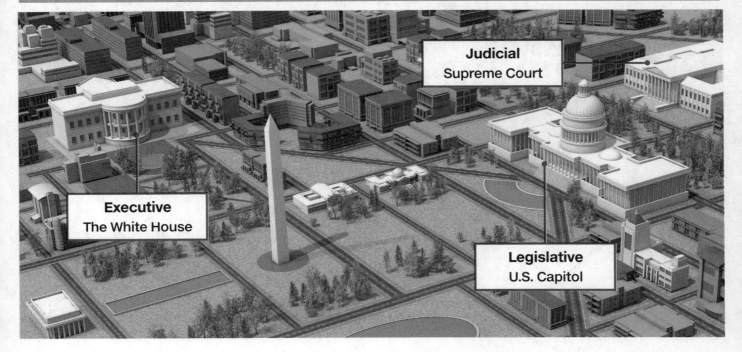

Judicial
Supreme Court

Executive
The White House

Legislative
U.S. Capitol

Checks and Balances

Why did the writers of the Constitution decide to separate the government into three branches? They thought that the government could become too strong and threaten people's rights, especially if one part of the government grew much stronger than other parts. To prevent this from happening, they came up with a system of **checks and balances**.

By dividing the government into three branches, the power was balanced. In addition, each part could check, or limit, the actions of the other two parts. These checks would keep any one branch of government from gaining too much **control**.

The checks and balances work for each branch of government. Congress, the legislative branch, has to pass all laws. Without the power to make laws, the president cannot act like a king.

Academic Vocabulary

control • *n.*, power, or command over something or someone

The system of checks and balances prevents any one branch from gaining too much power.

Checks and Balances

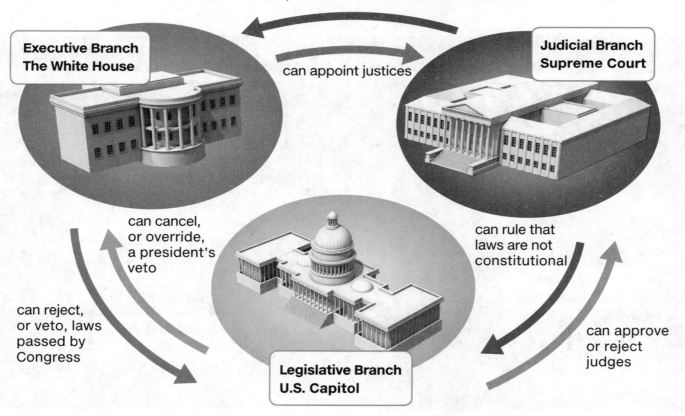

can rule that a president's acts are unconstitutional

**Executive Branch
The White House**

can appoint justices

**Judicial Branch
Supreme Court**

can cancel, or override, a president's veto

can rule that laws are not constitutional

can reject, or veto, laws passed by Congress

**Legislative Branch
U.S. Capitol**

can approve or reject judges

However, laws that are passed by Congress cannot go against the Constitution. If they do, the judicial branch can declare the laws unconstitutional. The judicial branch can also declare a president's orders unconstitutional.

The president has the right to veto, or reject, laws that Congress passes. In turn, Congress can override, or cancel out, the veto if two thirds of its members vote for the law. Although the president can pick Cabinet members and federal judges, which include justices for the Supreme Court, the Senate must approve the president's appointment. This provides a check against the president's power.

There are even checks and balances inside a single branch of government. You can see them in the way a law is approved. Before Congress sends a law to be signed by the president, both the House and the Senate must vote to approve the law.

All these checks and balances are known as the separation of powers. For more than 200 years, the system has served us well.

After President Barack Obama chose Sonia Sotomayor to become an Associate Justice of the Supreme Court, she had to first be approved by the Senate. In this picture, she is answering questions from senators.

2. **☑ Reading Check** **Explain** how Congress can check, or limit, the power of the president.

_____

_____

_____

_____

State and Local Government

The federal government is just one of three levels of government in the United States. The other two are state government and local government.

Each state has a state government. State governments follow their own state constitutions as well as the Constitution of the United States. Like the federal government, a state government has three branches. States also have a capital where the state government is located. The governor is head of the executive branch. For most states, the legislative branch includes a state senate and a state house of representatives. State courts and judges make up the judicial branch.

Local government includes the government of villages, towns, cities, and counties. Often, a mayor or a group of elected officials runs the government and makes local laws. A local government might also have its own courts.

Quest Connection

Draw a picture of a challenge your school or community faces. How might a local official be able to help?

 **INTERACTIVITY**

See examples of which officials or departments can help with certain issues.

Primary Source

The people of Atlanta have given us the gift of public trust, and for this we are grateful. But gratitude is not enough. Gratitude must be backed up with action, relentless, tireless action. Because at the end of the day, when it's all said and done, people elect you to win for them, to make their lives better, to care more about their future than you care about your own, and to keep your promise to come back for them, even when they weren't with you, or fought you every step of the way.

–Kasim Reed, Mayor of Atlanta, State of the City address, 2017

Academic Vocabulary

enforce • *v.*, to compel people to follow a rule or law

State and local governments create many of the laws we follow every day. The state government gives local governments the power to make and **enforce** laws. These include laws about speed limits, littering, and how your school is run. State and local governments collect taxes, just as the federal government does. These taxes are used to pay for services such as police, fire departments, schools, and libraries.

Some of the Founding Fathers didn't want all the government's power to be at the federal level. They wanted to **ensure** that the states would have a say in the government as well. Therefore, the Tenth Amendment to the Constitution says that all the powers that are not given to the federal government in the Constitution are reserved for the states and the people. This sharing and division of power is known as federalism.

Academic Vocabulary

ensure • *v.*, to make sure, or make certain

Levels of Government

Branches of Government	National	State	Local
Executive	President	Governor	Mayor
Legislative	Congress	State Legislature	City or Town Council
Judicial	Supreme Court	State Courts	Local Courts

3. ☑ **Reading Check** **Analyze** the chart. **Identify** and circle the head of a state's executive branch.

INTERACTIVITY

Check your understanding of the key ideas of this lesson.

☑ Lesson 2 Check

4. **Summarize Explain** how the Constitution shares power between the federal government and the states.

_____

_____

_____

5. **Sequence Describe** what happens after two thirds of Congress votes to approve a bill that the president has vetoed.

_____

6. **Understand the** *Quest* **Connections** Based on the problem you identified in the Quest Connection, which local official would you contact for help? **Explain** your answer.

_____

_____

Categorize

▶ VIDEO

Watch a video about categorizing.

To **categorize** means to organize things, ideas, or people based on related characteristics. A category is the group you put things in when you organize them. Everything in a category is related in some way. However, many things fit in more than one category. For example, an airplane and a train both go in the category of transportation, but the airplane could also go into the category of things that fly. Categorizing can also help us understand what we read and sort information when we are doing research.

To categorize anything, you can follow these steps:

1. Identify what you want to categorize.

2. Look for similarities among the things you want to categorize.

3. Decide on the categories that are the most useful.

4. Create a chart, as visual material, to analyze your information.

In Lesson 2, you read about different local, state, and federal governments. This chart categorizes the powers of our state and federal governments. What other category might be added to the chart?

Powers and Responsibilities of Government

Federal Government	State Government
• Print money	• Issue licenses
• Regulate trade within the country and internationally	• Regulate trade within the state
• Make treaties and conduct foreign policy	• Conduct elections
• Declare war	• Establish local governments
• Provide an army and navy	• Ratify amendments to the Constitution
• Establish post offices	• Take measures for public health and safety
• Make laws necessary to carry out these powers	• May exert powers the Constitution does not prohibit the states from using or delegate to the national government

In Lesson 2, you read about local, state, and national government. There are many ways you could categorize this information. Here are a few ideas for you to try.

1. **Identify** some places that have local governments.

   _____

2. **Identify** at least two things you could include in the Local Government category.

   _____

   _____

3. **Identify** the three branches of government for both state and national government.

   _____

   _____

4. Create a three-column chart to **categorize** information about the three branches of government.

Executive Branch	_____	Judicial Branch
signs or vetoes laws;	makes the laws;	_____
_____	divided into two parts	_____
_____		_____
_____		_____

Lesson 3 Our Rights and Responsibilities

INTERACTIVITY

Participate in a class discussion to preview the content of this lesson.

Vocabulary

jury
candidate
patriotism
symbol
petition

Academic Vocabulary

participate
convince

Unlock The BIG Question

I will know how citizens in a democracy have both rights and responsibilities.

JumpStart Activity

With a partner, plan and act out what you think it means to be a good citizen in your community. Then, present your idea to the rest of the class and identify what other groups are doing to show good citizenship.

The federal government protects the rights and freedoms of United States citizens. A person born in the United States is a United States citizen. Many people who move to this country can become citizens. They must follow a process and pass a test. The Constitution makes sure that citizens are treated fairly and that their rights are protected.

Citizens and Their Rights

The Constitution says that the United States government cannot pass any laws that would prevent Americans from expressing their opinions and ideas. Americans also have the right to their own religious beliefs. They have the right to travel freely. People who are accused of a crime have the right to a lawyer and a fair trial by a jury. A **jury** is a group of citizens who make a decision in a court of law. A jury's decision is based on the law and on facts that are presented by lawyers.

Some rights, such as freedom of speech, freedom of the press, and freedom of religion, were guaranteed by the Bill of Rights. Other rights have become law over time because of Constitutional amendments.

Thomas Paine was a writer who supported American independence. In 1794, years after the Bill of Rights had gone into effect, he wrote *The Age of Reason*, in which he explored freedom of religion.

Primary Source

I have always . . . supported the right of every man to his own opinion, however different that opinion might be to mine.

–Thomas Paine, *The Age of Reason*, January 27, 1794

Amendments Expand Citizens' Rights

When the Constitution was written, slavery was legal in the United States. On December 6, 1865, the Thirteenth Amendment ended this practice. This amendment said that no American could be enslaved. The Fourteenth Amendment gave all citizens equal protection under the law. The Fifteenth Amendment gave African American men the right to vote.

Women didn't have the right to vote when the Constitution was written. In 1920, women gained that right with the Nineteenth Amendment. Young people have gained rights, too. In 1971, the Twenty-sixth Amendment gave all citizens eighteen years and older the right to vote. Before this, the voting age was twenty-one in most states.

1. ☑ **Reading Check**
Analyze the picture.
Identify the people exercising their rights by circling them.

Our Responsibilities

Academic Vocabulary

participate • *v.*, to take part in an activity

In a democracy such as the United States, people have responsibilities as well as rights. To operate effectively, everyone needs to **participate**.

Voting is both a right and a responsibility. People cannot choose representatives unless they take the time to vote. Voters should learn about the candidates. **Candidates** are the people who run for a position in government. By reading newspapers, searching the Internet, or watching television, citizens can learn about the issues and how the presidential candidates, for example, view them. Voters can then elect a candidate they agree with on those issues.

Getting elected to public office is just one way to take part in government. A person can serve in government by being appointed, or selected, for a specific job, such as an employee of a government agency.

Americans also have a responsibility to obey laws. Otherwise, our communities can become more dangerous and disorderly. Adult citizens meet another responsibility when they serve on a jury. The right to a jury trial in America means that most adults must serve on juries.

2. ☑ Reading Check
Identify ways you can improve your community and school and add them to your citizenship to-do list.

Paying taxes is another responsibility. A tax is money that the government collects to pay for services such as roads, parks, schools, police, and the courts. Federal law requires us to pay income tax on the money we earn. Some state and local government laws add a sales tax on things we buy, such as clothes, and a property tax on our homes.

My Citizenship To-Do List

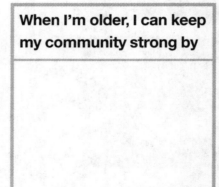

When I'm 18, my responsibilities include	When I'm older, I can keep my community strong by	I can help others in my community by

People also have a civic responsibility to take part in their community. Civics is the study of the rights and responsibilities of citizens. By being active in their community, people make sure their homes, towns, and cities are good places to live. For example, when it snows, people should shovel the sidewalk in front of their homes. They can also volunteer at a church or raise money for the school library.

Like adults, young people have responsibilities, too. They must obey the law, and some laws are aimed especially at children. For example, the law requires children to go to school or be educated at home. Children also have a responsibility to learn about United States history and government. That way, when they grow up, they will be informed citizens.

At school, students can take part in making the rules for their school. For example, groups of students have helped start recycling programs. To keep your school a safe and pleasant place to learn, you can help students who are being bullied, or pushed around. If you feel safe, you might ask the bully to stop. Or you might report the bullying to your teacher.

All people, whatever their age, have a responsibility to treat others with respect. This includes people who are different from you. In a strong, healthy democracy, all people benefit from a society that they themselves work to create and improve.

3. ☑ Reading Check   **Identify** and underline a law that applies to young people.

 Quest Connection

Highlight phrases that tell how you can make positive changes in your school.

👆 **INTERACTIVITY**

Learn how to match solutions to problems or issues in your community.

Recycling is a way for students to participate in their school community.

National Pride

Americans are proud of their nation, their people, and their government. This pride and support is called **patriotism**. We celebrate this pride each Independence Day. On Veterans Day and Memorial Day, we honor those soldiers who have served our country in war. On Martin Luther King, Jr. Day and Presidents' Day, we honor important people in our nation's history.

Americans have symbols to display their pride. **Symbols** are images, designs, or things that stand for ideas. For example, the American flag, a symbol of our nation, has 50 stars and 13 stripes. The stars stand for today's 50 states. The stripes stand for the country's original 13 states.

The Great Seal of the United States appears on the one-dollar bill. The motto, or saying, on this symbol is *E Pluribus Unum,* which is Latin for "Out of Many, One." This means that many states joined together with the federal government to form one union. Americans also honor their country when they recite the Pledge of Allegiance. In the Pledge, people state their loyalty to the nation and its symbol, the flag.

The number 13, which stands for the original 13 states, is shown in the 13 stars, stripes, arrows, and leaves on the olive branch of the Great Seal.

4. ☑ **Reading Check**
Compare the Great Seal to the American flag. How are they similar?

_____

_____

_____

_____

States have symbols, too. There are state flags and seals, which are official symbols. Many states have state animals. The ladybug is New York's insect. Pennsylvania has its own state toy, the Slinky, which was invented in Pennsylvania.

State symbols may show up on official state papers, Web sites, and license plates. License plates often display a state's motto, or saying, as well. Illinois plates say "Land of Lincoln." They point out the state's pride in the famous president from Illinois.

Citizens often take part in choosing state symbols. In 2005, for example, the orca became Washington State's official marine mammal because of students at Crescent Harbor Elementary School. The students created a petition to **convince** state officals. A **petition** is a formal request. Eventually, the Washington State legislators agreed with their choice and made the orca an official symbol of the state.

The honeybee is the state insect of Georgia.

Academic Vocabulary

convince • *v.*, to persuade

 INTERACTIVITY

Check your understanding of the key ideas of this lesson.

☑ Lesson 3 Check

5. **Summarize Explain** how constitutional amendments have changed our nation.

_____

_____

_____

6. You are designing a United States postage stamp to show what is special about this country. What symbol would you put on the stamp? **Explain** your choice.

_____

_____

7. **Understand the** *Quest* **Connections** What change do you think needs to happen in your school or neighborhood? Why is it important?

_____

_____

Compare Points of View

VIDEO

Watch a video about comparing points of view.

It is important to identify the point of view of a text when you read. This will help you understand why the author has written the text and what he or she wants you to learn, believe, or do. When you read two or more texts on the same topic, compare and contrast their points of view. Look for main ideas as well as words or examples that are used to influence readers.

In 2016, voters in San Francisco considered a measure that would have allowed sixteen-year-olds to vote in local elections. Not everyone agreed that this was a good idea. People in favor said that because sixteen-year-olds pay taxes, work jobs, and drive cars, they should be able to vote. Opponents believed that sixteen-year-olds are too young to make such an informed decision. In the end, the measure was not approved. Below, read the two official opinions about the issue from the San Francisco Elections Office. Then use the organizer on the next page to describe the points of view.

Point of View 1

... we need to do all we can to increase voter participation, both now and in the long run ... the earlier someone casts their first vote, the more likely they are to continue participating as a ... voter ... furthermore, research shows that ... 16-year-olds possess the same level of civic knowledge as 21 year olds ...

—Official Argument in Favor, San Francisco Elections Office

Point of View 2

Changing existing voting law in hopes of finding less worldly-wise citizens ... does not seem to be too prudent [wise] ... to reduce the average education and experience of San Francisco's voters might be a really dumb idea. The people pushing this so-called "reform" want younger and more trusting voters, who will ask fewer questions, have less education ...

—Official Argument Against, San Francisco Elections Office

1. Complete this organizer to list each point of view on lowering the voting age in San Francisco.

Point of View 1	Point of View 2
_____	_____
_____	_____
_____	_____
_____	_____

2. Use your answers from the organizer to write one or two sentences that **explain** the different points of view.

_____

_____

_____

_____

_____

3. Which opinion do you agree with? **Explain** why and include details from the point of view to support your answer.

_____

_____

_____

_____

Quality:
Leadership

The Purple Heart has a picture of George Washington on it because the medal was originally his idea. Washington wanted to honor brave soldiers in some way.

Tammy Duckworth (1968–)
Veteran and United States Senator

Tammy Duckworth is a United States Senator, representing Illinois as a Democrat. She is the first disabled woman elected to Congress.

Tammy Duckworth was born in Thailand, a country in Asia. When she was 16 years old, her family moved to Hawaii. After graduating from college, she joined the United States National Guard, which is part of the United States military. Members of the National Guard serve their country when asked to by the president. In 2004, Tammy Duckworth was called to active duty in the Iraq War. She worked as a helicopter pilot, and was severely injured in a battle. She lost both her legs and part of her right arm. She was awarded the Purple Heart, a special medal for bravery.

Tammy Duckworth did not let her injuries slow her down, however. She began a career in politics, winning seats in the United States House of Representatives and then the Senate. As a senator, she is a leader on veterans' issues. Many veterans come home from war with physical and emotional challenges, and she believes veterans deserve more support. She is also a leader in the struggle for equal rights for Americans with disabilities. In all her roles, Tammy Duckworth has been, and still is, a leader.

Find Out More

1. In what way does Tammy Duckworth show leadership?

_____

_____

_____

_____

2. Interview a veteran in your community. Ask him or her what it means to be a leader.

Use these graphics to review some of the vocabulary, people, and ideas from this chapter.

Federal Branches of Government

Executive	Legislative	Judicial
Who? President, Vice President, and Cabinet	**Who?** Congress	**Who?** Supreme Court; judges and courts
Role: enforces and carries out laws; head of the armed forces; can veto laws	**Role:** creates and passes laws; can override a veto	**Role:** settles disagreements about laws; decides if laws are constitutional

Rights and Responsibilities of Citizens

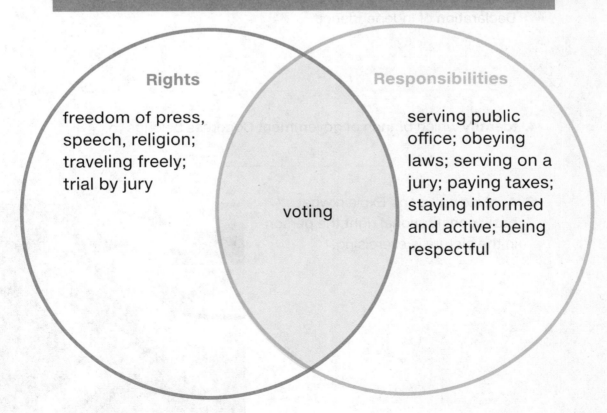

Rights

freedom of press, speech, religion; traveling freely; trial by jury

voting

Responsibilities

serving public office; obeying laws; serving on a jury; paying taxes; staying informed and active; being respectful

☑ **Assessment**

 GAMES

Play the vocabulary game.

Vocabulary and Key Ideas

1. **Identify** which person works at the national level of government. Fill in the circle next to the best answer.

   Ⓐ firefighter

   Ⓑ governor

   Ⓒ mayor

   Ⓓ senator

2. **Explain** how the Bill of Rights protects citizens' rights.

   _____

   _____

   _____

3. **Describe** one principle about our government that comes from the Declaration of Independence.

   _____

   _____

4. **Identify** which branch of government Congress belongs to.

   _____

5. **Analyze an Image** Explain what basic constitutional right the person in the picture is exercising.

   _____

   _____

Critical Thinking and Writing

6. **Explain** what two things can happen after the president vetoes a law.

_____

_____

_____

7. **Explain** how the Nineteenth and Twenty-sixth Amendments affected the rights of Americans.

_____

_____

_____

_____

8. **Identify** which of the following citizens are required to do by law. Fill in the circle next to the best answer.

Ⓐ pay taxes

Ⓑ run for office

Ⓒ volunteer at a school

Ⓓ volunteer at a hospital

9. **Revisit the Big Question** What is special about American government? **Explain** how the Constitution and the Bill of Rights still affect Americans today.

_____

_____

_____

10. **Writing Workshop: Write Informative Text** On a separate sheet of paper, write a paragraph explaining why the American flag has 13 stripes and 50 stars, and what each of these numbers stands for.

Analyze Primary Sources

SEC. 2. (a) Every person may freely speak, write and publish his or her sentiments [thoughts] on all subjects, being responsible for the abuse of this right. A law may not restrain or abridge [shorten] liberty of speech or press.

-California Constitution, Article I Declaration of Rights, May 7, 1879

11. What do you think is meant by the phrase "not restrain or abridge liberty of speech or press"? How does this section of the California Constitution illustrate both rights and responsibilities?

_____

_____

_____

_____

_____

_____

Categorize

12. Use the chart to **categorize** the words and phrases in the box. Write the letter of each item in the correct column, depending on whether it has to do with the Declaration of Independence, the United States Constitution, or the Bill of Rights.

(A) written by Thomas Jefferson   (E) "all men are created equal"

(B) "We the People"   (F) a plan for government

(C) freedom of speech and religion   (G) the first ten amendments

(D) has 27 amendments   (H) July 4, 1776

Declaration of Independence	United States Constitution	The Bill of Rights

Quest Findings

👆 **INTERACTIVITY**

Use this activity to help you write your letter to a local official.

Write Your Letter

You've read the lessons in this chapter, and now you're ready to write a letter to a local official. Remember that the goal of your letter is to convince or persuade the official to help you address an issue in your community. Follow these steps:

1 Prepare to Write

Create an outline that includes the issue you think is most important to address in your community, why it is important, and how you think your local government can help.

2 Research Your Local Government

Research your local government online to find which official might best be able to help address the issue you have identified. You will address your letter to this person.

3 Write a Draft Letter

Use your outline and the answers from your Quest Connections to write the most persuasive letter you can. Make sure your letter answers the following questions:

- What issue in your community do you want to address?
- Who does it affect?
- Why is it important to address it?
- How can local government officials help?

4 Share With a Partner

Exchange your draft letter with a partner. Invite your partner to ask questions about your letter and to make suggestions. When it is your turn, do the same for your partner.

5 Revise

Make changes to your letter after sharing it with your partner. Correct any grammatical or spelling errors.

The BIG Question

 VIDEO

How does the economy meet our needs and wants?

Jumpstart Activity

 INTERACTIVITY

Think about the things you and your family have in your home. Which do you need? Which could you do without? Fold a piece of paper in half. Write "Need" on one side and "Do Not Need" on the other. List three things for each category.

Wants and Needs

Preview the chapter **vocabulary** as you sing the rap.

Goods and services are bought and sold in an **economy**,
See they're set up to satisfy both wants and needs.
Producers make and sell goods or services,
Consumers buy the goods and services, you've heard
   of this.

When you buy something you use money to pay,
Currency is the type of money used in a place.
When you're deciding between two items,
The **opportunity cost** is the value of the one you
   didn't buy.

If **supply** is high, but **demand** is low,
Consumers may not buy, producers' profits won't grow.
Entrepreneurs take risks,
They have an idea, and then decide to open a
   business.

The Nation's Economy

Airplanes
Coal
Crude oil
Needles
Phones
Electronics
Lobsters
Electronics
Chips
Soybean oil
Tractors
Trucks
Diamonds
Gold
Soda ash
Coal
Iron and steel waste
Airplanes
Beef
Corn
Airplanes
Petroleum
Meds
Gold
Gold
Gasoline
Meds
Coal
Cars
Airplanes
Beef
Soybeans
Arms
Airplanes
Trucks
Airplanes
Airplanes
Electronics
Airplanes
Airplanes
Medical appliances
Airplanes
Airplanes
Cars
Petroleum
Cars
Airplanes
Petroleum
Airplanes
Airplanes

Zinc

Airplane parts

Where are goods sold in America?

This map shows the top-selling exports for each state in America.

Locate your state. What does it sell the most of?

_____

TODAY
The United States is one of the top sellers of goods in the world.

What happened and When?

Read the timeline to find out about the events that shaped the American workforce.

1700s

1700s
Workers live locally and trade goods.

1800s

1850s
Workers move from farms to factory jobs in cities.

Who will you meet?

Alexander Hamilton was a political leader who believed in a strong national government and economy.

Janet Yellen is an economist who became the first female to oversee the central bank of the United States.

Yelitsa Jean-Charles is an entrepreneur known for her groundbreaking line of empowering dolls.

Henry Ford was an inventor and businessman whose automobile changed America.

 INTERACTIVITY

Complete the interactive digital activity.

1900s　　　　　**2000s**　　　　　**Present**

1930s
Workers lose jobs and the U.S. government steps in to help.

1960s
Workers gain rights for fair and equal treatment.

TODAY
Workers find more jobs in services, technology, and worldwide markets.

129

Join the Economy: Start Your Own Business

Quest Kick Off

I'm Dion, and I own a dog walking business. My work makes me happy. I'm curious about what kind of work other kids might enjoy doing. What kind of business would you like to start? Use the information in this chapter to help you write a business plan.

1 Ask Questions

What will your business be? Will you sell something? Will you provide a service? Brainstorm a list of things you like to do and write down your ideas.

....

....

....

....

2 Build a Team

Starting a business can be hard work, so you will need help. Ask friends and family members to be on your business team. Ask them to work on tasks that you might not be ready to do on your own, such as driving to the store for supplies.

INTERACTIVITY

Complete the digital activities to get started on your business plan.

3 Look for *Quest* Connections

Begin looking for Quest Connections that will help you write your business plan.

4 *Quest* Findings
Write Your Business Plan

Use the Quest Findings page at the end of the chapter to help you write your business plan.

What Is the Economy?

INTERACTIVITY

Participate in a class discussion to preview the content of this lesson.

Vocabulary

producer
consumer
free enterprise system
market economy
command economy
private property

Academic Vocabulary

involve
individual

Unlock **The BIG Question**

I will know that economies exist to satisfy people's needs and wants.

Jumpstart Activity

Identify your favorite local store and the items you buy there. Explain how you, your family, and the people in your community depend on the store and the items it sells.

When you buy something or use it after you bought it, you are taking part in our economy. The economy is how the resources of an area or country are produced, delivered, and used. Every town, region, and state has an economy. Economies around the world may vary, but they all have things in common.

Needs and Wants

Economies are set up to satisfy both needs and wants. Needs are the things you must have to survive, such as food, clothing, and shelter. Wants are things you would like to have but can do without, such as a skateboard or a ticket to a movie.

There are two types of needs and wants that are called goods and services. Goods are actual products that you can buy, such as a car, apples, or shoes. Services are things that other people do for you, such as cutting your hair or giving you music lessons.

Making Choices

All economies produce, or make, goods and services for people to buy and use. A person or a company who makes a good or service to sell to others is known as a **producer**. A person or a company who buys a good or service is known as a **consumer**.

In this country, there are many different producers. That means that consumers have many choices of products and places to shop. If you decide to buy something for yourself, you could look in a store or you could shop online. Because you have choices, you might spend time deciding what to buy. Maybe you would end up buying a video game instead of a soccer ball.

Being part of an economy **involves** choices. By buying the video game, you fulfilled one of your wants. But now you have no money left to purchase a soccer ball. Buying the video game may mean that you have lost the chance to play soccer. Consumers must weigh their needs and wants before spending their money.

Academic Vocabulary

involve • *v.*, to take into account; include

1. ☑ **Reading Check**
   Categorize the following items as either needs or wants by adding them to the correct place on the chart: a bicycle, a home, shoes, a vacation, food, dance class

Needs	Wants
• drinking water	• lemonade
•	•
•	•
•	•

In a market economy, businesses decide what to manufacture, or produce. This factory worker is making windows.

Types of Economies

All types of economies answer three basic questions: What goods and services should be produced? How should they be produced? For whom should they be produced?

Around the world you will find different answers to these questions. In the United States, the economy is based on the free enterprise system. A **free enterprise system** is one in which producers have the right to create any goods or services they want. The government does not tell producers what they can create or sell. Producers also set the prices and quantities for their goods and services.

Another name for a free enterprise system is a **market economy**. A market in this sense is not like a store. Instead, it refers to an entire area or country in which things are bought and sold freely.

Not every country has a market economy. Some have a command economy, such as Cuba. In a **command economy**, the government decides what goods and services can be made and sold. The government tells people and businesses how much of something to produce. Often it is the government, not the producers, that sets prices.

2. ✅ **Reading Check** **Identify** details about each type of economy and complete the sentences.

Types of Economies	
Market Economy	**Command Economy**
• _____ decide what to produce. • The government does not decide how much of a product should be made.	• The government tells producers what to produce. • _____ decides how much of a product should be made.

Parts of the Economy

In every economy, producers use resources to create goods and services. These may be natural resources, such as trees, or human resources, such as truck drivers. They may even be capital resources, which are human-made products used to make goods and services. For example, the oven in a bakery is a capital resource.

Different parts of the United States economy use these resources to produce a variety of goods and services. Our giant economy is divided into important parts, or sectors.

The agricultural part, or sector, grows much of the food you eat, while the mining sector provides materials such as coal for electricity. The manufacturing sector makes many of the goods your family buys. The transportation portion gets people and goods from place to place in cars, trains, and planes. The services sector includes all the people who provide services for others, such as teachers, doctors, and the person who sells you a movie ticket. The entertainment sector includes the companies and people who make the songs and films you enjoy.

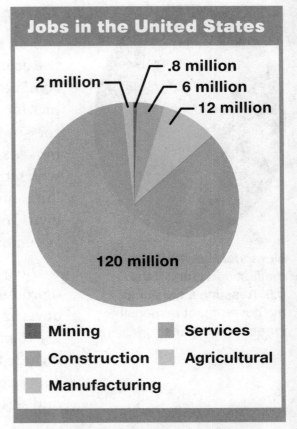

Jobs in the United States

2 million
.8 million
6 million
12 million
120 million

Mining
Services
Construction
Agricultural
Manufacturing

*Full-time Employment Only, Numbers approximated; Source: U.S. Bureau of Labor Statistics

Certain parts of the economy are more important in different regions. In the West, entertainment is important to California's economy. In the Southwest, ranching, or raising livestock, plays a large role in the Texas economy.

In the Midwest, manufacturing and transportation contribute to Michigan's economy. In the Southeast, mining provides many jobs in West Virginia. Tourism, which is part of the services sector, is important in Florida. The services sector is also important in the Northeast, in places like New York.

3. ☑ Reading Check **Analyze** the chart. **Compare** the number of services jobs to the number of manufacturing jobs.

_____

_____

Government and the Economy

Even though the United States government does not run the economy, it still has important economic responsibilities. A market economy needs certain rules. The government provides these rules. For example, people want the things they own to be protected, or secure. So the government makes stealing against the law. This is one of the ways in which the government protects **private property**, or the land, homes, stores, and goods that people or companies own. This is important in a free enterprise system, since the system is based on the buying and selling of private property.

The government also takes part in our economy as a producer and consumer. Most goods and services a government produces are public. This means everyone can use them, including those who cannot pay. Public goods include things like roads or schools. Public services include education and mail delivery. Citizens pay for public goods and services with taxes.

Alexander Hamilton was the first secretary of the U.S. Treasury, a division of the government responsible for economic rules.

4. ☑ **Reading Check** **Describe** what the government's activities are as a producer. Write your answers below.

The Government's Role in Our Economy

The Government Makes Laws
The government makes rules and protects private property.

The Government as Consumer
The government buys goods, such as computers and paper.

The Government as Producer

In what can it [the government] be so useful, as in promoting and improving the efforts of industry?

–Alexander Hamilton, *Report on Manufactures*, 1791

The government is also a consumer. As a consumer, the government buys goods and services from companies and **individuals**. For example, the government may buy planes for the navy or police cars from a private company. Or the government may buy the services of a teacher to teach at a public school.

In the United States, both the people and the government take part in the economy. Both are producers and consumers. Both provide goods and services needed in our daily lives.

Academic Vocabulary

individual • *n.*, a single human being

5. ☑ Reading Check **Identify** a good and a service that the government buys by underlining the text.

INTERACTIVITY

Check your understanding of the key ideas of this lesson.

☑ Lesson 1 Check

6. **Main Idea and Details Describe** the main purpose of an economy.

_____

_____

_____

7. Suppose you are going camping. **Identify** four things you will bring. **Categorize** them as either a need or a want.

_____

_____

8. Work with a partner. **Explain** a time when you were a producer. Then **explain** a time when you were a consumer.

_____

_____

_____

Make Predictions

VIDEO

Watch a video about making predictions.

When you look at a book title, you often have an idea of what that book will be about. That's because you are a smart reader! You can predict that *The Journey of a Young Boy* is going to be about a boy, not a dog. What about *A Wrinkle in Time*? Since time doesn't really have wrinkles, do you think this book is a kind of fantasy?

When you make a prediction, you make an educated guess about what is going to happen or what something will be about. It's like being a detective. You are using clues to figure something out by analyzing the information.

Suppose you were about to read Chapter 4. What clues would tell you what the chapter will be about? What does *the nation's economy* mean? The economy is how the resources of an area or country are produced, delivered, and used. You can predict that the chapter will be about how the nation makes, sells, and uses things.

Then look at the lesson titles. What word tells you that Lesson 2 will be about exchanging things? Look at the first heading in the lesson. What can you learn from it?

You can use a graphic organizer to keep track of clues and predictions as you read. Now look at the map about car manufacturing in Lesson 4 and read the "Globalization and Interdependence" section. Make a prediction about how car manufacturers in the United States and other nations are interdependent.

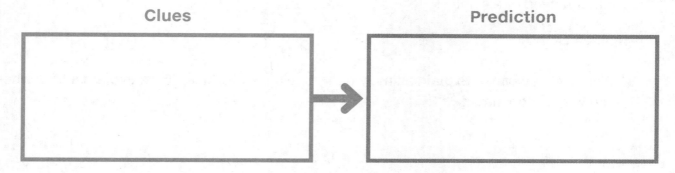

Clues

Prediction

Your Turn!

1. Skim through the title, images, and headings in Lesson 2. **Analyze** the information to make predictions on what the lesson is about.

   _____

   _____

   _____

2. **Analyze** the image at the beginning of Lesson 3. Then use the graphic organizer to make a prediction about what the lesson will be about.

Clues		Prediction
	→	

3. Think about a change that has happened in your life. Suppose you are going to write a story about it. **Identify** the title of your story and four headings that will help a reader predict what happens.

   _____

   _____

   _____

   _____

   _____

   _____

Trade and Markets

INTERACTIVITY

Participate in a class discussion to preview the content of this lesson.

Vocabulary

currency
barter
inflation
profit
income
supply
demand

Academic Vocabulary

borrow
available

Unlock The BIG Question

I will understand that businesses supply goods and services to match demand.

JumpStart Activity

Discuss with a partner at least three ways that people can pay for the things they buy.

Long ago, items such as seashells and pieces of metal served as money. Today, paper bills and metal coins are the most common forms of currency. **Currency** is the type of money used in a particular place. In the United States, our currency is the United States dollar.

Primary Source

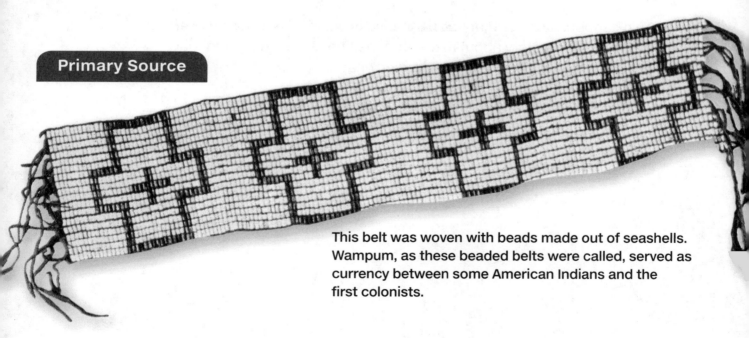

This belt was woven with beads made out of seashells. Wampum, as these beaded belts were called, served as currency between some American Indians and the first colonists.

Trade and Money

People have been exchanging things to get the goods and services they need and want since ancient times. Before the development of money, people would barter. To **barter** means to trade one type of good or service for another type. Animal furs, for example, might be traded for food.

Today, bartering is still used. A music teacher might trade guitar lessons to a baker. In return, the baker might give the teacher fresh bread. Both get what they need and want.

Bartering, however, has problems. What if the person who has what you need or want isn't interested in what you have to trade? That would make it impossible for a trade to happen. For this reason, modern economies use money to trade. Money can be traded for anything. Money is also easy to carry, can be divided into smaller quantities, and it is uniform, which means each piece of money is like another.

Prices and Inflation

The buying power of our currency can change as the prices of things change. Sometimes, prices go down—a pair of headphones that cost $50 last year might cost $40 this year. Sometimes, prices go up. Next year, the headphones might cost $60. A rise in the usual price of many goods and services is called **inflation**.

Inflation means you can buy fewer things for the same amount of money. Headphones are a want, not a need, so the rising price of a pair wouldn't threaten people's lives. However, inflation can cause serious problems when it causes the price of needs to rise. When the cost of food, shelter, or basic clothing rises, it can be hard for families to buy the things they need. This is especially true if the money a family earns decreases or stays the same.

These boys are trading playing cards. Each boy trades a card to get a card he wants.

1. **☑ Reading Check** A video game costs $20 before inflation in January. The same video game costs $25 in June because of inflation. **Identify** how much you think it will cost in August if inflation continues.

Businesses and Markets

When you buy something, your goal is to satisfy a want or a need. The goal of the business you buy from is to make a profit. **Profit** is the money a business has left over after it pays all its costs.

It might cost a bakery about $370, for example, to make bread each day. This cost includes expenses, such as the price of flour, rent on the building, and the money paid to employees. Employees are the workers who bake and sell the bread. If the bakery makes $470 a day in sales, then the difference, or profit, is $100. The profit that a business earns over a period of time, such as a year, is called **income**.

Businesses want to make a profit. They try to keep costs down, since they can't always raise prices. Competition is the reason. If a business sells a product at a high price, another business may open and sell the same product at a lower price. If the first business does not lower its prices or make its product better, it may lose customers. Businesses that can't match the prices or quality of their competitors often close down.

Quest Connection

What expenses might your business have? Do research on the costs of your business.

INTERACTIVITY

Explore the costs of doing business.

2. ☑ **Reading Check** This chart shows the monthly income and costs of a bakery. **Calculate** the monthly profit and write it in the chart.

Nelson's Bakery

Monthly Costs	
Rent	$3,500
Worker (Employee) Pay	$4,200
Ingredients and Packaging	$2,100
Equipment Rental	$800
Electricity and Gas	$425
Total Costs (Expenses)	$11,025
Total Sales	$14,100
Profit (Sales – Costs)	$

Entrepreneurs

There are many reasons businesses fail. Competition is just one of them. Opening a new business means taking a risk. You have to spend money to rent a workspace, pay for materials, and hire employees. If the business fails, all this money will be lost.

A person who takes a risk and opens a business is called an entrepreneur. An entrepreneur believes that his or her ideas for a business can make money and are worth that risk. Many of our country's most important companies have been started by entrepreneurs. Some entrepreneurs use their own savings to start their business, while others **borrow** money from a bank or from investors. An investor is someone who loans money in the hopes of making a profit when the new business has grown. Investors gave money to Yelitsa Jean-Charles. She is a young designer who started a natural-hair doll company. The goal of her business is to promote a positive and healthy self-image for girls.

Kids can be entrepreneurs, too. Suppose you decided to create a comic book business. You might spend money on paper, art supplies, and printer ink. If you didn't sell many comic books, you wouldn't make this money back. However, if your comic books sold well, you would make this money back plus a profit. Entrepreneurs have good ideas. They are willing to take risks for the chance to see their business succeed.

3. ☑ Reading Check **Identify** some costs of opening a new business by underlining them.

Yelitsa Jean-Charles is holding the prototype, or early model, of one of her Healthy Roots dolls.

Academic Vocabulary

borrow • *v.*, to take and use something with the agreement of returning it at a later time

Supply and Demand

A free enterprise system like the one in the United States is based on supply and demand. **Supply** is the amount of a product that businesses have **available** to sell. **Demand** is the amount of a product that consumers are willing to buy. Entrepreneurs have to be good judges of both to succeed.

The most successful businesses create products or services that have high demand. For example, if there is a product in great demand in your community, people are more likely to pay a high price for it. A business can charge a price well above what it costs to produce the item. This will result in larger profits.

If there is low demand for a product or service, then the situation is reversed. People will not be willing to pay a high price for the item. A business will be forced to lower prices to attract customers. The business's profits may be small.

Supply will usually respond to demand in a pattern.

4. ☑ **Reading Check** **Explain** why the store on the left is having a sale.

_____

_____

This store is having a sale on clothing.

Demand: Low

Customers came to this store to buy supplies before a big snowstorm.

Demand: High

If the amount supplied is low and the amount demanded is high, the price of an item will rise. Since large profits can be made by selling the item, businesses will increase the amount that is supplied. An entrepreneur, for example, may expand his or her business to make more of a product. Then the amount supplied may increase too much, and prices will likely fall.

These people are lining up for a sale. A sale can increase the demand for goods.

5. ☑ Reading Check **Identify** and underline the sentence that tells what happens if the amount supplied is low and the amount demanded is high.

☑ Lesson 2 Check

 INTERACTIVITY

Check your understanding of the key ideas of this lesson.

6. **Main Idea and Details Explain** why entrepreneurs are willing to take the risk of putting their money into a new business.

_____

_____

_____

7. Work with a partner. **Identify** a good or service you use. Then **discuss** what might cause the price of that good or service to go down.

8. **Understand the** *Quest* **Connections Think** about the product for the business you would like to start. **Explain** why there would be a demand for your product. **Describe** the kind of customers who might buy it.

_____

_____

_____

_____

People and the Economy

INTERACTIVITY

Participate in a class discussion to preview the content of this lesson.

Unlock The BIG Question

I will understand that both individuals and families make economic decisions.

Vocabulary

scarcity
opportunity cost
incentive
advertising
interest

Academic Vocabulary

promote
prefer

JumpStart Activity

You promised your friend you would go to the movies, but your soccer team has a game at the same time. How will you spend your day? Will you skip soccer or the movies? Explain your choice.

The economy provides you with needed goods, such as food and clothing, and also extras like movies and recorded music. Every day, you and your family take part in the economy by consuming or producing.

Babysitting is one way you can take part in the economy. You can earn money for things you need and want.

The Economy and You

When you get dressed in the morning, the clothes you wear are the result of economic activity. The clothes are produced by a business. You or someone you know made the choice to buy them. Your breakfast is also the result of economic activity and choice. Someone worked to get money to pay for the food. Someone also chose one food, such as a favorite cereal, over another food.

Economic choices are personal. You make choices all the time about your food or clothing. Should you buy the expensive pair of shoes? Maybe you should buy the cheaper pair? After all, you might outgrow them in a few months, and it would be good to save the money.

As you grow older, you will be making choices about more important economic questions. How will you pay for your basic needs? What kind of job will you have to earn money? What kind of home will you live in?

The Things We Want

Because of scarcity, we can never satisfy all our needs and wants. **Scarcity** means that the amount of a resource is limited. For example, water is scarce in a desert. You may be thirsty and want to fill your water bottle, but the water available to you is limited.

Labor can be scarce, too. During spring planting, a farmer may hire three workers to help him. Come fall, those same workers may not be available to help him with the harvest.

What if your favorite team was in the Super Bowl? Because there are a set number of seats in the stadium, and many thousands of fans who want to attend the game, those seats are scarce. The scarcity of those seats can make them costly.

For many consumers, the resource that may be scarce is money. You may come up with a list of things you want to buy, but the money to buy those things is limited, or scarce.

1. ☑ Reading Check Turn and talk to a partner. **Identify** an item your family buys that you help choose.

Making Choices

If you earned money by babysitting, how would you spend it? By deciding what you want to buy, you are making a choice. Before spending your money, you must make up your mind carefully. Once the money is spent, you won't get a chance to spend it again.

The money we earn is important to us. If we are lucky, we can spend it on something we want. But for most of us, satisfying our wants must wait until we have spent money on our basic needs. This means the money we have to spend on wants is limited.

Individuals and families must take care of basic needs first. Then extra money can be spent on wants. Keep in mind that there will always be new wants. If you spend a lot on a want today, there may not be enough money to pay for future wants. Managing these wants is part of being in charge of your personal spending.

Buying something always has an **opportunity cost**. When you choose between two items, the opportunity cost is the value of the item you didn't buy. If you spend money on something now, you lose the opportunity to spend that money on something else later.

2. ☑ Reading Check This boy has $20 to spend. **Describe** what the opportunity cost is if he buys the baseball cap.

_____

_____

Incentives

Why do we choose one product or service over another? Incentives play a big part in our decision. **Incentives** are things that encourage us to take an action, such as making a purchase. Sales and coupons are incentives. A low price on an item is a monetary incentive for people to buy it. Monetary means having to do with money. A negative incentive might be a fine on an overdue library book.

People usually learn about sales through advertising. **Advertising** is the use of public notices to bring attention to a product or service. Ads may appear in newspapers and magazines, on posters and billboards, or on the radio, television, and the Internet.

Advertising also uses nonmonetary incentives to make a product seem attractive or cool. Some ads try to convince consumers that a want is really a need. Ads can appeal to your emotions, making you think that you'll feel good if you purchase a product or service. Eye-catching packaging can make one product seem more attractive than another.

Location is an incentive, too. A restaurant owner may choose a street with convenient parking as an incentive to attract customers. Manufacturers try to **promote** their products by putting them near the cash registers so that it is easy for shoppers to see and buy the items.

Academic Vocabulary

promote • *v.*, to make widely known

3. ☑ **Reading Check** **Analyze** and **identify** each type of incentive shown below as *monetary* or *nonmonetary* by labeling it.

Making a Living

To provide for their wants and needs, most people must have an income, which is money people make from work or from property or businesses they own. The need for money is an incentive to find work.

Incentives play a role in job choice, too. The location of the job is one. Many people **prefer** jobs that are close to home. Income is another incentive. People usually prefer jobs that pay more money. However, the income a person can earn depends on many things. High-paying jobs often require special skills and education. Doctors, for example, need many years of college and training to learn their skills.

Banking and Saving

Most people keep the income they earn in a bank. Banks are a safe place for people to save money. Banks are also businesses that lend money. Banks take the money people save and give it out as loans to borrowers, who must pay it back over time. The federal government has a bank, too. It is run by the Federal Reserve. Janet Yellen was the first woman to oversee the Federal Reserve.

Janet Yellen

Primary Source

If there is a job that you feel passionate about, do what you can to pursue that job. . .

–Janet Yellen, "NYU Commencement Remarks," 2014

Since banks need money from savers to loan out, they provide an incentive. When you keep money in a bank, the bank pays you extra money called **interest**. Interest is added to your account regularly, usually once a month. This can make saving money a better choice than spending it.

Some people use their savings to buy stocks, or portions of a company. Stocks are risky as their value can change. Stock owners can make money if they sell their stocks when the value is high, but lose money if they sell at a low value.

Saver and Borrower

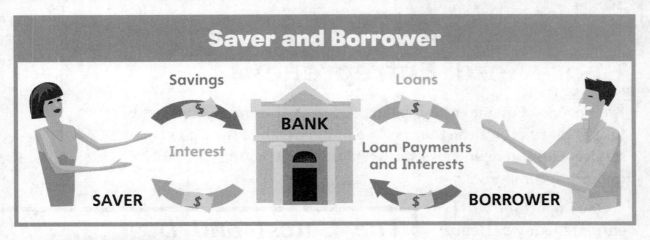

Savings

Loans

Interest

BANK

Loan Payments and Interests

SAVER

BORROWER

4. ☑ **Reading Check** **Explain** how banks benefit savers, bankers, and borrowers.

_____

_____

_____

INTERACTIVITY

Check your understanding of the key ideas of this lesson.

☑ Lesson 3 Check

5. **Main Idea and Details Compare** nice packaging and store sales. What do they have in common?

_____

_____

_____

6. Suppose your school's basketball team has a scarcity of uniforms. **Describe** a way you can work with others to get the supplies you need.

_____

_____

7. **Understand the**  **Connections** **Think** of the product or service your new business will offer. **Identify** some incentives you could use to encourage customers to buy.

_____

_____

Henry Ford, Entrepreneur

You have read about entrepreneurs. These are business people who take great risks because they believe in the worth of their good or service. Entrepreneurs have started many of our country's most important companies.

One important entrepreneur was Henry Ford. He founded the Ford Motor Company in Detroit, Michigan, in 1903. At the time, few people owned cars or "horseless carriages," as they were called. They were too expensive to make and buy. Ford had a dream to create a vehicle that everyone could afford. Today, the company sells more than six million cars a year.

The Latest and Best . . . . .
. . . . Boss of the Road

THIS new light touring car fills the demand for an automobile between a runabout and a heavy touring car.

It is positively the most perfect machine on the market, having overcome all drawbacks such as smell, noise, jolt, etc., common to all other makes of Auto Carriages.

It is so simple that a boy of 15 can run it.

For beauty of finish it is unequaled—and we promise

IMMEDIATE DELIVERY

THE FORDMOBILE $850
... with detachable tonneau ...

We haven't space enough to enter into its mechanical detail, but if you are interested in the NEWEST and MOST ADVANCED AUTO manufactured to-day write us for particulars.

FORD MOTOR CO.
692 MACK AVENUE   DETROIT, MICH.

A 1903 advertisement for a Ford car

Vocabulary Support

for the majority of the population

engineering, *n*., the planning, designing, and construction of machinery

devise, *v*., to work out or create

salary, *n*., a fixed regular payment for work; income

"I will build a car for the great multitude. It will be large enough for the family, but small enough for the individual to run and care for. It will be constructed of the best materials, by the best men to be hired, after the simplest designs that modern engineering can devise. But it will be so low in price that no man making a good salary will be unable to own one..."

- Henry Ford, *My Life and Work*, 1922

Close Reading

1. **Identify** and underline a place where Ford refers to resources. Circle a place where he refers to pricing.

2. **Analyze** the advertisement. **Identify** one way it tries to get people to buy a Ford.

_____

_____

_____

_____

_____

_____

Wrap It Up

Henry Ford took great risks to change the way cars were made. Do you agree that it is important to take risks in business? Why or why not?

_____

_____

_____

_____

_____

Lesson 4 | A Global Economy

 INTERACTIVITY

Participate in a class discussion to preview the content of this lesson.

Unlock The BIG Question

I will understand how global trade affects my life.

Vocabulary

innovation
import
export
division of labor
specialization
productivity
outsourcing

Academic Vocabulary

task
benefit

Jumpstart Activity

Think about what would need to be done to clean up your classroom. Then make a plan for how you could divide the project into smaller jobs.

Some of the goods that your family uses probably come from your community. The milk might come from a local dairy or the bread from your neighborhood bakery. Most goods, however, come from other places. Your community is connected to the whole world in a web of trade.

Today, many goods are shipped in huge containers on large cargo ships.

Trade Then and Now

Transportation is what makes trade and services between different places possible. Agricultural products from the countryside can be brought to the city. Goods from city factories can be brought to the countryside. Georgia peaches can be bought in Illinois. A package from Texas can be delivered to a business in Michigan. No single place can provide everything that the people who live there need. Each region depends on the others.

Trade has existed for many thousands of years. However, while it once took barges, wagons, and stagecoaches weeks and months to make a delivery, a jet plane can now cross those same distances in hours. Today's cargo ships can hold more goods than ever before. They can transport those goods far more cheaply, too. More goods are shipped and received around the world than at any other time in history.

New Technologies

Supersized boats, jumbo jets, and high-speed trains are all transportation **innovations**, or new inventions or ways of doing things. These innovations have helped bring the world closer together.

Innovations have changed communications, or the sharing of information, too. Computers, the Internet, and e-mail have made global communication faster and cheaper. Information from one place can move to another place almost instantly.

Both communication and transportation innovations allow companies to do business in countries around the world. They can buy resources in different places. Businesses can have factories in different nations. In the past, bosses may have spent long hours traveling to their company's factories. Now, they can run those factories using a video camera.

These innovations affect your life every day. Your computer may have been made in China, with parts from the United States. You can snack on strawberries in winter because they were grown in a part of the world where it is summer.

Word Wise

Word Origins The word *cargo* comes from two Latin words: *carcare* meaning "to load" and *caruus* meaning "wagon or vehicle." How does the word origin help to determine the meaning of *cargo*?

1. ☑ **Reading Check**
Identify a communication innovation and explain how it affects your life. Discuss with a partner.

Car Manufacturing

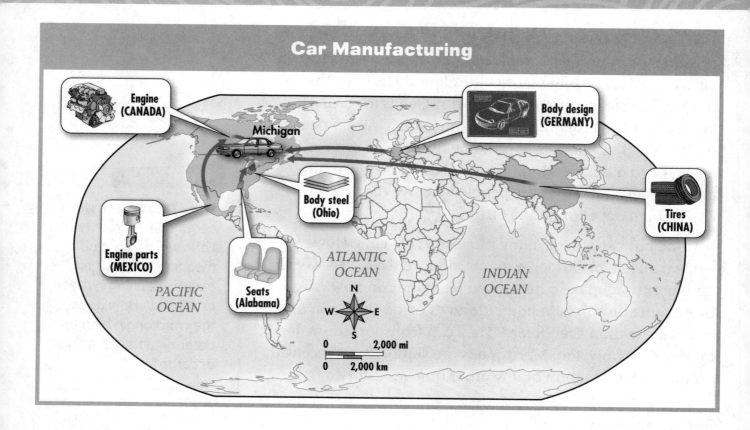

Engine (CANADA)

Michigan

Body design (GERMANY)

Engine parts (MEXICO)

Body steel (Ohio)

Seats (Alabama)

Tires (CHINA)

PACIFIC OCEAN

ATLANTIC OCEAN

INDIAN OCEAN

N W E S

0   2,000 mi
0   2,000 km

2. ☑ **Reading Check**

Main Idea and Details
The map shows a car being made in Michigan. **Explain** to a partner how the car is an example of globalization.

Globalization and Interdependence

The process through which goods and ideas spread between different countries is called globalization. Recently, the import and export of goods and services around the world has made trade grow. **Imports** are goods that are brought in from another country to be sold here. **Exports** are goods that are shipped to another country to be sold there. For example, bananas and figs might be imported into the United States, while wheat and apples may be exported to other countries.

Globalization makes the consumers and producers of different countries more connected to one another. A company can use parts or services from all over the world to create a product, such as the car on the map.

To do this, the company can have factories and workers in many places making the product. It can then sell this product to consumers almost anywhere. Through globalization, the world has become one giant market. This economic connection between countries is called interdependence. It means that one country's economy relies upon the economies in other countries to succeed.

Specialization and Productivity

The map of car manufacturing is also an example of the **division of labor**, or the separation of a work process into a number of different jobs. In a car factory, one group mounts the car's engine while another paints the body. The **task** of building the car has been split into different steps.

Division of labor is what allows for **specialization**. Specialization is the ability of a company, group, or person to focus on a single task. Focusing on a single job helps make people faster and more skilled at what they do. The people who mount car engines don't have to learn how to paint the car properly. Specialization often leads to innovation. Someone who is an expert at something is more likely to figure out ways to improve the product or process.

Specialization and the division of labor can also lead to greater **productivity**. Productivity is the amount a company can produce with a certain amount of labor. A person who only paints cars can paint more cars faster than a person who does other jobs as well.

Greater productivity can bring economic growth. A car company that increases productivity can supply more cars in the same amount of time. This means that the cars are probably cheaper to produce. The cost savings get passed on to consumers, which increases demand for the cars. It also means that consumers have more money to spend on other goods, such as food and clothes.

Academic Vocabulary

task • *n.*, a piece of work to be done

Primary Source

Henry Ford was one of the first business owners to use division of labor in his car factories.

3. ☑ **Reading Check**
Analyze the photo. Then **identify** different jobs that the division of labor creates by circling them.

The Benefits and Costs of Globalization

Academic Vocabulary

benefit • *n.*, an advantage gained from something

Globalization has many **benefits**. For the consumer, globalization means more choices. At the mall, you can choose from a vast selection of clothes and electronics. Because of globalization's division of labor, you can often buy these goods for less than you would if they were made entirely in the United States. If a part can be made more cheaply in another country, that lowers the cost of the entire product for you.

Globalization can also increase the number of jobs. If consumers in other countries can afford to buy American goods, it means American companies need to hire more workers to create, sell, and ship these goods.

Globalization has costs, too. It increases competition for sales and jobs. For example, strawberry farmers in the United States must compete for sales with strawberry farmers in Mexico. Although some jobs are gained, others are lost. If workers in another country will work for less money than workers in the United States, American companies may move jobs to that country. This process of hiring people to work outside of a company is called **outsourcing**. Globalization has led to competition among different countries for a share of the world's jobs. Globalization has environmental costs as well. For example, jet fuel, which is used to fly goods across the ocean, pollutes the air.

4. ☑ **Reading Check**
Analyze the map. Compare the number one and two trading partners of the United States. How are they different? Discuss with a partner.

The Top United States Trading Partners, 2017

Source: U.S. Census Bureau

5. ☑ **Reading Check** **Identify** some benefits and costs of globalization.

Globalization	
Benefits	**Costs**
_____	_____
_____	_____
_____	_____
_____	_____
_____	_____
_____	_____

INTERACTIVITY

Check your understanding of the key ideas of this lesson.

☑ **Lesson 4 Check**

6. **Cause and Effect Explain** how specialization leads to better-quality products.

_____

_____

_____

7. Suppose you wanted to make and sell toys. **Describe** the materials and workers you would need to create your product.

_____

_____

_____

8. **Explain** how you use division of labor at home.

_____

_____

Analyze Costs and Benefits

When we are making a decision, we need to analyze the costs and benefits of that decision. A cost is what you give up when you decide to do something. A benefit is what you gain by making a decision.

Conducting a cost-benefit analysis is a key part of making a decision. For example, when you are choosing a job, there are both costs and benefits to consider. Income is a major consideration. Most people prefer jobs that pay more money.

One benefit would be having more money to buy the things you want and need. However, high-paying jobs often require special skills and education. The cost of spending extra time and money might outweigh the benefits.

The suburbs experienced a housing boom after World War II.

Read the paragraph below that identifies another situation that had costs and benefits. It involves an economic shift that happened in the United States.

After World War II, many servicemen and servicewomen came back to the United States. Many of them settled in the suburbs, or neighborhoods outside of cities. New homes needed to be built. Building new homes provided jobs to people who worked in the construction industry. But, valuable farmland was lost in the process. This hurt small family farmers. Construction also destroyed trees and wetlands, killing birds and fish. Still, there were benefits to having so many new homes. The cost of housing was very low.

1. Use the graphic organizer to summarize the costs and benefits of the situation described in the paragraph. Include information about costs in the first column and write about benefits in the second column.

▶ VIDEO

Watch a video about analyzing costs and benefits.

Costs	Benefits

2. Go back to Lesson 3 and re-read the section titled "Banking and Saving." Use the graphic organizer to summarize the costs and benefits of buying stocks. If the costs and benefits are not clearly stated, try to draw conclusions.

Costs	Benefits

3. Choose an event that is currently going on in your school or community and conduct a cost-benefit analysis. Use a separate piece of paper and organize your work in a graphic organizer like the ones you completed on this page.

Quality:
Problem Solving

Bill Gates (1955–)
Professional Problem Solver

William Henry "Bill" Gates was born in Seattle, Washington, in 1955. When he was growing up, computers were rare and not many people used them. They were huge, expensive machines that could take up an entire room. Mostly large companies, the government, and universities used computers.

When he grew up, Gates formed a company called Microsoft with his friend Paul Allen. The two men began creating software for a new type of computer. This computer was smaller and meant for homes and offices. It was called the personal computer, or PC.

At the time, PC makers needed a type of software called an operating system. This is the basic program a computer needs to run. Without an operating system, a computer is not that useful. With an operating system, however, a computer can do all kinds of amazing things. In 1981, Microsoft made an operating system for IBM, one of the world's biggest computer makers.

By the 1990s, Microsoft software was on millions of computers all over the world. The company provided jobs for thousands of people, including computer programmers, designers, and accountants. Today, Microsoft's products are used on nearly every continent.

Find Out More

1. Identify the problem Bill Gates was faced with and how he solved it.

_____

_____

_____

2. Bill Gates helped to solve a problem. Follow your teacher's directions to identify and research a problem in your community. How did it start? How do you think it could be solved?

Visual Review

Use these graphics to review some of the vocabulary, people, and ideas from this chapter.

Supply and Demand

Consumers buy *more* of a good when its price goes down.
They buy *less* of a good when its price goes up.

When price goes down...	...Demand goes up.	When price goes up...	...Demand goes down.
↓	↑	↑	↓

Globalization

Benefits	Costs
Increase in some jobs	Loss of some jobs
Increase in sales of some products	Loss of sales in some areas
Greater availability of goods	Increase in harm to environment
Lower price of goods	

☑ Assessment

🎮 GAMES

Play the vocabulary game.

Vocabulary and Key Ideas

1. **Identify** the definition for each word.

a rise in the prices of many goods and services	**inflation**
the amount of a product that businesses have to sell	**currency**
the type of money used in a particular place	**supply**

2. **Explain** why an entrepreneur is willing to take risks.

_____

3. **Categorize** items in the list below. Underline each want. Circle each need.
   food, movie tickets, shelter, skating lessons

4. **Describe** how savers benefit from using a bank.

_____

5. **Analyze an Image Explain** what tools this farmer is using to sell her pumpkins.

_____

_____

_____

_____

_____

_____

Critical Thinking and Writing

6. **Identify** what describes the free enterprise system.

   _____ can decide what goods or services to sell.

7. **Main Idea and Details Describe** a problem with the barter system that the use of currency solved.

   _____

   _____

   _____

   _____

8. **Form Opinions** Do you agree or disagree with the following statement: All goods made locally are better than those made thousands of miles away. Explain your answer.

   _____

   _____

   _____

9. **Revisit the Big Question** What is the role of musicians in our economy? Do they meet a need or a want?

   _____

   _____

   _____

10. **Writing Workshop: Write a Narrative** Think about your future role in the United States economy. On a separate piece of paper, write two or three paragraphs about how you can prepare yourself to take part in it.

Analyze Primary Sources

"I believe that if you show people the problems and you show them the solutions they will be moved to act." -Bill Gates, Live 8, July 3, 2005

11. Rephrase what Bill Gates said here in your own words.

_____

_____

Analyze Costs and Benefits

12. As you have learned, specialization is the ability of a company, group, or person to focus on a single task. In the graphic organizer below, the benefits of specialization have been summarized for you. Think about a possible cost of specialization. Fill out the column with your analysis.

Costs	Benefits
	With specialization, a person can become an expert in a task, which may lead to innovation. He or she also can focus more and, therefore, move faster, which increases productivity.

Quest Findings

INTERACTIVITY

Use this activity to help you prepare to write your business plan.

Write Your Business Plan

You've read the lessons in this chapter and now you're ready to write your business plan. Remember that the goal of your plan is to explain what your business will do and how it will fill a need in your community.

1 Prepare to Write

Write down the name of your business. List the resources and supplies your business will need. Then write a sentence explaining why the business is important. This outline will help you write your plan.

2 Write a Draft

Use your outline and the answers from your Quest Connections to write the best business plan you can. Make sure your plan answers these questions:

- What is the name of your business?
- What does your business do?
- How will you advertise your business?
- Why is your business important or needed?

3 Share With a Partner

Exchange your draft business plan with a partner. Invite your partner to ask questions about your plan and to make suggestions. When it is your turn, politely do the same.

4 Revise

Make changes to your business plan after meeting with your partner. Correct any grammatical or spelling errors, or make changes to content if you need to.

Chapter 5

Regions: The Northeast

GO ONLINE FOR DIGITAL RESOURCES

- ▶ VIDEO
- 👆 INTERACTIVITY
- 🔊 AUDIO
- 🎮 GAMES
- ☑ ASSESSMENT
- 📖 eTEXT

The BIG Question

▶ VIDEO

How does where we live affect who we are?

Jumpstart Activity

 INTERACTIVITY

Work together in a small group to guess what the shape of the Northeast looks like. Make a mental map, or visualize, to think about what states make up this region. Then write one or two facts that you know or questions that you have about the Northeast. Think about the states in this region, its location, its climate, and its resources as you write. Share with a partner in your group.

_____

_____

_____

Welcome to the Northeast

Preview the chapter **vocabulary** as you sing the rap.

Let's set sail on the Atlantic, the Northeast in sight,

Lighthouses along the coast
help to guide you in the night.

Let's go to Cape Cod, that's a **peninsula**, right?

Yeah, it's land that's almost surrounded
by water on all sides.

When it comes to resources, the Northeast is full!

There's underground coal, and valuable **minerals**.

Fishing is a way of life here, but they're working to stop

Overfishing which caused the fish population to drop.

Many immigrants have come here to the Northeast,

Some laid railroads, some worked in factories.

This helped lead to a rise in industry,

And new inventions like **steamboats**, powered by steam.

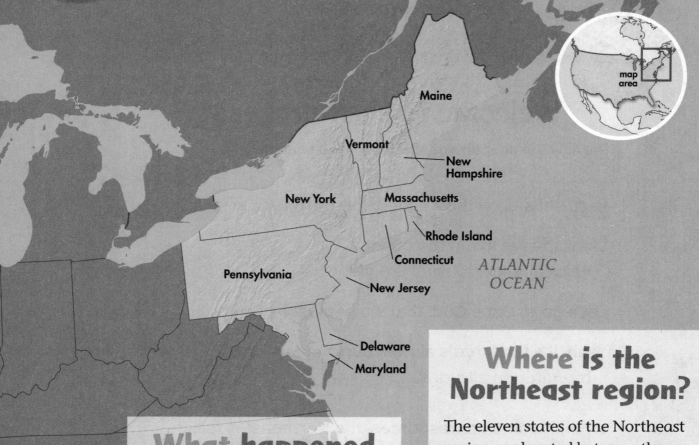

Maine

Vermont

New Hampshire

New York

Massachusetts

Rhode Island

Connecticut

Pennsylvania

New Jersey

ATLANTIC OCEAN

Delaware

Maryland

map area

Where is the Northeast region?

The eleven states of the Northeast region are located between the Great Lakes and the Atlantic Ocean. Beginning in the 1600s, people have come to the Northeast to make new lives for themselves. The birth of our government began here.

What happened and When?

Read and interpret the timeline to find out about the key events that happened in the Northeast region from early settlement to today.

1700

1800

1620
Settlers arrive and make the first English settlement in the Northeast at Plymouth.

1776
The Declaration of Independence is signed in Philadelphia.

TODAY
The Declaration of Independence is displayed at the National Archives Museum in Washington, D.C.

Who will you meet?

Benjamin Franklin was a Founding Father who helped write the Declaration of Independence and the United States Constitution.

Phillis Wheatley was the first African American to have a book of poetry published.

Elizabeth Cady Stanton was an an early leader of the women's rights movement.

Crispus Attucks was an African American who fought and died for freedom.

 INTERACTIVITY

Complete the interactive digital activity.

1900

2000

1879
Thomas Edison invents a new version of the electric light bulb.

1911
Many immigrants die in a factory fire.

2001
Terrorists attack the United States.

1892
Millions of immigrants arrive at Ellis Island.

TODAY
People can visit the National September 11 Memorial & Museum to commemorate those who died in the attack.

Immigrants and Workers' Rights

The United States drew many immigrants from Europe in the 1800s and early 1900s. Many immigrants, including men, women, and children worked in factories during the Industrial Revolution. This was a time of great change in the United States.

Quest Kick Off

Hi! I'm Sara, an immigrant from Italy. Your mission is to write a speech from the point of view of an immigrant who is trying to persuade others to join him or her in gaining more rights for workers. Think about what role workers of that time played in laws that protect workers today.

1 Think About Challenges

Think about reasons immigrants had for coming to the United States. What challenges did they face once they settled here?

....

....

....

....

2 Research

Find out more about the conditions that immigrants faced working in the factories.

INTERACTIVITY

Complete the digital activities to get started on your speech.

....

....

....

3 Look for Quest Connections

Begin looking for Quest Connections that will help you create your speech.

4 Quest Findings
Write Your Speech

Use the Quest Findings page at the end of the chapter to help you write your speech.

The Land of the Northeast

Vocabulary

lighthouse
peninsula
sound
glacier

Academic Vocabulary

surround
attract

Unlock The BIG Question

I will know that the Northeast has mountains, a long coast, and large lakes and rivers.

Jumpstart Activity

Work with a partner and together think about the coast of the Northeast. Make a word web with the word "ocean" in the middle and complete it by filling in activities that people can do if they live near the ocean. Show people doing one of the activities in a drawing.

Many people choose to live in the Northeast region of the United States. What makes this region so special? Is it the land? The people? The history? In fact, it is all of these things.

In parts of Pennsylvania, the land is used for farming.

Welcome to the Northeast

The Northeast is a diverse region. The region is known for the beauty of its land. It has rolling hills, mountains, farms, and thick forests. It has large busy cities and small quiet villages. Beach towns line the coast. The region has fast-running rivers, lakes, and the roaring waters of Niagara Falls. It also has trees with blazing colors in the fall. In winter, storms often cover the land in snow. All this variety is found in the smallest region of the United States.

The Northeast is made up of 11 states: Maine, New Hampshire, Vermont, Massachusetts, Rhode Island, Connecticut, New York, New Jersey, Pennsylvania, Maryland, and Delaware. Eight of these states are among the smallest states in the country. To the east of the region is the Atlantic Ocean. To the north is Canada. The Northeast is also bordered by two of the five Great Lakes.

1. ☑ **Reading Check**
Identify and circle the northern and western borders of the region. Then highlight the lakes that form part of the region's northwest border.

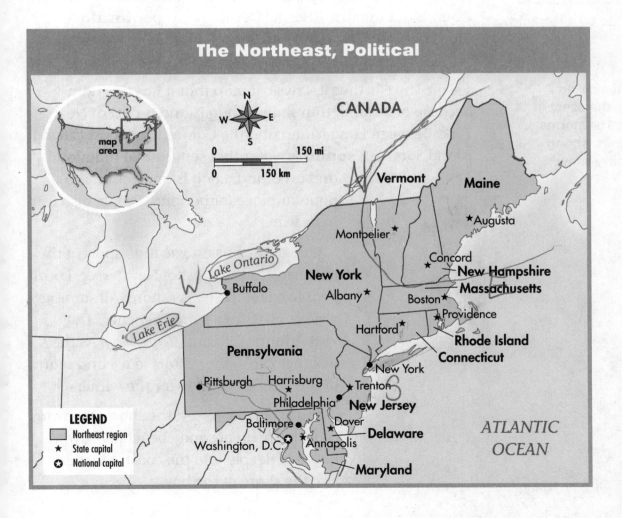

The Northeast, Political

CANADA

0 _____ 150 mi
0 _____ 150 km

Vermont

Maine
★Augusta

Montpelier ★

Concord
★

New Hampshire

Lake Ontario

Buffalo

New York
Albany ★

Boston ★
Massachusetts
Providence

Lake Erie

Hartford ★

Rhode Island
Connecticut

Pennsylvania

New York

Pittsburgh   Harrisburg
★

Trenton

Philadelphia   New Jersey

Baltimore   Dover
★   Delaware

Washington, D.C.   Annapolis

ATLANTIC OCEAN

Maryland

LEGEND
⬜ Northeast region
★ State capital
✪ National capital

The Atlantic Coast

All but two of the states in the Northeast, Pennsylvania and Vermont, are bordered by the Atlantic Ocean. The Atlantic coast is long and jagged as bays carve into the land. Islands lie just off the coast in many states, including Maine.

The coast of Maine is known for its rugged beauty. It is also known as the home to the easternmost point in the nation, Quoddy Head State Park. At Quoddy Head and other places on the Atlantic coast, waves crash against the rocks and cliffs. Dozens of lighthouses line the coast. A **lighthouse** is a tower with a bright light at the top called a beacon. The beacon shines to guide ships at sea during the night.

Some of the ships that travel along the Atlantic coast dock at one of the harbors in Massachusetts. People also come to the state to visit Cape Cod. The Cape, as it is often called, extends out into the Atlantic Ocean. It is a **peninsula**, or land that is almost **surrounded** on all sides by water.

Academic Vocabulary

surround • v., to be all around something

In winter, storms called nor'easters hit the coast of the Northeast. The storms often bring winds, strong waves, and heavy snow.

Farther south along the coast is Long Island. You can see on The Northeast, Physical map that it has this name because of its long, thin shape. Long Island is part of New York. Between Long Island and the Connecticut coast is Long Island Sound. A **sound** is water that separates a mainland and an island. Long Island Sound is a popular place for boating. People also fish in its waters.

One of the busiest vacation spots in the Northeast is the coast of New Jersey. Local people call it the Jersey shore. All summer, visitors fill its hot, sandy beaches. They visit Atlantic City and Cape May. As the weather cools, the visitors leave and many of the businesses close for the winter.

South of New Jersey, the short Delaware coast is a strip of sandy beach. Delaware Bay cuts deeply into the coast. Marshes line the shore of the bay.

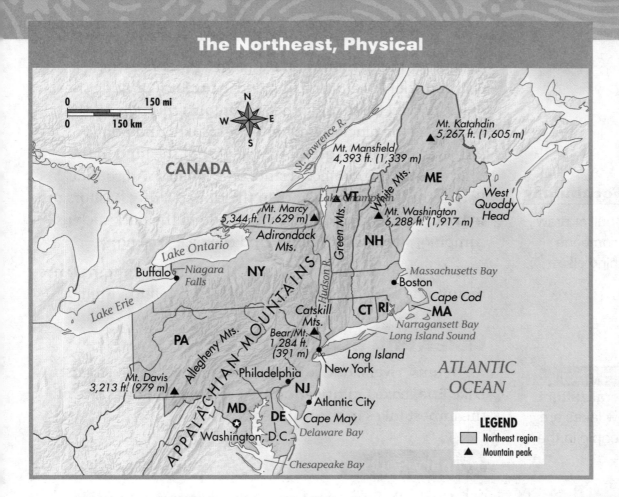

The Northeast, Physical

The Appalachian Range

Some of the oldest mountains on Earth, the Appalachian Mountains, are in the Northeast. The Appalachians stretch nearly 2,000 miles from Alabama, in the Southeast region, into Canada.

The Appalachian range is made up of several smaller mountain ranges. In the Northeast, they include the White Mountains in New Hampshire, the Green Mountains in Vermont, the Catskill Mountains in New York, and the Allegheny Mountains in Pennsylvania.

The White Mountains include Mount Washington, the tallest mountain in the Northeast. Its high elevation and its location in the path of storms often cause high winds on the mountain.

The Green Mountains run north and south through Vermont. Heavy winter snowfall in both the Green Mountains and White Mountains make them popular for winter sports.

The Catskill Mountains are north of New York City. The beautiful views are popular with hikers and skiers. Artists also visit the area to take photographs or paint pictures.

2. ☑ **Reading Check**
Locate the mountain peaks. **Identify** and circle the tallest mountains in New York state and New Hampshire.

Another major mountain range in New York is the Adirondack Mountains. Long ago, **glaciers**, or huge sheets of ice, carved these and other mountains throughout the region. As the glaciers began to melt, lakes and ponds formed. Forests also grew. A large part of the land in the Adirondacks is a protected state park. In fact, Adirondack Park is the largest state park in the United States. Visitors are **attracted** to the many activities to do in the park such as camping, swimming, hiking, and even ice-skating.

Many people also travel to the Allegheny Mountains. These mountains stretch from Pennsylvania south into Virginia.

Lakes and Rivers

Streams, rivers, and lakes are plentiful in the Northeast. Lake Erie, Lake Ontario, and Lake Champlain are some of the largest lakes in the Northeast.

Primary Source

> Gradually from week to week the character of each tree came out . . . reflected in the smooth mirror of the lake.
>
> –Henry David Thoreau, *Walden*, 1854

The region's four largest rivers, including the Hudson River, drain into the Atlantic Ocean. They are used for swimming and boating. Some rivers are also used for white-water rafting.

Academic Vocabulary

attract • *v.*, to pull or draw something or someone toward something else

3. ☑ **Reading Check**
Make Generalizations
Explain how lakes are useful to people in the Northeast.

They are useful for carrying goods on ships

White-water rafting is popular in the Northeast.

The rivers of the Northeast have been used for transportation for many years. In the 1600s and 1700s, rivers were the main transportation routes for settlers. Many cities, such as New York City, New York, and Baltimore, Maryland, were built at the mouths of rivers. The mouth is where a river flows into a larger body of water, such as a bay or ocean. These cities were important ports for people and goods that crossed the Atlantic Ocean, traveling to or from Europe.

Today, people still move goods on the rivers of the region. Large cargo ships carry vehicles, oil, fruit, and other goods on rivers such as the Delaware River and the Hudson River.

The Hudson River

INTERACTIVITY

Check your understanding of the key ideas of this lesson.

✓ Lesson 1 Check

4. **Make Generalizations Identify** one thing most Northeastern states have in common.

   What most Northeastern states have in common is they all have capitels

5. You and your family decide to take a trip to the Northeast. Choose one place to visit on your trip and **describe** it. Why did you choose that place?

   New York. How will I discribe New York is a lot of bilendings and a lot of stores.

6. **Explain** how rivers, lakes, and other bodies of water are used in the Northeast.

   To carry large cargo vehicles.

Resources in the Northeast

Vocabulary

mineral
quarry
overfishing
bog
tourist

Academic Vocabulary

allow
provide

Unlock The BIG Question

I will know that the Northeast is rich in natural resources and makes many products.

JumpStart Activity

Brainstorm with a partner a list of natural resources that you know. Then write down what products those resources make. Circle the natural resources that you think can be found in the Northeast.

Just as people everywhere do, people in the Northeast depend on natural resources to live. Luckily, this region has many resources to offer. Many of its resources come from the Northeast's forests.

Vermont and New York are the top two maple-syrup-producing states. In one year, the two states produced over two million gallons of maple syrup.

Forest Resources

People have used forest resources in many different ways. Long ago, American Indians used the wood from trees to build homes and fences. They also carved wooden boats. In the 1600s, settlers built with wood, too. They also cleared forests to start farms.

Maine, New Hampshire, and Vermont are the most thickly forested states in the region. The forest industry is important in these states. Workers in the industry cut down trees to make into lumber, paper, and other products.

Sugar maple trees are another forest resource. These trees grow throughout the Northeast. They are used to make maple syrup. To make syrup, people drill holes and put spouts in the tree trunks. People collect the sap that drips out. Then they boil the sap in large tubs. After many hours the water evaporates, leaving behind maple syrup.

Resources in the Earth

Some of the most valuable natural resources in the Northeast are found in the earth. For example, Pennsylvania has underground deposits of coal. Coal is used as fuel. The region also has valuable minerals. A **mineral** is a nonliving material that is found in the earth. Most stone or rocks, such as granite and marble, are a mix of minerals. These materials are often used for building.

New Hampshire is famous for its rock quarries. A **quarry** is a place where stone is dug, cut, or blasted out of the earth. In fact, the state nickname is the Granite State.

Vermont also has large amounts of granite. Vermont has marble, too. The first marble quarry in Vermont opened in Dorset, in 1785. Vermont marble has been used on well-known landmarks. It was used on the New York Public Library and the United Nations building in New York City.

Word Wise

Multiple-Meaning Words
Some words have more than one meaning. These are called multiple-meaning words. Try out both meanings of the word in a sentence. Figure out which makes more sense. What are the different meanings of the word *resource*?

The two narrow sides of the United Nations building are covered with marble from Vermont.

Water Resources

Academic Vocabulary

allow • *v.*, to let someone do something

provide • *v.*, to give or make something available

Blue crab from Maryland

The Atlantic Ocean is another important resource in the Northeast. For hundreds of years, fishing has been a way of life along the coast. Over time, people improved fishing gear and boats. This **allowed** them to stay out in the ocean for longer periods and catch more fish. In the 1970s, the fish populations dropped in many areas in the Northeast. One of the main reasons for this drop was that people were overfishing the waters. **Overfishing** is when people catch fish faster than natural processes can replace them. Today, people work to find solutions to overfishing. They often limit the amount of fish that people can catch.

People in the Northeast also catch other sea life such as shellfish and crabs. Maine is famous for its lobsters. Many lobster fishers have been fishing the same way for many years. The fishers lower a baited trap into the water. Days later, the fishers haul up the traps and collect the lobsters. Maryland, on the Chesapeake Bay, is famous for its blue crabs. People use nets and baited cages or traps to catch blue crabs.

Rivers are another resource. Many rivers in the Northeast are used as sources for drinking water. Others, such as the Niagara River, near Niagara Falls, are used by power plants to produce electricity. The Niagara River **provides** electricity for much of New York.

1. ☑ **Reading Check** **Cause and Effect** **Describe** an effect of overfishing by filling in the chart.

Overfishing in the Northeast

Cause

| People were overfishing the waters. |

Effect

People were limited to the amount of fish they catch

smaller fishing industry in Northeast

The Northeast, Land Use

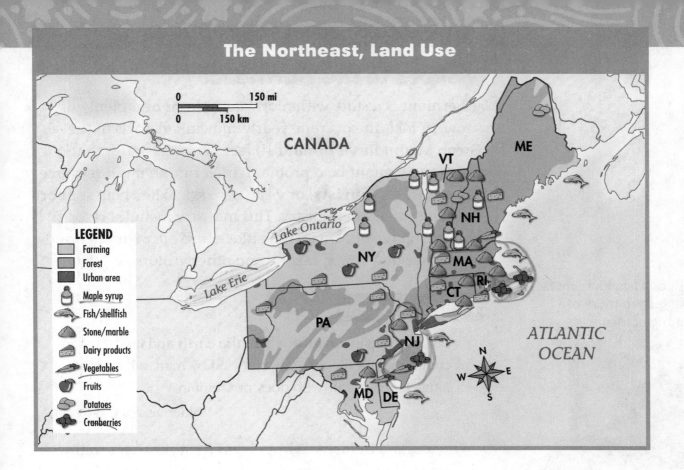

LEGEND
- Farming
- Forest
- Urban area
- Maple syrup
- Fish/shellfish
- Stone/marble
- Dairy products
- Vegetables
- Fruits
- Potatoes
- Cranberries

0   150 mi
0   150 km

CANADA

VT
ME
NH
Lake Ontario
NY
MA
RI
Lake Erie
CT
PA
NJ
ATLANTIC OCEAN
MD   DE

N W E S

Agriculture in the Northeast

The states in the Northeast with the most farms are New York and Pennsylvania. Farms in New York produce a variety of crops, including apples and grapes. New York also has many dairy farms. In Pennsylvania, farmers raise dairy cows, beef cattle, hogs, chickens, and sheep.

There are many farms in New Jersey, New Hampshire, and Vermont, too. Farmers in New Jersey grow many different fruits and vegetables. Most farms in Vermont are dairy farms. In fact, Vermont is a leading producer of milk in the Northeast.

In some parts of the region, such as Maine, the soil is rocky and not fertile enough for most crops. The climate is also cooler. However, certain crops, such as potatoes and blueberries, grow well there.

In Massachusetts, cranberries are a leading crop. These tart red berries grow in wet, marshy areas called **bogs**. The bogs near Cape Cod are perfect for growing them.

2. ✓ Reading Check **Analyze** the map. **Identify** the states where cranberries are grown by circling them on the map.

Visitors to the Northeast

Vermont is a state with many mountains and plenty of snow. In fact, the average yearly snowfall in parts of the Green Mountains is around 10 feet. In some states, that much snow might be a problem. In Vermont, it is a resource. Snow attracts **tourists**, or visitors, to ski. Skiers help support the state's tourism industry. This industry includes resorts, hotels, and restaurants. These places are busy summer and winter, serving skiers, hikers, and other visitors.

Primary Source

[Wilderness is] an area where the earth and its community of life are untrammeled by man, where man himself is a visitor who does not remain.

—Wilderness Act, 1964

The tourism industry is important in other states in the Northeast, too. The Adirondack Mountains and wilderness area as well as the mountains and lakes of New Hampshire attract tourists all year. So do cities such as Boston, Massachusetts, and New York City, New York. Coastal communities from Maine to Maryland attract many tourists in the summer.

Many people across the Northeast depend on tourism to earn a living. Workers in the tourism industry do many different jobs. They clean hotel rooms and serve food. They run ski lifts and give guided tours. They also sell T-shirts and rent bicycles.

3. ✔ **Reading Check**
Make Generalizations Identify and underline two sentences that make a generalization about the tourism industry in the Northeast region.

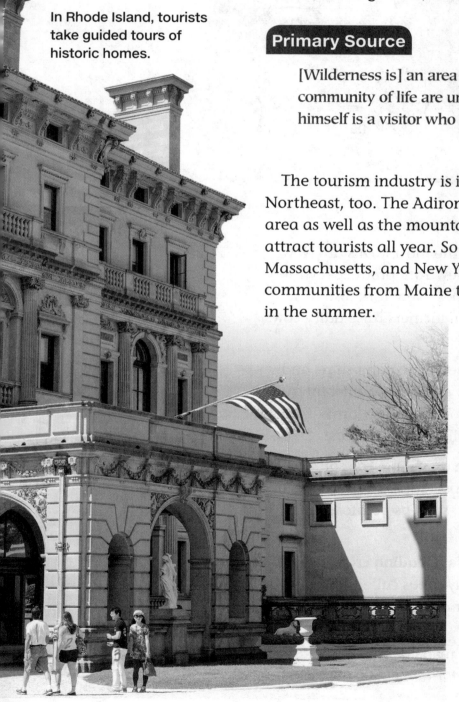
In Rhode Island, tourists take guided tours of historic homes.

4. ☑ **Reading Check** This picture shows snowboarders in the Northeast. Write a caption to **explain** how they help the industries in the region.

How they help the region is goeing to the region and paying money to go ski.

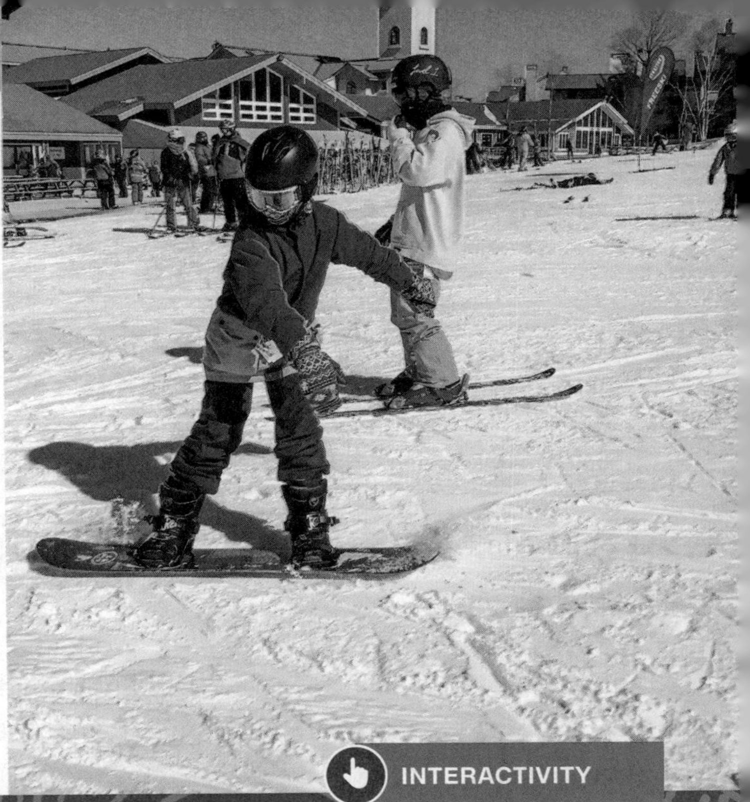

INTERACTIVITY

Check your understanding of the key ideas of this lesson.

☑ Lesson 2 Check

5. **Make Generalizations Describe** the causes of overfishing in the Northeast by making a generalization.

Be the causes is they take 400 fish out of the oecn

6. Big news! Your family is moving to the Northeast because your parents have found work there. Locate where you will live and **identify** what jobs your parents will be doing.

Fishing or work for tourism.

7. **Explain** how having plenty of natural resources in the Northeast affects the region's economy.

Coal and water, fish, lobster

INTERACTIVITY

Participate in a class discussion to preview the content of this lesson.

Vocabulary

sachem
wetu
suffrage

Academic Vocabulary

survive
oppose

Academic Vocabulary

survive • *v.*, to continue to live

Unlock The BIG Question

I will know that many of the events that led to the formation of the United States took place in the Northeast.

JumPstart Activity

Work in a small group to act out how you think the English settlers and American Indians met and lived in the Northeast. Show key activities in their daily lives.

Many of the events that led to the beginning of the nation took place in the Northeast. In fact, one of the first colonies was in what is now Massachusetts. In 1620, people from England arrived on the coast. They built a settlement they called Plymouth. Soon after, a cold, hard winter hit. Many of the settlers **survived** only with the help of the nearby Wampanoag (wamh puh NOH ag) people, an American Indian group.

Plimoth Plantation is a re-creation of an early English village. It shows how the settlement may have looked in 1627.

American Indians of the Northeast

Long before English settlers came to Plymouth, many different American Indian groups lived in the region. They lived in the forests and along the coast. Each group had its own beliefs, language, way of governing, and way of life.

The Wampanoag built their villages in forests. Each village had its own chief, or **sachem** (SAY chum). Families lived in **wetus** (wee TOOZ) made of poles covered with tree bark or reed mats. People wore clothing made of deerskins and fur. The Wampanoag hunted, fished, and grew corn and other vegetables.

The Wampanoag taught the settlers their ways of planting, fishing, and cooking. These skills helped the settlers adapt to the land. The English settlers brought with them goods from Europe. The goods included guns, metal tools, and cloth. These items were new to the Wampanoag.

At first, the Wampanoag and the English settlers helped each other and traded items. In time, more settlers came to the area. Many of them settled on land where the Wampanoag lived and hunted. In 1675, a war broke out. In a year of fighting, thousands of Wampanoag, Narragansett, and other American Indians were killed or forced out of their villages.

Farther inland lived the Mohawk, Oneida, Onondaga, Cayuga, and Seneca American Indians. Around 1600, these five groups joined together. They formed the Iroquois (IHR uh kwoi) Confederacy. This helped the groups live in peace. It also made them stronger in battles against the settlers from England and other European countries. For many years, the Iroquois were able to keep others off of their land.

1. ☑ **Reading Check**
Locate and circle the groups that made up the Iroquois Confederacy. **Identify** which Iroquois group lived farthest to the east.

_____

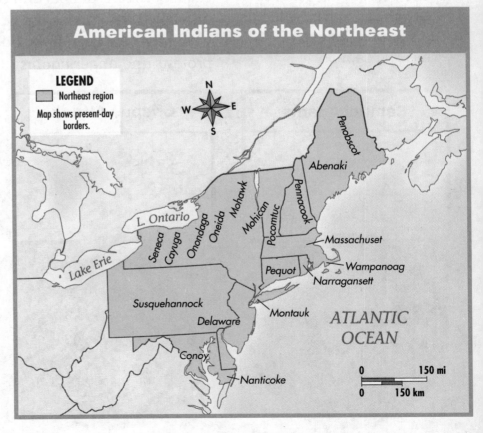

American Indians of the Northeast

LEGEND
▨ Northeast region
Map shows present-day borders.

N W E S

Penobscot
Abenaki
Pennacook
L. Ontario
Seneca
Cayuga
Onondaga
Oneida
Mohawk
Mohican
Pocomtuc
Massachuset
Lake Erie
Pequot
Wampanoag
Narragansett
Susquehannock
Montauk
Delaware
ATLANTIC OCEAN
Conoy
Nanticoke

0   150 mi
0   150 km

The Colonies Gain Independence

Word Wise

Multiple-Meaning Words
Some words have more than one meaning. Look for the word *founded* in the first paragraph. To figure out its meaning in this sentence, think of a meaning you already know. This may help you figure out the meaning that makes the most sense in this sentence.

Academic Vocabulary

oppose • *v.*, to go against

2. ☑ **Reading Check**
These images show key people from the colonies. **Describe** them by writing a sentence for each missing caption.

Settlers from England continued to set up colonies in North America. By the late 1700s, thirteen English colonies lined the Atlantic coast. Eight of them were in what is now the Northeast. Each was formed for a different reason. Rhode Island, Connecticut, and New Hampshire were settled by colonists from Massachusetts. New York was a Dutch colony that was taken over by English settlers. Pennsylvania was founded by William Penn. Penn wanted a colony where people had religious freedom. Delaware split off from Pennsylvania. New Jersey and Maryland were given to leaders by the king of Great Britain.

The colonies belonged to Great Britain. However, colonists held town meetings to discuss and vote on issues. In time, British leaders passed laws that the colonists were not allowed to vote on. Many colonists felt the laws were unfair and protested against them. Some of the first protests came from colonists in the Northeast. In Boston, Massachusetts, Samuel Adams wanted the colonists to **oppose** the laws.

Tensions between the colonists and British leaders grew. Soon, British soldiers were sent to Boston to keep order. In a clash between soldiers and colonists, five people were shot and killed. The first to die was Crispus Attucks. The fight was called the Boston Massacre. This fight led to even more protests and anger against Britain.

Samuel Adams	Crispus Attucks	Abigail Adams
Adams wanted the colonists to do oppose laws.	He fighted in Boston Massacre.	Adams wrote letters in support of freedom and liberty.

In 1775, the first battle of the American Revolution took place in the Northeast region. It was fought at Lexington, a town near Boston, Massachusetts. A year later, colonial leaders met in another area of the Northeast, in Philadelphia, Pennsylvania. There, they wrote the Declaration of Independence. This document marked the beginning of the United States of America.

3. ☑ **Reading Check**

Cause and Effect

Work with a partner and **explain** how different events in the Northeast affected the United States.

A New Plan of Government

In 1787, after the American Revolution was over, leaders from the states met again in Philadelphia. This time they met to make the states in the nation more united. They spent three months writing the United States Constitution. Benjamin Franklin from Pennsylvania played a key role. At 81, he was a respected leader. He helped settle disagreements between the states.

After the new United States government was formed, the nation's first capital was in the Northeast, in New York City. Here, George Washington was sworn in as the first president. In 1790, the capital moved to Philadelphia. It remained there until 1800, when it moved to the newly built city of Washington, D.C.

Joseph Brant	Benjamin Franklin	Phillis Wheatley
Brant was a Mohawk leader. He fought against the Americans during the American Revolution.	*When he was 81 he was repected leader*	Wheatley was a Boston poet who grew up in slavery. Her poetry celebrated the birth of the new nation.

Quest Connection

Why do you think the work of abolitionists helped to end slavery in the United States? Share your thoughts with a partner.

INTERACTIVITY

Explore the effects of the work of abolitionists in the United States.

The Abolitionists

Just as the Northeast region played an important role in the start of the nation, it played an important role in Americans' struggle for equal rights. The Declaration of Independence states that "all men are created equal" and that all people have the right to "life, liberty and the pursuit of happiness." Yet when the Declaration was written, many Americans were not free. Africans had been working as slaves in the colonies since the early days of settlement. In 1776, slavery was allowed in all 13 states.

Between 1777 and 1827, most of the states in the Northeast, except Maryland and Delaware, passed laws to end slavery. Many people in the Northeast also wanted to abolish, or end, slavery throughout the United States.

William Lloyd Garrison was a leading abolitionist. In 1833, he helped start the American Anti-Slavery Society in Philadelphia. Garrison was outspoken and fearless.

Many free African Americans and former slaves were part of the movement. Frederick Douglass and Sojourner Truth both had been slaves. They traveled and spoke about what life was like for a slave. Their speeches convinced many people to join the fight to end slavery. In 1865, the Thirteenth Amendment was added to the United States Constitution. The amendment made slavery illegal in the United States.

Stanton spoke to about 300 people who gathered at the Seneca Falls Convention.

Women's Rights

Many people who worked to end slavery also worked so that women could have equal rights. In the 1800s, women did not have the same rights as men. Women could not vote, and in most states they could not own property.

In 1848, Elizabeth Cady Stanton and Lucretia Mott organized a public meeting to talk about women's rights. It was to be a large convention held for this special purpose. It took place in Seneca Falls, New York. It was the first women's rights convention held in the United States.

The Seneca Falls Convention started the women's rights movement. Susan B. Anthony was a key leader in the women's rights movement. She led the struggle for women's **suffrage**, or the right to vote. An amendment to grant women suffrage was first introduced to Congress in 1878. However, the Nineteenth Amendment to the United States Constitution, which granted women the right to vote, did not pass until 1920.

4. ✓ **Reading Check** **Sequence** **Identify** which came first, the end of slavery or women's suffrage.

the end of Slavery

Like many abolitionists, Frederick Douglass supported women's rights at Seneca Falls.

 INTERACTIVITY

Check your understanding of the key ideas of this lesson.

✓ Lesson 3 Check

5. **Main Idea and Details** In the history of the Northeast, there are examples of conflicts and examples of how people worked together. **Identify** an example of each.

How people worked together is they tryed to stuggled to have equal rights

6. The Northeastern town where you live is near a Revolutionary War battle site. **Describe** what you might see in your town that shows its history.

I would see is a lot building destroy and a lot of bodies lying down on the ground. I wound sea some people getting out of town and some half dead soldiers

7. **Understand the** _Quest_ **Connections** **Explain** how people's lives would be different if the Thirteenth and the Nineteenth Amendments had not passed.

there will be a lot of war going on and allot of argeeement

Edward Winslow, *A Journal of the Pilgrims at Plymouth, 1622*

Edward Winslow was governor of Plymouth Colony, the first permanent European settlement. He came to Plymouth on the *Mayflower* with about 100 other settlers. After the ship landed, he was one of the leaders of the settlement who helped to influence others. Read an excerpt from Edward Winslow's journal before the landing at Cape Cod.

Vocabulary Support

different friends who lived there

the day we caught sight of land

gale, *n.*, a strong wind
dwelling, *n.*, a home or shelter
boisterous, *adj.*, strong
providence, *adj.*, divine care
deem, *v.*, judge

"Wednesday, the sixth of September, the winds coming east north east, a fine small gale, we loosed from Plymouth, having been kindly entertained and courteously used by divers friends there dwelling, and after many difficulties in boisterous storms, at length, by God's providence, upon the ninth of November following, by break of the day we espied land which was deemed to be Cape Cod."

–Edward Winslow, *Mourt's Relation: A Journal of the Pilgrims at Plymouth, 1622, Part I*

Fun Fact

The *Mayflower* was eventually broken up and sold off as scrap.

Close Reading

1. **Identify** and circle words that describe Winslow's mood, and **explain** whether it changes.

_____

_____

_____

_____

_____

2. **Draw conclusions** from the selection about Winslow's attitude about the journey and events that are taking place.

_____

_____

_____

_____

Wrap It Up

Find Cape Cod on a map. Then look for the location of England on a map or globe. Figure out how many miles the _Mayflower_ traveled. Then **explain** if you would have liked to make the journey.

_____

_____

_____

_____

Growth and Change in the Northeast

Vocabulary

steamboat
patent
sweatshop
labor union

Academic Vocabulary

advance
protect

Unlock The BIG Question

I will know that immigrants and growing industries brought change to the Northeast.

Jumpstart Activity

Make a list with a partner of items you would bring if you were immigrating to America in the 1800s. Explain why each of these items is important to bring.

Immigrants have been coming to the United States for hundreds of years. The settlers who started the colonies were immigrants. After the United States became a nation, many more immigrants came.

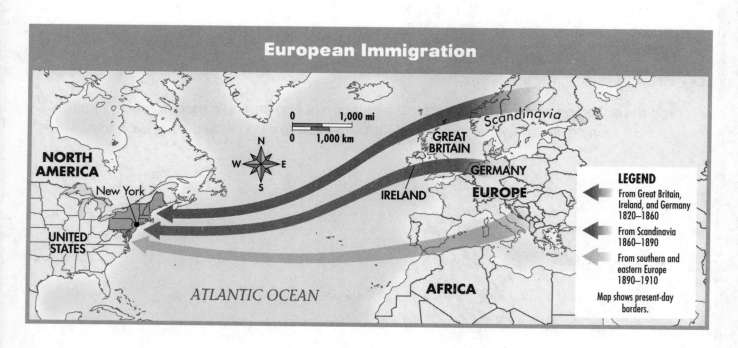

European Immigration

NORTH AMERICA

New York

UNITED STATES

ATLANTIC OCEAN

Scandinavia

GREAT BRITAIN

GERMANY

IRELAND

EUROPE

AFRICA

0   1,000 mi
0   1,000 km

N W E S

LEGEND

From Great Britain, Ireland, and Germany 1820–1860

From Scandinavia 1860–1890

From southern and eastern Europe 1890–1910

Map shows present-day borders.

Immigrants Come to the Northeast

Beginning in the early 1800s, immigrants came to the Northeast from many parts of Europe. From 1820 to 1860, most immigrants came from Ireland, Germany, and Great Britain. Newcomers from a part of northern Europe called Scandinavia came from 1860 to 1890. Many of them moved to the Midwest. Then from 1890 to 1910, immigrants came from countries in southern and eastern Europe.

Like today, immigrants came to the United States for many different reasons. Some came to find work. In the fast-growing cities in the Northeast, jobs in factories were plentiful. Others came to farm their own land. Still others came to escape war or a difficult life in their home country. Hope for a better life inspired them all.

Many immigrants came to the large port cities of the Northeast, such as Boston and New York City. New York was the busiest of these ports. In 1892, an immigration station opened on Ellis Island in New York Harbor. Millions of immigrants passed through its doors. At the station, government workers checked people's identification and other records. They examined eyes and throats to make sure the newcomers were healthy. Many of the newcomers were free to start their new lives. Those who did not pass the health checks were sent back to their home country.

Word Wise

Compound Words Did you know that compound words are two separate words put together to make a new word? Sometimes if you know the meaning of both words on their own, it can help you to understand the meaning of the compound word. What do you think the word *newcomers* means?

1. ✓ **Reading Check**
Make Generalizations Explain why immigrants came to the United States.

to live a new lifes and start a nice familys

Primary Source

Ellis Island

The Contributions of Immigrants

Immigrants have made many contributions to both the Northeast region and the rest of the nation. In the 1800s and 1900s, immigrants worked in factories and laid railroad tracks. Immigrants also planted and harvested crops.

Other immigrants made contributions to the study of science, to businesses, and to the arts. One well-known immigrant is Albert Einstein, a scientist from Germany. Irving Berlin came from Russia. He wrote songs. Alexander Graham Bell, the inventor of a telephone, was from Scotland.

Inventions and the Rise of Industry

The telephone was just one of many new inventions that changed the way Americans lived and worked. In 1807, Robert Fulton started the first steamboat service in the Northeast. A **steamboat** is a boat powered by a steam engine. Steamboats allowed people to travel more quickly from place to place.

Thomas Edison

In 1879, Thomas Edison invented a new version of the electric light bulb. In Menlo Park, New Jersey, Edison and his workers spent more than two years working with light and electricity. After many failed experiments, they had success. Edison applied for a patent. The **patent** gave him the right to make and sell the invention. Lewis Latimer, an African American inventor, found a way for light bulbs to last longer. Soon, light bulbs lit homes and city streets.

Fulton, Edison, and Latimer were not the only inventors to change the world. The first gasoline-powered automobile in the nation came out in 1885. Not long after, new roads linked cities. These and other new inventions helped bring the nation into the modern age. Together, they changed Americans' way of life.

New inventions and **advances** in technology helped industry grow. This change came first to the Northeast region, where there were already many factories and mills. In Massachusetts, Francis Cabot Lowell built a textile mill. His mill was one of the first to use a power loom to weave cloth.

In Pennsylvania, Andrew Carnegie, an immigrant from Scotland, used the Bessemer process to make steel. This led to rapid growth in the steel industry. Steel was used to make cars, railroad tracks, and bridges. Steel beams were also used to make tall buildings. After Elisha Otis of Vermont invented the brake for elevators in 1853, buildings could reach new heights. People could now use elevators to easily get to the upper floors. The tallest of these buildings were called skyscrapers.

The growth of industry had both helpful and harmful effects. Factories and mills provided jobs for immigrants and Americans. Workers turned natural resources into goods. As the amount of goods grew, many goods became less expensive.

However, industrial growth also created problems. Immigrants poured into the cities to find work. Cities grew so fast that there was not enough housing. Most newcomers lived in poorly built and unsafe buildings. Whole families were often crowded into one or two rooms. Some lived with no heat or hot water. In these poor conditions, diseases spread easily.

advance • *n.*, progress or a move forward

2. ☑ **Reading Check**
Identify inventions that brought America into the modern age and add them to the timeline.

Inventions from the Northeast

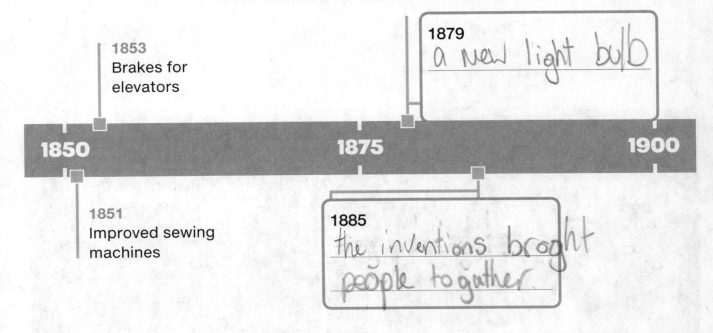

1853
Brakes for elevators

1879
a new light bulb

1850   1875   1900

1851
Improved sewing machines

1885
the inventions brought people togather

Movements for Reform

Quest Connection

Underline details about the working conditions of immigrants.

👆 **INTERACTIVITY**

Take a closer look at the living and working conditions that immigrants faced.

Academic Vocabulary

protect • v., to keep safe

Workers joined labor unions.

Working conditions in most mills and factories were poor. In New York City, most clothing factories were so crowded, dirty, and unsafe that they were known as **sweatshops**. Workers were often paid very little and worked long hours. Wages were so low that even children worked to help their families. Child workers were not able to go to school, and they were often hurt by the machines they worked with.

On March 25, 1911, dangerous conditions at a garment, or clothing, factory led to a tragedy. At the Triangle Shirtwaist Factory in New York City, a fire broke out. It raced through the top floors of the ten-story building. Many workers couldn't get out because the doors were locked. They went to the windows, hoping for rescue, but the firefighters' ladders were too short. Many people died, most of them young immigrant women.

The deadly fire angered many people in the Northeast region and across the country. People who wanted to reform, or improve, society worked together. These people were often called reformers. Reformers called for laws to **protect** workers. Groups of workers also banded together to form labor unions. A **labor union** is a workers' group that tries to gain better pay and working conditions. After the fire at the Triangle Shirtwaist Factory, many people joined the International Ladies' Garment Workers Union (ILGWU) and supported its demands for safer workplaces.

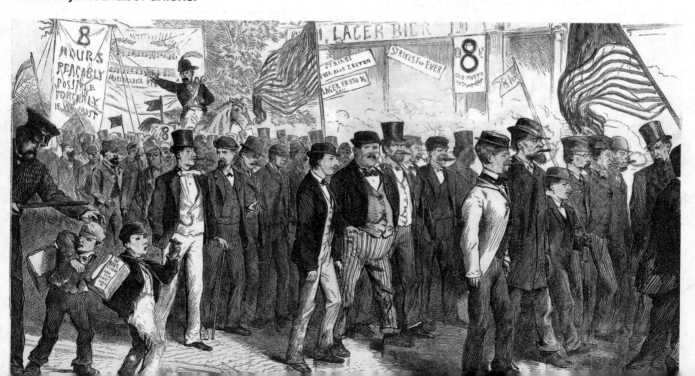

As industry grew in the Northeast, reformers continued to solve the problems that came with this growth. They pushed for laws to end child labor. In Massachusetts, the reformer Horace Mann worked to improve public schools. In New York City, reformers started community centers in poor immigrant neighborhoods. The centers offered child care, classes to teach English, and other help to immigrants.

Immigrant children at school

3. ☑ **Reading Check** **Draw Conclusions**
Explain how you think community centers changed immigrants' lives.

_____

_____

_____

INTERACTIVITY

Check your understanding of the key ideas of this lesson.

☑ **Lesson 4 Check**

4. **Cause and Effect** Choose one invention or industrial development of the 1800s. **Describe** its effects.

the effects are that new york city broke out in a fire

5. You have made a new friend. Your friend's grandparents came to the Northeast as immigrants from Europe. **Identify** three questions you would like to ask them about their experience.

did you like it your trip to Europe?
what is it like there?
did you ~~make~~ meet new people?

6. **Understand the** Quest **Connections** **Explain** how the growth of industry in cities impacted working conditions for immigrants.

to start a Job

_____

Cause and Effect

VIDEO

Watch a video about identifying causes and effects.

Identifying a cause and its effect can better help you understand what you read. A **cause** tells you why something happened. An **effect** is what happened. Sometimes writers use the words *cause* and *effect* to show readers how events are related. Other times, they use clue words such as *so, therefore, since, then,* or *because* to signal cause and effect. It is important to keep in mind that an effect can have more than one cause. Also, a cause can have multiple effects. This is especially true when you read about events in history.

Read the following passage. The causes have been underlined, and the effects have been highlighted. Try to locate any clue words that signal cause and effect for this selection.

Niagara Falls is located at the border of New York and Canada. A boat at the bottom of the falls, called the *Maid of the Mist*, carries tourists near the waterfall. The very first *Maid of the Mist* sailed in 1846.

Farther down the river from the falls are dangerous rapids, where the water rushes quickly. An exciting event happened here in 1861 when the *Maid of the Mist's* owner sold the steamboat. Therefore, the boat had to be taken through the rapids to its new owner.

Joel Robinson, the *Maid of the Mist's* captain, set out at 3:00 P.M. on June 6, 1861. The boat shot into the rapids. Since the rapids are fast-rushing water, huge waves crashed over the boat and tore off its smokestack.

Observers on the shore watched the boat being tossed about by waves. Soon, the boat hurtled into the Devil Hole's Rapids. Finally, the *Maid of the Mist* made it safely to Lake Ontario.

1. Using what you read on the previous page, fill in the graphic organizer with the effects of the sale of the *Maid of the Mist*.

Journey of *Maid of the Mist*

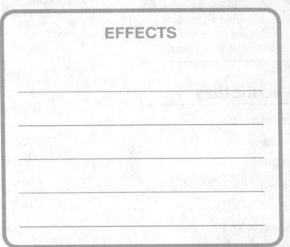

2. Read the second paragraph in the section "Immigrants Come to the Northeast" in Lesson 4. Then complete the graphic organizer with the causes and effects of the rise of industry in the Northeast.

The Rise of Industry

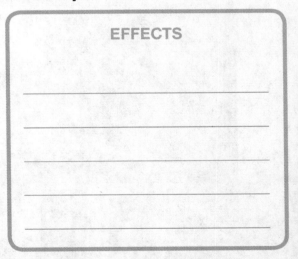

3. Re-read the section in Lesson 4 called "Movements for Reform". On a separate sheet of paper, take notes on the causes and effects of the Triangle Shirtwaist Factory fire. Then, fill in a graphic organizer like the ones shown here with the causes and effects of that event.

5 The Northeast Today

INTERACTIVITY

Participate in a class discussion to preview the content of this lesson.

Vocabulary

commerce
rural
urban
population density

Academic Vocabulary

pollution

Unlock
The **BIG**
Question

I will know that cities in the Northeast are centers of commerce and culture.

Jumpstart Activity

Work with a partner to discuss rural and city life. Write advantages for each in a two-column chart. Make a drawing of the one you prefer. Share your drawings and list of advantages with another group.

Since the 1900s, cities in the Northeast have continued to grow. Today, when people think of the region, they often think of big cities. They picture tall buildings, crowded sidewalks, and busy streets. The Northeast is known for its cities because it has some of the largest, oldest cities in the country.

The Growth of Cities

The three biggest cities in the Northeast are New York City, Boston, and Philadelphia. All three began as port cities in the colonies. Trade with Europe was important to the colonies. Ships brought people and goods to the colonies and took furs, wood, and other natural resources to other countries. The cities became centers of commerce. **Commerce** is the buying and selling of goods. The smaller port cities of Providence, Rhode Island, and Baltimore, Maryland, also grew from trade.

As settlers moved west, they started cities on inland waterways. Buffalo, New York, is a port city on Lake Erie. Pittsburgh, Pennsylvania, is located where three rivers meet. Boats brought people, animals, and goods to these cities, helping them grow.

The Northeast is not made up only of cities. It has rural areas as well. **Rural** areas have fewer people. In rural parts of the Northeast, there are small towns and farms. Most people live in houses with yards. They use cars or trucks to get where they want to go.

Urban areas are different. **Urban** areas are in or near cities. In urban areas, most people live in apartment buildings or houses with little or no land. Many people use public transportation systems to get around the city. Children play in parks and might take the bus or subway to school.

1. ☑ **Reading Check**
Make Generalizations
Compare rural and urban areas. How are the buildings people live in different in each area?

house with big yards and farm, apartments, skyscraper high rises

Public transportation in Boston

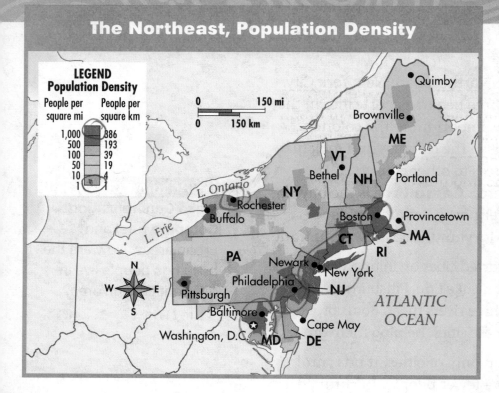

The Northeast, Population Density

LEGEND
Population Density

People per square mi	People per square km
1,000	886
500	193
100	39
50	19
10	4
1	1

Centers of Population and Commerce

In urban areas, people live close together. The closer together people live, the denser the population is. The number of people in an area of land is the area's **population density**. In places with a high population density, each square mile of land has many people living on it.

The population density of the Northeast varies from place to place. As the map shows, the most densely populated area is along the Atlantic coast. It is an area that includes Boston, New York City, Philadelphia, and Washington, D.C. The nation's capital has strong ties to Northeastern cities. It adds to the population density of the region.

Many people live in the Northeast because its cities are centers of activities. New York City is a center of shipping. In fact, it is the busiest port on the East Coast. Each year, imports and exports worth billions of dollars pass through the port. Imports are goods that are brought into a country for sale. Exports are goods that are sent to other countries for sale. Buffalo, New York, is also a key port. Many of the goods that travel to and from Canada go through Buffalo.

2. ☑ **Reading Check**

Locate and circle the area along the Atlantic coast where population density is high. Then **identify** two cities in this area.

Provincetown, Rochester
Newyork, Baltimore,
Philadadelphia,
Newark.

Camden Yards

Northeastern cities are hubs for other businesses as well. Wall Street, in New York City, is home to the world's leading financial companies and banks. Many high-tech businesses, such as computer software companies, are located in urban areas of the Northeast, too. Philadelphia is a leader in medical and health research. Boston is a leader in higher education. It has many colleges and universities.

City Sights and Landmarks

Each city in the Northeast has landmarks that make it unique. In Boston, people stroll on the Boston Common, or the Common, as it is often called. The Common is the oldest public park in the nation.

In Maryland, Oriole Park at Camden Yards is a favorite place to visit. This baseball stadium is located in downtown Baltimore. Nearly 50,000 people can fit in the ballpark at one time!

In New York City, visitors ride an elevator to the top of the Empire State Building. People also visit the National September 11 Memorial and Museum to remember those who died in the terrorist attack on the World Trade Center in 2001.

In Philadelphia, many people visit Independence Hall. It is where the Declaration of Independence and the Constitution were signed. Nearby is the famous Liberty Bell.

Independence Hall

3. ☑ **Reading Check**
Identify each picture by labeling it with the first letter of the city in which it is found. For example, write N next to a sight in New York.

Empire State Building

INTERACTIVITY

Take a closer look at Pittsburgh, Pennsylvania, and how it developed.

Academic Vocabulary

pollution • *n.*, chemical or physical waste that causes the air, water, and land to be dirty

Changing Times, Changing Cities

The cities of the Northeast have changed over time. One of the biggest changes has been economic. Manufacturing has become less important than it once was. Service industries have become more important. Banking and healthcare are examples of service industries. High-tech industries are also growing. They are built around technologies that were unknown a century ago.

Pittsburgh is a good example of how cities in the Northeast have changed. In the early 1800s, the city produced so much iron that it was known as the Iron City. Coal mining in the region provided the fuel for the furnaces used to make iron. Iron ore was brought by boat and railroads from the Midwest.

Then Pittsburgh turned to making steel. Steel brought money and jobs to the city for about 100 years. It also brought heavy **pollution**. Smoke dirtied the air and darkened the skies.

Primary Source

Men working in the city had to change their white shirts once a day because of the soot that dirtied them.

—A Pittsburgh resident, 1930s

After World War II, the demand for steel began to drop. The city passed laws to clean up the air. Pittsburgh changed once again. Today the city's steel industry is gone. Instead, it has high-tech industries, including businesses that make computer software, robots, and medical equipment. Service industries are important, too. Like all the Northeast's cities, Pittsburgh has changed with the times.

Pittsburgh today

4. ☑ **Reading Check** **Cause and Effect** Fill in the missing cause to **explain** how Pittsburgh has changed.

Effects of Industry

Cause

Pittsburgh's make steel

→

Effect

Pittsburgh's air was very polluted.

☑ **Lesson 5 Check**

INTERACTIVITY

Check your understanding of the key ideas of this lesson.

5. **Make Generalizations** Write a generalization to **describe** the impact of rivers in the region.

How I would describe the rivers in the region is they go down a path and though woods

6. One of your parents has been offered a new job working for a high-tech company. It will mean moving from your rural home to Pittsburgh. **Describe** your feelings about the move. Do you want to live in a city? Why or why not?

In between. Why, Because then I have to make new friends and new people and I think there he people will steal from our home.

7. **Understand the** *Quest* Connections **Explain** a negative effect that workers had to deal with in cities because of industrialization.

they had to deal with a lot of smoke

Work in Teams

A team is a group of people who work together to reach a goal. Many people in the United States have worked as a team to make changes to the nation. Women's groups, labor unions, and reformers have all worked as teams to reach their goals.

Being part of a team can be fun, but it can be a challenge, too. School projects, team sports, nature groups—all these activities are more successful when the people in them work together. The following steps will help you work in a team.

▶ **VIDEO**

Watch a video about working in teams.

1. Identify the team's goal. Make sure all team members agree on the goal.

2. Discuss what actions need to be taken. Take turns talking and listening. Make a list of tasks or jobs that need to be accomplished.

3. Decide who will complete each task. Try to divide the responsibilities equally.

4. Check in with each other as you work. Ask questions, give each other helpful ideas, and keep each other on schedule.

5. Meet to make sure all jobs have been accomplished.

At school, students often work in teams.

Your Turn!

Suppose you have been given the following assignment. Read the assignment. Add your name to the team. Then answer the questions.

> Work as a team to create a newspaper about well-known people and events in the history of the Northeast. Be creative! Due in three weeks.
>
> Team members: _____, Katie, Vanessa, Brad

1. **Identify** your team's goal.

   _____

   _____

2. Vanessa suggests brainstorming a list of topics for articles. Then you can each choose one you like. **Explain** why this is good idea.

   _____

   _____

3. Brad tells the group he doesn't want to write any articles. He says he doesn't write very well. **Describe** what you might say.

   _____

   _____

   _____

4. Members of the team check in with Katie the day before the newspaper is due. She hasn't even started her article. **Explain** what your team can do.

   _____

   _____

   _____

Quality:
Respect for the rights of others

Jacob Riis (1849–1914)
Helping Immigrants

Jacob Riis was a Danish immigrant, journalist, and photographer in New York City in the late 1800s. He came to the United States at the age of 21 and had a hard time finding work and sometimes had no food to eat. Finally, he got a job as a police reporter. Riis soon learned about the poor conditions that many immigrants were living in. He took photographs of tenements in the Lower East Side, where many immigrants lived in unsanitary and crowded conditions.

Riis could not believe what he saw. He felt that immigrants should have the same rights and respect as other Americans. He wanted to raise awareness about the poor conditions and treatment that many immigrants faced in New York so he decided to publish a book to share what he discovered. His book, *How the Other Half Lives*, included many of his photographs.

People were shocked when they read Riis's book and saw the photographs. One reader in particular was horrified. That person was Theodore Roosevelt—the police commissioner who would later become president of the United States. Roosevelt responded at once to help. Riis's work led to improvements in housing, sanitation, and overall living conditions for New York City's immigrants.

Find Out More

1. What do you think Jacob Riis meant by "the other half"? **Explain.**

_____

_____

_____

_____

2. Jacob Riis's photographs of immigrants living in tenement houses shocked many Americans. Today, people still work hard to fight for better living conditions for everyone. Work with a partner to find a local group that helps improve living conditions.

Quest Findings

Write Your Speech

INTERACTIVITY

Use this activity to help you write your speech.

You've read the lessons in this chapter and now you're ready to write your speech. Remember that the goal is to persuade others to support your cause: to gain more rights for immigrant workers. Follow these steps:

1 Prepare to Write

Talk with a partner about some of your ideas that you want to include in your speech. Then talk about how to organize these ideas. Consider talking about the problem and then tell a possible solution.

2 Write a Draft

Use your notes to write your draft. Make sure your draft answers the following questions:

• What challenges did immigrant workers face during this time period?

• How did immigrants help to improve working conditions during industrialization?

3 Share with a Partner

Exchange your draft speech with a partner. Invite your partner to ask questions about your speech and to make suggestions. When it is your turn, politely do the same.

4 Revise

Make changes to your speech after your meeting with your partner. Correct any grammatical or spelling errors.

6 Regions: The Southeast

GO ONLINE FOR
DIGITAL RESOURCES

▶ VIDEO

👆 INTERACTIVITY

🔊 AUDIO

🎮 GAMES

☑ ASSESSMENT

📖 eTEXT

The **BIG** Question ▶ VIDEO

How does where we live affect who we are?

Jumpstart Activity 👆 INTERACTIVITY

Imagine you live near a large body of water, like an ocean or a large river. In small groups, act out different things you do for fun in, on, or near the water.

Down in the Southeast

Preview the chapter **vocabulary** as you sing the rap.

From the Appalachians Mountains where there's lots
  of trees,

All the way down to Florida's **keys**.

The Southeast is a place people go to see, and,

Its warm climate allows for a long **growing season**.

But weather here can be dangerous too, be warned.

Hurricanes can form, those are powerful storms.

There are many farms found in the Southeast,

Agribusiness is farming as an industry.

So much culture here, African and English roots,

And other backgrounds like Cajun and Asian, too.

This region has also grown many kinds of music,

Like rock, gospel, **jazz**, country and blues.

map area

ATLANTIC OCEAN

West Virginia
Kentucky
Virginia
Tennessee
North Carolina
Arkansas
South Carolina
Mississippi
Alabama
Georgia
Louisiana
Florida

Where is the Southeast region?

The Southeast region includes twelve states. The Appalachian Mountains stretch along the upper states and an extensive coastline, starting along the Atlantic Ocean and running to the Gulf of Mexico, borders the lower states. The warm climate of the region makes it a popular tourist spot.

What happened and When?

Read the timeline to find out about key events in the history of the Southeast region.

1500

1600

1700

1513
Ponce de León claims Florida for Spain.

1682
French explorer Robert de La Salle sails down the Mississippi River.

1718
The French settle New Orleans.

TODAY
New Orleans is well-known for its French-influenced foods, such as *beignets*, which are square-shaped pastries.

Who will you meet?

Kasim Reed was elected as mayor of Atlanta, Georgia, in 2010.

Zora Neale Hurston was an author who wrote stories about African American culture in the Southeast region.

Cockacoeske was Queen of the Pamunkey, an American Indian cultural group in Virginia.

George Washington Carver was a scientist who worked to help farmers in the Southeast region.

 INTERACTIVITY

Complete the interactive digital activity.

1800

1900

2000

1865
The U.S. Civil War ends.

1968
Martin Luther King, Jr. is assassinated.

2005
Hurricane Katrina hits the Gulf Coast.

TODAY
People visit the Martin Luther King, Jr. Center for Nonviolent Social Change in Atlanta, Georgia.

Save the Southeast Coast!

The Southeast region has a beautiful coast along the Atlantic Ocean. However, it may not be beautiful for much longer! Humans are responsible for damaging the natural environment of the Southeast coast. The good news is—there are things we can do to protect it!

Quest Kick Off

Your mission is to research how people are impacting the environment of the Southeast coast. Create a blog in which you suggest how to protect and conserve, or save, that area.

1 Ask Questions

Learn about the Southeast coast. What landforms are there? What places do people visit?

....

....

....

....

2 Research

Use the Internet and research the environmental concerns people have about the Southeast coast. How are people impacting that area?

....

....

....

....

INTERACTIVITY

Complete the digital activities to get started on your blog.

3 Look for Quest Connections

Begin looking for Quest Connections that will help you write your blog.

4 Quest Findings Create Your Blog

Use the Quest Findings page at the end of the chapter to help you create your blog.

1 Land and Water of the Southeast

Unlock The BIG Question

I will know that the Southeast's geography is varied, from the Appalachian Mountains to the Gulf and Atlantic coasts.

Vocabulary

wetland
barrier island
piedmont
fall line
watershed
endangered species
extinct

Academic Vocabulary

occupy
transfer

Jumpstart Activity

Turn and talk to a partner about different jobs people might have if they live along the Mississippi River.

The Southeast region of the United States is made up of 12 states. Virginia, West Virginia, Kentucky, Tennessee, Arkansas, Louisiana, Mississippi, Alabama, Georgia, South Carolina, North Carolina, and Florida are all part of the Southeast. Something that makes the Southeast region unique is that it has two coasts.

The Southeast, Political

map area

West Virginia
★ Charleston
★ Richmond

★ Frankfort
Kentucky
Virginia

★ Nashville
Tennessee
Raleigh ★

Arkansas
★
Little Rock

Columbia ●
Atlanta ★
North Carolina

Alabama
Montgomery
South Carolina

Louisiana
★ Jackson
Mississippi
Georgia
ATLANTIC OCEAN

Baton Rouge ★
★ Tallahassee

● New Orleans

Florida

Gulf of Mexico

● Miami

N W E S

LEGEND
▢ Southeast region
— Fall line
★ State capital

Two Coasts

The Atlantic Ocean forms the eastern edge of the Southeast region. The Gulf of Mexico forms the southern edge. Thousands of miles of beaches line the two coastlines. In some areas, however, the coastlines are made up of wetlands. A **wetland** is an area sometimes covered with water. Swamps, marshes, and bogs are all kinds of wetlands.

Groups of long, narrow, islands called barrier islands lie off part of the Southeast's coast. **Barrier islands** lie between the mainland and the ocean. They began as sand dunes along the coast thousands of years ago. Then when glaciers melted, the ocean waters rose, and the dunes became islands.

From the Coast to the Mountains

As you move inland from the shore, the land is flat. This is the Coastal Plain of the United States. It stretches along both the Atlantic Ocean and the Gulf of Mexico. Wetlands such as the Great Dismal Swamp are found on the Coastal Plain.

As the elevation rises, there are rolling hills covered with forests. This area is called the **piedmont**. *Piedmont* means "foot of the mountain." The piedmont is high land at the foot of the Appalachian Mountains.

Rivers flow down from the mountains to the ocean. There is a drop-off between the higher land of the piedmont and the lower land of the Coastal Plain. In places at the drop-off, rivers tumble down in waterfalls. The falls form a line where the piedmont meets the Coastal Plain. That drop-off line of waterfalls is called the **fall line**. Several cities of the Southeast grew along the fall line, where falling water provided power for factories.

Word Wise

Greek and Latin Roots
The word *piedmont* is formed from the Latin root word *ped*, which means "foot." Think about how *ped* is used in the words *pedal* and *pedestrian*. What do those words mean?

As the Potomac River flows downhill through Virginia, it drops and forms the Great Falls.

The Appalachians

The Appalachian Mountains **occupy** much of the land of the Southeast. Different parts of the range have their own names. The Allegheny, Great Smoky, and Blue Ridge mountain chains are in the Southeast.

The mountains hold rich natural resources. Today, one-third of the nation's coal comes from Appalachia, the land in the mountains. The area's forests have long provided wood.

Every year, thousands of hikers follow the Appalachian Trail. The trail is more than 2,000 miles long. It begins in Maine and ends in Georgia. They say it takes 5 million footsteps to walk the whole trail. Many of those steps are in the Southeast.

1. ☑ **Reading Check** **Locate** the Mississippi River and **draw** a line along its path. Then do the same for the Savannah River. **Identify** which river is east of the Appalachian Mountains. What body of water does it empty into?

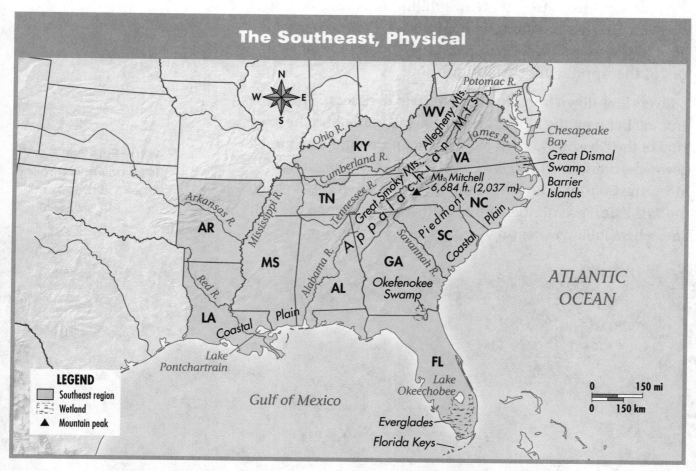

The Southeast, Physical

LEGEND
- Southeast region
- Wetland
- ▲ Mountain peak

Rivers of the Southeast

The largest river in the United States passes through the Southeast on its way to the Gulf of Mexico. The Mississippi is long, deep, and wide. It is a water highway through the center of the country. Ships and barges carry cargo along the river and out to the ocean.

In the high elevations there are watersheds. A **watershed** is an area where all the water drains in one direction. On the east side of the Appalachians, for example, rivers flow toward the Atlantic. On the other side of the Appalachians, the rivers flow to the west. The Tennessee River, for instance, travels west, from the Appalachians into the Ohio River. The Cumberland River does the same thing. Then the Ohio flows west into the Mississippi. By the time the Mississippi reaches the Gulf, it **transfers** the water of many rivers along its route.

Academic Vocabulary

transfer • *v.*, to move from one place to another; carry

Kentucky Bluegrass

In northern Kentucky, the Bluegrass region is known for its rich soil. Pastures of bluegrass (which is not actually blue) cover much of the land. Livestock and racing horses are bred there. It is home to Kentucky's biggest cities, like Louisville. It is also home to the state capital, Frankfort.

2. ☑ **Reading Check** **Explain** why the Mississippi River is called a water highway.

_____

_____

_____

_____

The Cumberland River flows through Kentucky and Tennessee.

Quest Connection

Highlight sentences that tell how people have impacted wildlife in the Southeast.

INTERACTIVITY

Explore how people have impacted landforms and wildlife in the Southeast.

Animals and Birds of the Southeast

In the late 1960s, alligators were an endangered species. An **endangered species** is a kind of plant or animal that is in danger of disappearing.

Back then, people were killing too many alligators for food or for their hides. Alligator hunting is now carefully controlled. Today, there are more than 1 million American alligators. Almost all of them live in the Southeast. Many live in wetlands, rivers, and canals in Florida and Louisiana.

The Southeast is home to many different kinds of birds. Some are endangered. The red-cockaded woodpecker is one. These birds depend on certain kinds of very old pine trees that grew in the Southeast. They make their nests and find their food in trees more than 80 years old. More and more of those trees have been cut down. So the woodpeckers are in danger of becoming **extinct**, or disappearing.

Primary Source

The goal of the U.S. Fish and Wildlife Service's red-cockaded woodpecker recovery program is to conserve the species ... Red-cockaded woodpeckers have increased in number ... from an estimated 4,694 active clusters in 1993 to 6,105 in 2006.

–U.S. Fish and Wildlife Service, December 19, 2016

The Southeast is home to many different kinds of plants and animals.

Landforms of the Southeast

bold cypress
mountains
spanish moss
piedmont
coastal plain
armadillo
alligator
wetlands
manatee

Trees, Plants, and Flowers

About 250 different kinds of trees grow in the Southeast. They are a valuable resource. Wood from trees is used to make furniture and build houses. Some wood is ground up and used to make paper.

Some trees, plants, and flowers grow especially well in the Southeast. The warm and humid climate is good for Spanish moss, for example. Trees hanging with moss are sometimes a symbol of the region.

3. **☑ Reading Check** **Fact and Opinion Identify** and underline a fact about the camellia in the photo caption. Then write a sentence giving an opinion about the flower.

Camellias come from warm Asian climates. They grow well in the Southeast. The camellia is Alabama's state flower.

_____

_____

☑ Lesson 1 Check

INTERACTIVITY

Check your understanding of the key ideas of this lesson.

4. **Summarize Describe** the Southeast's major physical features.

_____

_____

_____

5. You have been hired to create an advertisement for the Southeast. Your goal is to attract new business. **Explain** why the region's land would be a good place for a business.

_____

_____

_____

6. **Understand the Quest Connections Identify** one way people are helping to protect wildlife today.

_____

Use a Road Map and Scale

It's fun to explore new places. On a driving trip, a road map is the perfect tool to help you find your way. You can find a road map in an atlas, online, or on a Global Positioning System (GPS). A road map shows highways and other roads, as well as the location of important places. Road maps also show distance.

VIDEO

Watch a video about maps.

Suppose your family is visiting Georgia. The road map below could help you on your trip. You start out at Stone Mountain Park. You want to drive to Grant Park. Which road do you take? Find Stone Mountain Park on the map. You decide to take Highway 78 to a larger road, Interstate 285. Then you go south to Interstate 20. Then you take it west to Grant Park.

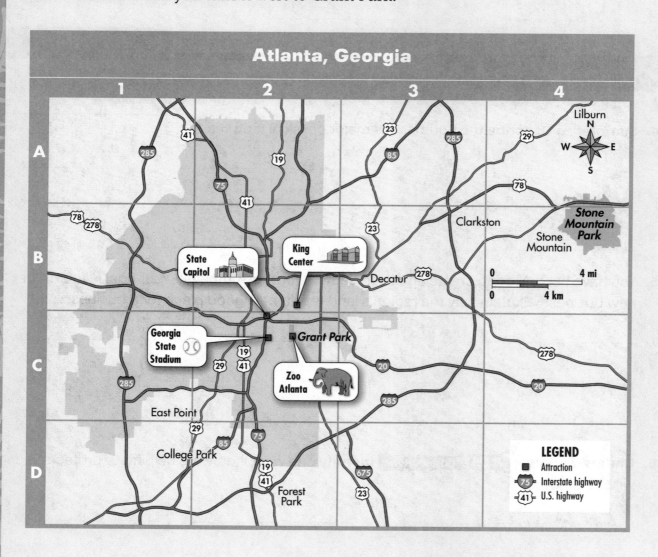

Atlanta, Georgia

To find out distance on a map, you need to use the map scale. Look at the map scale, and determine the length of the bar that equals 4 miles on land. Use a ruler or a piece of paper to measure the distance of your trip from Stone Mountain Park to Grant Park. You will discover that it is about 21 miles.

Many road maps have grids. A grid is a pattern of squares labeled with numbers and letters. A map index will tell you the number and letter of the square where you can locate a place on the map.

In Atlanta, you want to visit many different places. Use the map, the scale, and the grid to answer these questions.

1. **Locate** the State Capitol building on the map and circle it.

2. You'd like to visit the King Center next. This is a memorial to Dr. Martin Luther King, Jr. **Identify** and underline the label for the King Center on the map.

3. **Locate** and draw the route described that your family will take to drive from Stone Mountain Park to Grant Park.

4. Use the map scale to **calculate** how many miles it is between Georgia State Stadium and the King Center. Write your answer.

_____

5. **Locate** the grid square where Grant Park is located. Write your answer.

_____

6. **Apply** Now **create** and **label** a map of your desk on a separate piece of paper. Use a ruler to measure the length and width of your desk in inches. Create a scale for your map where one inch on your map equals four inches of your desk. Now place two objects on your desk. Measure the objects with your ruler. Then draw them on your map to scale.

2 Climate of the Southeast

👆 **INTERACTIVITY**

Participate in a class discussion to preview the content of this lesson.

Vocabulary

growing season
key
hurricane
storm surge
levee
evacuation

Academic Vocabulary

generate
consequence

Unlock The BIG Question

I will know that the Southeast's location gives the region a warm climate and varied weather.

JumPstart Activity

Imagine you live in the Southeast, which has a mild climate. In small groups, act out different things you do for fun.

"Heading south" is something many Americans like to do in the winter. A cold January day in Chicago is likely a warm January day in Miami. The Southeast's climate is not all the same, however. It changes from the coast to the mountains. It changes from north to south. And it changes from season to season.

Climate of the Southeast

The climate of the Southeast is mild. In most of the Southeast, average January temperatures are above freezing. A warm climate means a long growing season. A **growing season** is the part of the year when temperatures are warm enough for plants to grow. In some parts of the Southeast, the growing season can be as long as 300 days a year.

Living in a Mild Climate

Across the Southeast, people can enjoy the outdoors for much of the year. People spend time hunting, fishing, hiking, and playing on sandy beaches.

With its miles of coastline, the Southeast is a perfect place for water sports. Cape Hatteras (HAT ur uhs), North Carolina, was the nation's first national seashore. Visitors swim, camp, and explore about 30,000 acres there. At Virginia Beach, Virginia, surfers compete in surfing competitions every year.

Key West is another favorite. A **key** is a low island. Key West is one of a string of keys off Florida's southern coast. More than 1 million people visit it every year. They come to dive in the warm waters, eat fish, and find shells.

Climate affects how people build their homes, too. In Florida many houses have a screened porch called a Florida room. You can be inside and outside at the same time. Sometimes it is too hot to be outdoors. People turn on the air conditioning inside to solve that problem.

Quest Connection

Highlight sentences that tell how people interact with the Southeast coast for fun.

INTERACTIVITY

Explore how people are working to protect the Southeast coast.

Millions of tourists visit Florida's Miami Beach each year.

Hurricanes

Sometimes the Southeast's weather can be dangerous. Hurricanes strike the Southeast more than any other region. A **hurricane** is a powerful storm. Hurricanes form in warm areas such as the waters off the Southeast. Warm air rises from the ocean and hits cooler air above. The temperature difference can **generate** strong winds.

Hurricanes begin as tropical storms. The National Weather Service gives each storm a name. When the winds reach 74 mph, the storm becomes a hurricane. About six storms become hurricanes each year. In 2005, one particular hurricane was very severe—Hurricane Katrina.

A hurricane's winds move in a circle. At its center is the eye of the storm. The strong winds can cause a **storm surge**. This is when the ocean's level rises as water is pushed toward shore. Hurricanes also bring heavy rain, huge waves, and flooding.

Academic Vocabulary

generate • *v.*, to produce or create

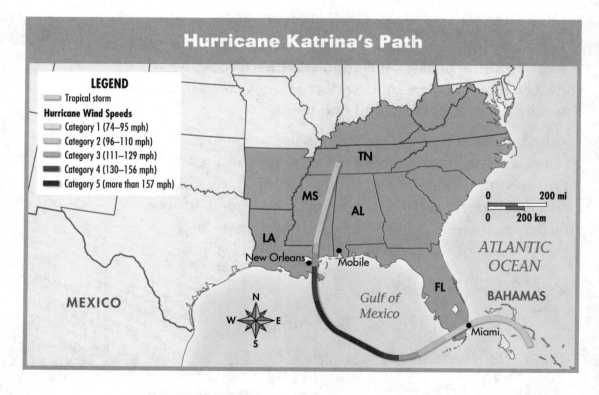

Hurricane centers track the power and path of each hurricane.

1. ☑ **Reading Check** **Analyze** the map. Find out how strong Hurricane Katrina was when it passed Miami and New Orleans. Which city likely had more damage? Explain your answer.

Effects of Hurricanes

The hurricane season lasts from June to the end of November. During this period, hurricanes form in the Atlantic and the Gulf of Mexico. Some are small. Some move in a direction away from the land. Others lose their strength before they hit the land. But some hurricanes cause severe damage when they hit the Southeast.

Every few years a major hurricane strikes the region. Hurricane Andrew hit Florida hard in 1992. It caused more than $26 billion in damages. In 2005, Hurricane Katrina became the costliest natural disaster in American history, with over $100 billion in damages. When it hit land in Mississippi, the storm surge was more than 26 feet high. In New Orleans, the storm caused terrible flooding. More than 1 million people had to leave the city and surrounding area. Overall, more than 1,800 people died as a result of Katrina. It was a terrible storm.

Primary Source

We must take a careful look at what went wrong and make sure it never happens again.

–Louisiana Governor Kathleen Blanco, September 14, 2005

After Katrina, people across the nation wanted to help. More than 1 million people volunteered to rebuild Louisiana and Mississippi. People came to build houses. Others provided medical care. Many helped by giving money or serving food.

2.   **Reading Check**
Cause and Effect Describe one effect of Hurricane Katrina.

Cause
Hurricane Katrina

↓

Effect

Volunteers gave millions of hours of service after Hurricane Katrina.

Handling Floods

Hurricanes are not the only time when water is a danger. The Mississippi River travels through five states in the Southeast. Sometimes the river floods. When the nation's largest river floods, there can be major **consequences**.

Along the Mississippi River, people have built levees. A **levee** is a dirt or concrete wall. It keeps water from overflowing the riverbanks. When the water gets too high, however, it can overflow or break through a levee.

What causes the high water? Often, heavy rains swell the river. The flood of 1927 was one of the worst floods in the nation's history. Heavy rains began in late 1926. By January 1927, the Mississippi River flooded 27,000 square miles. That May, the river water spread across 70 miles of land near Memphis, Tennessee.

In May 2010, there were terrible floods in Tennessee, Kentucky, and Mississippi. More than 13 inches of rain fell in just two days. The Cumberland River flooded and water spread out over Nashville, Tennessee, causing damage.

3. ☑ **Reading Check**
Fact and Opinion Read the statements. **Identify** and underline the opinion.

Many people take action when a river floods. The National Weather Service alerts people living near the river when it rises. National, state, and local workers and volunteers pile bags of sand to raise the levees. When towns are flooded, groups like the American Red Cross help, too.

I think floods are worse than hurricanes.

The flood of 1927 was one of the worst floods in American history.

Being Prepared

Most of the time, people in the Southeast enjoy good weather. When the weather turns bad there, people are prepared.

Today, people can get weather news quickly and easily. Televisions, computers, and even cell phones can give weather alerts. When there is danger, officials may call for **evacuation** of an area. This means that people are moved to safety.

In coastal areas, people need protection from hurricanes. They need houses that can stand up to strong winds or high waves. In Florida and the Carolinas, new houses have special roofs and windows. Whatever the weather, the people of the Southeast are ready.

Houses near a coast have special designs. They may be built high up to avoid damage from a storm surge.

INTERACTIVITY

Explore the key ideas of this lesson.

☑ Lesson 2 Check

4. **Make Generalizations Describe** the weather in the Southeast region and **explain** how it changes.

_____

_____

_____

_____

5. You have a new job in the Southeast. You are working at the nation's main weather channel. **Describe** the weather on a day when a hurricane is forming in the Atlantic.

_____

_____

6. **Understand the** *Quest* **Connections Describe** how the environment of the Southeast coast might be harmed by tourism.

_____

_____

A Land of Many Resources

INTERACTIVITY

Participate in a class discussion to preview the content of this lesson.

Vocabulary

timber
pulp
agribusiness
livestock
fossil fuel
hydroelectric power
heritage

Academic Vocabulary

mastery
restore

Hot red peppers grown on Avery Island, Louisiana, are used to make a very spicy sauce.

Unlock
The **BIG** Question

I will know that the Southeast is rich in natural resources.

Jumpstart Activity

As a class, make a list on the board of everyone's favorite foods. Then put a check mark next to the foods that are grown in the region in which you live.

Take a ride around New Iberia, Louisiana. You'll get a picture of the Southeast's many different resources. At nearby Avery Island, you'll see fields of hot red peppers. You can visit a factory where hot sauce is made. Then you can drive down to the nearby Gulf of Mexico. Along the way, you can talk to some people who catch fish for a living and watch workers leave for their jobs on oil rigs in the Gulf. Just like the whole Southeast, New Iberia is rich in resources.

Using the Land and Water

The Southeast's land and water offer valuable resources. These resources vary across the region. On the Coastal Plain, there are wide stretches of good farmland. Trees cover half of most of the states in the Southeast. Coal is mined in the mountains. Oil and natural gas come from the Gulf Coast area. In the Atlantic and the Gulf of Mexico, fishing boats bring up the resources of the sea.

Resources offer more than food and products. They create jobs. The people of the Southeast earn money at these jobs.

Forest Resources

Much of the land of the Southeast is forested, or covered with trees. In most Southeastern states, at least half the land is forested. Forests provide timber. **Timber** is trees that are grown and cut for wood. Much of the Southeast's timber comes from the region's many tree farms.

The forest industry plants millions of acres of trees. Most are pine trees. They grow quickly and well in the region's sandy soil. The forest industry brings thousands of jobs and billions of dollars to the region.

The region's timber is raw material. It is used for making many different products. At mills, trees are turned into lumber used for building homes. Wood is also crushed by machines into pulp. **Pulp** is a mix of ground-up wood chips, water, and chemicals. The pulp is used for products from paper to cardboard to diapers.

The Southeast's trees are important to the environment, too. They give off oxygen and help cool Earth. They provide homes for birds and other animals.

Quest Connection

Turn to a partner and talk about how people are using the land and water of the Gulf Coast.

INTERACTIVITY

Explore how people are using resources found in the Southeast region.

At a sawmill in Georgia, timber is cut into lumber.

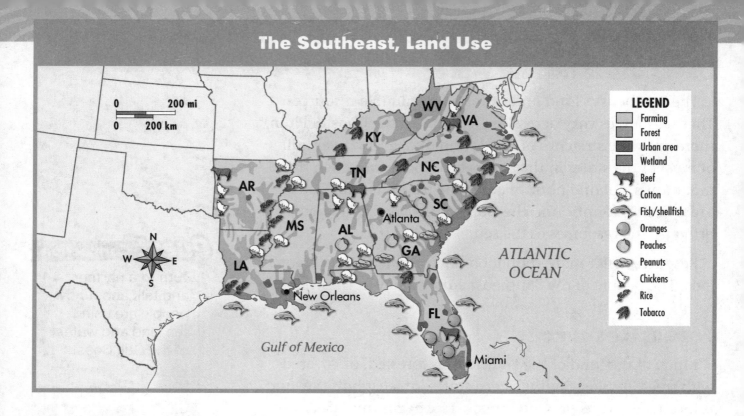

The Southeast, Land Use

LEGEND
- Farming
- Forest
- Urban area
- Wetland
- Beef
- Cotton
- Fish/shellfish
- Oranges
- Peaches
- Peanuts
- Chickens
- Rice
- Tobacco

ATLANTIC OCEAN

Gulf of Mexico

1. ☑ **Reading Check**
Analyze the map.
Identify where oranges and cotton are grown. Turn and talk with a partner to compare locations.

A Great Region for Farming

The Coastal Plain of the Southeast has all the conditions for good farming. The land is flat, temperatures are warm, and there is plenty of rain. In the long growing season, farmers can grow many different crops. Many of these crops, such as cotton and sugar cane, do not grow well in colder regions.

The region is also a good place for agribusiness. **Agribusiness** is farming as an industry. Some companies own huge farms. They ship agricultural products around the country and the world. Florida produces about 8 million tons of citrus fruit each year, for example. Citrus fruits include oranges, lemons, and grapefruit. That's a lot more fruit and juice than the people of Florida can eat and drink. Companies ship most of it out of the state.

Growing Food

Georgia raises more peanuts, peaches, and pecans than any other state. Arkansas and Louisiana are leading growers of rice. In fact, almost half of all the rice grown in the United States comes from Arkansas.

Other main crops include strawberries, corn, and soybeans. Soybeans are used to make food for livestock, vegetable oil, and other foods.

Peanuts and soybeans have not always been major Southeastern crops. In the 1700s and 1800s, the region mostly grew cotton. However, growing cotton damaged the soil. An agricultural scientist named George Washington Carver helped farmers with this problem. Carver's **mastery** in growing crops led him to the answer. While working at the Tuskegee Normal and Industrial Institute in Alabama in the 1880s, he discovered that growing peanuts and soybeans **restored** the soil.

Today, many Southeastern states, including Georgia and Alabama, still grow a lot of cotton. Because of this, some textile manufacturers are located in the Southeast. A textile is cloth used to make clothes. In factories, workers produce cloth and clothing from southern cotton.

Raising Animals

The land and climate of the Southeast also make it a good place to raise animals. In Virginia, for example, more than two thirds of the money made from agriculture comes from livestock. **Livestock** are animals raised for sale. Georgia, Arkansas, and Alabama are the nation's leading producers of broilers, or young chickens. North Carolina is a major producer of hogs and turkeys. Raising beef cattle is also important in several Southeastern states.

Academic Vocabulary

mastery • *n.*, great knowledge or skill in a particular field
restore • *v.*, to bring back to health

Word Wise

Compound Words
The word *livestock* is a compound word, which means it is made from two words: *live* and *stock*. The word *stock* means "animals that are farmed." What does the word *live* tell you about the definition of *livestock*?

Primary Source

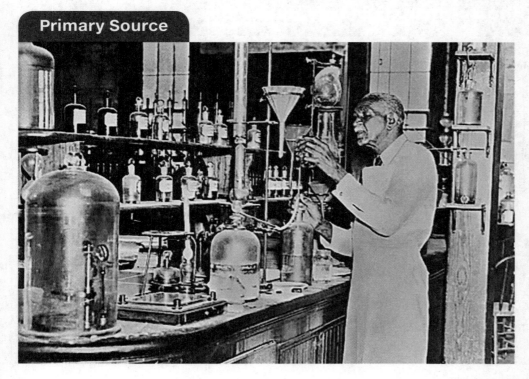

George Washington Carver experimented with growing peanuts. He found that many things could be made from peanuts, including milk, ink, and soap.

Energy Resources

Coal is one of the most important energy resources in the United States. Electricity comes from a power plant, and almost half of our power plants get their energy from coal. In the Southeast, coal is mined in Appalachia.

In the Southeast, coal, oil, and natural gas are found both underground and underwater. Each is a **fossil fuel**, formed in the earth from the remains of plants or animals. Fossil fuels are millions of years old. They are a nonrenewable resource.

Another source of energy is falling water. Power plants capture the energy of falling water and turn it into electricity. Electricity that is created by the force of falling water is called **hydroelectric power**.

2. ☑ **Reading Check** **Compare and Contrast** Pick two states in the region. **Compare** and contrast their energy resources.

_____

_____

_____

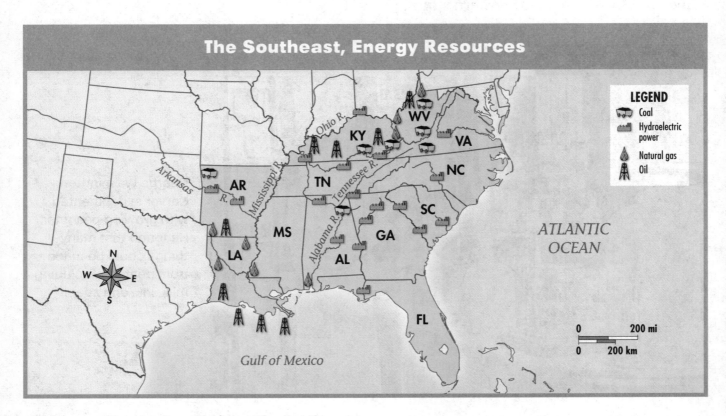

The Southeast, Energy Resources

LEGEND
🚃 Coal
🏭 Hydroelectric power
⛽ Natural gas
🛢 Oil

Tourism and the Land

The land of the Southeast is a resource in another way, too. Its beauty brings tourists to the region. There are national parks in many Southeastern states. Some are so special that they are World Heritage Sites. This means that they are preserved as part of the cultural heritage of everyone in the world. Your **heritage** is the beliefs and customs passed down from one generation to another. There are 21 World Heritage Sites in the United States. Four are in the Southeast.

Mammoth Cave National Park is a World Heritage Site located in Kentucky. Tourists can explore its deep caves.

INTERACTIVITY

Explore the key ideas of this lesson.

✓ Lesson 3 Check

3. **Summarize Identify** one resource in the Southeast. Summarize its importance to the region.

_____

_____

_____

_____

_____

4. You are going to start a business in the Southeast, using one of the region's resources. **Describe** your business. What resources will it use?

_____

_____

5. **Understand the** *Quest* **Connections Describe** how people could protect the land and the water of the Gulf Coast.

_____

Distinguish Fact From Opinion

How can you tell the difference between a fact and an opinion? A fact is a statement of information that you can prove to be true. Facts tell what actually happened. An opinion is a statement of feelings that cannot be proven true or false. Opinions usually contain words such as *I believe, I think, favorite,* and *probably.* Another way to think about this is that facts do not change, no matter who says them, where opinions may change from person to person.

When you read, it's important to be able to distinguish— or tell the difference between—facts and opinions. Read the paragraph below and look for statements of fact and opinion.

▶ **VIDEO**

Watch a video about distinguishing facts from opinions.

The Southeast region is a terrific place for agribusiness. Large farms owned by companies ship fruits, vegetables, and other agricultural products all over the world. For example, Florida produces about 9 million tons of citrus fruit each year. Citrus fruits include oranges and grapefruit. Citrus fruits are delicious, but I believe there are too many of them for just the people of Florida. As a result, companies ship most of Florida's citrus fruit crop out of the state.

1. What are the facts and opinions included in the paragraph? Fill in the organizer with sentences from the paragraph.

FACT	OPINION

2. Read the following sentences. Decide if each one is a fact or an opinion and check the appropriate box. Then explain why you think the statement is an example of a fact or an example of an opinion.

I think Florida should grow apples, too.

☐ Fact   ☐ Opinion

_____

_____

Florida also grows cucumbers, tomatoes, watermelons, and strawberries.

☐ Fact   ☐ Opinion

_____

_____

Settling the Southeast

INTERACTIVITY

Participate in a class discussion to preview the content of this lesson.

Vocabulary

indentured servant
plantation
pioneer
emancipation

Academic Vocabulary

intent
ruins

Unlock
The **BIG**
Question

I will know that the Southeast has a history of crisis and rebuilding.

JumpStart Activity

Imagine you could interview someone who long ago settled in the region you live in. What questions would you want to ask that person? Get up and add your questions to a class list on the board.

In the town of Cherokee, North Carolina, you can hear people speaking the Cherokee language, and you can hear storytellers pass on Cherokee traditions. Long before people came from Europe and Africa, this was Cherokee land.

American Indians of the Southeast

For thousands of years, American Indians have lived in the Southeast. Even before Europeans came, the Southeast had a large population. Many different groups lived in the region. For example, the Cherokee lived in southern Appalachia. The Powhatan were on the coast of Virginia. These and other groups developed different cultures.

Like others in the region, the Cherokee lived in villages. Their lives were shaped by their environment. They built houses from wood and clay. For food, they hunted, fished, and farmed. They made clothing from the skins of animals they hunted.

Modern Cherokee keep their culture alive. This Cherokee man performs a traditional dance.

Explorers and Settlers

In the early 1500s, the American Indians' world changed. That's when Europeans began to explore North America. Many of the first explorations began in the Southeast. Juan Ponce de León and Hernando de Soto landed first in Florida. In 1513, Ponce de León claimed Florida for Spain. In the 1560s, Spanish and French explorers settled along the Atlantic coast.

About 20 years later, the English settled off the coast of what is now North Carolina. Then, in 1682, French explorer Robert de La Salle arrived. He sailed down the Mississippi River. He claimed the entire Mississippi Valley for France. In 1718, the French settled New Orleans.

The Europeans met the American Indians who lived there. Sometimes the meetings were peaceful. Other times there was conflict. The American Indians were threatened by these newcomers. The Europeans had guns and steel armor, unlike the American Indians.

One American Indian who tried to avoid conflict was Cockacoeske. She was Queen of the Pamunkey, an American Indian group in Virginia. In 1676, the Pamunkey were attacked by English settlers. However, Cockacoeske agreed to help the settlers defend themselves against other American Indian groups. Her actions helped ease the conflict between the Pamunkey and the English.

The early explorers mostly passed through the region. Some settled down while others kept moving. They left behind something deadly, however: germs. European diseases would kill thousands of American Indians.

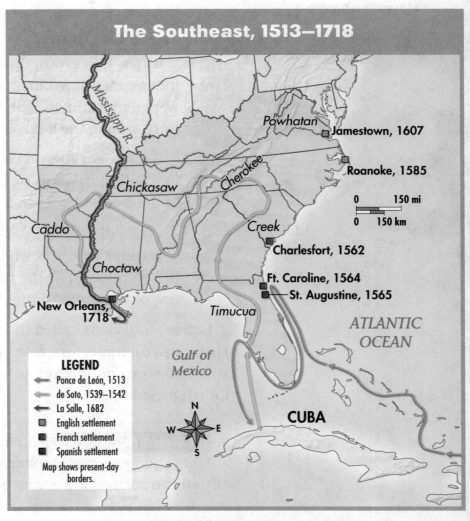

The Southeast, 1513–1718

Mississippi R.

Powhatan
Jamestown, 1607

Roanoke, 1585

Chickasaw
Cherokee

0   150 mi
0   150 km

Caddo

Creek

Charlesfort, 1562

Choctaw

Ft. Caroline, 1564
St. Augustine, 1565

New Orleans, 1718

Timucua

ATLANTIC OCEAN

LEGEND
← Ponce de León, 1513
← de Soto, 1539–1542
← La Salle, 1682
■ English settlement
■ French settlement
■ Spanish settlement
Map shows present-day borders.

Gulf of Mexico

N
W   E
S

CUBA

The English Colonies

In 1607, a group of 104 English men and boys set up a colony in what is now Virginia. They called it Jamestown, after the English king. The early days of the colony were hard. The Powhatan, a group of American Indians, helped the colonists. They traded food with the colonists. Jamestown became the first successful English colony in North America.

By the early 1700s, the English had 13 colonies along the Atlantic. Four of them were in the Southeast: Virginia, North Carolina, South Carolina, and Georgia.

The colonies grew as Europeans made new lives in America. Many came as indentured servants. An **indentured servant** signed an agreement in which he or she promised to work for free for a period of time. Others came to America against their will. Many enslaved Africans worked on large farms called **plantations**. They helped build the colonial economy and culture from the beginning.

George Washington and Thomas Jefferson are carved into Mount Rushmore.

Three Virginians

By the late 1700s, the colonies were on the road to independence. Women and men from the Southeast were important on that journey. Three men from Virginia were among the leaders in the creation of a new nation.

George Washington led the colonial army in the Revolutionary War. He became the first President of the United States in 1789. As the "Father of His Country," he was an example for later presidents.

Thomas Jefferson wrote the Declaration of Independence. As the third president, he doubled the size of the United States with the Louisiana Purchase.

James Madison is called the Father of the Constitution. He played an important role in creating the document that still guides our nation today. Madison was the nation's fourth president.

1. ☑ **Reading Check** **Fact and Opinion Identify** and underline facts about George Washington and Thomas Jefferson. Then, turn to a partner and exchange opinions about each leader.

Pioneers Head West

Even before American independence, settlers pushed west. They wanted to find more land. Daniel Boone was an early pioneer. A **pioneer** settles a place, leading the way for others. In 1775, Boone led a group into Kentucky. They went through the Cumberland Gap. This was a gap, or pass, in the Appalachians. They built the Wilderness Road. It became a main route for settlers moving west.

Many settlers moved west, **intent** on finding better land for growing cotton. These were the days when cotton was "king." Plantation owners planted more and more of the crop. To run the plantations, they depended on a growing number of enslaved Africans.

As people moved west, new states were formed. Kentucky and Tennessee became states in the late 1790s. Alabama, Mississippi, and Louisiana joined the Union in the 1810s. By 1845, Arkansas and Florida were states, too.

Conflict with American Indians increased in these years. Settlers wanted to farm Cherokee land, but the Cherokee did not want to move. The Cherokee fought in the courts but did not win. Then the United States ordered the American Indians to give up their land. Some Cherokee escaped, but most were forced to move. They went to a territory that today is part of Oklahoma. Their journey was so terrible that it is called the Trail of Tears.

Academic Vocabulary

intent • *adj.*, focused on a specific purpose

2. ☑ **Reading Check**
Cause and Effect
Explain to a partner what caused new states to form.

Historians believe that as many as 15,000 American Indians died during the Trail of Tears.

Academic Vocabulary

ruins • *n.*, the remains of something that has been badly damaged or destroyed

Slavery and the Civil War

On February 4, 1861, men from six Southeast states met in Montgomery, Alabama. They represented South Carolina, Mississippi, Florida, Alabama, Georgia, and Louisiana. They created the government of a new country. They called it the Confederate States of America, or the Confederacy.

These states, and Texas, had already seceded from the United States. In a few months they were joined by Virginia, Arkansas, North Carolina, and Tennessee. These 11 states were the Confederacy. Only Kentucky and West Virginia among the Southeastern states remained in the Union.

The Civil War between North and South lasted from 1861 to 1865. Conflicts over slavery were the main cause of the war. About 3.5 million enslaved Africans lived in Confederate states. In 1863, President Abraham Lincoln issued the Emancipation Proclamation. **Emancipation** means freeing someone from slavery. It freed all enslaved people in the Confederacy. Many learned they were free only after the Civil War had ended.

The Confederacy lost the war. Much of the Southeast lay in **ruins**. Almost 500,000 soldiers died or were wounded. Buildings and homes were destroyed. The slave-based economy was also destroyed. The Southeast had to rebuild.

Primary Source

After the Civil War ended, the city of Richmond, Virginia, lay in ruins.

The Southeast After Slavery

After the war, the nation had to be joined together again. To rejoin the United States, each Confederate state promised African Americans their civil rights.

Without slavery, people had to learn new ways of living and working together. For almost 100 years, segregation separated African Americans and whites in the Southeast. This changed in the civil rights movement of the 1950s and 1960s. Some people called the civil rights movement "the second Reconstruction."

Many of the leaders of the civil rights movement were from the Southeast. Rosa Parks was born in Tuskegee, Alabama. Dr. Martin Luther King, Jr. was born in Atlanta. Today you can visit the King Center there. It is a memorial to Dr. King and the entire civil rights movement.

Today, more than 150 years after the Civil War, Richmond is a thriving, modern city.

INTERACTIVITY

Explore the key ideas of this lesson.

☑ Lesson 4 Check

4. **Make Generalizations Explain** how one of the following signficant people influenced the lives of other people in the Southeast: Robert de La Salle, Daniel Boone, Abraham Lincoln.

_____

_____

_____

5. **Sequence** Organize these settlements in order of earliest to most recent: New Orleans, Jamestown, St. Augustine.

_____

6. You are going to take a historical tour of one of the early European settlements in the Southeast. Which would you choose? **Explain** your answer.

_____

_____

Cherokee Syllabary

The Cherokee are an American Indian group who have lived in the Southeast region for many hundreds of years. Beginning in 1809, a Cherokee named Sequoyah worked to develop a syllabary. A syllabary is a system used for writing down the words of a language. In a syllabary, a symbol stands for a syllable, or a part of a word.

Sequoyah believed that if the Cherokee had a way to write down their language, they could more easily exchange knowledge and ideas. He began by teaching his daughter Ayoka his simple system of 85 characters. Sequoyah's fellow Cherokee came to believe in his system when they saw him send messages to other Cherokee living in the Southeast region. Soon, Sequoyah was teaching many Cherokee how to use his syllabary. Eventually, the Cherokee would write their own constitution, works of literature, and a newspaper, the *Cherokee Phoenix*.

Fun Fact

Sequoyah fought against the British under the command of General (and later President) Andrew Jackson during the War of 1812!

Sequoyah developed his syllabary over a period of 12 years, from 1809 to 1821.

Close Reading

1. **Explain** what a syllabary is and why Sequoyah believed the Cherokee needed one.

_____

_____

_____

_____

_____

2. **Describe** what Sequoyah did to convince other Cherokee that his syllabary worked.

_____

_____

Wrap It Up

Do you think the Cherokee Syllabary is an important part of the history and culture of the Southeast region? **Explain** your reasoning.

_____

_____

_____

_____

_____

_____

_____

Vocabulary

Gullah
jazz
folklore
craft
port

Academic Vocabulary

essential
perspective

Unlock The BIG Question

I will know that the Southeast is home to cultural traditions that have influenced the nation and the world.

JumpStart Activity

Raise your hand, and when your teacher calls on you, share a tradition that you have learned from your family. For example, a grandparent might have asked you to help cook a certain kind of food.

It's May and you are visiting Memphis, Tennessee. You are there for the city's big celebration called Memphis in May. At the Beale Street Music Festival, you hear the best in rock and blues music. Later, you wander over to the World Championship Barbecue Cooking Contest. In one day, you've gotten a wonderful taste of Southeast culture.

The Culture of the Southeast

As in every region, the Southeast has a special culture. We use the word *culture* to talk about things like music, painting, dance, literature, and cooking. Whether you are listening to a banjo player or eating barbecue, you are sharing part of the culture of the Southeast.

The culture of the Southeast is a rich mix of many traditions. Most people in the region come from English or African American backgrounds. Others have different cultural roots. For example, the Cajuns of Louisiana have French backgrounds. On the Gulf Coast, you may enjoy a Vietnamese meal. In South Carolina, you can hear the Gullah language. The **Gullah** are African Americans in the Southeast who have kept much of their African heritage. All of these are part of Southeastern culture.

Music in the Southeast

Many of America's favorite kinds of music have their roots in the Southeast. Rock, blues, gospel, bluegrass, country, and ragtime all began or grew in the region.

One unique kind of music that began in the Southeast is jazz. **Jazz** music was mostly created by African American musicians. The music they played in New Orleans in the early 1900s soon spread to other cities.

Rock and roll music was also born in the Southeast. In the 1950s, both African American and white musicians developed this new form of music. Memphis and Nashville, Tennessee, were centers of rock and roll.

The gospel songs of southern black churches inspired others. Singers like Aretha Franklin made gospel music popular. Beginning in the 1920s, radio programs broadcast gospel and other music across the nation. Today, the Internet brings it to the world.

Music in the Southeast has changed over time. For example, electronic instruments like keyboards might be heard in jazz bands today.

Today, millions of people travel to New Orleans each year to hear jazz bands.

Cultural Traditions

Academic Vocabulary

essential • *adj.*, absolutely necessary

perspective • *n.*, point of view; outlook

Writers tell the stories of each region. These stories are **essential** in helping us understand the past and learning how they shaped the present. Diaries like *Mary Chestnut's Civil War* report one person's **perspective**. William Faulkner wrote fiction about life in Mississippi. Zora Neale Hurston records the African American experience in her novels. Hurston also made important studies of the folklore of African Americans in the Southeast. **Folklore** refers to the traditions and beliefs of a group of people.

Primary Source

WHEN I was a boy on the old plantation,
Down by the deep bayou,
The fairest spot of all creation,
Under the arching blue;
When the wind came over the cotton and corn,
To the long slim loop I'd spring
With brown feet bare, and a hat brim torn,
And swing in the grapevine swing.

–Samuel Minturn Peck, "The Grapevine Swing," 1892

1. ☑ **Reading Check**
Identify any unfamiliar words in the poem by Samuel Minturn Peck. Look up their meaning and then discuss the poem with a partner.

The Southeast has a long tradition of crafts. A **craft** is an object made by hand. In Appalachia, for example, people make musical instruments such as banjos. The quilters of Gee's Bend live in Alabama. Their quilts are in museums today.

Sports are an important part of life in the Southeast. One of the most popular is NASCAR racing. NASCAR is the National Association for Stock Car Auto Racing. Millions of fans watch the races. Most of the racing teams are based in North Carolina.

Fans all over the Southeast enjoy NASCAR races.

The New South

A century ago, most people in the Southeast lived in rural areas. Today, most live in cities. Georgia is a good example: in 1900, more than eight out of every ten people in Georgia lived in the country. Today, about eight out of every ten live in cities, and the cities of the Southeast are still growing.

The Southeast moved away from an economy based on agriculture. In Birmingham, Alabama, industry grew quickly. Crowded with steel mills, it was called the Pittsburgh of the South. Like most other Southeastern cities, however, Birmingham is no longer an industrial center. Most people in Birmingham work in service industries today. The city is a leader in medical research and banking.

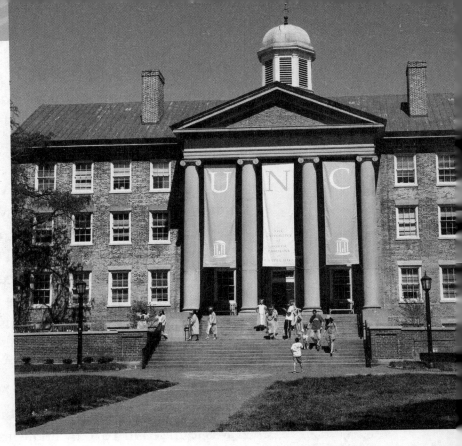

The University of North Carolina at Chapel Hill is one of the universities that makes up the Research Triangle in North Carolina.

One area of North Carolina called the Research Triangle is also growing quickly. The cities of Raleigh, Durham, and Chapel Hill are there. This area is a center for research in medicine, computers, business, and education.

In Arkansas, too, service industries lead the economy. Especially important are businesses that sell things. Arkansans sell everything from automobiles to groceries.

Some of the world's biggest service providers are in the Southeast. The headquarters of many communications, technology, and Internet companies are in northern Virginia.

2. ✓ **Reading Check** **Main Idea and Details** **Describe** one way the economy of the Southeast has changed.

_____

Fast-Growing Cities

Many cities in the Southeast lead the country in population growth. Of the 100 fastest-growing United States cities, 16 are in the Southeast.

New Orleans

New Orleans, Louisiana, is known for its food and its music. Founded in the early 1700s, the city is a busy port on the Mississippi River. A **port** is a place where people or goods can enter or leave a country. Large ships move products up and down the Mississippi between the Southeast and the Midwest. Thousands of ocean-going ships connect New Orleans and the world. In 2005, Hurricane Katrina caused a lot of damage to the city. The people of New Orleans survived many challenges as they rebuilt their city. The rebuilding of New Orleans continues today.

Charleston

Charleston, South Carolina, is one of the Southeast's oldest cities. It was founded in 1670 by English settlers. It is a mix of old and new. Many tourists come to see the colonial buildings and beautiful gardens. Near Charleston's harbor is the South Carolina Aquarium. There you can see plants and animals from all areas of the state. Also at the harbor is the Fort Sumter National Monument. It marks the place where the first shots of the Civil War were fired. Like the rest of Charleston, it is a good place to see how the Southeast has changed.

Nashville is one of the largest cities in the Southeast region.

Atlanta

Atlanta, Georgia, is one of the leading cities of the Southeast. The capital of Georgia, Atlanta began as a railroad center in the 1830s. Today, Atlanta is still a center of transportation. In fact, it has the world's busiest airport.

Atlanta is growing quickly. Shiny new buildings are going up, and new businesses are moving in. Kasim Reed, mayor from 2010 to 2018, helped to make Atlanta one of the top "green" cities in the United States through the large city-wide recycling program. The city is a center of communications and finance. Atlanta is one of the cultural capitals of the Southeast.

3. ☑ **Reading Check** Draw a picture postcard that shows your favorite thing about the Southeast region. **Explain** why to a partner.

☑ **Lesson 5 Check**

INTERACTIVITY

Explore the key ideas of this lesson.

4. **Fact and Opinion Describe** a fact about Southern life. Then write an opinion on the same subject.

_____

_____

5. **Cause and Effect Explain** how Southeastern culture has influenced American music.

_____

_____

6. You have a chance to learn more about quilting, jazz trumpeting, or barbecue cooking. What would you pick? **Explain** your answer.

_____

_____

Quality:
Courage

Rosa Parks (1913–2005)
Mother of the Civil Rights Movement

Rosa Parks was born in Alabama in 1913. At that time, in many parts of the United States, and particularly in the Southeast, African Americans faced severe racial discrimination. They were segregated from white Americans in many places including schools, restaurants, and public transportation. In fact, there were laws in place that mandated, or ordered, segregation.

On December 1, 1955, Parks was riding a city bus in Montgomery, Alabama. She was asked to give up her seat so that a white man could sit down. She refused. As a result, she was arrested and sent to jail. African Americans in Montgomery, including Dr. Martin Luther King, Jr., protested her unfair treatment.

During the 1950s and 1960s, African Americans worked to end segregation, fight racism, and gain their civil rights. Rosa Parks' courageous act that day is believed to be the beginning of the United States civil rights movement. Civil rights are the rights to freedom and equality that all people should have.

Rosa Parks was a leader in the struggle to end discrimination against African Americans.

Find Out More

1. How did Rosa Parks demonstrate, or show, courage?

_____

_____

2. Think about a time when you showed courage. It could be something as simple as raising your hand in class to answer a question. How did you feel afterwards? Why should people show courage?

6 Visual Review

Use these graphics to review some of the vocabulary, people, and ideas from this chapter.

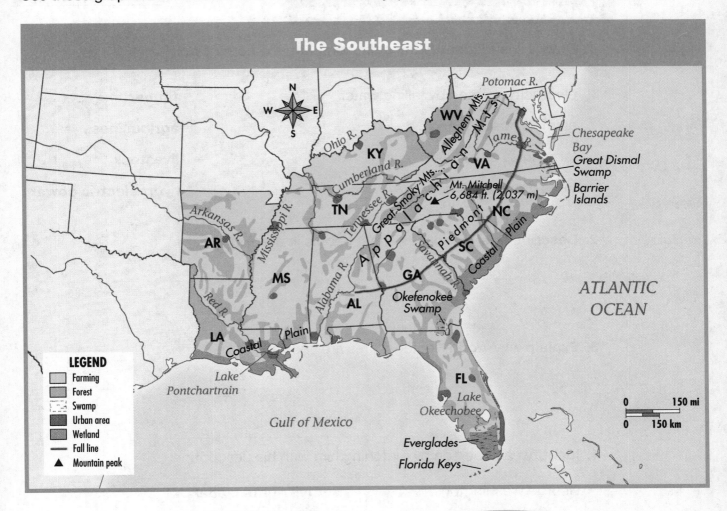

The Southeast

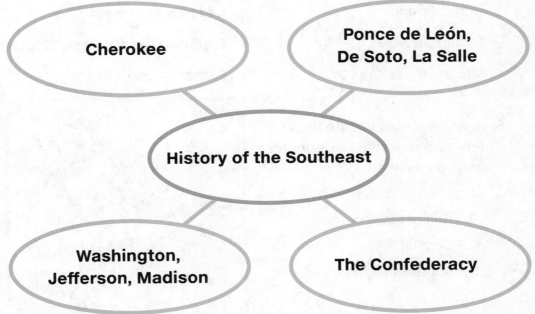

Cherokee

Ponce de León, De Soto, La Salle

History of the Southeast

Washington, Jefferson, Madison

The Confederacy

🎮 **GAMES**

Play the vocabulary game.

Vocabulary and Key Ideas

1. Draw a line to **identify** the definitions with the correct words.

electricity created by falling water   **timber**

animals raised for sale   **agribusiness**

farming as an industry   **livestock**

trees grown for wood   **hydroelectric power**

2. **Describe** how hurricanes affect people in the Southeast.

_____

_____

3. **Explain** why World Heritage Sites are special.

_____

_____

4. **Identify** each person by matching him with his description.

George Washington   **Civil rights leader**

Daniel Boone   **Led pioneers west**

Robert La Salle   **Explored the Mississippi River**

Martin Luther King, Jr.   **Father of his country**

5. **Analyze a Map Locate** these features and write the letter for each on the map.

   A. Atlantic Ocean

   B. Gulf of Mexico

   C. Coastal Plain

   D. Appalachian Mts.

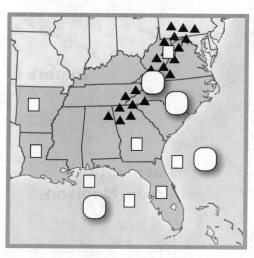

Critical Thinking and Writing

6. **Analyze** the map used for question 5. Read the list of resources below. Write the number of each resource near an area where you could find it.

   1. fish and shellfish

   2. coal

   3. citrus fruits

   4. peaches

   5. oil

   6. rice

7. **Sequence** these events: Reconstruction, Civil War, secession.

   _____

8. **Fact and Opinion Describe** the culture of the Southeast. Write one fact and one opinion.

   _____

   _____

   _____

9. **Revisit the Big Question** How does having two coasts affect the Southeast? Then explain how cities affect the Southeast.

   _____

   _____

   _____

   _____

10. **Writing Workshop: Write Narrative Text** On a separate sheet of paper, write two short paragraphs that might have appeared in your journal if you had seen Sequoyah exchange messages with Cherokee living in other areas of the Southeast. Describe the reaction of other Cherokee. Be sure to include details about the Cherokee Syllabary.

Analyze Primary Sources

11. What can you tell about the people who made this quilt? How does the quilt represent the Southeast traditions?

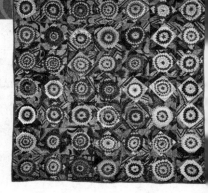

Gee's Bend quilt

_____

_____

_____

_____

_____

Use a Road Map and Scale

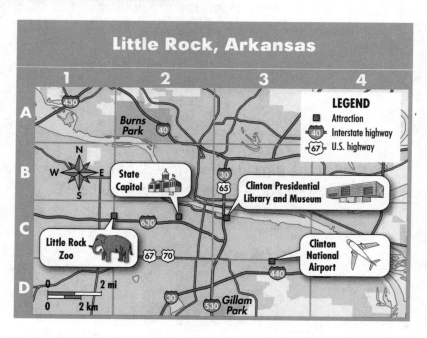

12. Analyze the road map of Little Rock, Arkansas. Use the map, the grid, and the scale to answer the following questions.

a. You and your family would like to visit the Clinton Presidential Library and Museum. **Locate** it on the map and circle it. Then write the grid square that it is located in. _____

b. Imagine your family wants to drive from the Clinton Presidential Library and Museum to the Little Rock Zoo. Draw the route on the map.

c. Use the map scale to **identify** how many miles on the highway it is from the State Capitol to Gillam Park. Write your answer. _____

Quest Findings

Create Your Blog

You've read the lessons in this chapter and now you're ready to create your blog. Remember, your goal is to create a blog in which you suggest ways to conserve the Southeast coast.

1 Prepare to Write

Write down the ways that humans impact the physical environment of the Southeast coast. Then write a few sentences describing how it can be conserved and protected. These notes will help you create your blog.

2 Write a Draft

Use your outline and the answers from your Quest Connections to create your blog. Make sure your blog covers these topics:

- What landforms are part of the Southeast coast?
- Where do people go to visit in the Southeast coast?
- How do humans impact the Southeast coast?
- How can people help conserve and protect the Southeast coast?

3 Share With a Partner

After you have written a first draft of your blog, exchange it with a partner. Take turns asking each other questions about your blogs. Make polite suggestions about ways your partner could improve his or her blog. Listen to your partner's suggestions about yours.

4 Revise

Make changes to your blog after you and your partner have finished your exchange. Also correct any spelling errors and grammatical errors.

GO ONLINE FOR
DIGITAL RESOURCES

 VIDEO

 INTERACTIVITY

 AUDIO

 GAMES

 ASSESSMENT

eTEXT

 **The BIG Question**

 VIDEO

How does where we live affect who we are?

JumpStart Activity

INTERACTIVITY

Long ago, the rich farmland and many rivers of the Midwest attracted settlers. Soon, cities grew in the region. Then more people came to work in these cities. Think about your community. Talk with a partner about what might attract people to move to where you live.

_____

_____

_____

_____

_____

AUDIO

The Heart of the Nation

Preview the chapter **vocabulary** as you sing the rap.

The Midwest sits between two mountain ranges,
The Rocky Mountains way out to the Appalachians.
You can see farmlands, forests, **prairies, plains,**
Rivers, and lakes, it's the heart of the nation.

With farming, the Midwest is near the top,
The land is **arable,** or capable of growing crops.
In this region they have coal so mining is a big deal,
So is manufacturing like making iron into steel.

American Indians have lived for a long time in this place,
And many Europeans came because of the fur trade.
They set up **trading posts** along waterways,
And many grew into cities as more people came.

Chapter 7 Regions: The Midwest

Where is the Midwest region?

The twelve states of the Midwest region are located in the heart of the country. It is known for its prairies, pastures, and fertile farms. The rivers and lakes of the region have long been important trade routes. Great cities have grown on the shores of the waterways.

What happened and When?

Read the timeline to learn about settlement patterns in the Midwest.

10,000 BC   **1600**   **1700**

10,000 BC
American Indian groups settle in the Midwest.

1600s
French fur traders arrive in the Midwest.

1780s
Northwest Ordinance brings settlers to the Midwest.

TODAY
Members of about 34 American Indian groups live in the Midwest.

Who will you meet?

Ojibwa Indians were one of many American Indian groups in the Midwest.

Jacques Marquette was a French priest who explored the Midwest with Louis Jolliet.

John Deere was an inventor who changed how people farmed.

Jean Baptiste Point DuSable was a pioneer and trader who settled Chicago.

 INTERACTIVITY

Complete the interactive digital activity.

1800

1900

2000

1800s
Wave of immigrants come to the Midwest.

1869
Railroad brings settlers to the Midwest.

1950s
Interstate highway system grows population.

2000s
Jobs in technology bring people.

TODAY
Many of the largest U.S. cities are in the Midwest.

Quest

In the Mix: Music of the Midwest

The Midwest has a rich and diverse population. As people moved to the area, they shared their culture through music and influenced people and parts of society. Many different genres, or styles of music, have developed as a result.

Quest Kick Off

Hi! My name is Camila. I work at a recording studio. We're looking for a song for a new album. It will have a mix of musical styles from the Midwest. Your mission is to research music genres from the region, the cultures represented, and its influence on society. Then identify a song to present to your class and explain why it belongs on the album.

1 Think About Music

Think about different styles of music. How many can you identify? Write down as many as you can think of.

....

....

INTERACTIVITY

Complete the digital activities to get started on your song presentation.

2 Plan

How can you learn about musical genres from the Midwest? What kind of resources might help you find your song? Write down some ideas here.

....

....

....

....

3 Look for Quest Connections

Begin looking for Quest Connections that will help you present your song.

4 Quest Findings
Present Your Song

Use the Quest Findings page at the end of the chapter to help you present your song.

CORDING

Lesson 1: In the Heart of the Nation

INTERACTIVITY

Participate in a class discussion to preview the content of this lesson.

Vocabulary

Great Plains
prairie
Central Plains
blizzard
tornado
Badlands

Academic Vocabulary

situate
account

Unlock The BIG Question

I will know that the lives of people in the Midwest are affected by its landforms and bodies of water.

JumpStart Activity

With a small group, talk about how cold and hot weather can change the choices you make in daily life. Then vote with the class to say if cold or hot weather affects people the most.

The Midwest region is located in the middle of the country. It stretches from Ohio in the east to Nebraska and Kansas in the west. In the north, it includes states that border Canada, such as Michigan and North Dakota.

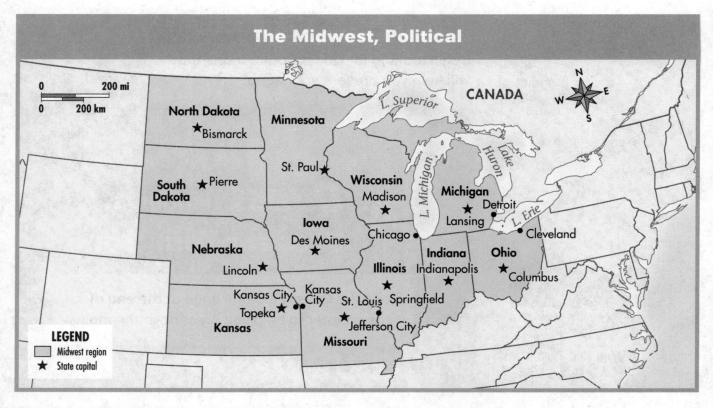

The Midwest, Political

CANADA

L. Superior

North Dakota
★ Bismarck

Minnesota

St. Paul ★

South Dakota
★ Pierre

Wisconsin
Madison ★

L. Michigan

Lake Huron

Michigan
★ Lansing
Detroit

L. Erie
Cleveland

Iowa
Des Moines ★

Chicago ●

Nebraska

Lincoln ★

Indiana
Indianapolis ★

Ohio
★ Columbus

Illinois
Springfield ★

Kansas City
Kansas City

St. Louis ●

Topeka ★

Kansas

Jefferson City ●

Missouri

LEGEND
☐ Midwest region
★ State capital

0 ___ 200 mi
0 ___ 200 km

Midwestern Land

Academic Vocabulary

situate • *v.*, to set in a particular location

You can think of the Midwest as **situated** in the area between two mountain ranges. To the west are the Rocky Mountains. To the east are the Appalachians. Though there are hills and mountains in the Midwest, much of the land is level. The region includes farmland, forests, and open grasslands. In western parts of the Midwest, the land is higher and drier, as it stretches toward the Rocky Mountains. This area is called the **Great Plains**. Much of the Great Plains is prairie. **Prairie** is level or gently rolling land covered in grasses, with few trees. The eastern part of the Midwest is called the **Central Plains**.

Thousands of years ago, glaciers covered much of the region. Glaciers changed the land. They flattened hills and carved out valleys. Some valleys filled with water, creating river valleys. Glaciers also left behind moraines when they melted. A moraine is a mound or ridge of rock and gravel.

Great Rivers

Rivers have shaped the Midwest, too. The nation's two longest rivers run through the region.

The greatest river of all is the Mississippi River. The Mississippi carries more water than any other river in North America. It flows from north to south. The river begins in the lakes of Minnesota and travels 2,350 miles. Along its journey, other rivers, such as the Missouri and the Ohio, flow into it. The Mississippi begins as a small stream and expands to more than 11 miles wide in places. Its waters drain into the Gulf of Mexico.

The Missouri River is one of the longest in the country. It runs 2,315 miles. The Missouri begins in Montana and runs east and south through the Dakotas. It marks part of the borders between Nebraska and Iowa and between Kansas and Missouri.

The Ohio River is another long Midwestern river. It is more than 981 miles long. It flows west out of Pennsylvania along the southern edges of Ohio, Indiana, and Illinois.

1. **☑ Reading Check** The Ohio River creates the southern borders of Ohio, Indiana, and Illinois. On the map, **identify** the Ohio River. Then draw a line along it and label it.

The Great Lakes

Not only does the Midwest have the country's largest rivers, it also boasts its biggest lakes. There are five Great Lakes: Lake Erie, Lake Huron, Lake Michigan, Lake Ontario, and Lake Superior. All the lakes are connected to each other. All but Lake Ontario are in the Midwest. The Great Lakes **account** for one fifth of the world's fresh water. Unlike seawater, fresh water is not salty. Each of the Great Lakes is huge. If you stand on one side of a Great Lake, the opposite shore will be far out of sight. Winds can whip up large waves on the lakes, making them seem like oceans.

The Great Lakes were formed long ago by glaciers. As the glaciers moved across the land, deep pits formed in the earth. When the glaciers melted, water filled the pits.

Though all the Great Lakes are inland, they connect to the Atlantic Ocean. The St. Lawrence River flows out of Lake Ontario and east to the ocean.

Academic Vocabulary

account • *v.*, to make up or provide

2. ☑ **Reading Check**
Analyze the smaller map that shows where glaciers were long ago. **Identify** and circle which large bodies of water are in those areas today.

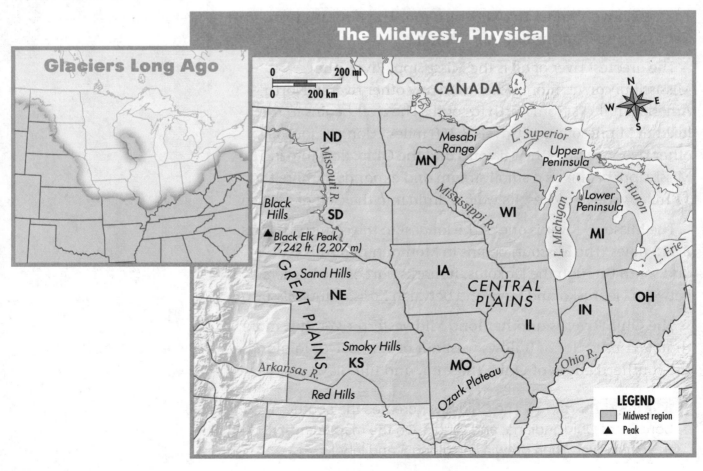

Glaciers Long Ago

The Midwest, Physical

CANADA

ND

MN
Mesabi Range

Missouri R.

L. Superior

Upper Peninsula

Lower Peninsula

L. Huron

Black Hills
SD
▲ Black Elk Peak
7,242 ft. (2,207 m)

Mississippi R.

WI

L. Michigan

MI

L. Erie

GREAT PLAINS
Sand Hills
NE

IA

CENTRAL PLAINS

IL

IN

OH

Arkansas R.

Smoky Hills
KS

MO

Ohio R.

Red Hills

Ozark Plateau

LEGEND
☐ Midwest region
▲ Peak

Climate of the Midwest

The Midwest is located far from the coasts. This affects its climate. Coastal places are cooled in the summer and warmed in the winter by the fairly steady temperature of ocean water. Oceans moderate the temperatures on land nearby. Inland, temperatures can be extreme. In the Midwest, summers can be very hot and winters very cold.

Winters are especially cold in states like North Dakota, Minnesota, Wisconsin, and Michigan. Snow is common there. Blizzards sometimes sweep through the region. A **blizzard** is a heavy snowstorm with powerful winds. Summers can bring heat waves and hot temperatures.

The western part of the Midwest tends to be much drier than the eastern part. That's because of the Rocky Mountains. The Rockies block moisture-filled air. Rain falls to the west of the Rockies, and then dry air passes into the Midwest. In the Great Plains, less than ten inches of precipitation falls in an average year. Farther east, states like Indiana and Ohio get about 40 inches of precipitation each year. Moist air blows up from the Gulf of Mexico and meets cool Canadian air. This brings rain and snow to these states.

While being inland means Midwesterners don't have to fear hurricanes, they do have to watch out for other kinds of extreme weather. When dry Midwestern air meets hot, wet air coming up from the Gulf of Mexico, big thunderstorms can result. So can tornadoes. Tornadoes are both common and dangerous in the Midwest. A **tornado** is a destructive column of spinning air with winds that can reach more than 300 miles per hour. Part of the Midwest is located in an area called Tornado Alley. Tornadoes are common there in spring and summer.

Midwestern winters can bring blizzards and freezing temperatures.

Word Wise

Antonyms Find the adjective *destructive*. Do you know what it means? Its antonym, or opposite, is *constructive*. How does that help you understand its meaning?

3.  **Reading Check** **Summarize Explain** how the inland location of the Midwest affects the region's weather.

_____

_____

_____

Wildlife of the Midwest

The Midwest is home to a great variety of wildlife. Deer, sheep, and snakes live in the dry, rocky hills of the Badlands. The **Badlands** is an area of rough land in western South Dakota. Vegetation is light in the Badlands, and few trees grow there. The black-footed ferret, one of North America's most endangered animals, has been brought back to Badlands National Park.

The Midwest's prairie is home to the American bison. Millions of these animals once roamed the plains. Long ago, they were almost hunted out of existence. Today, there are thousands of bison once again. They share the area with pronghorn antelope, prairie dogs, and coyotes. The wide-open grasslands are also perfect for ranching. Ranchers raise cattle across much of this region.

Prairie dogs are common in the Midwestern grasslands. They live in holes called burrows that they dig in the ground.

Primary Source

"Grasslands challenge our senses, calling us to open our eyes to impossibly broad horizons and then, in the very next breath, to focus on some impossibly tiny critter hidden in the grass."

–Candace Savage, *Wild Prairie*, 2005

To the north and east, other animals like squirrels, raccoons, and deer are common, especially in forests. The gray wolf, which almost became extinct, is now found in parts of Wisconsin and Minnesota.

The Midwest is home to many species of birds, such as owls and hawks. Bald eagles make their nests along rivers and lakes. There, these birds can find fish to eat. Birds that migrate, or fly long distances when the seasons change, visit the Midwest. Ducks, geese, and cranes can be seen in marshes. A marsh is a grassy wetland.

Many kinds of fish live in the Midwest's rivers and lakes. Lake fish such as pike, perch, bass, and carp fill the waters of the Great Lakes. Huge catfish live on the muddy bottom of the Mississippi River.

The Midwest is home to many different kinds of birds.

4.  **Reading Check** **Categorize** **Identify** one animal that lives in each type of land.

Wildlife of the Midwest	
prairie	
dry, rocky hills	
forest	
rivers, lakes, and wetlands	

INTERACTIVITY

Check your understanding of the key ideas of this lesson.

✓ **Lesson 1 Check**

5. **Compare and Contrast** What is the difference in climate between the western part of the Midwest and the eastern part? **Explain** why they are different.

_____

_____

_____

6. You are planning a summer trip to the Midwest. Think about the region's climate. **Identify** the best and worst reasons for going in summer.

_____

_____

_____

7. Minnesota is sometimes called "the Land of 10,000 Lakes." **Discuss** with a partner why there are so many lakes in the state.

_____

_____

Give an Effective Presentation

Suppose everyone in your class had to give a social studies presentation. Some of the presentations would be interesting. Others might not be. What is the difference between an effective, interesting presentation and a weaker one? You might guess it is the subject matter. Think again. You can make anything interesting if you know how to prepare. To give an effective and interesting presentation, follow the steps below:

1. **Know your audience.** It is always important to keep in mind the people to whom you'll be speaking. How much do they already know?

2. **Identify your main idea and state it at the beginning and the end.** Your audience needs to know right away what your presentation is about. Otherwise, they may lose interest. It is also good to remind people of your main idea before you close.

VIDEO

Watch a video about how to give an effective presentation.

3. **Choose your details carefully.** Your audience does not need to know every single detail you found in your research. Choose only the most interesting details that support your main point.

4. **Speak clearly and loudly.** A presenter who mumbles or whispers will quickly frustrate his or her listeners. Audiences lose interest when they cannot hear clearly. Also make sure you look up at your audience from time to time when you make a presentation.

5. **Use visuals.** A visual, such as a map or picture, gives the audience something else to focus on. Using visuals is also a great way to illustrate your point.

6. **Practice before you present.** Effective presenters practice their presentations so that they feel comfortable with their material.

Your Turn!

Analyze this student's notes for a presentation about the Great Lakes. Then answer the questions.

Great Lakes Presentation

I am doing a presentation about the Great Lakes. My main idea is that the Great Lakes are important to the states that border them, especially Illinois, and to the port of Chicago. I will speak clearly and loudly when I present.

1. Review the steps to an effective presentation. **Identify** three things that the student is missing.

   _____

2. What do you think is the most important step to an effective presentation? **Explain** your answer.

   _____

   _____

   _____

3. Plan a presentation **explaining** something you find interesting about the Midwest. Write your notes for the presentation in the space provided. Remember to include all the steps for giving an effective presentation.

   Topic: _____

   _____

   Notes: _____

   _____

   _____

   _____

Lesson 2

Resources and Farming

INTERACTIVITY

Participate in a class discussion to preview the content of this lesson.

Vocabulary

nutrient
arable
crop rotation

Academic Vocabulary

combine
critical

Unlock The BIG Question

I will know why the Midwest is one of the world's most important agricultural areas.

Jumpstart Activity

Work with your class to show population growth. Some students will stand and hold hands to form the regional borders of the Midwest. Your teacher will name economic activities such as farming, mining, and manufacturing. Walk inside the "borders" when an activity that interests you is named.

The Midwest has different kinds of land; some of which is good for farming.

To successfully grow crops, a farmer needs sunshine, water, rich soil, level ground, and a long growing season. In the Midwest, all of these resources are plentiful.

Farming Resources

Successful farms need certain resources. For example, planting crops is easier on level or gently rolling land. With its plains, prairies, and low hills, much of the Midwest is perfect for farming. Deep soil that contains many nutrients is also important. **Nutrients** are substances that help plants grow. Some of the richest soil in the country is found in the Midwest.

Crops also need water. Much of the Midwest gets enough rainfall to raise crops. This is particularly true in the Central Plains. In the drier Great Plains, farms can get water from rivers and underground wells. Using irrigation, farmers bring water to their fields.

Sunshine is the final ingredient for successful farming. With its long growing season and hot summers, the Midwest gets plenty of sun. That sunshine, **combined** with everything else, makes the Midwest one of the most productive farming regions in the world.

Academic Vocabulary

combine • *v.*, to join
critical • *adj.*, of major importance

A Region for Farming

Farming is important in the Midwest because the region has much more arable land than the other regions in the country. **Arable** means capable of growing crops.

So thanks to the Midwest, the United States is one of the world's leading producers of farm products. For example, each year the United States produces an enormous amount of corn. In fact, it produces almost twice as much corn as China and far more than any other country. The United States is the world's biggest producer of soybeans. More than a third of the world's crop is grown here. Our country is also one of the world's top producers of dozens of other farm products, from blueberries to cheese.

The food that is grown in the Midwest is used and eaten in the United States. It is also sold to other countries. That makes Midwestern agriculture a **critical** part of the nation's economy.

1. ✓ **Reading Check** **Summarize** **Explain** what makes the Midwest great for farming.

Wheat grows well in the drier Great Plains. Besides being ground into flour for bread, wheat can be used to make animal food, glue, and plastic.

Regions Within a Region

Not every part of the Midwest is the same. Because the region includes different landforms and climates, it produces a variety of crops.

The Central Plains are perfect for growing corn. In fact, the area that includes Ohio, Illinois, Iowa, southern Minnesota, Missouri, Kansas, and Nebraska is known as the Corn Belt. Farmers in this area grow soybeans as well as corn. Often, they switch between the two crops, growing corn one year and soybeans the next. This is called **crop rotation**.

Farms in the Great Plains to the west don't get as much rain as those in the Central Plains. As a result, farmers there grow crops that require less water, such as wheat and oats. They might also use irrigation to grow corn and soybeans.

2. ☑ Reading Check **Compare and Contrast Compare** how farmers on the Great Plains and Central Plains use their land differently. **Explain** why.

_____

_____

_____

_____

Farm Products

Of course, wheat, corn, and soybeans are just some of what is grown in the Midwest. In the north central region, states such as Michigan are famous for their fruit. Orchards are crowded with apple and cherry trees. Fields of berries are everywhere. In the summer and fall, these fruits, along with peaches and grapes, fill local farmers' markets.

Dairy farms are also common in the Midwest. Dairy farmers raise cows for their milk. Dairy is especially important in northern states, such as Wisconsin. This state is famous for its milk, cheese, butter, and other dairy products.

Raising animals for meat is also a huge part of Midwestern agriculture. Much of the country's pork comes from states such as Minnesota and Iowa. A lot of corn is grown in these states, and hogs feed on the corn. This makes the area a natural fit for raising hogs. For the same reason, a lot of beef is produced in the Midwest. Chickens are raised for meat and eggs in the Midwest. Iowa is the nation's top egg-producing state.

3. ☑ **Reading Check**
Analyze the map with a partner. **Identify** one state that produces dairy products and another that produces wheat.

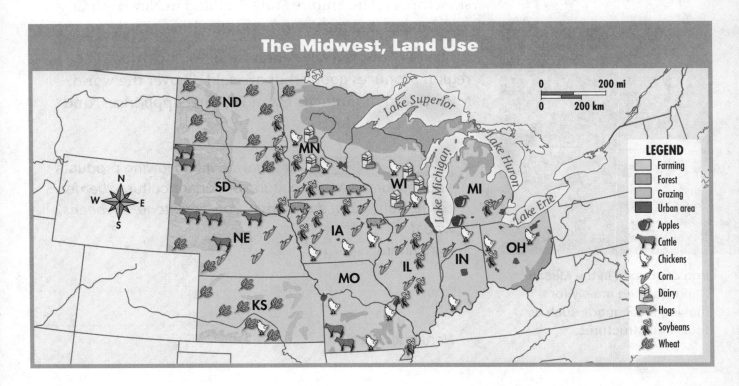

The Midwest, Land Use

LEGEND
Farming
Forest
Grazing
Urban area
Apples
Cattle
Chickens
Corn
Dairy
Hogs
Soybeans
Wheat

Word Wise

Prefixes When you see an unfamiliar word, try using prefixes to understand the meaning. For example, read the word *nonagricultural.* The prefix *non-* means "not," or "the opposite of." What do you think *nonagricultural* means?

Iron ore mined in the Mesabi Range is used mainly for making steel goods such as tools and structures.

Other Resources

Agricultural goods are not the Midwest's only products. Many nonagricultural resources contribute to the region's economy, as well.

Mining is important in the region. Mining for coal has provided jobs for people in Illinois for many years. Today, the state still has a quarter of the nation's supply of coal. Illinois coal provides power for millions of homes.

Minnesota's Mesabi Range is rich in iron. Between 1900 and 1980, the mines there produced more than half of the nation's supply of iron. Michigan is also a source of iron.

In Indiana, limestone is an important natural resource. The stone is dug out of huge deposits in the ground. These deposits form an underground layer of rock in the earth.

Manufacturing

The many natural resources of the Midwest help make the region a leader in manufacturing. For example, iron from Minnesota is manufactured into steel. The steel is used in construction and making machines. Indiana limestone is cut into blocks and used to build houses, bridges, and skyscrapers. The Empire State Building in New York City was constructed partly with Indiana limestone.

The Midwest is a key center for manufacturing. The region produces goods that are sold all over the world. Midwestern manufacturers make cars, appliances, and many other products.

4. ☑ **Reading Check** **Categorize** the following products and resources as agricultural or nonagricultural: *berries, cattle, coal, corn, dairy, eggs, iron, limestone, soybeans, wheat*
Agricultural

_____

_____

Nonagricultural

_____

Resources From Lakes and Rivers

The lakes and rivers of the Midwest also contain important resources. Fishing has long played a role in the economies of the Great Lakes states. American Indians fished the waters of Lake Huron and Lake Michigan. Commercial fishing was a major industry there for many years. But pollution led to a decline in fish populations in the region. This caused commercial fishing to collapse.

Today, recreational fishing, or fishing for fun, is popular on Midwestern rivers and lakes. Even in winter, fishers cut holes in the ice, drop a line, and wait to catch trout or perch.

Ice fishing is a traditional winter pastime in the Midwest.

INTERACTIVITY

Check your understanding of the key ideas of this lesson.

☑ Lesson 2 Check

5. **Summarize Explain** how the Midwest's physical environment enables farmers to do their jobs. Then **explain** how farmers change the physical environment as they farm.

_____

_____

_____

6. On a trip to the Midwest, you plan to meet a farmer. **Identify** the kind of farmer you would like to meet. Then write a few questions you might ask him or her.

_____

_____

7. **Explain** why the Midwest is one of the world's most important agricultural areas.

_____

_____

_____

Settling in the Midwest

Unlock
The **BIG**
Question

I will know that the rich farmland and other resources of the Midwest attracted thousands of settlers.

Vocabulary

nomad
missionary
trading post
Northwest Ordinance
plow

Academic Vocabulary

permit
extensive

JumpStart Activity

Suppose you are visiting a new place. You meet people who do not speak your language and who have a very different culture. How do you approach this new group? How will you work with them? Stand up and act out a meeting between the two groups.

American Indians have lived in the Midwest for thousands of years. Because the Midwest has varied landscapes, these groups lived in different ways.

American Indians of the Midwest

Missouri R.

Ojibwa

L. Superior

L. Huron

Mandan

Mississippi R.

Lakota

Sauk

L. Michigan

Potawatomi

L. Erie

Fox

Iowa

Erie

Omaha

Chicago

Pawnee

Miami

Missouri

Illini

Shawnee

Kansa

Cahokia

Ohio R.

0   200 mi
0   200 km

LEGEND
Midwest region
Trading post

American Indians of the Midwest

American Indian groups lived in the forests, river valleys, and flat areas of the eastern Midwest. Groups like the Fox and the Shawnee farmed corn, beans, and squash.

Wisconsin, Michigan, and Minnesota were home to the Ojibwa, also known as the Chippewa. The Ojibwa did little farming. Instead, they adapted to the Midwest's geography. They hunted in the forests. They fished in the region's many lakes and rivers. They gathered berries, fruit, and wild rice.

Other groups lived on the Great Plains. Eastern Plains groups like the Omaha and the Iowa farmed in river valleys. Western Plains groups like the Lakota were nomads. A **nomad** is a person who moves from place to place. Western Plains groups followed the bison.

The Fur Trade

Some of the first Europeans to arrive in the Midwest were missionaries. **Missionaries** are religious people who set up settlements to teach religion. Other settlers, many of them French, came because of the fur trade. Beaver, otter, and mink furs were valuable in Europe. They were used to make hats and coats.

French fur traders explored the Midwest from the north to the south. In 1673, explorers Jacques Marquette and Louis Jolliet traveled by canoe down some Midwestern waterways. They started on Lake Michigan. Then they explored parts of the Mississippi River.

Soon, the French were building forts and trading posts along waterways. A **trading post** is a small settlement where goods are traded. They traded European goods to American Indians for furs. Often, the trading posts were built near American Indians who would farm and trade their food with the Europeans. Some of these trading posts later grew into cities. Chicago is one of them. This major city began as a trading post.

The Objibwa Indians lived in the Midwest.

1. ☑ **Reading Check** **Analyze** the map. Locate the trading posts. **Explain** what most of them have in common.

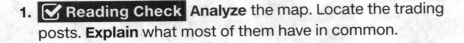

Farmers Settle the Land

Farmers came to the Midwest as early as the 1770s. They were attracted to the region's rich farmland. They came from the East. The first to come settled in the Ohio River valley. Later, as farmland became harder to find there, settlers moved farther west. Many new settlers came west through the Great Lakes.

At the time of the Revolutionary War, the Midwest was part of the frontier. Then, in the 1780s, the new United States government began organizing the region. Much of the Midwest became part of the Northwest Territory. In 1787, Congress passed the **Northwest Ordinance**. This law said the Northwest Territory must be divided into "not less than three nor more than five states." It also said these new states could not **permit** slavery. Five states came from this territory: Ohio, Illinois, Indiana, Wisconsin, and Michigan.

In the early 1800s, pioneers began coming to the Midwest by the thousands. Most wanted land to farm. The government was offering cheap land. There was a conflict, however. American Indians were already living on much of this land. So the government forced the American Indians to sell their land and move to reservations. By 1890, all of the Midwest had been organized into states.

2. ☑ **Reading Check** **Compare and Contrast** When families moved to the Midwest, their lives changed. For example, living in log cabins (left) or sod houses (right) may have been unfamiliar. **Describe** to a partner other challenges families might have faced.

Academic Vocabulary

permit • *v.*, to allow to do something

Immigrants Come to the Midwest

In the mid-1800s, immigrants from Europe started coming to the Midwest. These settlers looked for land in the Northeast first. Soon however, the Midwest became the first choice for new immigrants. Many of these immigrants came from northern and central Europe. They came from countries such as Germany, Ireland, Sweden, Norway, and Hungary. Some of these new immigrants started farms. Others moved to growing Midwestern cities, port towns, and trading posts.

Primary Source

"I was little and homesick and lonely . . . So the country and I had it out together and by the end of the first autumn the shaggy grass country had gripped me with a passion that I have never been able to shake."

–Willa Cather, *Omaha Bee*, 1921

Farming Changes

Although Midwestern land was great for farming, it was hard work to clear it. Farmers had to remove trees. They had to clear prairie grass from the plains. Then they had to turn over the soil to get it ready for planting. The tool they used for this was a **plow**. But plows had a hard time digging through the thick prairie grass roots.

Then, in 1837, a man named John Deere invented a new steel plow. This plow made farming easier. It could break through the toughest prairie grass roots. Soon, oxen or horses were pulling bigger plows. Years later, plows were pulled by tractors. This made it possible to farm **extensive** areas of the Midwest's prairies. More and more pioneers began settling the Great Plains. They hoped to start big, successful farms.

3. ☑ **Reading Check** **Identify** the kinds of plows that allowed more people to settle the Great Plains.

_____

_____

Quest Connection

Take notes on the different cultural communities that settled in the Midwest.

 INTERACTIVITY

Learn more about Midwestern settlers.

Academic Vocabulary

extensive • *adj.*, far-reaching

This illustration shows Chicago, Illinois, as it looked in 1820. The artist has painted Jean Baptiste Point DuSable's cabin on the right.

Midwestern Cities

As more people settled the Midwest, some trading posts grew into towns and cities. These communities were often on waterways used for transportation. As trade grew, so did the communities.

In 1784, African American pioneer Jean Baptiste Point DuSable established a trading post. It was at the mouth of the Chicago River, near Lake Michigan.

Soon DuSable's trading post was the largest in the Midwest. It had a bakery, a mill, and livestock. In the early 1830s, Chicago had a few hundred people. By 1890, it had more than a million. Today, it is the largest city in the Midwest and the third-largest city in the country.

Other Midwestern cities began as trading posts. In 1701, a French trader founded Detroit on a river that connected Lake Huron to Lake Erie. Cleveland was founded in 1786 on the Cuyahoga River. In 1764, another French trader settled St. Louis on the Mississippi River. St. Louis soon became a center of shipping and transportation. This was true for other Midwestern cities. Slowly, the Midwest was becoming more urban.

4. ☑ **Reading Check**
Summarize Chicago started as a trading post. Write a sentence to **explain** why so many Midwestern cities grew near waterways.

_____

_____

_____

_____

_____

From Trade to Factories

As the United States became more industrial in the late 1800s, so did the Midwest. Many Midwestern cities were good sites for factories because they were on the water. The raw materials used to manufacture goods could be shipped to these cities easily. Finished products could also be shipped easily.

In the early 1900s, Detroit became the center of the car industry. Companies like the Ford Motor Company were located there. Soon almost every car in the United States was made in Detroit. The city was nicknamed "the Motor City."

Of course, all these new industries brought people in search of jobs and better lives. Some of these new settlers were immigrants from other countries. Others were African Americans from the Southeast. They came to escape segregation and to find jobs.

Car factories provided jobs to many residents of Detroit during the 20th century.

Lesson 3 Check

 INTERACTIVITY

Check your understanding of the key ideas of this lesson.

5. **Summarize Explain** how the Midwest's geography affected the way it was settled.

_____

_____

6. During a trip to the Midwest, you want to visit a city. Which city would you choose? **Explain** your choice.

_____

_____

7. **Understand the** *Quest* **Connections** On a separate piece of paper, **identify** a group of people who settled in the Midwest. **Research** and write a paragraph about how they affected the culture of the region.

Willa Cather, *Roll Call on the Prairies*

Willa Cather was an American author who was raised in Nebraska. This selection comes from a magazine article she wrote during World War I.

Vocabulary Support

World War I, a global war from 1914–1918

eastern Nebraska

black clothes sewn to mourn or honor the dead

experiencing war

draft, *n.*, when the government requires citizens to become soldiers during a time of war

customs, *n.*, activities, or ways of behaving, which is usual or traditional in a particular society

military service, *n.*, a period of time in which a soldier works for a country's armed forces

casualty, *n.*, a person who is injured or killed in a war

Early in the summer of 1917, I stopped in the eastern part of the state and went to see a fine German farmer woman whom I had always known. She looked so aged and broken that I asked her if she had been ill.

"Oh, no; it's this terrible war. I have so many sons and grandsons. I am making black dresses."

"But why? The draft is not called yet. Your men may not even go. Why get ready to bury them?"

She shook her head. "I come from a war country. I know."

The next summer she was wearing her black dresses.

When I was a child, on the farm, we had many German neighbors, and the mothers and grandmothers told me such interesting things about farm-life and customs in the old country—beautiful things which I can never forget—that I used to ask them why they had left such a lovely land for our raw prairies. The answer was always the same—to escape military service. …

These people had left their country to get away from war, and now they were caught up in the wheels of it again. No one who read the casualty lists can doubt the loyalty of the foreign peoples in our country.

– Willa Cather, from *Roll Call on the Prairies*, 1919

Some people believed that immigrants were not loyal Americans. During the war, anti-German feelings were especially high. In reality, nearly half a million immigrants from Germany and 45 other nations served in the U.S. military. Many died or were injured defending our country.

Close Reading

1. **Identify** and circle words in the text selection that describe the condition of immigrants living in Nebraska in 1917.

2. **Describe** the photo and what the image suggests about immigrant life during the war.

_____

_____

_____

Wrap It Up

Did the immigrants have a good chance for a better life in the Midwest? Support your answer with information from the chapter. Refer to the image and use one quotation from the selection shown here in your answer.

_____

_____

_____

The Midwest on the Move

Vocabulary

junction
hub
interstate highway

Academic Vocabulary

develop
initial

Unlock The BIG Question

I will know how a central location made the Midwest important in the nation's transportation and trade.

JumpStart Activity

The Midwest is a center for many kinds of transportation. People and goods move by truck, train, and boat. Work with a partner and make a T-Chart with the headings "Products" and "Type of Transportation". Brainstorm products that come to your neighborhood and the types of transportation you think are used to get there. Write the product and the type of transportation in the appropriate columns.

The Midwest grew as more and more people settled there. These new Midwesterners farmed, ran stores, and worked in factories. All had one thing in common: they used and needed transportation.

In the 1200s, traders traveled to the bustling American Indian city of Cahokia.

American Indian Trade in the 1200s

Long before Europeans arrived, American Indians and goods moved all over the region. The Midwest's many lakes and rivers made transportation by water easy. Trading centers like Cahokia **developed**. Located in Illinois, Cahokia was the site of the largest American Indian city in what later became the United States.

Cahokia was close to the **junction**, or meeting point, of three rivers: the Illinois, the Missouri, and the Mississippi. These waterways connected Cahokia to the north, south, west, and northeast. Traders from the Great Lakes area shipped copper to Cahokia. Southern traders in the Mississippi valley shipped shells, jewelry, and pottery. Cahokia was a meeting place of many cultures.

Academic Vocabulary

develop • *v.*, to grow

Changes in Transportation

In the early 1800s, few roads existed west of the Appalachian Mountains. The best way to travel was on the water. This was especially true in the Midwest, with its many rivers and lakes. Most transportation in the region was by boat.

Until the early 1800s, boats needed wind or human power to move them. Sailing ships could travel down the St. Lawrence River and around the Great Lakes. On the shallower rivers, such as the Mississippi, people had to use canoes or flatboats. Flatboats could float downstream, but they had to be paddled upstream. The upstream journeys were long and difficult.

The invention of the steamboat changed everything. These new boats were bigger and faster than human-powered boats. By the 1830s, steamboats carrying tons of cargo and hundreds of passengers sailed up Midwestern rivers daily. Such steamboats turned the great rivers of the Midwest into major water highways.

1. ☑ **Reading Check** **Cause and Effect** **Describe** how steamboats affected river transportation.

Railroads and Shipping

This ship is entering the locks on the St. Lawrence Seaway.

By the mid-1800s, the steamboat was no longer the most modern form of transportation. Trains had taken over. In 1869, the transcontinental railroad was completed. Now goods could travel from the Midwest to either coast. The Midwest became the **hub**, or center, of the country's rail transportation network. It was now even easier for Midwesterners to trade goods.

Shipping continues to be very important to the Midwest. Large ships are able to carry people and goods more cheaply than trains. And, because of the St. Lawrence Seaway, ships can travel from the Atlantic Ocean all the way to the Great Lakes. The St. Lawrence Seaway is a system of canals and waterways that connects the Midwest to the Atlantic Ocean. Because of the value of shipping, many important ports developed in the Midwest. Like Chicago, Detroit, and Cleveland, cities such as Milwaukee, Wisconsin, and Duluth, Minnesota, became major shipping centers.

Today, these port cities remain important shipping centers. More than 160 million tons of cargo crosses the Great Lakes and their waterways each year. As in the 1850s, this cargo includes iron ore, coal, limestone, grain, and other farm products.

2. **☑ Reading Check** You need to send iron ore from Duluth to Cleveland. Work with a partner to **analyze** the chart. Would you ship by land or by water? **Explain** your answer.

Shipping From Duluth, MN to Cleveland, OH		
Category	Land	Water
Cargo	iron ore	iron ore
Travel Time	2.2 days	1.7 days
Distance	813 miles	549 miles
Cost	$2,811	$1,725

Highways

In the early 1900s, cars became very popular in the United States. **Initially**, there were few good roads. Then the United States government began building better ones. In 1956, the government began building an **interstate highway** system. This system of wide, fast roads connected all the states.

Trucks used the new highways, too. Soon, trucks became a popular way of transporting goods. Today, most of the goods we buy are shipped by truck. Because of the Midwest's central location, its highways are important truck routes.

Academic Vocabulary

initial • *adj.*, at first

New Industries

Though farming and manufacturing are still important in the Midwest, its economy has changed. Today, many Midwesterners have jobs in the technology and service industries. There are many new companies in the Midwest. Companies go where the workers are. A quarter of the nation's workforce is in the Midwest.

Today, instead of working in a car factory, Midwesterners might work at a factory that manufactures solar panels. Instead of farming, they might work in the health care field.

As the Midwest's economy has changed, so has life for Midwesterners. For example, people might live in apartment buildings that were once factories. They might also live along cleaned-up rivers that were once polluted by those factories.

3. ☑ **Reading Check**
Categorize The economy of the Midwest is changing. **Identify** and underline examples of new industries in the text.

Indianapolis, Indiana, is one of the fastest growing cities in the Midwest.

It took hundreds of workers more than six years to shape the figures on Mount Rushmore in the Black Hills of South Dakota.

Mount Rushmore, South Dakota

Tourism in the Midwest

Another important industry in the Midwest is tourism. Many Midwesterners work in this field. They might be tour guides in Chicago or lead canoe trips across lakes in Michigan.

There is plenty for tourists to see and do in this region. Tourists depend on the Midwest's many forms of transporation to plan their visits. Visitors might drive on highways to visit Mount Rushmore in the Black Hills of South Dakota. Or they might fly into Chicago's busy O'Hare International Airport. Then they could take a train into the city and spend the afternoon in Millennium Park.

Arts and Culture

Arts and culture are thriving in the Midwest. The Chicago Symphony Orchestra is one of the world's best. And the Guthrie Theater in Minneapolis is second only to New York's Broadway. Music lovers visit the Rock and Roll Hall of Fame on the shores of Lake Erie in Cleveland. Millions of visitors have visited this museum since it opened in 1995.

4. ☑ **Reading Check**
Summarize **Explain** how tourism is an important industry in the Midwest.

_____

_____

_____

_____

CLEVELAND ROCKS

Quest Connection

Analyze this image of visitors at the Rock and Roll Hall of Fame in Cleveland, Ohio. With a partner, discuss how this genre of music influences culture.

INTERACTIVITY

Explore rock and roll.

INTERACTIVITY

Check your understanding of the key ideas of this lesson.

✅ **Lesson 4 Check**

5. **Compare and Contrast Describe** how the economy of the Midwest has changed since the mid-1800s. Then tell how it has stayed the same.

_____

_____

_____

6. What form or forms of transportation would you like to use on your trip to the Midwest? **Explain** your answer.

_____

_____

7. **Understand the Quest Connections** Why do you think millions of people visit the Rock and Roll Hall of Fame in Ohio? **Explain** your answer.

_____

_____

Identify Main Idea and Details

A **main idea** is the most important point in a passage. **Details** support the main idea. Identifying the main idea will help you better understand what you read, but finding the main idea is not always easy. Here are some clues to help you:

VIDEO

Watch a video about identifying main ideas and details.

- The main idea is often (but not always) stated at the beginning of a passage.

- If the main idea is not stated, you can use the important details to figure out the main idea.

- Details give supporting information about the main idea, such as facts and examples.

The invention of the steamboat changed life for Midwesterners. Until the early 1800s, boats needed wind or human power to move them. Flatboats could float downstream, but they had to be paddled upstream. Steamboats, however, were bigger and faster than human-powered boats. These new boats could go both downstream and upstream easily. They could carry hundreds of passengers and tons of cargo daily. Steamboats turned the great rivers of the Midwest into major water highways.

The American riverboat *Senator* sailing the Ohio River in the 1930s.

1. **Identify** the main ideas and details of the paragraph on the facing page. Fill in the organizer showing the main ideas and details of the paragraph.

The Invention of the Steamboat

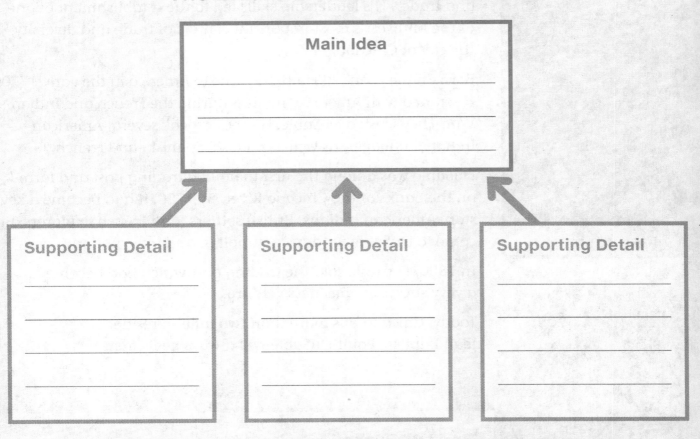

2. Reread the paragraphs in Lesson 4 under the heading "Highways." **Analyze** the information and **identify** the main idea. Then **identify** one supporting detail. Write a statement that summarizes the content.

_____

_____

_____

_____

_____

Quality:

Leadership

Jean Baptiste Point DuSable

(About 1750–1818)

The Father of Chicago, Illinois

Jean Baptiste Point DuSable was an African American pioneer and trader. His leadership skills led to the establishment of one of the Midwest's most important centers of trade and diversity, the city of Chicago, Illinois.

Born on the island of Haiti, he came to America in the early 1770s. He traded with American Indians during the French and Indian War. They trusted DuSable. He could speak several American Indian languages, as well as English, Spanish, and French.

DuSable was among the first to build a trading post and farm on the banks of the Chicago River. By 1790, it had become a key stop. American Indians, British settlers, and French explorers all came to DuSable for advice, supplies, and information.

In 1800, DuSable sold the trading post which had become a very successful business venture.

Today, Chicago has more than two million residents. Jean Baptiste Point DuSable will always be its first.

Find Out More

1. How was Jean Baptiste Point DuSable a leader?

_____

_____

_____

_____

_____

2. Talk to your parents, friends, or classmates about the characteristics of a good leader.

7 Visual Review

Use these graphics to review some of the vocabulary, people, and ideas from this chapter.

The Midwest

Natural Resources

- Midwestern wildlife includes bison and many kinds of birds and fish.

- The agricultural resources of the Midwest make it one of the world's leading producers of farm products.

- The Midwest has other natural resources, such as iron, coal, and limestone that give the region a balanced economy.

People

- American Indian groups were the first to live in the Midwest.

- French missionaries and fur traders were the first Europeans to settle in the Midwest, followed by other pioneers.

- Settlers turned the Midwest into a productive region of farms and cities.

Culture and Economy

- Waterways, railroads, and highways are all used for transportation.

- The Midwest's railroads, ports, and highways make it a shipping hub.

- New industries and dynamic cities show that the culture and economy of the Midwest are thriving.

☑ **Assessment**

🎮 **GAMES**

Play the vocabulary game.

Vocabulary and Key Ideas

1. **Define** *prairie* and use it in a sentence.

_____

_____

_____

2. **Compare** parts of the Midwest by completing the sentences.
   The _____ Plains are great for growing corn. The drier _____
   Plains are better for growing wheat.

3. **Identify** which of the following Midwestern cities began as a trading post.
   - (A) Detroit
   - (B) Chicago
   - (C) Cleveland
   - (D) all of the above

4. **Analyze Images Describe** who might live in the place shown in the photograph and what kind of work they might do. Would that work be different if they lived somewhere else?

_____

_____

_____

_____

_____

Critical Thinking and Writing

5. **Analyze** Which of these best describes the climate of the Midwest?

   (A) hot and dry

   (B) wet and humid

   (C) mild winters and cool summers

   (D) cold winters and hot summers

6. **Explain** why the Midwest is so important to the nation's transportation and trade.

   _____

   _____

   _____

7. **Compare and Contrast Compare** the Shawnee to the Lakota. How were these American Indian groups different?

   _____

   _____

   _____

8. The Midwest is sometimes called "the nation's breadbasket." **Explain** why you think it was given this nickname.

   _____

   _____

   _____

9. **Revisit the Big Question** How did the physical environment of the Midwest affect Cahokia's success as a trading center?

   _____

   _____

10. **Writing Workshop: Write an Opinion Piece** Choose two industries that are important to the Midwest. On a separate sheet of paper, write a short paragraph that explains which industry you think is more important and why.

Analyze Primary Sources

"Cleveland has a diverse and exciting culinary food history! Cleveland's melting pot of immigrant groups and their various culinary traditions have long played an important role in defining the local cuisine and students don't have to go far to immerse themselves in it."

—Case Western Reserve University, "Dining Services" website, 2017

11. **Explain** what the university meant when it said the immigrant groups of Cleveland are a "melting pot."

_____

_____

_____

_____

Identify Main Idea and Details

By the mid-1800s the steamboat was no longer the most modern form of transportation. Trains had taken over. In 1869, the transcontinental railroad was completed. Now goods could travel from the Midwest to either coast. The Midwest became the hub, or center, of the country's rail transportation network.

12. On the lines below, **identify** the main idea and one detail. Then, **explain** how you know the difference.

_____

_____

_____

_____

Quest Findings

INTERACTIVITY

Use this activity to help you present your song.

Present Your Song

You've read the lessons in this chapter and now you're ready to present your song. Remember that the goal of your presentation is to share how a person or group of people who lived in the Midwest shared their culture through music. Follow these steps:

1 Prepare to Write

Work with a partner and focus on a music genre from the Midwest. Research and identify a song from this region. Take notes.

2 Write a Draft

Use your notes to write your presentation. Make sure your draft answers the following questions:

- What style of music is your song?
- Why did that particular style of music develop in the Midwest?
- What does it tell you about the culture of the Midwest represented by this song?
- How did this music influence society?

3 Revise

Make changes to your presentation after discussing it with another group. Correct any grammatical or spelling errors. Discuss what you like about their presentation and what could use improvement. Be polite when you provide suggestions.

4 Present Your Song

Take turns with your partner when presenting your song to the class. Include any recordings you found of the song, to create more interest. Answer any questions the class may have.

Chapter 8

Regions: The Southwest

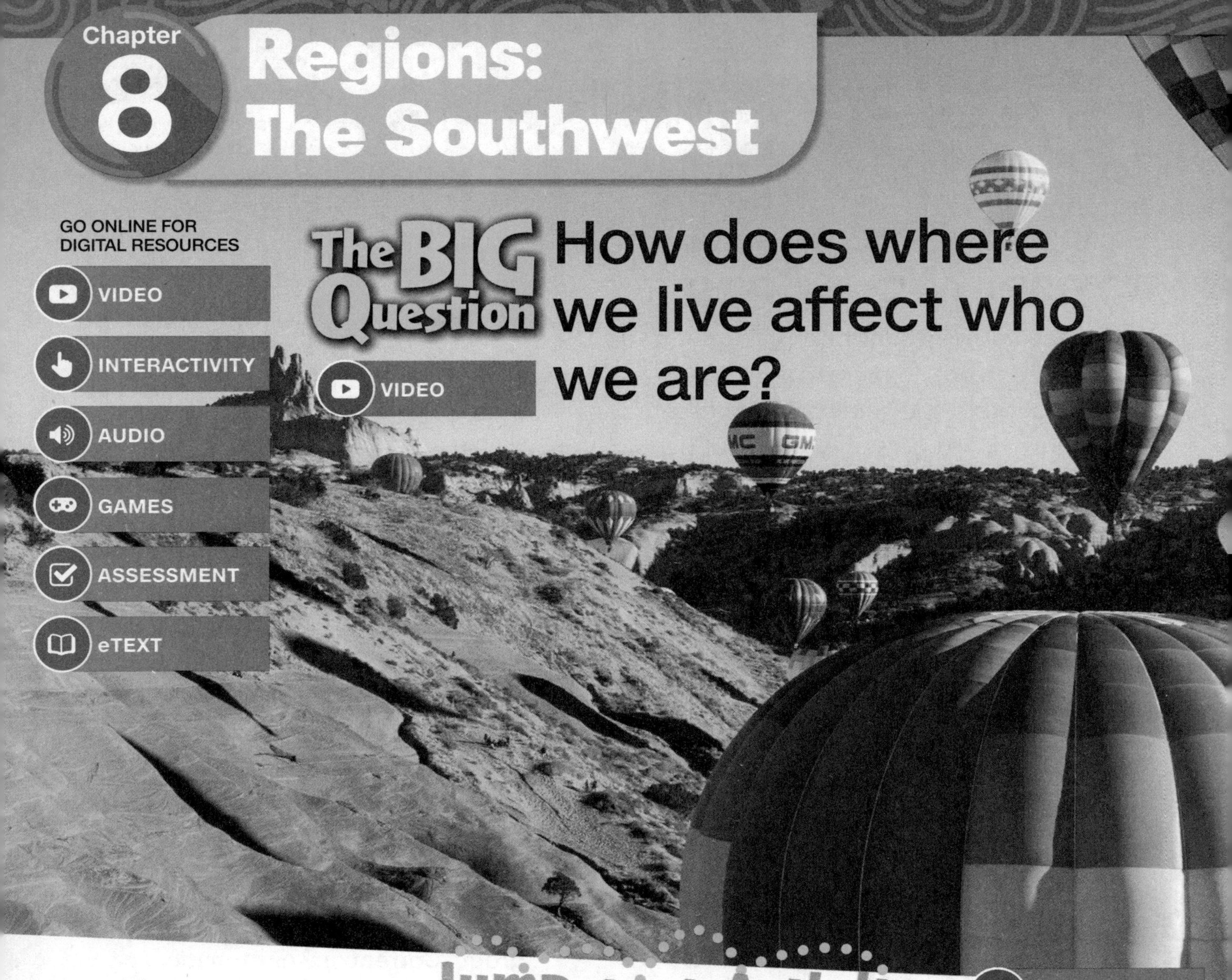

GO ONLINE FOR DIGITAL RESOURCES

- VIDEO
- INTERACTIVITY
- AUDIO
- GAMES
- ASSESSMENT
- eTEXT

The BIG Question

How does where we live affect who we are?

VIDEO

Jumpstart Activity

INTERACTIVITY

Make a list of items you would bring if you traveled to the Southwest. Think about what the climate is like and the activities you could do. Share your list with a partner.

AUDIO

Life in the Southwest

Preview the chapter **vocabulary** as you sing the rap.

Let's take a flight, the Southwest is where
    we're landing.
We'll see plains, plateaus and the Grand Canyon.
Landforms vary, so does climate, right?
Yeah, some areas are **arid** or very dry.

See they go without rain for long stretches of time,
Semiarid climates get some rain but are still dry.
People have built dams where water is stored,
In a lake that's called a **reservoir**.

Ancient Puebloans lived in the Southwest long ago,
In cliffs in **cliff dwellings** where they made
    their homes.
Many groups lived in large villages, or **pueblos**,
And built an irrigation system so their crops
    could grow.

8 Regions: The Southwest

Arizona

New Mexico

Oklahoma

Texas

map area

What happened and When?

Read and interpret the timeline to find out about the key events that happened in the Southwest region from early settlement to today.

Where is the Southwest region?

The four states of the Southwest region are located north of the United States' border with Mexico. Dry, hot desert spreads across much of the region. The Grand Canyon, one the natural wonders of the world, can be found in the Southwest region.

1500   **1600**   **1700**   **1800**

1528
Spanish explorer Cabeza da Vaca's expedition lands in Texas.

1687
Father Kino founds a mission in Arizona.

1821
Stephen F. Austin leads settlers into Texas (Mexico).

TODAY
People visit the Alamo, a symbol for Texas's fight for freedom from Mexico.

Who will you meet?

Sam Houston became the first president of the Republic of Texas before Texas was annexed to the United States.

Francisco Vásquez de Coronado was a Spanish explorer who searched much of the Southwest for cities made of gold.

Margaret Borland was a female cattle ranch owner in Texas who was the only known woman to have led a cattle drive.

Father Eusebio Kino started three missions in what is now Arizona where he taught the Pima and Yuma American Indians.

 INTERACTIVITY

Complete the interactive digital activity.

1900   2000

1901
Oil is found at Spindletop, Texas.

1930s
Hoover Dam is built.

2010
The people of Santa Fe celebrate its 400th anniversary.

TODAY
Santa Fe hosts the International Folk Art Market every year.

Quest
Project-Based Learning

Welcome to Our Class Cultural Festival!

My name is Pari. My class is having a cultural festival to celebrate the cultures of the Southwest! Learning about cultures can help us to better connect the past to the present.

Quest Kick Off

Your job is to plan a cultural festival at your school. Learn about a culture that makes up the Southwest region. Then, show what you have learned by planning and creating a booth at your festival.

1 Ask Questions

What should you include in the festival to represent the culture? Write two questions of your own.

....

....

....

....

2 Research

Learn about cultures in the Southwest. How does the culture's past connect to the culture's present?

....

....

....

....

👆 INTERACTIVITY

Complete the digital activities to get started on planning your cultural festival.

3 Look for Quest Connections

Begin looking for Quest Connections that will help you plan your cultural festival.

4 Quest Findings

Plan Your Cultural Festival

Use the Quest Findings at the end of the chapter to help you plan and create your cultural festival.

Southwestern Land and Water

INTERACTIVITY

Participate in a class discussion to preview the content of this lesson.

Vocabulary

erosion
natural gas
refinery

Academic Vocabulary

reveal
commodity

Unlock
The **BIG**
Question

I will know about the landforms and natural resources in the Southwest.

JumpStart Activity

Form small groups. Think of the landforms and natural features found in the Southwest. Make a human monument of one of the landforms or natural features. Show it to the class and explain why it is important to the region.

Flying over the Southwest, you cross four states: Texas, Oklahoma, New Mexico, and Arizona. On your flight, you will see some of the landforms of the region. In Texas and Oklahoma, farms and cities stretch across the plains. Farther west, the land rises. On the high plateaus, you see herds of cattle. Forests cover some mountains.

At the southern border of the region, the Rio Grande winds through Big Bend National Park.

The Land

Much of Texas and Oklahoma is flat. The Coastal Plain extends inland from the Gulf of Mexico. It covers almost half of Texas. The Great Plains sweep south through the Midwest into Oklahoma, Texas, and New Mexico.

Much of New Mexico and Arizona is plateaus and mountains. In fact, most of New Mexico lies more than 4,000 feet above sea level. In southern New Mexico and Arizona, many mountain ranges rise up from the land. The ranges are separated by basins. Basins are low, slightly hollowed areas of land.

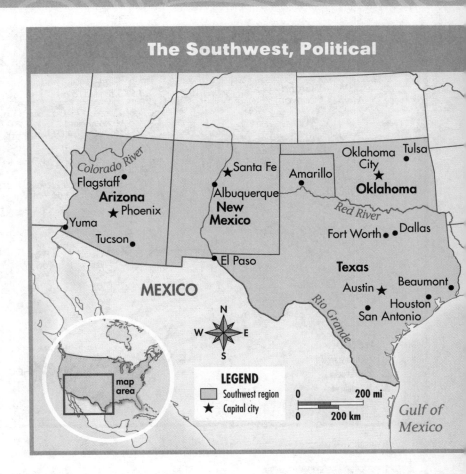

The Southwest, Political

LEGEND
- Southwest region
- ★ Capital city

0   200 mi
0   200 km

Rivers and the Gulf

The states of the Southwest form part of the southern border of the United States. In Texas, the Gulf of Mexico and the Rio Grande form part of the border. The Rio Grande separates Texas and Mexico.

The Rio Grande is one of the great rivers of the nation. In fact, its name means "great river" in Spanish. The Rio Grande begins in the Rocky Mountains in the state of Colorado. It is one of the longest rivers in North America. It flows 1,900 miles south and east to the Gulf of Mexico.

The Colorado River is another major river. It begins in the Rocky Mountains and empties in the Gulf of California. The Colorado River drains a large part of North America. That means that the rivers in the area flow into the Colorado River. This river also forms most of the western border of Arizona.

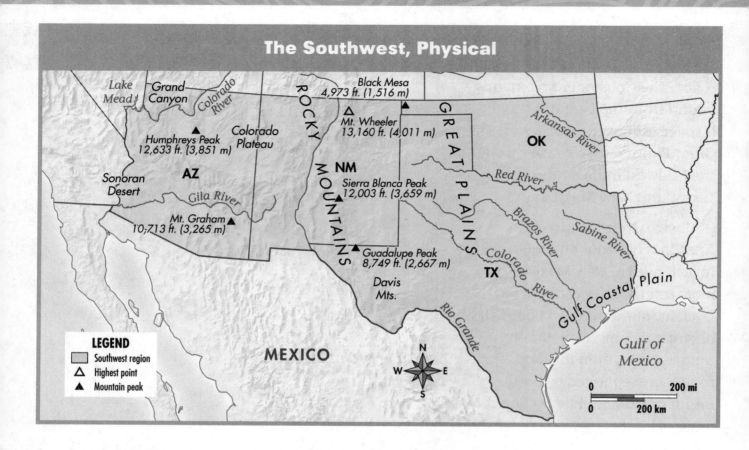

The Southwest, Physical

Lake Mead
Grand Canyon
Colorado River
Humphreys Peak 12,633 ft. (3,851 m)
Colorado Plateau
Sonoran Desert
AZ
Gila River
Mt. Graham 10,713 ft. (3,265 m)
ROCKY MOUNTAINS
Black Mesa 4,973 ft. (1,516 m)
Mt. Wheeler 13,160 ft. (4,011 m)
NM
Sierra Blanca Peak 12,003 ft. (3,659 m)
Guadalupe Peak 8,749 ft. (2,667 m)
Davis Mts.
GREAT PLAINS
Arkansas River
OK
Red River
Brazos River
Colorado River
Sabine River
Rio Grande
TX
Gulf Coastal Plain
Gulf of Mexico
MEXICO

LEGEND
Southwest region
△ Highest point
▲ Mountain peak

N W E S
0 200 mi
0 200 km

The Remarkable Grand Canyon

1. ☑ **Reading Check**

Draw Conclusions
Discuss with a partner why the Grand Canyon is a World Heritage Site.

Suppose that you are in northwest Arizona, about to begin a hike down into the Grand Canyon. Looking out, you understand why over 5 million people visit each year. The canyon seems to go on forever. In places, the Grand Canyon is more than 18 miles wide. It is 6,000 feet deep at its deepest point. That is more than one mile!

Birds fly thousands of feet below you in the canyon, including the rare California condor. At the bottom is the Colorado River. The land near the river is desert-like. There, rattlesnakes hunt their prey. At the top of the canyon are forests. The different types of vegetation make a journey down into the canyon like a trip from Canada to Mexico.

The Grand Canyon is a World Heritage Site. This means it is one of more than 1,000 places on Earth that is prized for its unique cultural or natural environment.

The Work of Erosion

No one knows exactly how the Grand Canyon was formed. Scientists do know that erosion played a big part in it. **Erosion** is a gradual process of wearing away soil and rock. These small pieces of rock and soil are then moved and deposited elsewhere. Scientists say that the rushing water of the Colorado River helped wear away the rock to form the Grand Canyon. This process may have taken millions of years. The water itself gradually wears away the rock. Sand, gravel, and boulders in the river also cut the canyon walls.

Erosion is not only caused by rivers. It can also be caused by rainwater, by melting and moving glaciers, and even by the wind. Rainwater causes erosion when it washes away dirt, soil, and rock such as limestone.

Wind plays a role in erosion when it picks up sand and blows it against rocks or mountains. Even though sand seems harmless, its small, sharp edges wear away the surface of the rocks and mountains.

Every minute of every day, erosion is taking place in the canyons and in other places. The changes happen very slowly over many years.

2. **Reading Check** Cause and Effect **Identify** and **describe** the effect.

Erosion

Cause
River water flows over rock.

Effect

Window Rock, in Arizona, was formed through the process of erosion.

Natural Resources

Rich mineral resources are found underground in the Southwest region. In the highlands of New Mexico and Arizona, mining is important to the economy. The Arizona Mining Association **reveals** the importance of mining in its motto: "Minerals make it possible." Copper is a key **commodity** in Arizona. In fact, Arizona is the country's leading producer of copper. Today, Arizona copper is mined in two ways. Some mines are underground. Others are what are called open-pit mines. In these, miners blast copper out of the ground at the surface. Copper from Arizona is used in everything from coins to computers. The region also has gold, silver, and coal mines.

Just as oil is found underground, so is natural gas. **Natural gas** is a fossil fuel like oil. Texas produces more oil and natural gas than any other state. There is oil under more than two thirds of the state, and there are thousands of oil wells there. Oil is processed, or made into useful chemicals, at a **refinery**.

Academic Vocabulary

reveal • *v.*, to make known

commodity • *n.*, an economic good such as oil, natural gas, or copper

3. ✓ **Reading Check** **Analyze** the map. Circle the symbols for oil and natural gas. Where is most of the oil in the Southwest found?

_____

_____

_____

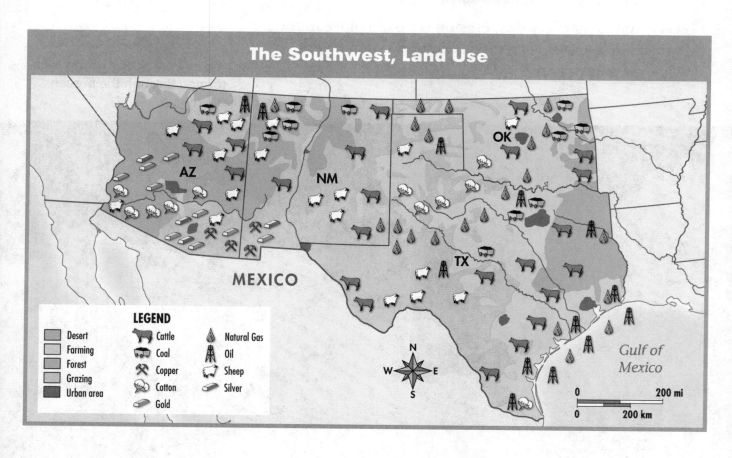

The Southwest, Land Use

AZ

NM

OK

TX

MEXICO

Gulf of Mexico

N W E S

LEGEND
- Desert
- Farming
- Forest
- Grazing
- Urban area
- Cattle
- Coal
- Copper
- Cotton
- Gold
- Natural Gas
- Oil
- Sheep
- Silver

0   200 mi
0   200 km

People in the Southwest also farm. Even though there are many mountains and deserts, the Southwest also has productive farmland. Texas and Arizona are among the nation's largest producers of cotton, and Texas has more farms than any other state. In Oklahoma, farmers raise large crops of wheat.

The grasslands of the region are used to raise livestock. People in Texas and Oklahoma raise cattle, goats, and sheep. The Navajo people have been raising sheep in the region since the 1500s.

A Navajo family watches their sheep.

4. ✅ **Reading Check** **Explain** how both oil production and farming are important to Texas.

_____

_____

INTERACTIVITY

Check your understanding of the key ideas of this lesson.

✅ Lesson 1 Check

5. **Fact and Opinion Describe** the Grand Canyon. Write one fact and one opinion.

_____

_____

_____

6. Suppose you were moving to the Southwest from another country. Where would you want to live? **Explain** your answer.

_____

_____

7. **Explain** the process of erosion.

_____

_____

_____

Latitude and Longitude

The equator is a line that divides Earth halfway between the North Pole and the South Pole. It separates the globe into the Northern and Southern Hemispheres. The location of the equator is labeled 0°, or zero degrees latitude. Lines of latitude are drawn east to west and are always an equal distance from one another. The North Pole is at 90°N and the South Pole is at 90°S. All locations north of the equator are marked with an *N*, and all locations south of the equator are marked with an *S*.

VIDEO

Watch a video about using latitude and longitude to find places.

The prime meridian is an imaginary line that is drawn from the North Pole to the South Pole on a globe. The prime meridian passes through Europe and Africa. It divides Earth into the Eastern Hemisphere, or all those locations east of the prime meridian, and the Western Hemisphere, or all locations west of the prime meridian. Just as the equator is the starting point for latitude, the prime meridian is the starting point for lines of longitude. The prime meridian is labeled 0°, or zero degrees longitude. Lines of longitude are labeled from 0° to 180°. All locations east of the prime meridian are marked with an *E*, and all locations west of the prime meridian are marked with a *W*.

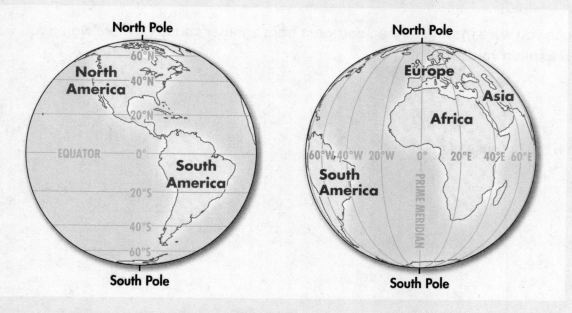

Your Turn!

Use what you have already learned and the map of Texas to help you answer the questions.

1. In which hemispheres is Big Bend National Park located?

_____

_____

2. What is the latitude and longitude of Big Bend National Park?

_____

3. Which attraction is located at about 29°N, 101°W?

_____

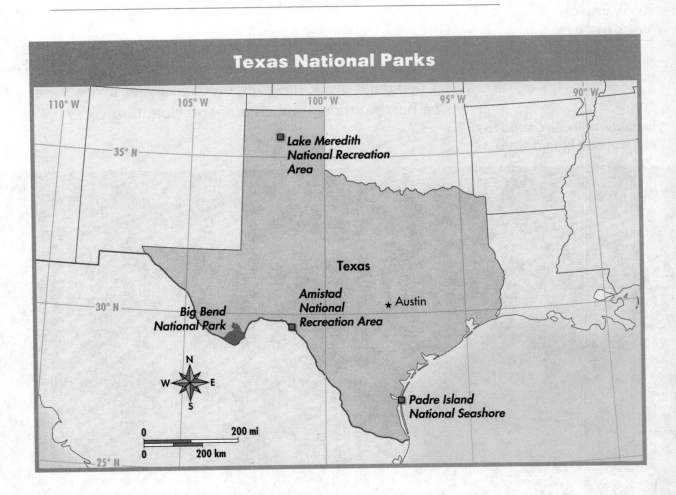

Texas National Parks

Climate of the Southwest

INTERACTIVITY

Participate in a class discussion to preview the content of this lesson.

Vocabulary

arid
semiarid
air mass
savanna

Academic Vocabulary

typical
petrified

In eastern Texas, Caddo Lake is a wet and humid area.

Unlock The BIG Question

I will know that the climate of the Southwest ranges from dry deserts in the west to damper lands in the east.

JumpStart Activity

With a partner, act out a scene that shows the climate of the Southwest. Consider what props you might use. Perform your skit for others in a small group.

Just as the landforms of the Southwest vary, so does the climate. In Arizona, the summers are hot and dry. More than 1,000 miles away, however, on the coast of Texas, it will still be hot, but there is much more precipitation.

A Range of Climates

Some parts of the region, such as southern Arizona and New Mexico, have an **arid**, or very dry, climate. They may receive some rain, but often go for a long time with little or no rain. Other parts of Arizona and New Mexico receive more rain, but they are still dry, or **semiarid**.

Texas has contrasting climates. The western half of the state is semiarid. As you travel east, however, the climate becomes wetter and more humid. In fact, a storm in Texas holds the record for the most rain in one day. It rained 43 inches!

Primary Source

The storm damaged farms and refineries, knocked out telephone service to thousands of customers, and damaged some 20,000 homes. The total damage was estimated at about $750 million by federal officials.

–David Werst, editor, *The Big Lake Wildcat*, Vol. 54, No. 32, Ed. 1. August 9, 1979

Like Texas, Oklahoma is semiarid in the west and wetter in the east. In one year, western Oklahoma received less than 15 inches of rain, but in the east, it rained 57 inches.

Tornado Alley

The weather in the Southwest can change quickly. Large storms can develop. Then you might see a tornado come out of the sky.

Both Texas and Oklahoma are part of Tornado Alley. On the map, you see how different **air masses** meet in the Southwest. An air mass is a body of air with the same temperature and humidity. Tornadoes can form when the contrasting air masses clash.

The strong winds of a tornado can rip roofs off houses and overturn cars. In one year, Oklahoma suffered more than $1 billion in property damage as a result of tornadoes.

Tornado Alley

LEGEND
Tornado Alley
Cold, dry air
Warm, dry air
Warm, moist air

Climate and Vegetation

Academic Vocabulary

typical • *adj.*, common or usual

petrified • *adj.*, made into a fossil

Word Wise

Compound Words
To help you figure out what a compound word means, you can look at the meaning of both words on their own and then put them together. Use this strategy to figure out what the word *grassland* means.

Since the climate changes from the western part of the region to the eastern part, the types of vegetation change, too. In western Arizona is the Sonoran Desert. Here cactus such as the barrel cactus and the prickly pear are **typically** found. There are also large saguaro cactus. Like other plants in the region, this cactus grows long, shallow roots to get water from underground. Its trunk and branches also expand to store the water so that it will survive during the long, dry periods.

Arizona is home to a **petrified** forest. The remains of these very old logs have been replaced by minerals over time. Petrified wood can be orange, red, and even green.

As you move across the region to the east, there is enough precipitation to keep the soil moister. The land changes to prairie and grassland. In fact, the Cibola (SEE boh lah) National Forests and National Grasslands cover more than 263,000 acres of land in northern New Mexico, western Oklahoma, and northern Texas.

Farther east, in parts of Texas and Oklahoma, there is an area called Cross Timbers. This area includes a **savanna**, or a grassland with few, scattered trees. It also has thick forests. The forests of the Cross Timbers were often viewed as a starting point for settlers traveling to the West.

Along the eastern edge of the Southwest, in Texas, are swamps and wetlands. In this watery, humid area, reeds and other marsh plants grow. Some areas of land are covered with water most of the year.

1. ☑ **Reading Check** **Describe** how the vegetation of the Southwest relates to the climates.

_____

_____

_____

_____

_____

_____

A desert owl in a cactus

An egret in a wetland

Animals of the Southwest

Suppose you could visit one of the Southwest's deserts, such as the Sonoran Desert in Arizona. You might think there were no animals there. You could easily see a golden eagle in the sky, but where are the animals on the ground? They are hiding from the sun. Some, like elf owls and lizards, find protection in the saguaro cactus. Rattlesnakes take shelter under rocks. Gila monsters are poisonous lizards. Like snakes, they find protection under rocks and in holes in the ground.

The prairies and grasslands of the region are home to many different animals. Deer, armadillos, and even bald eagles are found here. American bison graze on the grasslands of Oklahoma. Other animals, such as coyotes, can be found across the grasslands, too. Bighorn sheep live high up in the mountains and forests of New Mexico.

Farther east, in Texas, there are more than 300 miles of coast on the Gulf of Mexico. At Padre Island National Seashore, nearly 400 different kinds of birds live in or pass through the parkland each year. You can find seagulls, egrets, and pelicans here. There are also sea turtles that lay their eggs on the beaches.

Quest Connection

How might animals of the Southwest relate to the cultures of the Southwest?

INTERACTIVITY

Explore the influence of the environment on cultures of the Southwest.

2. ☑ **Reading Check** **Explain** how animals like rattlesnakes survive in the desert.

_____

_____

The Higher You Go . . .

Not only does the climate change as you travel from west to east, but also it changes from lower to higher. One hot afternoon in Phoenix, Arizona, you decide to go someplace cooler. A drive to Flagstaff changes everything. If Phoenix is more than 100°F, Flagstaff, might be 30 degrees cooler. The two cities are just 150 miles apart, but the difference in elevation is huge. Phoenix is a little more than 1,000 feet above sea level. Located in the mountains, Flagstaff is almost 6,000 feet higher. They are both in one state, but their climates are very different.

Taos Mountain

In Phoenix, the land is drier as well as lower. When you move to higher elevations, there is more precipitation. In the Sonoran Desert, for example, the lowest areas are at sea level, and the temperatures are high most of the time. But in parts of the Sonoran Desert, there are mountain peaks. The highest is 9,000 feet above sea level. In the low areas, you will see cactus plants. In the mountains, there is enough precipitation so that you will see ponderosa pine trees and aspen trees. These trees grow well in the damper high elevations.

3. ☑ **Reading Check** **Compare** the climates in Phoenix and Flagstaff. Why are they different?

_____

_____

_____

People's activities vary according to elevation, too. In the low areas of Arizona and New Mexico, people bike and hike on nature trails. People also go on guided horseback tours through places such as the Sonoran Desert. In the mountains, people also hike, but they can ski, sled, and snowboard in addition. Another popular sport in the mountains is mountain biking. Wherever you are in the Southwest, elevation matters.

People climb the large rocks and boulders in the region.

INTERACTIVITY

Check your understanding of the key ideas of this lesson.

Lesson 2 Check

4. **Summarize Explain** how the climate of the Southwest changes as you travel from the west to the east.

_____

_____

_____

5. **Draw Conclusions Explain** why you think climate changes at higher elevations.

_____

_____

_____

6. **Understand the** _Quest_ **Connections** Sometimes an animal represents a culture. A bald eagle is the national bird of the United States. Think about an eagle flying in the sky over the Southwest. **Explain** how an eagle might represent American culture.

_____

_____

_____

Lesson 3 · The Southwest's Past

INTERACTIVITY

Participate in a class discussion to preview the content of this lesson.

Vocabulary

cliff dwelling
pueblo
mission

Academic Vocabulary

radiant
architecture

An Ancient Puebloan cliff dwelling

Unlock The BIG Question

I will know that American Indians and Spanish settlers have shaped the history and culture of the Southwest.

Jumpstart Activity

Work in a small group to draw and label a picture that shows American Indian life before the Spanish arrived. Share your pictures with the class and discuss how the American Indians' lives most likely changed.

In 1908, George McJunkin, an African American ranch manager, made an amazing discovery. He found bones from long ago near Folsom, New Mexico. At the site was a spear point made by humans more than 10,000 years ago. Twenty-one years later, near Clovis, New Mexico, bones and a spear point were discovered that were even older. Archeologists learned that humans lived in the area far earlier than anyone had thought.

Ancient Cultures of the Region

More than 3,000 years ago, many different groups lived in what is now the Southwest. One of the earliest of these groups was the Ancient Puebloans, or Anasazi (ah nuh SAH zee). The Ancient Puebloans built **cliff dwellings**, or homes in the cliffs, in present-day New Mexico and Arizona. The Hohokam lived in what is now central Arizona. They built a system of canals. These canals brought water from the Salt River and the Gila River to their farms. The Mogollon people lived along rivers in Arizona and New Mexico. There, they farmed and hunted.

American Indians in the 1500s

The Ancient Puebloans, Hohokam, and Mogollon groups are the ancestors to some of today's American Indians. Like the Ancient Puebloans, the Hopi and Zuni built large villages. When the Spanish came, they called these villages **pueblos**. That is the Spanish word for "village." The Hopi and Zuni farmed crops such as corn, beans, and cotton.

The Pima people were farmers, too. They used the canal systems that the Hohokam built to irrigate their crops. The Mojave and Yuma farmed in the river valleys.

Some American Indians, such as the Apache and Comanche, came to the Southwest from the north. Both the Apache and the Comanche were nomads. Nomads are people who move from place to place. The Navajo people came from the north, too. Like other groups, they were farmers and raised sheep.

Quest Connection

As you read through the lesson, list different groups who have lived in the Southwest. Compare and contrast the groups with a partner.

INTERACTIVITY

Find out more about the cultural groups of the Southwest.

Coronado explored much of the Southwest. He searched for, but never found, cities of gold.

The Spanish Arrive

In the 1500s, Spain sent explorers to the Americas. Álvar Núñez Cabeza de Vaca was part of an early expedition. In 1528, the expedition landed on the coast of what is now Texas. Soon, however, Cabeza de Vaca was one of only four survivors. Another was an African, Estevan. Cabeza de Vaca and Estevan set out to reach Mexico City. It was the capital of New Spain located in what is now Mexico. When they arrived in the city, they said that they heard about rich "cities of gold" while they were traveling. These cities could be found in what is now the Southwest region.

In 1539, Estevan and Father Marcos de Niza set out to find the cities. Father Marcos de Niza was a Spanish missionary. When they reached southeastern Arizona, Father Marcos de Niza saw what he thought were cities of gold shining **radiantly** in the sun.

When the governor of New Spain heard of cities with "walls of gold blocks . . . and streets paved with silver," he wanted to find them. In 1540, he sent Francisco Vásquez de Coronado to find the golden cities, called Cíbola.

Academic Vocabulary

radiant • *adj*., glowing brightly

1. ☑ **Reading Check**
Cause and Effect
Identify and underline the effects of the arrival of Cabeza de Vaca and Estevan in Mexico City.

Primary Source

[S]ome Indians who were natives of other provinces beyond these had told me that in their country . . . they had lords who ruled them, who were served with dishes of gold, and other very magnificent things. . . .

—Letter from Francisco Vásquez de Coronado to the King of Spain, sent from Tiguex on October 20, 1541

Near the present-day border of New Mexico and Arizona, Coronado reached the Zuni pueblo. He found that it was not made of gold after all.

The Colonial Period

Some Spanish explorers would not give up the dream of finding gold in the Southwest. One was Juan de Oñate. In 1598, he led 400 settlers north to build a colony and to find riches. The settlers found no riches, and many were afraid of the American Indians that lived nearby. As a result, most of them returned to Mexico. However, the Spanish soon built other colonies in the Southwest.

At the heart of the Spanish colonies were missions. A **mission** is the headquarters of missionaries. The goal of the missions was to claim land and teach Christian beliefs to the American Indians. The Spanish set up missions across the Southwest. Near many, they built settlements called presidios. Soldiers lived at the presidios so that they could protect the missions.

At the missions, American Indians were given food and protected from enemies. They were put to work farming or making goods. Sometimes, they were forced to live and work at the missions. At times they were treated poorly. At other times, however, the Spanish treated them with kindness.

In 1687, Father Eusebio Kino (eh oh SEH bee oh KEE noh) started the first of three missions in what is now Arizona. Here, he taught the Pima and Yuma groups for 25 years.

Word Wise

Multiple-Meaning Words
Some words have more than one meaning. Look at the word *settlements*. The word *settlement* can mean "an agreement," or it can mean "a community." Determine the best meaning based on the sentence.

2. ✓ **Reading Check**
Turn and Talk Analyze the mission. **Identify** clues that show the people on missions grew or made most of what they needed. **Discuss** with a partner.

San José Mission in Texas

Bell Tower

Orchard

Garden

Gate

Church

Flour Mill

Livestock

Influences Past and Present

Like much of the nation, the Southwest has great diversity, or mixture of cultures. People from all over the world have come to live in the region. Yet the Spanish, Mexican, and American Indian cultures have been especially influential in the Southwest.

In Arizona, New Mexico, and Texas, many people speak both English and Spanish. You see Spanish-style **architecture**, and you can eat Mexican and Spanish foods. People in the Southwest also celebrate two important holidays from Mexico. One is Cinco de Mayo on May 5, which celebrates a Mexican military victory. The other is on September 16, which is Mexican Independence Day.

The Southwest region is still home to American Indians. Many Navajo, Hopi, and Mojave live on reservations. The Navajo Reservation covers about 27,000 square miles. Other American Indian reservations in the region include the Gila River Reservation and the Colorado River Indian Tribes Reservation in Arizona and California.

Academic Vocabulary

architecture • *n.*, building or structure design

People in the Southwest perform traditional dances from Mexico.

3. **☑ Reading Check** Draw Conclusions **Identify** and underline three of the different cultures in the Southwest. **Explain** which culture you think influences the region the most.

_____

_____

_____

_____

_____

_____

Visiting the Southwest

Every year, millions of people visit the Southwest. Many of these people come to experience the mix of cultures. They come to see the cultural life in places from San Antonio, Texas, to Santa Fe, New Mexico. They attend festivals, eat Mexican food, hear music, and see settlements that were once missions. In 2010, the people of Santa Fe celebrated its 400th anniversary.

Tourists come, too, to visit American Indian sites. At places like Canyon de Chelly, they see the carvings and cliff dwellings of ancient American Indians. They also visit pueblos. They learn more about the Navajo, Hopi, and Zuni people. They learn that, like Mexican and Spanish culture, American Indians and their culture are a key part of the Southwest.

Weavings, pottery, and jewelry made by Navajo artists are popular with collectors.

☑ Lesson 3 Check

 INTERACTIVITY

Check your understanding of the key ideas of this lesson.

4. **Draw Conclusions Explain** how the arrival of Spanish settlers changed the lives of American Indians.

_____

_____

5. **Explain** how people from ancient cultures of the Southwest lived.

_____

_____

_____

6. **Understand the Quest Connections Identify** one American Indian group from this lesson. Write one question you would ask if you could visit the group.

_____

_____

Lesson 4 Growth of the Southwest

INTERACTIVITY

Participate in a class discussion to preview the content of this lesson.

Vocabulary

annex
meat-packing
homestead
gusher
metropolitan area

Academic Vocabulary

significant
notable

Unlock The BIG Question

I will know that the Southwest continued to grow as settlers from the United States moved into the region.

Jumpstart Activity

With a partner, make a list of reasons why a place grows. Think about causes and effects of growth.

In 1821, an American named Stephen F. Austin led a group of American settlers into Texas. At this time, Texas was part of Mexico. Over the next 15 years, more settlers from the United States moved to Texas. With each married man promised more than 4,000 acres, many Americans saw opportunity in this land.

The Alamo

Breaking Away

By the 1830s, many Texans wanted to break away from Mexico. Soon, a war started between Mexico and Texas. During the Texas Revolution, several thousand Mexican soldiers attacked the Alamo in 1836. The Alamo was a Spanish mission in present-day San Antonio, Texas. Nearly 200 Texan soldiers died. Although the Mexican victory at the Battle of the Alamo was **significant**, Mexico lost the war. Those who lived in Texas declared it a new country, the Republic of Texas. Sam Houston, a settler and soldier, became its president.

In 1845, Texas went from being a country to a state. It was annexed to the United States. To **annex** means to add to. The battles with Mexico were not over, though. The annexation of Texas led the United States into the Mexican-American War. At the end of the war, the United States won even more land. This land included what is now New Mexico and California, and most of Arizona.

Changing Life for American Indians

Settlers from other states poured into Texas, Arizona, and New Mexico. So did immigrants from Europe. Many of these settlers moved to the river valleys, including the Pecos and Rio Grande valleys. Here there was both water and good soil for farming. Some of this land was used by American Indians. Since the 1830s, the United States had forced many American Indians to move to reservations. The largest reservation was the Indian Territory, in present-day Oklahoma.

In 1863 and 1864, the Navajo were driven from their land. The United States government wanted to stop the fighting between the Navajo and settlers in New Mexico. United States soldiers forced the Navajo to move to a reservation. The Navajo had to walk about 300 miles during the winter months. During the walk, many Navajo died. This difficult journey is called "The Long Walk."

In 1868, the government returned some of the land in present-day Arizona, New Mexico, and Utah, to the Navajo. This land is still the home of the Navajo Nation today.

Members of the Navajo Nation today

Cattle Country

Settlers in Texas raised cattle to sell. In 1867, a man named Philip Armour started the largest meat-packing plant in Chicago, Illinois. A **meat-packing** plant processes the meat from animals for food. In time, this plant and others began to process beef.

People in Texas could raise cattle on their ranches to supply the beef. A ranch is a large farm where livestock is raised. The challenge was getting the cattle to the meat-packing plants. How did the cattle get there? Cattle drives and the railroad were the answer. Cowhands "drove" the cattle north along cattle trails.

Cattle drives were dangerous. One **notable** ranch owner drove cattle over 1,500 miles from Texas to Kansas on the Chisholm Trail. Margaret Borland earned the name of Trail Boss. She was the only known woman to have led a cattle drive. These cattle trails met the railroads at large cities. The freight cars carried the cattle to meat-packing plants in Chicago and Kansas City.

1. ☑ **Reading Check** **Compare** the routes. What do they have in common?

Nat Love was a well-known African American cowhand on the cattle trails of the Southwest.

Academic Vocabulary

notable • *adj.*, worthy of attention or notice

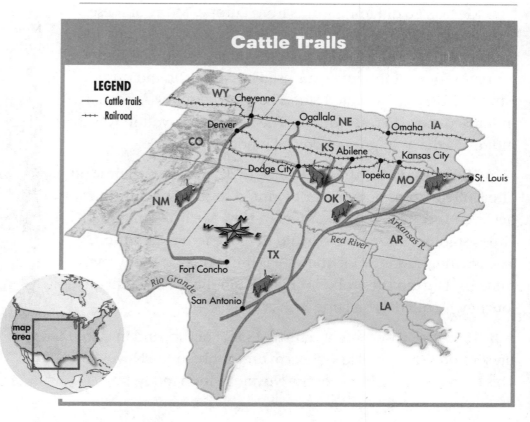

Cattle Trails

LEGEND
— Cattle trails
+++ Railroad

Cheyenne · WY
Denver · CO
Ogallala · NE
Omaha · IA
KS Abilene
Kansas City
Dodge City
Topeka · MO
St. Louis
NM
OK
AR
Arkansas R.
Red River
TX
Fort Concho
Rio Grande
San Antonio
LA

map area

Cattle ranching quickly became a big business. As the demand for beef grew, so did ranching. Ranches were started across the Southwest, as well as in the states of the northern plains. These lands where bison once grazed were now filling with cattle.

Over time, however, ranching changed. Railroad lines were laid in the Southwest. Also, more settlers were moving to the region. The government gave them land to start farms called **homesteads**. To protect their crops, homesteaders, as the farmers were called, put up fences. Cattle could no longer freely roam the grasslands, and the routes the cattle drives followed were often blocked by fences. The days of the long cattle drives came to an end.

Birth of the Oil Industry

More changes came to the Southwest in the 1900s. Anthony Lucas, a mining engineer, began to drill for oil in Texas in 1900.

Primary Source

I went to Beaumont, Texas, about seventy miles west of Lafayette. There I was attracted by an elevation, then known locally as Big Hill, although this hill amounted merely to a mound rising only twelve feet above the level of the prairie.

—Anthony Lucas, *Interviews with Mining Engineers*, 1922

On January 10, 1901, Anthony Lucas and other workers were drilling an oil well at Spindletop, near Beaumont, Texas when suddenly the well exploded. Mud, gas, and then oil shot up more than 100 feet in the air. It took workers nine days to stop the flow of oil called a **gusher**.

The discovery of oil at Spindletop amazed people. Few had ever seen this much oil before. Soon, land around Spindletop went from $150 to $50,000 for one lot. Oil derricks, or the frames that hold the drills, became common. Workers and oil companies rushed to the area. Oil companies spent billions of dollars looking for oil and natural gas in the Southwest. Today, the oil industry is still important to the region.

Oil derricks covered the land over oil fields in Texas.

2. ☑ **Reading Check**
Draw Conclusions
Explain how land might be used near an oil field.
Discuss with a partner.

Quest Connection

How have people who are originally from other places influenced the culture of the Southwest?

INTERACTIVITY

Explore how different groups of the Southwest contributed to the region's past and present.

Still Growing

The Southwest is still a region of wide-open spaces. However, it is also a region of large cities and growth. In fact, Houston, Texas; San Antonio, Texas; Dallas, Texas; and Phoenix, Arizona, are four of the nation's fastest growing metropolitan areas. A **metropolitan area** is a large city and its surrounding area. Texas has more farms than any other state. However, most of the population lives in cities. So do most of the people in Arizona. In New Mexico and Oklahoma, too, most people live in cities.

Why are people moving to cities in the Southwest? High-tech industries and medical centers draw people to cities like Dallas and Houston. Many people come to Phoenix to work in the service industry. Across the region, "snowbirds," or people from states with cold climates, come to enjoy the warm weather of the Southwest and its beauty. People retire to the region for the same reasons. Immigrants come, too, largely from Mexico and Central America.

Not all of the people in cities in the Southwest have come to live there. Tourists come to experience the beauty of the region. In fact, tourism is New Mexico's largest industry.

The area around Phoenix is called the Valley of the Sun.

3. ✓ **Reading Check** **Compare and Contrast Identify** the reasons that people settled in the Southwest by filling in the chart.

Reasons for Settlement	
Group	Reasons
Early American settlers	land
Homesteaders	to start farms
Oil workers	
Retired people	

 **Lesson 4 Check**

 **INTERACTIVITY**

Check your understanding of the key ideas of this lesson.

4. **Draw Conclusions Describe** how railroads changed cattle ranching.

_____

_____

5. **Explain** the challenge of getting cattle to meat-packing plants.

_____

_____

_____

6. **Understand the** *Quest* **Connections** What cultures influenced the history of the area where you live? **Explain** what you would tell tourists about your area.

_____

_____

_____

Draw Inferences

An inference is something you figure out based on clues and information that you already know. Drawing inferences is a way to better understand what you read.

Authors don't state everything when they write. Sometimes meanings and connections are not completely clear. Drawing an inference is a way to fill in some information.

To draw an inference, begin by analyzing the clues in the text. Make sure you understand them. Then think about any related information you already know. Combine the text clues with what you already know to draw an inference.

Read the lines from a cowboy song, "The Old Chisholm Trail." Then read the information below to see how to draw an inference.

▶ **VIDEO**

Watch a video about drawing inferences.

Oh come along, boys, and listen to my tale,
I'll tell you all my troubles on the ol' Chisholm trail.

(chorus)

Come a-ti yi youpy youpy yea youpy yea
Come a-ti yi youpy youpy yea

On a ten dollar horse and a forty dollar saddle,
I was ridin', and a punchin' Texas cattle.

We left ol' Texas October twenty-third
Drivin' up the trail with the U-2 herd.

I'm up in the morning before daylight,
And before I sleep the moon shines bright.

Clues: The cattle are called the U-2 herd.

What I already know: Ranchers branded their cattle to identify them.

Inference: The cattle were from the U-2 ranch and had the U-2 brand.

1. **Draw an inference** by analyzing the last two lines of the song.

   Clues: Cowboys get up before dawn and sleep when the moon shines.

   What I already know: From sunup to night takes about 14 hours.

   Inference: _____

2. Read this passage. **Draw an inference** about why the price of cattle was much lower in Texas than to the north.

   > *After the Civil War, Texas ranchers faced a problem. Cattle in Texas were worth only $3 or $4 each. The same animal in a northern city might be worth $30 or $40. The ranchers needed a way to get their cattle to the north.*

   Clues: _____

   _____

   What I already know: _____

   _____

   Inference: _____

   _____

3. Go back to an earlier chapter. Find a passage in which you drew an inference. **Explain** why your inference was helpful.

   _____

   _____

   _____

4. **Create** an inference outline like the ones above. Use the passage you found for question 3 and show how you drew the inference.

   _____

   _____

   _____

Life in a Dry Land

INTERACTIVITY

Participate in a class discussion to preview the content of this lesson.

Vocabulary

reservoir
aqueduct
drought
gray water

Academic Vocabulary

crucial
shortage

Cacti grow in the desert because they can survive with very little water.

Unlock
The **BIG**
Question

I will know that people in the Southwest have limited water resources.

JumPstart Activity

Brainstorm ideas as a class to conserve water. As your teacher calls out each way, stand up if you practice this. Then write a sticky note that you can stick on your bedroom wall to help you remember other ways to conserve water.

People cannot live without water. Neither can plants or animals. Yet water has always been a scarce resource in the Southwest. Even though some places in the Southwest get plenty of rainfall, remember that much of the region has a climate that is either arid or semiarid.

Lake Mead, created by Hoover Dam, is one of the world's largest human-made lakes.

Where Does the Water Come From?

Anywhere in the world, there are two main sources of water: groundwater and surface water. Groundwater is water that is underground. Groundwater resources are called aquifers. Rainwater and melted snow soak into the ground and become part of an aquifer. When people dig wells, they are tapping into aquifers.

Surface water is water found in lakes, streams, and rivers. Of course, the oceans are also surface water, but salt water is not useful for most human needs. In the Southwest, there are two main sources of surface water: the Colorado River and the Rio Grande.

The Colorado River is especially important. It is the main supply of water for more than 30 million people. High in the mountains, the source of the river is rain and melting snow. States in the Southwest and the West agree on how to share the Colorado's water. In the 1930s, the United States built Hoover Dam on the river, and the dam created a reservoir. A **reservoir** is a lake where water is stored. The Lake Mead reservoir was created by Hoover Dam. It extends more than 100 miles behind the dam. It is a **crucial** part of the Southwest's water supply.

Academic Vocabulary

crucial • *adj.*, of great importance

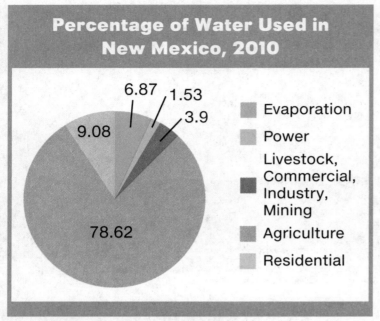

Percentage of Water Used in New Mexico, 2010

6.87 1.53 3.9 9.08 78.62

- Evaporation
- Power
- Livestock, Commercial, Industry, Mining
- Agriculture
- Residential

Source: NM Office of the State Engineer
https://www.nps.gov/state/tx/index.htm

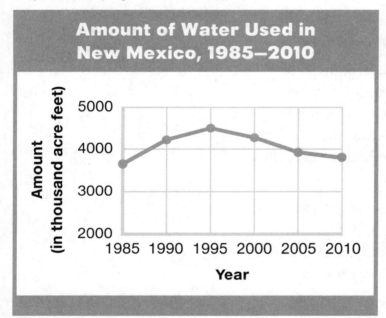

Amount of Water Used in New Mexico, 1985–2010

Amount (in thousand acre feet)

5000
4000
3000
2000

1985 1990 1995 2000 2005 2010

Year

Source: US Geological Survey
https://waterdata.usgs.gov/nm/nwis/wu

Who Uses the Water and How?

In both Arizona and New Mexico, most of the water is used for agriculture. Through irrigation, farmers turn dry soil into rich farmland. That takes a lot of water, though. Experts say that it takes over 1,200 gallons of water to grow the food needed for a typical family dinner.

Who uses the rest of the water? Cities supply water to their residents, or the people who live there. Many businesses use water, too. Other water is used by power plants. These plants use flowing water to turn machines to produce electricity. Dams are one of the places that produce electricity. In fact, Hoover Dam produces electricity for more than 8 million people.

Experts study the water supply and the amount of water that people use. They try to predict future needs. Many expect that more water will be used in residences, or homes, in the future. Why? The answer is "more people." The population in the dry areas of the Southwest continues to grow.

1. ☑ **Reading Check** **Draw Conclusions** **Predict** the amount of water that will be used in 2065. **Explain** why water use may increase or decrease.

_____

_____

_____

Life in a Hot, Dry Land

The warm climate has drawn people to the Southwest for many years. People have adapted to both the heat and the limited amount of water.

If it is 104°F in New Mexico, you may not want to stand outside in the sun. Most likely, you would rather be in your cool home or even a movie theater. Today, most public places are air conditioned. Air conditioning was invented more than 100 years ago. The first large air-conditioned office building opened in San Antonio, Texas, in 1928. Air conditioning made life in the Southwest more comfortable. People could go inside to escape the heat. Since life in the region became less harsh, the population grew.

As more people moved to the Southwest, cities grew in areas without much water. Phoenix, Arizona, is one of these cities. How does Phoenix supply enough water for people to live? It uses aqueducts. **Aqueducts** are systems with pipes that carry water long distances. Aqueducts bring water from the Colorado River to Phoenix. Farmers also use aqueducts to bring water to their farms.

Evidence of how people have adapted to the Southwest can be found at people's homes. This home has a yard that uses less water than a yard filled with grass.

2. ☑ **Reading Check** **Cause and Effect Identify** the effects and fill them in on the chart.

Ways People Adapt

CAUSES	EFFECTS
People use air conditioning to cool homes and businesses. →	
Aqueducts bring water to cities. →	

Water Shortages

The Southwest is one of the fastest-growing regions in the country. Arizona is a good example. Its population is nearly four times larger now than it was just 40 years ago. This means there is a need for more water.

However, for the past decade there has been a water **shortage**. Parts of Arizona and New Mexico have experienced a drought. A **drought** is a period of time when there is little or no rain. When there is a drought, less water is available for use. In times of severe drought, there may not be enough water for farmers to raise crops. Animals in the wild may also have less water as rivers and streams dry up.

The people in the Southwest are meeting the challenge of the water shortage. Scientists, experts, and ordinary citizens are working to use water more wisely. Farmers have developed ways to use less water for irrigation. Many now use drip irrigation. In drip irrigation, less water is lost through evaporation since the water drips directly onto the base of the plants.

Cities and industries are helping, too. Some use new sources of water. They use "gray water" to water public lands or in factories. **Gray water** is recycled water. It is not safe for drinking by people or washing the fruit and vegetables that people eat, but it is useful in other ways.

Academic Vocabulary

shortage • *n.*, a situation in which something that is needed cannot be obtained

Primary Source

In the 1930s, a severe drought in the Great Plains lasted many years. The drought left farmers in Oklahoma, Texas, and New Mexico with dry, dusty soil.

Families are also working to save water. In the last twenty years, for example, people in Phoenix, Arizona, have cut their water use by about 20 percent. Many new showers, toilets, and washing machines are designed to use less water. Families also try to use less water outdoors. They follow city guidelines that recommend that they water their yard less often and water only at night or early morning. This way, less water is lost through evaporation. Many people also have stopped washing their cars to save water. Across the Southwest, people know that their lives and their region depend on water.

3.  **Reading Check** **Identify** two ways you and your family can save water.

_____

_____

_____

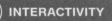 **INTERACTIVITY**

Check your understanding of the key ideas of this lesson.

☑ Lesson 5 Check

4. **Summarize** **Explain** how technology helps people adapt to the Southwest.

_____

_____

_____

_____

5. "The bigger, the better" is a saying in American culture. But growth brings challenges. **Develop** a new saying that takes a shortage of resources into account.

_____

6. Why is water so important in the Southwest?

_____

_____

"They Dance for Rain and Rainbows"

The Pueblo American Indians have a strong cultural heritage. Many of the traditions started long ago are still practiced today. The Pueblo have passed on traditions through storytelling, dancing, and singing.

Ceremonies vary during each season. Everyone in the group helps to prepare costumes and other traditional objects needed for the event. Musicians and dancers practice for many days.

This song describes a traditional ceremony performed on a particular Feast Day.

Vocabulary Support

copying what the Comanche warriors did

elders, *n.*, older people from an earlier generation

plaza, *n.*, a public area or square

Fun Fact

The Tewa are a Pueblo tribe. The Comanche were their enemies long ago.

"On Feast Day the Pueblo Indians celebrate in Old San Juan
The Tewa tribe will be dancing to honor the sun and
　　Saint John
Oh how I long to see the Pueblos
Dancing in New Mexico
They show the earth great respect
And they dance for rain and rainbows
The Tewas dance out in the plaza
　　imitating Comanche warriors
The dancers pray and give thanks
All the children and the elders
Oh how I long to see the Pueblos dancing in New Mexico
They show the earth great respect and they dance
For rain and rainbows
For rain and rainbows"

—Sam Jones, "They Dance for Rain and Rainbows"

Close Reading

1. **Identify** and circle words that describe the setting of the song, or where the song takes place.

2. Why are the Pueblo dancing?

_____

_____

_____

3. **Explain** how the image supports the text.

_____

_____

_____

_____

Wrap It Up

Find out more about the Pueblo. Research other traditions that they still practice today. Share your findings with your class.

_____

_____

_____

Quality:
Individual Responsibility

Henry Chee Dodge (about 1857–1947)
Peacekeeper and Community Leader

Henry Chee Dodge faced many hardships as a child. His father died when Dodge was very young. He was forced to march with his people on "The Long Walk" at age six and was separated from his mother during this time. So, Dodge was mostly raised among the Navajo.

After the U.S. government allowed the Navajo to return home in 1868, Dodge learned to speak English. He soon began to interpret for the U.S. agents governing the Navajo. Later, he worked to keep the peace between his people and the government agents. When the first Navajo Tribal Council was formed in 1923, Dodge became chairman and served until 1928. During this time, he worked to help the Navajo receive money for the oil that was discovered under the land where the Navajo reservation was located. He felt it was his responsibility to take on this challenge for the Navajo and get what he thought was rightfully theirs.

In 1945, Henry Chee Dodge was awarded the Achievement Medal from the Indian Council Fire for being an outstanding citizen who worked to better his community. He was the first Navajo to be awarded this achievement.

Find Out More

1. Why do you think Dodge worked as an interpreter?

_____

_____

_____

2. Research to find out more about Dodge's legacy and how some of his children continued their father's work.

_____

_____

_____

_____

Visual Review

Use these graphics to review some of the vocabulary, people, and ideas from this chapter.

The Southwest

Land and Water

- The Southwest region includes four states: Texas, Oklahoma, New Mexico, and Arizona.
- Landforms of the Southwest include plains, mountains, and canyons.
- Along with the Gulf of Mexico, the Colorado River and the Rio Grande shape the region.

Resources

- The Southwest is a rich source of minerals, but water is scarce.
- Availability of land and rich resources, such as oil, have drawn people to the Southwest for hundreds of years.
- Groundwater from aquifers and surface water from the Colorado River and Rio Grande are the region's main water sources.

Climate

- The range of climates, from humid to arid, affects the vegetation that grows in the region.
- Tornadoes are common in Tornado Alley.
- The climate in the Southwest changes as the elevation changes.

Culture and History

- American Indians have lived in the Southwest for thousands of years, and they continue to keep their cultures and traditions alive.
- Spanish explorers and missionaries influenced the region starting in the 1500s.
- Many American Indians were uprooted in the past.

☑ Assessment

GAMES

Play the vocabulary game.

Vocabulary and Key Ideas

1. **Identify** these words by matching them to their definitions.

plains   high, flat lands

basins   flat lands, good for farming

mountains   low, slightly hollowed areas

plateaus   high peaks

2. **Identify** and label one location for each item below.

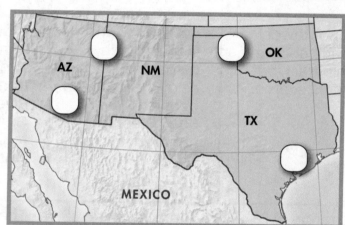

A Arid land

G Gulf Plains

T Tornado Alley

P Plateaus

3. **Sequence** these events. Number them 1 through 4, from the earliest to the latest event.

_____ The Hohokam farmed in Arizona.

_____ Coronado saw the Zuni pueblos.

_____ Folsom people carved spear points.

_____ Father Kino started missions.

4. **Identify** the word to complete the sentence.

In 1540, Coronado was sent to find cities made of _____.

5. **Draw Conclusions Explain** how the Southwest's history affects its culture.

_____

_____

Critical Thinking and Writing

6. Cause and Effect Identify the missing cause in the chart.

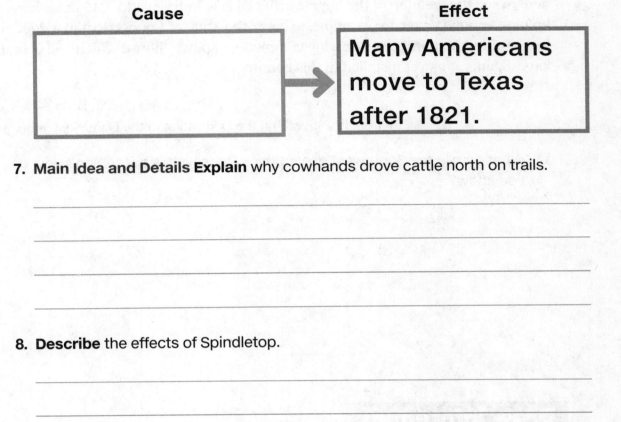

Cause

Effect

Many Americans move to Texas after 1821.

7. Main Idea and Details Explain why cowhands drove cattle north on trails.

_____

_____

_____

_____

8. Describe the effects of Spindletop.

_____

_____

9. Revisit the Big Question How were the people of the Southwest affected by where they lived?

_____

_____

_____

10. Writing Workshop: Write Informative Text Describe ways people are adapting to the dry land in the Southwest. On a separate sheet of paper, write two short paragraphs that explain how people are adapting.

Analyze Primary Sources

"We are here to celebrate the completion of the greatest dam in the world. . . we are here to see the creation of the largest artificial lake in the world—115 miles long, holding enough water, for example, to cover the State of Connecticut to a depth of ten feet; and we are here to see nearing completion a power house which will contain the largest generators yet installed in this country."

—President Franklin D. Roosevelt, excerpt
from his Speech on the Dedication of the Dam, September 30, 1935

11. What dam in the Southwest do you think Roosevelt is describing? How do you know?

_____

_____

_____

_____

_____

Draw Inferences

12. Why is the water problem such an important issue for the people of the Southwest region to resolve?

_____

_____

_____

_____

_____

Quest Findings

INTERACTIVITY

Use this activity to help you plan your cultural festival.

Plan Your Cultural Festival

You've read the lessons in this chapter and now you're ready to plan your cultural festival. Remember that the goal is to show others all about the culture you researched and its contributions to the Southwest in the past and present. Follow these steps:

1 Brainstorm Your Ideas

Think of the key aspects of culture that you would like to present at the class cultural festival. Make a list of your ideas.

2 Make an Outline

Use your notes to write an outline of your plan. Make sure your outline answers the following questions:

- Why is this cultural group important to the Southwest?
- What contributions has the group made in the past and in the present?
- How are past and present contributions connected?

3 Revise Your Outline

Exchange your outline with a partner. Tell your partner what you like about the plan and what could use improvement. Be polite when you provide suggestions.

4 Create Your Cultural Booth

Use your revised outline to create a booth at your class cultural festival. Be creative. Make decorations, draw pictures, show a video, or make a special food that is important to the culture you researched.

GO ONLINE FOR
DIGITAL RESOURCES

▶ VIDEO

👆 INTERACTIVITY

🔊 AUDIO

🎮 GAMES

☑ ASSESSMENT

📖 eTEXT

The BIG Question

▶ VIDEO

How does where we live affect who we are?

JumpStart Activity

👆 INTERACTIVITY

As a class, make a list of jobs that people do in your region where they interact with their physical environment. Write your notes here. Then, make a class list on the board. Add your ideas to the list.

_____

_____

_____

Headed Out West

Preview the chapter **vocabulary** as you sing the rap.

A range of climates in the West affects the places
  we'll go,
Like in the **tundra** where it's so cold that trees
  can't grow.
West of the Cascades gets a lot of rain and snow,
But the east side gets less, it's in a **rain shadow**.

In California's **Central Valley** rivers flow,
And farmers irrigate crops so that they can grow.
Early Spanish settlers were given plots of land,
Where they could raise cattle and sheep out on
  the **ranch**.

During the **gold rush**, people came from
  all around,
To search for gold and created towns
  called **boomtowns**.
In the Silicon Valley the tech industry would start,
They used **silicon** from rocks to create
  computer parts.

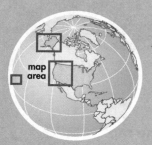

PACIFIC
OCEAN

map
area

Washington

Montana

Oregon

Idaho

Wyoming

Nevada

Utah

Colorado

Alaska

California

Hawaii

Where is the West region?

The eleven states of the West region make up the western border of our country. The outermost states touch the waters of the Pacific Ocean. As a result, shipping is a major industry. The West region is home to the Rocky Mountains and other mountain ranges. Mining and ranching are part of its rich history.

What happened and When?

Read the timeline to find out about key events in the history of the West region.

1800   1850   1900

1848
Gold is discovered at Sutter's Mill.

1869
Transcontinental railroad is completed.

TODAY
Visitors to the Golden Spike National Historic Site can watch a reenactment of the final spike being driven into the railway.

Who will you meet?

Junípero Serra was a Spanish priest who founded many of California's 21 missions.

John Sutter was a California settler who built the fort where gold was discovered in 1848.

William F. "Buffalo Bill" Cody was an entertainer whose "Wild West show" told popular stories about the West to people all over the world.

Senator Mazie Hirono is a United States senator from Hawaii who is the first Asian American woman elected to the Senate.

 INTERACTIVITY

Complete the interactive digital activity.

1950 **2000**

1959
Alaska becomes the forty-ninth state.

1992
Ben Nighthorse Campbell of Colorado becomes the first American Indian elected to the U.S. Senate.

TODAY
The population of Alaska is over 700,000 people.

On a Wagon Train: Journey to the West

In the 1800s, people began migrating, or moving, from the eastern United States to the West on wagon trains. They moved for different reasons. Some journeyed during the gold rush to find riches. Others were drawn by the fur-trapping and logging industries. Still others moved to find religious freedom.

Quest Kick Off

Imagine you are on a wagon train in the 1800s. Write a journal entry describing why you and your family are migrating to the West. Also, describe what you see during your journey, as well as how you feel. Tell about what is challenging, as well as what is interesting and fun! Later, you will share your journal entry with your classmates.

1 Ask Questions

What questions do you have about wagon trains during the 1800s?

....

....

....

2 Research

 INTERACTIVITY

Complete the digital activities to get started on your journal entry.

Use the Internet to find answers to your questions. Then choose one of the reasons people migrated and research places and events related to it.

....

....

....

....

3 Look for *Quest* Connections

Begin looking for Quest Connections that will help you write your journal entry.

4 *Quest* Findings
Write Your Journal Entry

Use the Quest Findings page at the end of the chapter to help you write your journal entry and conduct your class discussion.

A Varied Land

Vocabulary

volcano

geyser

magma

tsunami

Academic Vocabulary

accumulate

recall

Unlock The BIG Question

I will know that the land of the West is varied and sometimes reshaped by earthquakes and volcanoes.

Jumpstart Activity

In a group, pretend you are standing in or on a different landform of the West. One group at a time, stand up and describe what you "see."

The West is a region with many different landforms. A person could hike a mountain trail in the morning and then splash in the Pacific Ocean in the evening. The West has been shaped by volcanoes and earthquakes and mighty rivers that wind like ribbons through the region. The West includes the states of California, Oregon, Montana, Wyoming, Colorado, Utah, Nevada, Idaho, Washington, Alaska, and Hawaii.

The Rocky Mountains are made up of more than 100 smaller mountain ranges, such as the Elk Mountains in Colorado.

Mountains of the West

From Alaska, through Canada, and on south through New Mexico, the Rocky Mountains form the largest mountain range in North America. They stretch more than 3,000 miles in length and more than 300 miles in width in some places.

The Rockies, as they are often called, rise up in steep peaks and form the western border of the Great Plains. Coming west from the east, they tower over the plain's flat lands.

West of the Rocky Mountains is another mountain range located in eastern California and western Nevada called the Sierra Nevada. Some of these mountains are more than 14,000 feet above sea level. Sea level is the height of the surface of the ocean.

Another mountain range, called the Cascades, extends from northern California up through Oregon and Washington. Mount Rainier, the tallest mountain in this range, is more than 14,400 feet above sea level.

The Long Coast

The Pacific Coast is the land along the western border of the United States. This is where the land meets the Pacific Ocean. California, Oregon, Washington, and Alaska are the states that share this coastline.

Sea arches and sea stacks are unusual landforms that visitors can spot along the coast. A sea arch is formed by waves wearing away large rocks along a coast. Over time, the waves erode the middle of a rock to form an arch. As erosion continues, part of the arch may break. The pile of rocks that is left behind is called a sea stack.

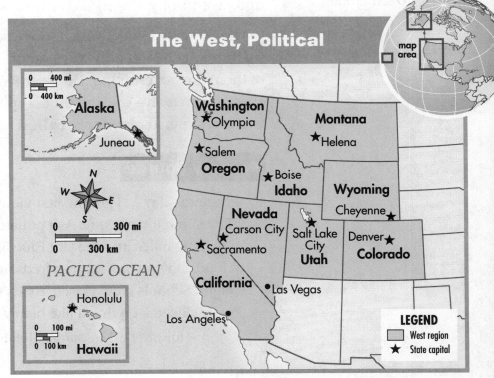

The West, Political

map area

0 400 mi
0 400 km
Alaska
Juneau

N
W   E
S

0   300 mi
0   300 km

PACIFIC OCEAN

0 100 mi
0 100 km
Honolulu
Hawaii

★**Washington**
Olympia
★Salem
Oregon
Montana
★Helena
★Boise
Idaho
Wyoming
Cheyenne ★
Nevada
Carson City
★
★Sacramento
Salt Lake City
Utah
Denver ★
Colorado
California
• Las Vegas
Los Angeles •

LEGEND
West region
★ State capital

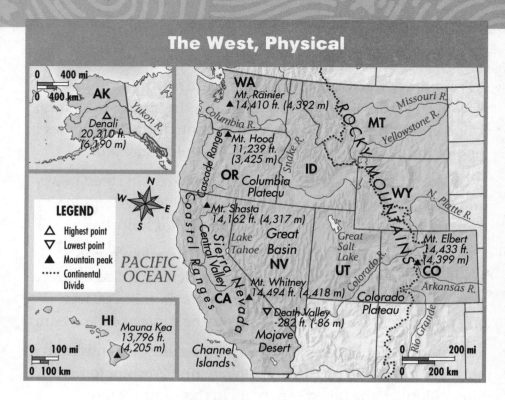

The West, Physical

LEGEND
△ Highest point
▽ Lowest point
▲ Mountain peak
····· Continental Divide

1. ✓ **Reading Check**
Locate and circle the region's highest and lowest points.

Academic Vocabulary

accumulate • *v.*, to build up
recall • *v.*, to remember

Volcanoes

A **volcano** is an opening in the surface of Earth through which gas, ash, and lava are forced out. As hot lava flows from the volcano, it begins to cool and harden. More lava flows on top and begins to **accumulate**, creating land.

Hawaii formed from undersea eruptions millions of years ago. Eventually, the islands rose above the Pacific Ocean.

The Cascade Range, which spreads from northern California up through Oregon and Washington, has many volcanoes. Most of them are not erupting. However, Washington's Mount Saint Helens is an active volcano that erupted violently in 1980. Twenty-five years later, a reporter **recalled** what he had witnessed:

Primary Source

The next day … I got my first view of the mountain. The summit was gone. Ash poured out of the new crater, climbing miles into the sky. Blue lightning flashed in the cloud. Downwind, for hundreds of miles, day turned to night. Schools were closed, roads were closed, airports were closed.… Ash fell like heavy snow.

–Howard Berkes, National Public Radio reporter, 2005

Geysers and Hot Springs

In Wyoming's Yellowstone National Park, more than 10,000 hot springs and hundreds of geysers attract tourists from around the globe. A **geyser** is a hot, underground spring that shoots steam and boiling water high into the air. The park's most famous geyser is Old Faithful, which erupts about every 60 to 110 minutes.

The geysers and hot springs of Yellowstone occur because groundwater there is heated by **magma**, or melted rock that is underneath Earth's surface. Pools of heated water that form are known as hot springs. Only when these pools of hot water erupt, such as Old Faithful does, are they called geysers.

During an eruption, Old Faithful can spray more than 8,000 gallons of water into the air in about five minutes.

Earthquakes

A fault is a break in Earth's crust that is created by the movement of giant blocks of Earth. These massive blocks sometimes overlap or slip past each other. When the blocks finally break free of each other, the energy that is released is an earthquake. There are a great number of faults in the West, especially along the coastline.

Earthquakes can cause terrible damage. Landslides of rocks, mud, snow, and ice can slide down mountains, knocking down forests and burying buildings. When huge blocks of Earth shift along the fault lines, roads, highways, and railroads can split apart. Buildings and bridges can collapse from the shaking.

In March 1964, an earthquake hit Prince William Sound in Alaska and created a number of tsunamis. A **tsunami** is a wall of water that can be 100 feet higher than an average wave. These enormous waves are dangerous when they crash along the shore.

2. **☑ Reading Check Cause and Effect Explain** why the West is more likely to suffer an earthquake than other regions.

_____

_____

Quest Connection

Highlight the names of rivers in the West.

INTERACTIVITY

Explore bodies of water found in the West.

Rivers and Lakes of the West

When people first settled in the West, they often made their homes near rivers, streams, and lakes. The main reason is that people and their animals needed water to survive. Another reason is that long ago, it was easier for people to travel and transport goods by water than by land.

One important western river is the Columbia, which begins its journey of more than 1,200 miles in the Rocky Mountains of Canada. It then winds south and west through Washington and Oregon before spilling into the Pacific Ocean. Over time, the river cut through rock to form the beautiful Columbia River Gorge, a deep valley that is set between mountains.

The many dams on the Columbia River and its tributaries, or the smaller rivers that flow into the Columbia, provide electricity for homes and businesses. The energy produced by this blocked water is a valuable resource in the region. However, the dams have not been good for the river's fish. The salmon population has decreased sharply since the dams were built. Scientists and other experts are studying the problem and looking for ways to solve it.

The Willamette River is an important river in Oregon that feeds into the Columbia. As the Willamette drains, the rich soil stays behind in the Willamette Valley. The soil provides ideal conditions to grow a variety of fruits and vegetables.

The Columbia River Gorge forms part of the boundary between Washington and Oregon.

Many lakes in the West are freshwater lakes. Alaska has more than 3 million lakes. Lake Iliamna, about 200 miles southwest of Anchorage, is Alaska's largest lake.

Utah's Great Salt Lake is a saltwater lake. This lake is also known as a sump lake because it does not flow into another body of water. The Great Salt lake has an even higher salt content than the oceans. Rivers that feed into the lake carry small amounts of salt in their water. As the water evaporates, the salt is left behind and the lake becomes saltier.

3. ☑ **Reading Check** **Compare and Contrast** **Explain** how a sump lake is different from other lakes.

_____

_____

INTERACTIVITY

Check your understanding of the key ideas of this lesson.

☑ Lesson 1 Check

4. **Summarize** **Describe** how the islands of Hawaii were formed.

_____

_____

_____

5. On your vacation to the West, you saw a sea arch, a landform created by wind and water. Write a postcard to a friend to **describe** the sea arch and how it was formed.

_____

_____

_____

6. **Understand the** *Quest* **Connections** Why do you think pioneers would not have seen any dams when they journeyed west in the 1800s?

_____

_____

Climate of the West

INTERACTIVITY

Participate in a class discussion to preview the content of this lesson.

Vocabulary

tundra
rain shadow
nocturnal

Academic Vocabulary

impress
camouflage

The hottest temperature ever recorded on Earth took place in Death Valley, California. On July 10, 1913, the temperature hit 134°F.

Unlock The BIG Question

I will know how weather and climate vary in different parts of the West.

JUMPstart Activity

Gather again in your landform groups. Your group will be assigned a type of climate. One group at a time, stand up and describe what you feel and what activities you can do there.

From the baking heat of a summer day in the desert to a snowy, frozen plain in winter, the West region has a range of climates. Climate is the average weather patterns in an area throughout a year.

Extreme Heat and Cold

Many areas in the West have hot summers. Death Valley, a desert in southern California, has the most extreme heat. In the summer, temperatures often rise to 120° F. The extreme heat of Death Valley has **impressed** people for many years:

Primary Source

At different times according to the experiences of travelers, temperatures varying from 120 to 135 [Fahrenheit] have been reported. . . . We recall a heavy and firmly constructed table . . . that warped and twisted [because of the heat] . . .

–Goldthwaite's Geographical Magazine
on Death Valley, 1892

People who live in Idaho, Montana, Wyoming, Colorado, and parts of Washington are used to heavy snows and freezing winter temperatures. However, the most extreme winter temperatures occur in Alaska, our northernmost state.

Tundra is a level, frozen area in the far north where the temperatures are so cold that trees cannot grow. In winter, the Alaskan tundra often has extremely cold temperatures.

Academic Vocabulary

impress • *v.*, to amaze or have an impact on

Trees cannot grow on the Alaskan tundra because temperatures are too cold.

Moderate and Tropical Climates

Many areas in the West have climates that are more moderate. This means that the temperatures are warm, not hot, in the summer. Winters are cool, not cold. In some areas of California, such as San Diego, people enjoy mild temperatures throughout the year.

Hawaii has a tropical climate, meaning it is warm all year. The average high temperature for Hawaii is about 85° F. The average low temperature is about 70° F. Tropical rain forests filled with plants and flowers grow on some of Hawaii's islands.

Precipitation

Just as temperatures vary in the West, so does rainfall. Extreme examples of rainfall include Death Valley, California, and Mount Waialeale, Hawaii. In one part of Death Valley, between October 3, 1912, and November 8, 1914, no precipitation fell. Two years with no rain! At the other extreme is Hawaii's Mount Waialeale. It receives about 450 inches of rain in an average year.

The Rain Shadow Effect

The tall mountains that make up the Cascade Range affect the amount of precipitation that falls nearby. In parts of Washington's Olympic Peninsula, which lies to the west of the Cascades, the yearly precipitation averages about 140 inches. However, Yakima, Washington, which is east of the Cascades, receives less than 8 inches of precipitation each year.

How do mountains affect the amount of rain or snow that falls on an area? Warm, moist air is carried in from the Pacific Ocean. As the warm air blows to the east, it forms clouds. As the clouds rise up over the mountains, they become cooler and can no longer hold as much moisture.

The water inside the cooled clouds falls as rain or snow. When the clouds begin to pass over the eastern side of the mountains, they have little moisture left inside. Because the eastern side of the Cascades lies in the **rain shadow**, it receives less rain than the western side.

The Rain Shadow Effect

Warm, moist air from the Pacific Ocean rises and moves up the mountains.

Moisture falls from the cooled clouds as rain or snow.

As the clouds reach the eastern side, they have lost most of their moisture.

The area in the rain shadow receives little moisture.

Pronghorns roam on the high plains of Montana and Wyoming.

Wildlife of the Western Plains and Deserts

The Great Plains is a large area of land that lies in the rain shadow created by the Rocky Mountains. Most of the Great Plains is a prairie, a place where grass grows well but trees are scarce. The Great Plains often experiences hot summers and cold winters. This area is also known for sudden storms that seem to form without warning. Animals that make their home in the Great Plains must adapt to this grassland area where the weather can change quickly.

Pronghorns are found mostly in the high plains area of Wyoming and Montana. The light brown coat of the pronghorn helps it to blend in with the dry, brown grasses of the high plains. But the pronghorn also relies on its speed and keen eyesight. These are important since this animal needs to see and outrun wolves and coyotes.

Desert animals have found interesting ways to survive the hot and sandy environment of Death Valley. Some animals spend the hottest part of the day asleep in a hole in the ground. The Mojave rattlesnake is **nocturnal**, meaning that it is only active at night. The desert jackrabbit survives by feeding on small desert plants. The jackrabbit's long ears move heat away from its body, helping it to stay cool. The fringe-toed lizard has scales on its feet that help it run quickly across the sand to escape predators.

Quest Connection

What about the climate of the western plains might have been challenging for the pioneers?

INTERACTIVITY

Explore the climate of the West.

1. ☑ **Reading Check**
Turn to a partner and **describe** the Great Plains in your own words.

The arctic fox has white fur in the winter.

Wildlife of Alaska

Many people think of Alaska as a land of ice and snow. But Alaska has many climates. Areas in its southern climate zone have average winter temperatures of about 20 to 40° F. Average summer temperatures are about 40 to 60° F.

Alaska is home to a variety of wildlife, including birds such as snowy owls and tundra swans, as well as black and white puffins that live near the arctic waters.

Down in the cold sea, walruses keep warm with a thick layer of blubber, or fat. Other sea creatures, such as dolphins, sharks, and whales, live in the waters off Alaska's coast.

Alaskan mammals include the arctic fox, which has a white coat in the winter. In the summer, its coat turns reddish brown to provide **camouflage** while it moves through the native grasses. This helps the fox sneak up on its prey without being seen.

Academic Vocabulary

camouflage • *n.*, the disguising or blending in with one's surroundings

Wildlife of Hawaii

The ocean surrounding the Hawaiian Islands is home to dolphins, sharks, whales, and the monk seal, which is one of Hawaii's native mammals.

The nene, or Hawaiian goose, is the state bird. The nene is often spotted in the Hawaii Volcanoes National Park showing off its tan and black feathers.

Hawaiian honeycreepers are colorful birds found in the tropical rain forests. They feed on insects, snails, fruit, seeds, and the nectar from flowers.

The nene is Hawaii's state bird.

2. **☑ Reading Check**
Compare and Contrast Use the Venn diagram to **identify** two animals that have adapted to Alaska and two that have adapted to Hawaii. In the shared section, **identify** two animals that have adapted to both places.

Alaska **Hawaii**

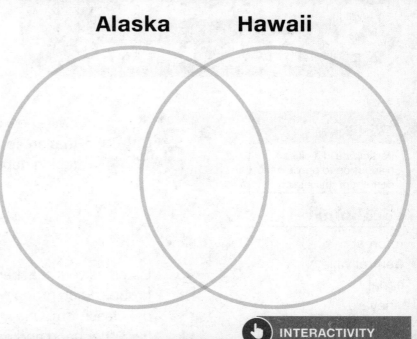

INTERACTIVITY

Explore the key ideas of this lesson.

☑ Lesson 2 Check

3. **Cause and Effect Explain** how the Cascade Range affects the climate east of the mountains.

_____

_____

_____

4. You are packing for a vacation to see the Great Salt Lake in Utah. Because the West has so many different climates, **identify** what you need to know about Utah to help you pack.

_____

_____

_____

5. **Understand the** _Quest_ **Connections** How would you and your fellow pioneers have handled the climate of the western plains?

_____

Western Resources

Vocabulary

reforest
Central Valley
canal
vineyard

Academic Vocabulary

favorable
considerable

Unlock The BIG Question

I will know about the different resources that are found in the West and how the region depends on them.

JumpStart Activity

Listen as your teacher divides the class into two groups. Each group will stand in a different area of the classroom. One student in the first group will raise his or her hand and name an animal, plant, or mineral. Then that student will call out someone's name from the second group. That student should tell a way that we use that resource.

The West is a region rich in natural resources. People in the Western states use their land, forests, and waters to produce goods that are shipped from the West to other regions and overseas.

Idaho is home to many large sheep ranches.

The Great West

Although the West contains many mountain ranges, farmers use valleys and broad, level plateaus to grow vegetables, fruits, and grains. These same plateaus are just right for cattle and sheep ranching. In fact, animals that are raised on farms and ranches are the main source of farming income in some Western states. This includes beef from ranches, as well as milk from dairy cows. Sheep and sheep products, such as wool, are also important.

Western forests provide trees to make many different products. Trees are cut down and then sawed into lumber. The lumber is used to build homes and furniture. Other wood products include paper to make paper towels and books. To keep forests productive, timber companies usually **reforest**. This means they plant new trees to replace the ones that have been cut.

Fishing is important to the Western coastal economy. In Alaska, the harvesting and processing of fish brings in billions of dollars each year to the state's economy. Government groups and others help protect fish in the West. They alert the public about fish that are in danger because too many are being caught.

Mountains and Minerals

Certain areas of the West, especially the mountains, are rich in minerals, such as silver, copper, gold, and lead. Other areas are rich in fuels, such as coal and oil. Colorado has a large supply of coal, gold, and lead. Coal is burned to produce electricity in power plants. It is also used to make steel. Silver, which is mined in Nevada and Utah, is used to make jewelry and coins. The Bingham Canyon Mine in Utah is a leading copper producer. Because copper has an excellent ability to carry electricity and heat, it is often used in electrical wiring and pots and pans. Gold is used to make jewelry and computer parts. California's Kennedy Gold Mine is one of the world's deepest gold mines. A tunnel that was first dug in 1898 eventually reached almost 6,000 feet.

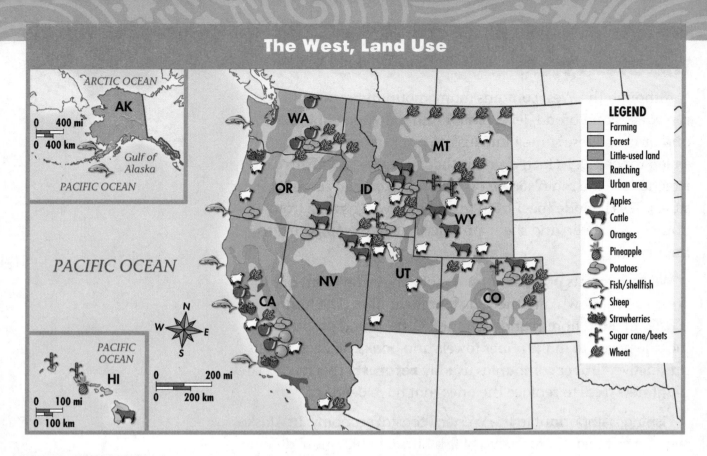

Western Agriculture

The West, with its variety of climates, produces many different agricultural products. The large plateau of the Great Plains is an ideal location to grow wheat and to raise cattle and sheep. Livestock has been an important product of these grasslands since the cattle drives of the 1870s. Back then, cowboys would round up the cattle and move them to another grazing area or to a market to be sold.

In parts of Washington, where the climate is perfect for growing apples, orchards dot the land. Apples and apple products, such as juice, jellies, jams, and applesauce, are shipped to countries all over the world. Washington is also known for its cherries, pears, and potatoes. Farms in Oregon's rich Willamette Valley produce strawberries, nuts, berries, and a variety of vegetables.

The tropical climate of Hawaii makes it a good place to grow sugar cane and pineapples, the state's most important crops. Sugar cane is a type of grass that produces long stalks or canes. The canes are boiled and processed to make sugar. Macadamia nuts and coffee are also well-suited to Hawaii's year-round warmth.

1. ☑ **Reading Check**
Compare and Contrast
Compare land use in Washington and Utah. How are they different? **Discuss** with a partner.

Word Wise

Context Clues Context clues are words and phrases near an unfamiliar word that can help clarify its meaning. Find the word *orchard* in the second paragraph. What context clues help you know that an orchard is a place where apples are grown?

California Agriculture

California is the top-producing farm state in the nation. Of all the states in the West, California produces the widest variety of agricultural goods. Many crops are grown in California's **Central Valley**, the long valley set between the Sierra Nevada mountain range to the east and the Coastal Range to the west. Rich soil and a long growing season make this area **favorable** for farming. Although the Central Valley doesn't receive a lot of rainfall, farmers irrigate their crops with water from rivers that flow down from the mountains. The water is transported in canals. **Canals** are waterways that are dug to hold water.

Primary Source

The grandest and most telling of California landscapes is outspread before you. At your feet lies the great Central Valley glowing in the sunshine, extending north and south farther than the eye can reach, one smooth, flowery, lake-like bed of fertile soil.

–John Muir, *The Mountains of California,* 1894

Almonds are an important crop in California's Central Valley. This area produces almost 100 percent of the nation's almonds. California is also a key producer of garlic. This member of the onion family is a central ingredient in many dishes all around the world.

California farmers grow strawberries, oranges, tomatoes, and broccoli. **Vineyards**, or places that grow grapes, are an important part of California's agriculture, too. Climate, precipitation, and the amount of sunlight all contribute to making this an ideal spot for growing red and white grapes. Grapes are also used to make dried grapes, or raisins, and jelly.

The Imperial Valley in southeastern California is known for its farmland, though it receives little rainfall. A canal from the Colorado River irrigates the land. Farmers in this valley grow citrus fruit, figs, and dates. Farmers here also grow vegetables, such as onions, peppers, carrots, spinach, and lettuce.

Academic Vocabulary

favorable • *adj.*, acceptable or fitting

Napa Valley, in Northern California, is well-known for its grape-growing vineyards.

2. **☑ Reading Check**
Discuss with a partner how the California farmers grow crops in areas with little rainfall.

Top Western Fishing Ports

Fishing Port	Pounds of Fish Landed (in millions)	Dollar Value of Fish Landed (in millions)
Dutch Harbor-Unalaska, AK	777	$174
Astoria, OR	153	$28
Los Angeles, CA	141	$19
Westport, WA	120	$32
Honolulu, HI	24	$64

Source: National Ocean Economics Program

Fishing in the West

The fishing industry is very important to Alaska. Salmon, cod, perch, and halibut are just a few of the fish pulled from the chilly Alaskan waters. The fisheries where the fish, crab, and shrimp are made ready for shipping provide thousands of jobs for workers.

Based on the amount of seafood that is caught there, Dutch Harbor in Unalaska, Alaska is one of the nation's largest fishing ports. One important resource in the area is the king crab. Fishing for king crabs takes place during the freezing winter months and is a dangerous job. Fishers must protect themselves from the cold temperatures and the rough waters where the king crab is found.

Academic Vocabulary

considerable • *adj.*, rather large or great

Another busy fishing port in Alaska is Kodiak. Commercial fishing fleets catch **considerable** numbers of fish and several types of crab in that area.

Off the California and Oregon coasts, sardines, crab, sole, shrimp, tuna, and swordfish are caught. In Hawaii, tuna and swordfish are major catches. Washington fishers bring in salmon, tuna, halibut, and shrimp.

3. ☑ Reading Check **Analyze** the table. **Identify** the western state with the busiest fishing port.

Where Are the Salmon?

Salmon is a native fish that lives both in the ocean and in the fresh water of streams and rivers. A salmon begins its life in the fresh water of the Pacific Northwest. As they mature, the fish travel downstream to the Pacific Ocean, where they live as adults. When it is time to spawn, or lay their eggs, salmon swim back to the rivers and streams where they were born. The fish that survive the journey lay their eggs in the same stream where they were hatched.

About 50 years ago, many dams were built along the rivers where the salmon spawn. The salmon population began to decline. The dams blocked salmon that were heading upstream. Some fish that made it past the dams into the reservoir, or pooled water behind the dam, became confused. The fish couldn't find their way to the waters where they needed to lay their eggs. Today, dams are being changed to give the salmon a better chance to make the journey to their spawning ground.

Salmon are able to leap up steep rapids as they swim upstream to the place where they will lay eggs.

INTERACTIVITY

Explore the key ideas of this lesson.

☑ Lesson 3 Check

4. **Compare and Contrast Identify** some Western resources that come from land and some resources that come from the ocean.

_____

_____

5. You are leading a group that is fishing for Alaskan king crab. Write a plan for your trip that **explains** how to protect your crew.

_____

_____

6. **Explain** how ranching in the West creates income.

_____

_____

VIDEO

Watch a video about making generalizations.

Make Generalizations

A generalization is a broad statement or rule that applies to many examples. These clue words are often part of a generalization: *all, most, many, some, sometimes, usually, seldom, few,* or *generally.* Making generalizations helps you see similarities between ideas that might not be apparent at first. Read the table and compare the information for the four states.

The Geography of the West

State	Major Landforms	Economic Activity and Resources	Climate
Montana	Rocky Mountains	minerals coal	very cold winters snow
	forests	lumber paper	
	high plains and plateaus grasslands	sheep and cattle ranching livestock some farming	rain shadow effect: rain and snow sudden storms
California	Sierra Nevada Cascade Mountains	minerals, gold	cold, snowy winters
	Central Valley	farming: fruits, nuts, vegetables, grain	milder temperatures dry
	Pacific Coast	fishing	
	Imperial Valley (desert)	farming: citrus, figs, dates, vegetables	extremely hot, dry
Alaska	Rocky Mountains	minerals, gold	cold, snowy winters
	Pacific Coast	fishing	milder summers
	tundra	none	extremely cold
Hawaii	islands (volcanoes) rain forests	farming: sugar cane, pineapples, coffee	tropical heat very rainy
	Pacific Coast	fishing	hot summers

When you want to make a generalization, you start by gathering information. Then you analyze the facts and details. Finally, you make a verbal or written statement that brings the information together. Make sure the facts support your generalization. Use a clue word such as *many, seldom,* or *generally* to make it clear you are making a generalization.

You can make generalizations about the geography of the West. Think about how the four states in the table are similar. Use the similarities to help you make a generalization. For example, the Pacific Coast is a landform in three of the four states. A generalization might be this: *Some western states border the Pacific Ocean.*

Use the table and what you know about these states to answer the questions.

1. **Identify** an economic activity that is found in two of the states. Write the economic activity and the states.

   _____

   _____

2. **Analyze** the information above and make a generalization.

   _____

   _____

3. What generalization can you make about fishing?

   _____

   _____

4. What generalization can you make to **explain** why irrigation takes place in California's Imperial Valley?

   _____

   _____

Growth of the West

INTERACTIVITY

Participate in a class discussion to preview the content of this lesson.

Unlock The BIG Question

I will know how growth has affected the states in the West.

Vocabulary

totem pole
ranch
gold rush
boomtown

Academic Vocabulary

seek
maintain

JumpStart Activity

Think about the largest cities and towns in your region. Raise your hand and name one characteristic about that city or town. It might be a word that describes it, like *busy*, or it might be something people like to do there, like *go to a museum*.

The West's rich lands and resources have long attracted people to the region. From the first people who came to the West thousands of years ago to those who live there today, all have contributed to the region's growth.

A Tlingit totem pole

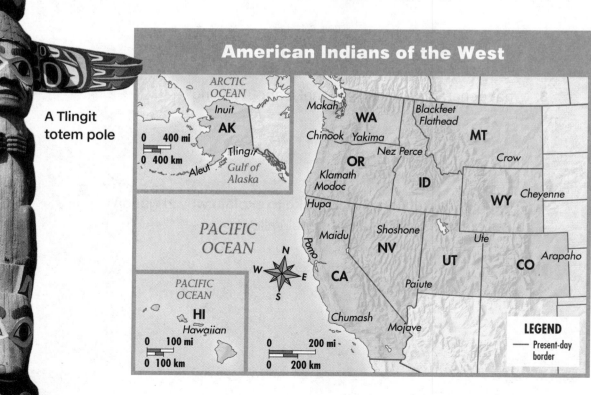

American Indians of the West

ARCTIC OCEAN

Inuit
AK

0   400 mi
0   400 km

Tlingit
Aleut   Gulf of Alaska

PACIFIC OCEAN

PACIFIC OCEAN

0   100 mi
0   100 km

HI
Hawaiian

Makah   WA
Chinook Yakima
Nez Perce
OR
Klamath
Modoc   ID
Hupa

Maidu   Shoshone
Pomo   NV
W   CA   Paiute
Chumash
Mojave

Blackfeet
Flathead
MT
Crow
WY   Cheyenne
Ute
UT   CO   Arapaho

0   200 mi
0   200 km

LEGEND
— Present-day border

American Indian Past

The forests and rivers of Alaska's southeastern coast offered plenty of fish and game for the American Indians who settled there long ago. One such group, the Tlingit (TLING giht), built their homes from large planks cut from trees found in the forests. Some Tlingit families placed a totem pole outside their homes. A **totem pole** is a tall post carved with the images of people and animals. The Tlingit traded canoes, wool blankets, and seal oil with other American Indians. Today, many Tlingit people still live in the region. They live on lands where their families have survived for hundreds of years.

The Inuit live in the Arctic region of northern Alaska. They have survived on fish and game. But for a few months each year, the tundra thaws and the Inuit add berries to their meals. The Inuit passed their history and culture down to their children through stories and songs.

The Blackfeet people have lived in what is now Montana for many years. In the past, the Blackfeet worked together to gather food and to protect their villages. Each group, or band, had a leader known as the chief. There was also a council of older people that met to make important decisions.

The Chumash lived along the California coast for thousands of years before explorers from Europe arrived. They fished in the ocean using canoes made from redwood trees. The Chumash were known for the tools they made from stone, wood, and the bones of whales.

Long ago, people from Polynesia migrated to the islands of Hawaii. Polynesia is a group of islands far to the west in the Pacific Ocean. These people told stories about Pele, the goddess of fire. They believed she was responsible for the volcanoes and lava flows on the islands.

Chumash homes were made of a kind of grass called tule.

Early Spanish Settlers

Word Wise

Word Origins *Ranch* is not the only English word that comes from a Spanish word. So do the words *alligator*, *cafeteria*, *Florida*, *hurricane*, and *mosquito*. Choose one word and look up the Spanish word it comes from. Does the Spanish word have a different meaning?

In 1542, the explorer Juan Rodriguez Cabrillo sailed from the west coast of what is now Mexico and headed north. Like Christopher Columbus, Cabrillo was exploring on behalf of Spain. His plan was to search the Pacific coast for riches and a possible route to connect the Pacific and Atlantic oceans. Cabrillo was probably the first European to land along the California coast. Eventually, Spanish explorers would travel up the coast as far as Alaska.

Spain later sent other explorers to California. The Spanish wanted to start colonies in this new land, even though native people had been there for thousands of years. Spanish explorers eventually started settlements as far up the coast as Alaska.

By 1769, a priest named Father Junípero Serra (hoo NEE peh roh SEHR rah) built the first mission in what is now San Diego, California. Other California cities such as Santa Barbara and San Francisco also began as missions. By 1823, 21 missions had been built to serve both the Spanish settlers and the American Indians.

To encourage settlement of the area around the missions, the Spanish government gave land and supplies to settlers. These plots of land, which were used mostly for raising cattle and sheep, were called *ranchos*. It is from this Spanish word that we get the word **ranch**. A ranch is a large area of land set aside for raising livestock.

1. ☑ **Reading Check**
   Identify some cities in California that began as missions.

_____

_____

Mission San Diego de Alcalá was founded by Junípero Serra in 1769.

Gold mining was difficult, dirty work.

In Search of Opportunity

Jedediah Smith was a New Yorker who joined a group of fur traders who wanted to explore the West. In 1826, Smith crossed the Mojave Desert into what is now California. Smith may have been the first white man to enter the region from the East. Later, other American explorers and some settlers began to head west.

In 1848, a man named James Marshall was building a sawmill for a businessman named John Sutter. The mill was on the American River in the foothills of the Sierra Nevada. In the water, Marshall saw sparkling yellow flakes that he recognized as gold. News of his discovery spread quickly, and thousands of people came to California in what became known as the **gold rush**.

This sudden increase in people and business activity created towns called **boomtowns**. The prospectors, or people who search for gold or other minerals, were nicknamed "forty-niners." This was because it was in 1849 when the rush of gold miners first hit the area.

Life was hard for people in the crowded mining camps. The tunnels the miners dug to find the gold often collapsed. It took a long time to find small amounts of gold by chipping away at rocks deep underground or searching for it in streams.

Other groups that came to the West included Russian settlers who moved into northern California and the Alaskan territory for the fur-trading industry. Many Easterners moved west for opportunities in farming and logging. Some traveled hundreds of miles by wagon trains over the Oregon and California Trails.

Some settlers came west for religious freedom. The Mormons, a religious group, settled in the area that is now Salt Lake City, Utah.

Quest Connection

Turn to a partner and talk about some of the reasons why pioneers moved west in the 1800s.

INTERACTIVITY

Explore important events in the history of the West.

Growth Continues

Academic Vocabulary

seek • *v.*, to try to get, find, or discover something
maintain • *v.*, to preserve; to continue

As news of the 1849 gold rush spread, people from all across the globe came to the West. People in China saw flyers from mining companies advertising for workers. Some Chinese came for the work while others were **seeking** gold. Companies building railroads also hired foreign workers. The transcontinental railroad, or a railroad that crossed the entire continent, was one such project. The completed railroad made it possible for new businesses in the West to ship their products east. The railroad also sped up communication.

2. ☑ **Reading Check**
Describe how the United States acquired the Alaskan territory. **Tell** a partner.

Almost one hundred years after the gold rush, in 1959, Hawaii became a state. How did this chain of islands in the Pacific Ocean become a state? As trade increased between the United States and Asia, the Hawaiian Islands were an important stop on the trading route. Passengers could get off the ship when it reached the Hawaiian Islands to refuel and take on supplies. Hawaii was also an important base in the Pacific for the United States Navy. In 1900, Hawaii became a U.S. territory. Today, leaders like Senator Mazie Hirono work to **maintain** Hawaii's economic strength as well as its military importance.

Alaska was another territory that became a state in the 1950s. The United States bought it from Russia in 1867. Many thought this land of snow and ice a waste of money. When gold and oil were discovered there, the public changed its mind. Alaska became a state in 1959.

Primary Source

On May 10, 1869, a ceremony was held in Promontory Summit, Utah, to celebrate the completion of the transcontinental railroad.

Cities in the West

As farmers, loggers, miners, ranchers, and railroad workers moved to the West, the number of people who lived in the region grew quickly. By 1900, the West had a population of about 4 million people. This number was still smaller than any other region in the United States. Many of these people lived in cities.

By 1920, Western cities had grown so much that four of them were among the 25 largest cities in the United States. These were Los Angeles and San Francisco in California, Seattle, Washington, and Denver, Colorado.

Today, Western cities are just as varied as the region's land and climates. Although Anchorage, Alaska, does not have a very large population, at 1,697 square miles, it has the largest area of any city in the nation.

The Denver Art Museum is known for its excellent collections of Western American art and American Indian art.

INTERACTIVITY

Explore the key ideas of this lesson.

☑ Lesson 4 Check

3. **Compare and Contrast Explain** how a boomtown is different from a ghost town.

_____

_____

4. You are living in the Hawaiian territory in the 1950s. People are talking about Hawaii becoming a state. Write a diary entry to **describe** how this may affect life in Hawaii.

_____

_____

_____

5. **Understand the** _Quest_ **Connections** Why was the gold rush such an important event in the history of the West?

_____

_____

VIDEO

Watch a video about analyzing images.

Analyze Images

A member of the Pomo California American Indian group weaves a basket.

Images can be used as primary sources. An image can tell you something in a way that writing cannot. When you analyze an image, you look at it closely and in a new way. You can look at the people, objects, details, and activities in the image to learn what is happening.

California's American Indians, such as the Pomo, are famous for the beautiful baskets they weave. Using reeds and grasses, they have made baskets for all occasions and many uses. They carried babies in baskets. They gathered food in baskets, cooked in baskets, and sometimes ate from baskets. They also used them to help carry heavy items.

Study the image here. What can you learn about basketmaking from the image? Look carefully at what the woman is doing, what she is using, and what the basket looks like.

Your Turn!

1. **Analyze** the image. What can you tell about the basket and the basketmaker by studying this image? Describe what you see next to each topic.

   Size _____

   _____

   Materials _____

   _____

   Design _____

2. **Analyze** the picture of the Chumash house in Lesson 4. What is one detail that can you learn from that image?

   _____

   _____

   _____

3. Imagine you were looking at a photo of your classroom today. **Identify** three clues that would show it is a classroom and not another kind of room.

   _____

   _____

   _____

   _____

Lesson 5 · The West Today

The West Today

Vocabulary

silicon
Pacific Rim
international trade

Academic Vocabulary

pace
guarantee

Unlock The BIG Question

I will know about work and recreation in the West today and the challenges in its future.

JumpStart Activity

Work in a small group and come up with a list of all the technology you use each day. Think about cell phones, computers, and even stoplights. Then stand up, go to the board, and compile a class list. Ask your teacher if he or she had these things when he or she was your age.

Over time, the West has changed. Communities have grown into cities, and many cities have grown into large urban areas. There are still wide-open spaces in the West, but not as many as before. People continue to move to the West for jobs. Many visitors also come to see the region's national parks and exciting cities.

Working in the West

In the early 1900s, southern California's sunny weather drew film and then television companies to the West. Entertainment has been important to the area's economy ever since. Another part of California is often called "Silicon Valley." **Silicon** is obtained from rocks. It is used to make key computer parts. Starting in the 1970s, computer companies began popping up in this area and started a high-tech industry. High-tech refers to computers and other goods that are made using advanced processes.

Surfing in Hawaii is just one of many activities that tourists love to do in the West.

The economy of Seattle, Washington, grew quickly during World War II when large numbers of planes were needed. At the time, the Boeing Company of Seattle, a maker of military planes, became one of the city's largest employers.

Another boom began in the 1970s in northern Alaska. After large amounts of oil were discovered there, an 800-mile pipe was built to move the oil. This pipe system is still used to carry the oil from the Arctic coast down to harbors on Alaska's southern coast. From there it is shipped around the world.

Nevada has recently become a leader in producing energy that is clean and renewable. This includes geothermal energy, in which heat from deep inside Earth is used to produce electricity. Solar energy is also produced in Nevada and other sunny Western states.

Tourism in the West

Tourism has long been an important part of the West's economy. One of the most famous tourist attractions of the past was "Buffalo Bill" Cody's Wild West show. At the show, people could see cowboys ride horses and perform rope tricks. Wild animals were on display, and American Indians performed war dances.

Today, Wyoming's Yellowstone National Park, California's Yosemite National Park, and Montana's Glacier National Park let visitors enjoy beautiful views of mountains and forests. These parks offer many trails for hikers. These states also have many natural areas where people can hunt and fish.

The mountains of the West have many fine spots for winter skiing. During the spring and summer, the water flows so quickly on some rivers that it looks white. Tourists can test their skills and enjoy the thrill of taking a raft down these fast-running rivers.

California and Hawaii have warm beaches and big waves that are popular with surfers. Other tourists may prefer to spread a towel on the sand and relax.

"Buffalo Bill" Cody's Wild West show began in 1883 and ran until 1916.

Primary Source

BUFFALO BILL'S WILD WEST
AND CONGRESS OF ROUGH RIDERS OF THE WORLD.

A COMPANY OF WILD WEST COWBOYS. THE REAL ROUGH RIDERS OF THE WORLD WHOSE DARING EXPLOITS HAVE MADE THEIR VERY NAMES SYNONYMOUS WITH DEEDS OF BRAVERY.

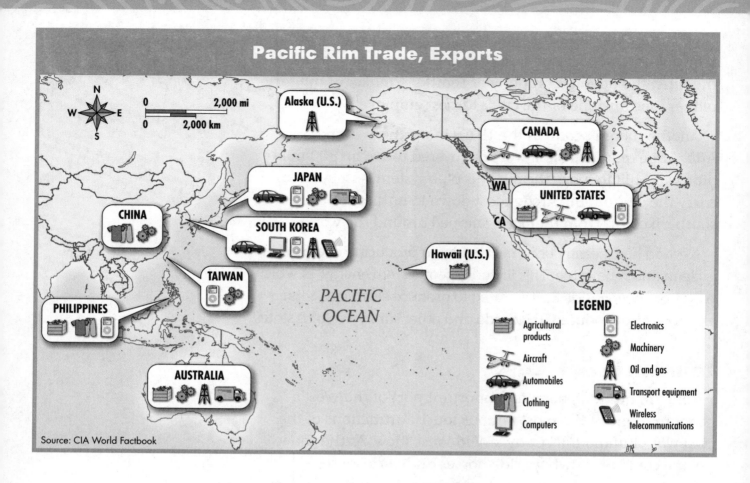

Pacific Rim Trade, Exports

0 — 2,000 mi
0 — 2,000 km

Alaska (U.S.)

CANADA

JAPAN

WA

UNITED STATES

CHINA

SOUTH KOREA

CA

TAIWAN

Hawaii (U.S.)

PHILIPPINES

PACIFIC OCEAN

AUSTRALIA

LEGEND

Agricultural products

Electronics

Aircraft

Machinery

Automobiles

Oil and gas

Clothing

Transport equipment

Computers

Wireless telecommunications

Source: CIA World Factbook

The Pacific Rim and International Trade

The **Pacific Rim** is a geographic area made up of countries that border the Pacific Ocean. Because Pacific Rim nations all face the Pacific, they trade many resources, goods, and services with each other. The map above shows goods that Pacific Rim nations export to other nations.

In the past, much of the United States' **international trade**, or the trade with other countries, was with European nations. Beginning in the 1960s, however, Japan and then other East Asian nations began exporting goods to the United States on a large scale. An export is an item that is sent from one country to be sold in another. When an item enters a country, it is called an import, or an item from abroad that is offered for sale.

It is not just the trading of goods and services that increase with international trade. Languages, ideas, and cultural traditions are shared, too.

1. ☑ **Reading Check**
Analyze the map. Which country might you buy clothing from? Which country might you buy a computer from?

_____

_____

_____

Imports and Exports

Most imports and exports that are traded between countries of the Pacific Rim are shipped from one nation's ports to another. In the West, three ports that move at a very busy **pace** are in Los Angeles and San Francisco in California, and Seattle, Washington.

Imports that come into Western ports include electronic equipment and automobiles from Japan. From Australia, the United States receives meat and minerals. Cargo ships from China bring clothing, food, electronics, and toys.

The United States exports products to other Pacific Rim nations from the same ports that receive imports. Los Angeles, California, with its busy entertainment industry, exports movies. Computer software from Silicon Valley and Seattle are major United States exports, too. Alaska's busy ports export seafood and minerals. Hawaii ships out agricultural products, including pineapples, coffee, and sugar cane.

2. ☑ **Reading Check** Compare and Contrast **Explain** how imports are different from exports.

_____

_____

_____

Academic Vocabulary

pace • *n.*, the rate at which something moves or grows

Word Wise

Prefixes The words *import* and *export* have prefixes, which are letters placed before a word to give a new meaning. The prefixes *im-* and *in-* mean "in," and the prefix *ex-* means "out." Review what *import* and *export* mean. What do *include* and *exclude* mean?

A cargo ship heading to port passes through the Port of Seattle.

The Western Future

For more than 200 years, the West has continued to grow and change. Some changes result in challenges. As the West continues to grow, these challenges must be met to **guarantee** a promising future for the region.

In many areas of the West, farmers and ranchers depend on rain and snow to provide water for their land. But what happens when there isn't enough rainfall, and water is in short supply, or scarce? Also, as the population increases in large urban areas such as Los Angeles, California, and Las Vegas, Nevada, the water needs of the population increase as well. Water scarcity is a major challenge in the West.

The problem of making sure there is enough water for everyone is difficult to solve. Learning to conserve water helps, but it also takes cooperation and enforcement. Some states, such as California, have rules that homes must have plumbing that uses water efficiently. Other states try to educate the public. Utah's Division of Water Resources reminds the state's residents that, "We live in a desert."

3. ✓ **Reading Check** **Describe** how California's government is helping people to conserve water.

_____

_____

_____

Academic Vocabulary

guarantee • _v._, to secure or ensure something

So-called "green" buildings are built with recycled materials and are designed to use less energy. These "green" buildings are part of CityCenter in Las Vegas, Nevada.

Portland, Oregon, the largest city in the state, is known for being a successful "green" city. This means that the city has rules that help keep the city and its resources clean and green. Bike lanes throughout the city allow people to safely ride bikes to work, school, and markets. The city offers free public transportation in the downtown area to encourage people to leave their cars at home. With fewer cars on the road there is less air pollution.

Portland's farmers' markets offer fruits, vegetables, meats, and other food that is raised locally. This means that the products do not have to be shipped in from long distances. The city also has a strong recycling program. The people of Portland found ways to balance the needs of a growing city with the needs of our planet.

People can buy locally grown foods at the Portland Farmers Market.

☑ Lesson 5 Check

INTERACTIVITY

Explore the key ideas of this lesson.

4. **Summarize Predict** how the West might change in the future.

_____

_____

5. **Explain** why a part of California is often called "Silicon Valley."

_____

_____

6. You are making a Hollywood movie about sports in the West and must choose two locations for your film. **Identify** two locations and **describe** the scenes you would like to shoot.

_____

_____

A photograph of Yosemite's Half Dome by Ansel Adams.

Ansel Adams, *The Portfolios of Ansel Adams*

Yosemite National Park, one of the best-known national parks in the country, is located in California, within the Sierra Nevada. Inside the park, you can visit thick pine forests, giant rock cliffs, waterfalls, and streams. It attracts tourists from all over the world.

One person who visited Yosemite in the 1900s was the photographer Ansel Adams. He loved Yosemite and took famous photographs of it. He also wrote about the natural wonders he found in the Yosemite Valley.

Vocabulary Support

that can match the power

the huge size may be all you notice at first

we see and appreciate the details

edifice, *n.*, building, structure
patina, *n.*, thin layer
colossal, *adj.*, huge
dominate, *v.*, control

Yosemite Valley, to me, is always a sunrise, a glitter of green and golden wonder in a vast edifice of stone and space. I know of no sculpture, painting, or music that exceeds the compelling spiritual command of the soaring shape of the granite cliff and dome, of patina of light on rock and forest, and of the thunder and whispering of the falling, flowing waters. At first the colossal aspect may dominate; then we perceive and respond to the delicate and persuasive complex of nature.

– Ansel Adams, *The Portfolios of Ansel Adams*

Close Reading

1. **Identify** and draw a square around a place where Adams refers to large rock structures like Half Dome. Circle a place where he refers to waterfalls.

2. **Identify** three things Adams compares to the natural wonders in Yosemite.

_____

_____

_____

Wrap It Up

Ansel Adams worked to preserve the Yosemite Valley. Do you agree that it is important to preserve beautiful natural places? Why or why not?

_____

_____

_____

_____

_____

_____

_____

_____

Quality:

Speaking Out
for Equal Rights

Elizabeth Peratrovich (1911–1958)
Voice of the People

Elizabeth Peratrovich was a Tlingit Native Alaskan who led the struggle for equal rights for native Alaskans. Peratrovich and her husband moved to the Alaskan city of Juneau in 1941, when Alaska was still a United States territory. They experienced much anti-Native discrimination there. For example, many restaurants would not serve them. Businesses posted signs that said, "No Dogs, No Natives," and "No Natives Allowed." Peratrovich decided to fight for her equal rights.

Peratrovich and her husband wrote letters to local newspapers, saying that the signs were "un-American." They also argued that they were "the real Natives of Alaska by reason of our ancestors who have guarded these shores and woods for years past." Also, World War II was raging at the time, and Native Alaskans were fighting in the U.S. Army. That made the discrimination seem even more unfair.

Peratrovich's leadership led to the passage of a law called the Anti-Discrimination Act of 1945. Alaska's Territorial Senate approved it after listening to Peratrovich give a passionate speech in which she said, "I would not have expected that I . . . would have to remind the [senators] with 5,000 years of recorded civilization behind them of our Bill of Rights." Elizabeth Peratrovich fought for the equal rights of Native Alaskans and won.

Find Out More

1. What impact do you think Elizabeth Peratrovich had on other Native Alaskans?

   _____

   _____

2. Research to find a news article that shows someone who speaks out for equal rights.

Visual Review

Use these graphics to review some of the vocabulary, people, and ideas from this chapter.

mining minerals in
the mountains

farming in California
and on the Great Plains

Resources in the West

ranching on plateaus

fishing along the
Pacific coast

	Then		Now
Population	communities and cities	→	cities and large urban areas
Industry	World War II: Boeing airplanes made in Seattle	→	Silicon Valley, California: high-tech companies; clean energy in Nevada
Trade	with European countries	→	with Pacific Rim countries
Water and the Environment	water scarcity; fewer rules and less enforcement	→	water conservation; "green" cities and buildings

☑ Assessment

 GAMES

Play the vocabulary game.

Vocabulary and Key Ideas

1. Draw a line to **identify** the definitions with the correct words.

   a very cold area where trees cannot grow   **tundra**

   a large area of land set aside for growing livestock   **prairie**

   active at night   **nocturnal**

   an area where grass grows well but trees are rare   **ranch**

2. **Identify** five landforms that can be found in the West.

   _____

3. **Identify** the state that is the leading producer of agricultural products in the nation. _____

4. **Compare** the landforms of Hawaii and the Cascade Range. What do they have in common?

   _____

   _____

5. **Analyze an Image Identify** the material you think the Tlingit used to build this house.

   _____

   What does this detail tell you about how American Indians of the West used natural resources?

   _____

   _____

   _____

Critical Thinking and Writing

6. **Identify** which is an effect of the Cascade rain shadow. Fill in the correct circle.

    (A) The Cascades receive no rain.

    (B) The western side of the mountains receives more rain than the eastern.

    (C) The mountains have a desert climate.

    (D) The northern side of the Cascades receives more rain than the southern.

7. **Cause and Effect Identify** one reason that the West continues to grow.

    _____

    _____

8. **Compare and Contrast Explain** how the resources of Alaska and Hawaii are alike and different.

    _____

    _____

    _____

    _____

9. **Revisit the Big Question** How are people in the West affected by resources?

    _____

    _____

    _____

    _____

10. **Writing Workshop: Write Informative Text** On a separate sheet of paper, write how wildlife in the West adapts to its environment. Give specific examples as part of your answer.

Analyze Primary Sources

Let us leave a splendid legacy for our children. Let us turn to them and say, this you inherit: guard it well, for it is far more precious than money, and once destroyed, nature's beauty cannot be repurchased at any price.   —Ansel Adams, on the environment

11. What do you think Adams meant by the phrase "and once destroyed, nature's beauty cannot be repurchased at any price"?

_____

_____

_____

_____

Make Generalizations

12. Go back through the chapter and gather information about why people living in the West settled (and still settle) near bodies of water. Analyze the facts, and then make a generalization in which you bring the information together. The facts should support your generalization. Be sure to use a clue word like *many, sometimes,* or *generally.*

FACTS _____

_____

_____

_____

_____

GENERALIZATION _____

_____

_____

_____

Quest Findings

Write Your Journal Entry

 INTERACTIVITY

Use this activity to help you prepare to write your journal entry.

You've read the chapter and now you're ready to write your journal entry and have a class discussion. Remember, your goal is to describe the reasons you and your family moved west, where you moved to, and how you feel about what you experienced along the way.

1 Prepare to Write

Write down the reason you chose for moving to the West. Then write a few sentences summarizing your research on the places and events related to it. These notes will help you write your journal entry.

2 Write a Draft

Use your notes and the answers from the Quest Connections to write your journal entry. Make sure your entry includes answers to these questions:

- Why did my family and I migrate west?
- Where did we move to?
- What people, places, and events did we experience?
- How do I feel about what I saw and did on my journey?

3 Present to the Class

When it is your turn, read your journal entry to your class. Share the feelings and experiences you had on your western journey. Be sure to mention specific evidence from your research.

4 Listen, Learn, and Discuss

Listen as your classmates read their journal entries. Where did they go, and why did they move there? What experiences did they have? As a class, compare and contrast everyone's experiences.

The Declaration of Independence

In Congress, July 4, 1776
The Unanimous Declaration of the Thirteen
United States of America

The first part of the Declaration of Independence is called the Preamble. A preamble is an introduction, or the part that comes before the main message. The Preamble states why the Declaration was written.

The second paragraph lists the basic rights that all people should have. The founders called these **unalienable** rights, meaning that these rights cannot be taken or given away. If a government cannot protect these rights, the people must change the government or create a new one.

1. According to the Declaration, what are three "unalienable rights"? Circle these words in the text.

The third paragraph introduces the List of Grievances. Each part of this list begins with the words, "He has...." These words refer to King George III's actions in the colonies. To prove that the king had abused his power over the colonies, this list of 27 complaints described how the British government and the king had treated the colonists.

When in the Course of human events it becomes necessary for one people to dissolve the political bands which have connected them with another, and to assume among the powers of the earth, the separate and equal station to which the Laws of nature and of nature's God entitle them, a decent respect to the opinions of mankind requires that they should declare the causes which impel them to the separation.

We hold these truths to be self-evident, that all men are created equal, that they are endowed by their Creator with certain unalienable Rights, that among these are Life, Liberty and the Pursuit of Happiness. That to secure these rights, Governments are instituted among Men, deriving their just powers from the consent of the governed; That whenever any Form of Government becomes destructive of these ends it is the Right of the People to alter or to abolish it, and to institute new Government, laying its foundation on such principles and organizing its powers in such form, as to them shall seem most likely to effect their Safety and Happiness. Prudence, indeed, will dictate that Governments long established should not be changed for light and transient causes; and accordingly all experience hath shown, that mankind are more disposed to suffer, while evils are sufferable, than to right themselves by abolishing the forms to which they are accustomed. But when a long train of abuses and usurpations, pursuing invariably the same Object evinces a design to reduce them under absolute Despotism, it is their right, it is their duty, to throw off such Government, and to provide new Guards for their future security.

Such has been the patient sufferance of these Colonies; and such is now the necessity which constrains them to alter their former Systems of Government. The history of the present King of Great Britain is a history of repeated injuries and usurpations, all having in direct object the establishment of an absolute Tyranny over these States. To prove this, let Facts be submitted to a candid world.

He has refused his Assent to Laws, the most wholesome and necessary for the public good.

He has forbidden his Governors to pass Laws of immediate and pressing importance, unless suspended in their operation till his

Assent should be obtained; and when so suspended, he has utterly neglected to attend to them.

He has refused to pass other Laws for the accommodation of large districts of people, unless those people would relinquish the right of Representation in the Legislature, a right inestimable to them and formidable to tyrants only.

He has called together legislative bodies at places unusual, uncomfortable, and distant from the depository of their Public Records, for the sole purpose of fatiguing them into compliance with his measures.

He has dissolved Representative Houses repeatedly, for opposing with manly firmness his invasions on the rights of the people.

He has refused for a long time, after such dissolutions, to cause others to be elected; whereby the Legislative powers, incapable of Annihilation, have returned to the People at large for their exercise; the State remaining in the mean time exposed to all the dangers of invasions from without, and convulsions within.

He has endeavored to prevent the population of these States; for that purpose obstructing the Laws for Naturalization of Foreigners; refusing to pass others to encourage their migration hither, and raising the conditions of new Appropriations of Lands.

He has obstructed the Administration of Justice, by refusing his Assent to Laws for establishing Judiciary powers.

He has made Judges dependent on his Will alone for the tenure of their offices, and the amount and payment of their salaries.

He has erected a multitude of New Offices, and sent hither swarms of Officers to harass our people and eat out their substance.

He has kept among us in time of peace, Standing Armies, without the Consent of our legislatures.

He has affected to render the Military independent of, and superior to, the Civil Power.

He has combined with others to subject us to a jurisdiction foreign to our constitutions, and unacknowledged by our laws; giving his Assent to their Acts of pretended Legislation:

For quartering large bodies of armed troops among us;

For protecting them, by a mock Trial, from punishment for any Murders which they should commit on the Inhabitants of these States;

In the List of Grievances, the colonists complain that they have no say in choosing the laws that govern them. They say that King George III is not concerned about their safety and happiness. They list the times when the king denied them the right to representation. The colonists also state that the king has interfered with judges, with the court system, and with foreigners who want to become citizens.

2. There are many words in the Declaration that may be unfamiliar to you. Circle three words you do not know. Look the words up in the dictionary. Write one word and its meaning on the lines below.

_____

_____

_____

_____

_____

_____

_____

_____

This page continues the colonists' long List of Grievances.

3. In your own words, briefly sum up three grievances.

_____

_____

_____

_____

4. Match each word from the Declaration with its meaning. Use a dictionary if you need help with a word.

abolishing	tried to achieve
plundered	changing
suspending	doing away with
altering	stopping for a time
endeavored	robbed

Statement of Independence
After listing their many grievances, the signers begin their statement of independence. Because the king has refused to correct the problems, he is an unfair ruler. Therefore, he is not fit to rule the free people of America.

For cutting off our Trade with all parts of the world;

For imposing Taxes on us without our Consent;

For depriving us, in many cases, of the benefits of Trial by Jury;

For transporting us beyond Seas to be tried for pretended offenses;

For abolishing the free System of English Laws in a neighboring Province, establishing therein an Arbitrary government, and enlarging its Boundaries so as to render it at once an example and fit instrument for introducing the same absolute rule into these Colonies;

For taking away our Charters, abolishing our most valuable Laws, and altering fundamentally the Forms of our Governments;

For suspending our own Legislatures, and declaring themselves invested with Power to legislate for us in all cases whatsoever.

He has abdicated Government here, by declaring us out of his Protection, and waging War against us.

He has plundered our seas, ravaged our Coasts, burned our towns, and destroyed the lives of our people.

He is at this time transporting large Armies of foreign mercenaries to complete the works of death, desolation and tyranny, already begun with circumstances of Cruelty and perfidy scarcely paralleled in the most barbarous ages, and totally unworthy the Head of a civilized nation.

He has constrained our fellow Citizens taken Captive on the high Seas to bear Arms against their Country, to become the executioners of their friends and Brethren, or to fall themselves by their Hands.

He has excited domestic insurrections amongst us, and has endeavored to bring on the inhabitants of our frontiers the merciless Indian Savages whose known rule of warfare, is an undistinguished destruction of all ages, sexes, and conditions.

In every stage of these Oppressions We have Petitioned for Redress in the most humble terms. Our repeated Petitions have been answered only by repeated injury. A Prince, whose character is thus marked by every act which may define a Tyrant, is unfit to be the ruler of a free People.

Nor have We been wanting in attentions to our British brethren. We have warned them from time to time of attempts by their legislature to extend an unwarrantable jurisdiction over us. We have reminded them of the circumstances of our emigration and settlement here. We have appealed to their native justice and magnanimity, and we have conjured them by the ties of our common kindred to disavow these usurpations, which, would inevitably interrupt our connections and correspondence. They too have been deaf to the voice of justice and of consanguinity. We must, therefore, acquiesce in the necessity, which denounces our Separation, and hold them, as we hold the rest of mankind, Enemies in War, in Peace Friends.

We, therefore, the Representatives of the United States of America, in General Congress, Assembled, appealing to the Supreme Judge of the world for the rectitude of our intentions, do, in the Name, and by the Authority of the good People of these Colonies, solemnly publish and declare, That these United Colonies are, and of right ought to be Free and Independent States; that they are Absolved from all Allegiance to the British Crown, and that all political connection between them and the State of Great Britain, is and ought to be totally dissolved, and that as Free and Independent States, they have full Power to levy War, conclude Peace, contract Alliances, establish Commerce, and to do all other Acts and Things which Independent States may of right do. And for the support of this Declaration, with a firm reliance on the protection of Divine Providence, we mutually pledge to each other our Lives, our Fortunes, and our sacred Honor.

New Hampshire:
Josiah Bartlett
William Whipple
Matthew Thornton

Massachusetts Bay:
John Hancock
Samuel Adams
John Adams
Robert Treat Paine
Elbridge Gerry

Rhode Island:
Stephan Hopkins
William Ellery

Connecticut:
Roger Sherman
Samuel Huntington
William Williams
Oliver Wolcott

New York:
William Floyd
Philip Livingston
Francis Lewis
Lewis Morris

New Jersey:
Richard Stockton
John Witherspoon
Francis Hopkinson
John Hart
Abraham Clark

Delaware:
Caesar Rodney
George Read
Thomas M'Kean

Maryland:
Samuel Chase
William Paca
Thomas Stone
Charles Carroll of
  Carrollton

Virginia:
George Wythe
Richard Henry Lee
Thomas Jefferson
Benjamin Harrison
Thomas Nelson, Jr.
Francis Lightfoot Lee
Carter Braxton

Pennsylvania:
Robert Morris
Benjamin Rush
Benjamin Franklin
John Morton
George Clymer
James Smith
George Taylor
James Wilson
George Ross

North Carolina:
William Hooper
Joseph Hewes
John Penn

South Carolina:
Edward Rutledge
Thomas Heyward, Jr.
Thomas Lynch, Jr.
Arthur Middleton

Georgia:
Button Gwinnett
Lyman Hall
George Walton

In this paragraph, the signers point out that they have asked the British people for help many times. The colonists hoped the British would listen to them because they have so much in common. The British people, however, paid no attention to their demand for justice. This is another reason for why the colonies must break away from Great Britain.

In the last paragraph, the members of the Continental Congress declare that the thirteen colonies are no longer colonies. They are now a free nation with no ties to Great Britain. The United States now has all the powers of other independent countries.

5. List three powers that the signers claim the new nation now has.

_____

_____

_____

_____

_____

6. The signers promised to support the Declaration of Independence and each other with their lives, their fortunes, and their honor. On a separate sheet of paper, tell what you think this means. Then explain why it was a brave thing to do.

United States Constitution

PREAMBLE

This **Preamble** gives the reasons for writing and having a Constitution. The Constitution will form a stronger and more united nation. It will lead to peace, justice, and liberty and will defend American citizens. Finally, it will improve the lives of people.

We the People of the United States, in Order to form a more perfect Union, establish Justice, insure domestic Tranquility, provide for the common defense, promote the general Welfare, and secure the Blessings of Liberty to ourselves and our Posterity, do ordain and establish this Constitution for the United States of America.

ARTICLE I

Section 1.

All legislative Powers herein granted shall be vested in a Congress of the United States, which shall consist of a Senate and House of Representatives.

Section 1. Congress
The legislative branch of government makes the country's laws. Called the Congress, it has two parts, or houses: the House of Representatives and the Senate.

Section 2. The House of Representatives
Members of the House of Representatives are elected every two years. Representatives must be 25 years old and United States citizens. They must also live in the states that elect them.

The number of Representatives for each state is based on the population, or number of people who live there.

Section 2.

1. The House of Representatives shall be composed of Members chosen every second Year by the People of the several States, and the Electors in each State shall have the Qualifications requisite for Electors of the most numerous Branch of the State Legislature.
2. No Person shall be a Representative who shall not have attained to the age of twenty-five Years, and been seven Years a Citizen of the United States, and who shall not, when elected, be an Inhabitant of that State in which he shall be chosen.
3. Representatives and direct Taxes shall be apportioned among the several States which may be included within this Union, according to their respective Numbers, which shall be determined by adding to the whole Number of free Persons, including those bound to Service for a Term of Years and excluding Indians not taxed, three fifths of all other Persons. The actual Enumeration shall be made within three Years after the first Meeting of the Congress of the United States, and within every subsequent Term of ten Years, in such Manner as they shall by Law direct. The Number of Representatives shall not exceed one for every thirty Thousand, but each State shall have at Least one Representative; and, until such enumeration shall be made, the State of New Hampshire shall be entitled to choose three, Massachusetts eight, Rhode Island and Providence Plantations one, Connecticut five, New York six, New Jersey four, Pennsylvania eight, Delaware one, Maryland six, Virginia ten, North Carolina five, South Carolina five, and Georgia three.

1. Why do some states have more Representatives in Congress than other states?

_____

_____

_____

_____

Over the years, the Constitution has been altered, or changed. These altered parts are shown here in gray type.

4. When vacancies happen in the Representation from any State, the Executive Authority thereof shall issue Writs of Election to fill such Vacancies.
5. The House of Representatives shall choose their Speaker and other Officers; and shall have the sole Power of Impeachment.

Section 3.

1. The Senate of the United States shall be composed of two Senators from each State chosen by the Legislature thereof for six Years; and each Senator shall have one Vote.
2. Immediately after they shall be assembled in Consequences of the first Election, they shall be divided, as equally as may be, into three Classes. The Seats of the Senators of the first Class shall be vacated at the Expiration of the second Year; of the second Class, at the Expiration of the fourth Year; and of the third Class, at the Expiration of the sixth Year; so that one-third may be chosen every second Year; and if Vacancies happen by Resignation, or otherwise, during the Recess of the Legislature of any State, the Executive thereof may make temporary Appointments until the next Meeting of the Legislature, which shall then fill such Vacancies.
3. No Person shall be a Senator who shall not have attained to the Age of thirty Years, and been nine Years a Citizen of the United States, and who shall not, when elected, be an Inhabitant of that State for which he shall be chosen.
4. The Vice President of the United States shall be President of the Senate but shall have no Vote, unless they be equally divided.
5. The Senate shall choose their other Officers, and also a President pro tempore, in the Absence of the Vice President, or when he shall exercise the Office of President of the United States.
6. The Senate shall have the sole Power to try all Impeachments. When sitting for that Purpose, they shall be on Oath or Affirmation. When the President of the United States is tried, the Chief Justice shall preside: And no Person shall be convicted without the Concurrence of two thirds of the Members present.
7. Judgment in Cases of Impeachment shall not extend further than to removal from Office, and disqualification to hold and enjoy any Office of honor, Trust, or Profit under the United States: but the Party convicted shall nevertheless be liable and subject to Indictment, Trial, Judgment and Punishment, according to Law.

A state governor calls a special election to fill an empty seat in the House of Representatives.

Members of the House of Representatives choose their own leaders. They also have the power to impeach, or accuse, government officials of crimes.

Section 3. Senate

Each state has two Senators. A Senator serves a six-year term.

At first, each state legislature elected its two Senators. The Seventeenth Amendment changed that. Today, the voters of each state elect their Senators.

Senators must be 30 years old and United States citizens. They must also live in the states they represent.

2. How is the length of a Senator's term different from a Representative's term?

_____

_____

The Vice President is the officer in charge of the Senate but only votes to break a tie. When the Vice President is absent, a temporary leader (President Pro Tempore) leads the Senate.

The Senate holds impeachment trials. When the President is impeached, the Chief Justice of the Supreme Court is the judge. A two-thirds vote is needed to convict. Once convicted, an official can be removed from office. Other courts of law can impose other punishments.

Section 4. Elections and Meetings of Congress

The state legislatures determine the times, places, and method of holding elections for senators and representatives.

Section 5. Rules for Congress

The Senate and House of Representatives judge the fairness of the elections and the qualifications of its own members. At least half of the members must be present to do business. Each house may determine the rules of its proceedings and punish its member for disorderly behavior. Each house of Congress shall keep a record of its proceedings and from time to time publish the record.

3. Why is it important for Congress to publish a record of what they do?

_____

_____

_____

_____

Section 6. Rights and Restrictions of Members of Congress

The Senators and Representatives shall receive payment for their services to be paid out of the Treasury of the United States. Members of Congress cannot be arrested during their attendance at the session of Congress, except for a very serious crime, and they cannot be arrested for anything they say in Congress. No person can have a government job while serving as a member of Congress.

Section 4.

1. The Times, Places and Manner of holding Elections for Senators and Representatives, shall be prescribed in each State by the Legislature thereof; but the Congress may at any time by law make or alter such Regulations, except as to the Places of choosing Senators.
2. The Congress shall assemble at least once in every Year, and such Meeting shall be on the first Monday in December, unless they shall by Law appoint a different Day.

Section 5.

1. Each House shall be the Judge of the Elections, Returns and Qualifications of its own Members, and a Majority of each shall constitute a Quorum to do Business; but a smaller Number may adjourn from day to day, and may be authorized to compel the Attendance of absent Members, in such Manner, and under such Penalties, as each House may provide.
2. Each House may determine the Rules of its Proceedings, punish its Members for disorderly Behavior, and, with the Concurrence of two thirds, expel a Member.
3. Each House shall keep a Journal of its Proceedings, and from time to time publish the same, excepting such Parts as may in their Judgment require Secrecy; and the Yeas and Nays of the Members of either House on any question shall, at the Desire of one fifth of those Present, be entered on the Journal.
4. Neither House, during the Session of Congress, shall, without the Consent of the other, adjourn for more than three days, nor to any other Place than that in which the two Houses shall be sitting.

Section 6.

1. The Senators and Representatives shall receive a Compensation for their Services, to be ascertained by Law, and paid out of the Treasury of the United States. They shall in all Cases, except Treason, Felony, and Breach of the Peace, be privileged from Arrest during their Attendance at the Session of their respective Houses, and in going to and returning from the same; and for any Speech or Debate in either House, they shall not be questioned in any other Place.
2. No Senator or Representative shall, during the Time for which he was elected, be appointed to any civil Office under the Authority of the United States, which shall have been created, or the Emoluments whereof shall have been increased during such time; and no Person holding any Office under the United States, shall be a Member of either House during his Continuance in Office.

Section 7.

1. All Bills for raising Revenue shall originate in the House of Representatives; but the Senate may propose or concur with amendments as on other Bills.

2. Every Bill which shall have passed the House of Representatives and the Senate, shall, before it become a law, be presented to the President of the United States: If he approve, he shall sign it, but if not he shall return it, with his Objections to that House in which it shall have originated, who shall enter the Objections at large on their Journal, and proceed to reconsider it. If after such Reconsideration two thirds of the House shall agree to pass the Bill, it shall be sent, together with the Objections, to the other House, by which it shall likewise be reconsidered, and if approved by two thirds of that House, it shall become a Law. But in all such Cases the Votes of both Houses shall be determined by Yeas and Nays, and the Names of the Persons voting for and against the Bill shall be entered on the Journal of each House respectively. If any Bill shall not be returned by the President within ten Days (Sunday excepted) after it shall have been presented to him, the Same shall be a law, in like Manner as if he had signed it, unless the Congress by their Adjournment, prevent its Return, in which Case it shall not be a Law.

3. Every Order, Resolution, or Vote to which the Concurrence of the Senate and House of Representatives may be necessary (except on a question of adjournment) shall be presented to the President of the United States; and before the Same shall take Effect, shall be approved by him, or, being disapproved by him, shall be repassed by two thirds of the Senate and House of Representatives, according to the Rules and Limitations prescribed in the Case of a Bill.

Section 8.

The Congress shall have Power

1. To lay and collect Taxes, Duties, Imposts and Excises to pay the Debts and provide for the common Defense and general Welfare of the United States; but all Duties, Imposts and Excises, shall be uniform throughout the United States;

2. To borrow Money on the credit of the United States;

3. To regulate Commerce with foreign Nations, and among the several States, and with the Indian Tribes;

4. To establish an uniform Rule of Naturalization, and uniform Laws on the subject of Bankruptcies throughout the United States;

Section 7. How Laws are Made

All bills for raising money shall begin in the House of Representatives. The Senate may suggest or agree with amendments to these tax bills, as with other bills.

Every bill which has passed the House of Representatives and the Senate must be presented to the President of the United States before it becomes a law. If the President approves of the bill, the President shall sign it. If the President does not approve, then the bill may be vetoed. The President then sends it back to the house in which it began, with an explanation of the objections. That house writes the objections on their record and begins to reconsider it. If two thirds of each house agrees to pass the bill, it shall become a law. If any bill is neither signed nor vetoed by the President within ten days, (except for Sundays) after it has been sent to the President, the bill shall be a law. If Congress adjourns before ten days have passed, the bill does not become a law.

Section 8. Powers of Congress

Among the powers of Congress listed in Section 8 are:

- establish and collect taxes on imported and exported goods and on goods sold within the country. Congress also shall pay the debts and provide for the defense and general welfare of the United States. All federal taxes shall be the same throughout the United States.
- borrow money on the credit of the United States;
- make laws about trade with other countries, among the states, and with the American Indian tribes;
- establish one procedure by which a person from another country can become a legal citizen of the United States;
- protect the works of scientists, artists, authors, and inventors;
- create federal courts lower than the Supreme Court;

- declare war;
- establish and support an army and navy;
- organize and train a National Guard and call them up in times of emergency;
- govern the capital and military sites of the United States; and
- make all laws necessary to carry out the powers of Congress.

4. The last clause of Section 8 is called "the elastic clause" because it stretches the power of Congress. Why do you think it was added to the Constitution?

_____

_____

_____

_____

_____

_____

5. To coin Money, regulate the Value thereof, and of foreign Coin, and fix the Standard of Weights and Measures;
6. To provide for the Punishment of counterfeiting the Securities and current Coin of the United States;
7. To establish Post Offices and post Roads;
8. To promote the Progress of Science and useful Arts, by securing, for limited Times to Authors and Inventors the exclusive Right to their respective Writings and Discoveries;
9. To constitute Tribunals inferior to the supreme Court;
10. To define and punish Piracies and Felonies committed on the high Seas, and Offences against the Law of nations;
11. To declare War, grant Letters of Marque and Reprisal, and make Rules concerning Captures on Land and Water;
12. To raise and support Armies; but no Appropriation of Money to that Use shall be for a longer Term than two Years;
13. To provide and maintain a Navy;
14. To make Rules for the Government and Regulation of the land and naval Forces;
15. To provide for calling forth the Militia to execute the Laws of the Union, suppress Insurrections and repel Invasions;
16. To provide for organizing, arming, and disciplining the Militia, and for governing such Part of them as may be employed in the Service of the United States, reserving to the States respectively the Appointment of the Officers, and the Authority of training the Militia according to the discipline prescribed by Congress;
17. To exercise exclusive Legislation in all Cases whatsoever, over such District (not exceeding ten Miles square) as may, by Cession of Particular States, and the Acceptance of Congress, become the Seat of the Government of the United States, and to exercise like Authority over all Places purchased by the Consent of the Legislature of the State in which the Same shall be, for the Erection of Forts, Magazines, Arsenals, Dockyards and other needful Buildings;—And
18. To make all Laws which shall be necessary and proper for carrying into Execution the foregoing Powers and all other Powers vested by this Constitution in the Government of the United States, or in any Department or Officer thereof.

Section 9.

1. The Migration or Importation of such Persons as any of the States now existing shall think proper to admit, shall not be prohibited by the Congress prior to the Year one thousand eight hundred and eight, but a Tax or duty may be imposed on such Importation, not exceeding ten dollars for each Person.

2. The Privilege of the Writ of Habeas Corpus shall not be suspended, unless when in Cases of Rebellion or Invasion the public safety may require it.

3. No Bill of Attainder or ex post facto Law shall be passed.

4. No Capitation, or other direct, Tax shall be laid, unless in Proportion to the Census of Enumeration herein before directed to be taken.

5. No Tax or Duty shall be laid on Articles exported from any State.

6. No Preference shall be given by any Regulation of Commerce or Revenue to the Ports of one State over those of another: nor shall Vessels bound to, or from, one State, be obliged to enter, clear or pay Duties in another.

7. No Money shall be drawn from the Treasury, but in Consequence of Appropriations made by Law; and a regular Statement and Account of the Receipts and Expenditures of all public Money shall be published from time to time.

8. No Title of Nobility shall be granted by the United States: And no Person holding any Office of Profit or Trust under them, shall, without the Consent of the Congress, accept of any present, Emolument, Office, or Title, of any kind whatever, from any King, Prince, or foreign State.

Section 10.

1. No State shall enter into any Treaty, Alliance, or Confederation; grant Letters of Marque and Reprisal; coin Money; emit Bills of Credit; make any Thing but gold and silver Coin a Tender in Payment of Debts; pass any Bill of Attainder, ex post facto Law, or Law impairing the Obligation of Contracts, or grant any Title of Nobility.

2. No State shall, without the Consent of the Congress, lay any Imposts or Duties on Imports or Exports, except what may be absolutely necessary for executing its inspection Laws; and the net Produce of all Duties and Imposts, laid by any State on Imports or Exports, shall be for the Use of the Treasury of the United States; and all such Laws shall be subject to the Revision and Control of the Congress.

Section 9: Powers Denied to Congress

Congress cannot

- stop slaves from being brought into the United States until 1808;
- arrest and jail people without charging them with a crime, except during an emergency;
- punish a person without a trial; punish a person for something that was not a crime when he or she did it;
- pass a direct tax, such as an income tax, unless it is in proportion to the population;
- tax goods sent out of a state;
- give the seaports of one state an advantage over another state's ports; let one state tax the ships of another state;
- spend money without passing a law to make it legal; spend money without keeping good records;
- give titles, such as king and queen, to anyone; allow federal workers to accept gifts or titles from foreign governments.

5. Why do you think the writers included the last clause of Section 9?

_____

_____

_____

_____

_____

_____

Section 10: Powers Denied to the States

After listing what Congress is not allowed to do, the Constitution tells what powers are denied to the states.

State governments do not have the power to

- make treaties with foreign countries; print money; do anything that Section 9 of the Constitution says the federal government cannot;
- tax goods sent into or out of a state unless Congress agrees;
- keep armed forces or go to war; make agreements with other states or foreign governments unless Congress agrees.

6. What problems might arise if one state went to war with a foreign country?

_____

_____

_____

_____

_____

Article 2 describes the executive branch.

Section 1. Office of President and Vice President

The President has power to execute, or carry out, the laws of the United States.

Electors from each state choose the President. Today, these electors are called the Electoral College and are chosen by the voters.

Before 1804, the person with the most electoral votes became President. The person with the next-highest number became Vice President. The Twelfth Amendment changed this way of electing Presidents.

3. No State shall, without the Consent of Congress, lay any Duty of Tonnage, keep Troops, or Ships of War in time of Peace, enter into any Agreement or Compact with another State, or with a foreign Power, or engage in War, unless actually invaded, or in such imminent Danger as will not admit of delay.

Section 1.

1. The executive Power shall be vested in a President of the United States of America. He shall hold his Office during the Term of four Years, and, together with the Vice President, chosen for the same Term, be elected as follows:
2. Each State shall appoint, in such Manner as the Legislature thereof may direct, a Number of Electors, equal to the whole Number of Senators and Representatives to which the State may be entitled in the Congress: but no Senator or Representative, or Person holding an Office of Trust or Profit, under the United States, shall be appointed an Elector.
3. The Electors shall meet in their respective States, and vote by Ballot for two Persons, of whom one at least shall not be an Inhabitant of the same State with themselves. And they shall make a List of all the Persons voted for, and of the Number of Votes for each; which List they shall sign and certify, and transmit sealed to the Seat of the Government of the United States, directed to the President of the Senate. The President of the Senate shall, in the Presence of the Senate and House of Representatives, open all the Certificates, and the Votes shall then be counted. The Person having the greatest Number of Votes shall be the President, if such Number be a majority of the whole Number of Electors appointed; and if there be more than one who have such Majority, and have an equal Number of Votes, then, the House of Representatives shall immediately choose by Ballot one of them for President; and if no Person have a Majority, then from the five highest on the List the said House shall in like Manner choose the President. But in choosing the President, the Votes shall be taken by States, the Representatives from each State having one Vote; a quorum for this Purpose shall consist of a Member or Members from two thirds of the States, and a Majority of all the States shall be necessary to a Choice. In every Case, after the Choice of the President, the Person having the greatest Number of Votes of the Electors shall be the Vice President. But if there should remain two or more who have equal Votes, the Senate shall choose from them by Ballot the Vice President.

4. The Congress may determine the Time of choosing the Electors, and the Day on which they shall give their Votes; which Day shall be the same throughout the United States.

5. No Person except a natural born Citizen, or a Citizen of the United States, at the time of the Adoption of this Constitution, shall be eligible to the Office of President; neither shall any person be eligible to that Office who shall not have attained to the Age of thirty-five Years, and been fourteen Years a Resident within the United States.

6. In Case of the Removal of the President from Office, or of his Death, Resignation, or Inability to discharge the Powers and Duties of the said Office, the Same shall devolve on the Vice President, and the Congress may by Law provide for the Case of Removal, Death, Resignation or Inability, both of the President and Vice President, declaring what Officer shall then act as President, and such Officer shall act accordingly, until the Disability be removed, or a President shall be elected.

7. The President shall, at stated Times, receive for his Services, a Compensation, which shall neither be increased nor diminished during the Period for which he shall have been elected, and he shall not receive within that Period any other Emolument from the United States, or any of them.

8. Before he enter on the Execution of his Office, he shall take the following Oath or Affirmation: "I do solemnly swear (or affirm) that I will faithfully execute the Office of President of the United States, and will to the best of my Ability, preserve, protect and defend the Constitution of the United States."

Section 2.

1. The President shall be Commander in Chief of the Army and Navy of the United States, and of the Militia of the several States, when called into the actual Service of the United States; he may require the Opinion, in writing, of the principal Officer in each of the executive Departments, upon any Subject relating to the Duties of their respective Offices, and he shall have Power to Grant Reprieves and Pardons for Offences against the United States, except in Cases of Impeachment.

Congress decides when electors are chosen and when they vote for President. Americans now vote for the electors on Election Day, the Tuesday after the first Monday in November.

To become President, a person must be born in the United States and be a citizen. Presidents also have to be at least 35 years old and have lived in the United States for at least 14 years.

If a President dies or leaves office for any reason, the Vice President becomes President. If there is no Vice President, Congress decides on the next President. (In 1967, the Twenty-fifth Amendment changed how these offices are filled.)

7. Why is it important to agree on how to replace the President or Vice President if one should die or leave office?

_____

_____

_____

_____

The President's salary cannot be raised or lowered while he is in office. The President cannot accept other money or gifts while in office. Before taking office, the President must swear to preserve, protect, and defend the Constitution.

Section 2. Powers of the President

The President controls the armed forces and National Guard, and can ask for advice of those who run government departments. (These advisers to the President are members of the Cabinet.) The President can pardon, or free, people convicted of federal crimes.

The President can make treaties, but two thirds of the Senate must approve them. The President, with Senate approval, can name Supreme Court judges, ambassadors, and other important officials.

8. What is the Senate's ability to approve or reject treaties an example of?

_____

_____

Section 3. Duties of the President

From time to time, the President must talk to Congress about the condition of the nation. (Today, we call this speech the State of the Union address. It is given once a year in late January.) In an emergency, the President can call on Congress to meet. The President also meets with foreign leaders, makes sure the nation's laws are carried out, and signs the orders of military officers.

Section 4. Removal From Office

The President, Vice President, and other high officials can be impeached. If proved guilty, they are removed from office.

2. He shall have Power, by and with the Advice and Consent of the Senate, to make Treaties, provided two thirds of the Senators present concur; and he shall nominate, and by and with the Advice and Consent of the Senate, shall appoint Ambassadors, other public Ministers and Consuls, Judges of the supreme Court, and all other Officers of the United States, whose Appointments are not herein otherwise provided for, and which shall be established by Law: but the Congress may by Law vest the Appointment of such inferior Officers, as they think proper, in the President alone, in the Courts of Law, or in the Heads of Departments.

3. The President shall have Power to fill up all Vacancies that may happen during the Recess of the Senate, by granting Commissions which shall expire at the End of their next Session.

Section 3.

He shall from time to time give to the Congress Information of the State of the Union, and recommend to their Consideration such Measures as he shall judge necessary and expedient; he may, on extraordinary Occasions, convene both Houses, or either of them, and in Case of Disagreement between them, with Respect to the Time of Adjournment, he may adjourn them to such Time as he shall think proper; he shall receive Ambassadors and other public Ministers; he shall take Care that the Laws be faithfully executed, and shall Commission all the Officers of the United States.

Section 4.

The President, Vice President and all Civil Officers of the United States, shall be removed from Office on Impeachment for and Conviction of, Treason, Bribery, or other high Crimes and Misdemeanors.

Section 1.

The judicial Power of the United States, shall be vested in one supreme Court, and in such inferior Courts as the Congress may from time to time ordain and establish. The Judges, both of the supreme and inferior Courts, shall hold their Offices during good Behavior, and shall, at stated Times, receive for their Services, a Compensation, which shall not be diminished during their Continuance in Office.

Section 2.

1. The judicial Power shall extend to all Cases, in Law and Equity, arising under this Constitution, the Laws of the United States, and Treaties made, or which shall be made, under their Authority;— to all Cases affecting Ambassadors, other public ministers, and Consuls;— to all Cases of Admiralty and maritime Jurisdiction;— to Controversies to which the United States shall be a Party;— to Controversies between two or more States;— between a State and Citizens of another State;— between Citizens of different States;— between Citizens of the same State claiming Lands under Grants of different States, and between a State, or the Citizens thereof, and foreign States, Citizens, or Subjects.

2. In all Cases affecting Ambassadors, other public Ministers and Consuls, and those in which a State shall be a Party, the supreme Court shall have original Jurisdiction. In all the other Cases before mentioned, the supreme Court shall have appellate Jurisdiction, both as to Law and Fact, with such Exceptions, and under such Regulations as the Congress shall make.

3. The trial of all Crimes, except in Cases of Impeachment, shall be by Jury; and such Trial shall be held in the State where the said Crimes shall have been committed; but when not committed within any State, the Trial shall be at such Place or Places as the Congress may by Law have directed.

Article 3 deals with the judicial branch.

Section 1. Federal Courts

The judges of the Supreme Court and other federal courts have the power to make decisions in courts of law. If they act properly, federal judges hold their offices for life.

9. Do you think it's a good idea that federal judges hold their offices for life? Why?

_____

_____

_____

_____

_____

Section 2. Powers of Federal Courts

Federal Courts have legal power over
- laws made under the Constitution
- treaties made with foreign nations
- cases occurring at sea
- cases involving the federal government
- cases involving states or citizens of different states
- cases involving foreign citizens or governments

Only the Supreme Court can judge cases involving ambassadors, government officials, or states. Other cases begin in lower courts, but they can be appealed, or reviewed, by the Supreme Court. In criminal cases other than impeachment, trials are held in the state in which the crime took place. A jury decides the case.

Section 3. Treason

Treason is waging war against the United States or helping its enemies. To be found guilty of treason, a person must confess to the crime; or, two people must have seen the crime committed.

10. Name the three branches of federal government described in Articles 1-3.

_____

_____

_____

Congress decides the punishment for a traitor. The traitor's family cannot be punished if innocent.

Article 4 deals with relationships between the states.

Section 1. Recognition by Each State

Each state must respect the laws and court decisions of the other states.

Section 2. Rights of Citizens in Other States

Citizens keep all their rights when visiting other states.

A person charged with a crime who flees to another state must be returned to the state in which the crime took place.

A slave who escapes to another state must be returned to his or her owner. (The Thirteenth Amendment outlawed slavery.)

Section 3. New States

Congress may let new states join the United States. New states cannot be formed from the land of existing states unless Congress approves.

Congress has the power to make laws to govern territories of the United States.

Section 3.

1. Treason against the United States shall consist only in levying War against them, or in adhering to their Enemies, giving them Aid and Comfort. No Person shall be convicted of Treason unless on the Testimony of two Witnesses to the same overt Act, or on Confession in open Court.
2. The Congress shall have Power to declare the Punishment of Treason, but no Attainder of Treason shall work Corruption of Blood, or Forfeiture except during the Life of the Person attainted.

ARTICLE IV

Section 1.

Full Faith and Credit shall be given in each State to the public Acts, Records, and judicial Proceedings of every other State. And the Congress may by general Laws prescribe the Manner in which such Acts, Records and Proceedings shall be proved, and the Effect thereof.

Section 2.

1. The Citizens of each State shall be entitled to all Privileges and Immunities of Citizens in the several States.
2. A Person charged in any State with Treason, Felony, or other Crime, who shall flee from justice, and be found in another State, shall on Demand of the executive Authority of the State from which he fled, be delivered up, to be removed to the State having Jurisdiction of the Crime.
3. No Person held to Service or Labor in one State, under the Laws thereof, escaping into another, shall, in Consequence of any Law or Regulation therein, be discharged from Service or Labor, but shall be delivered up on Claim of the Party to whom such Service or Labor may be due.

Section 3.

1. New States may be admitted by the Congress into this Union; but no new State shall be formed or erected within the Jurisdiction of any other State; nor any State be formed by the Junction of two or more States, or Parts of States, without the Consent of the Legislatures of the States concerned as well as of the Congress.

2. The Congress shall have Power to dispose of and make all needful Rules and Regulations respecting the Territory or other Property belonging to the United States; and nothing in this Constitution shall be so construed as to Prejudice any Claims of the United States, or of any particular State.

Section 4.

The United States shall guarantee to every State in this Union a Republican Form of Government, and shall protect each of them against Invasion; and on Application of the Legislature, or of the Executive (when the Legislature cannot be convened) against domestic Violence.

ARTICLE V

The Congress, whenever two thirds of both Houses shall deem it necessary, shall propose Amendments to this Constitution, or, on the Application of the Legislatures of two thirds of the several States, shall call a Convention for proposing Amendments, which, in either Case, shall be valid to all Intents and Purposes, as Part of this Constitution, when ratified by the Legislatures of three fourths of the several States, or by Conventions in three fourths thereof, as the one or the other Mode of Ratification may be proposed by the Congress; Provided that no Amendment which may be made prior to the Year One thousand eight hundred and eight shall in any Manner affect the first and fourth Clauses in the Ninth section of the first Article; and that no State, without its Consent, shall be deprived of its equal Suffrage in the Senate.

ARTICLE VI

Section 1.

All Debts contracted and Engagements entered into, before the Adoption of this Constitution, shall be as valid against the United States under this Constitution, as under the Confederation.

Section 2.

This Constitution, and the Laws of the United States which shall be made in Pursuance thereof; and all Treaties made, or which shall be made, under the Authority of the United States, shall be the supreme Law of the Land; and the Judges in every State shall be bound thereby, anything in the constitution or Laws of any State to the Contrary notwithstanding.

Section 4. Guarantees to the States

The federal government guarantees that each state has the right to elect its leaders. The federal government will also protect the states from invasion and violent disorders.

11. There were only thirteen states when the Constitution was written. Do you think the framers expected the United States to grow in size? Why?

_____

_____

_____

_____

Article 5 describes the two ways the Constitution can be amended. Two thirds of the Senate and House of Representatives can suggest an amendment, or two thirds of the state legislatures can have a special convention to suggest an amendment. Once an amendment has been suggested, three fourths of the state legislatures or three fourths of the special conventions must approve the amendment.

Article 6 deals with national law and the national debt. The federal government promises to pay all its debts and keep all agreements made under the Articles of Confederation.

The Constitution and federal laws are the highest laws in the land. If state laws disagree with them, the federal laws must be obeyed.

Section 3. Supporting the Constitution

Federal and state officials must promise to support the Constitution. A person's religion cannot disqualify him or her from holding office. Nine of the thirteen states must approve the Constitution for it to become the law of the land.

Article 7 deals with ratifying the Constitution. On September 17, 1787, twelve years after the Declaration of Independence, everyone at the Constitutional Convention agreed that the Constitution was complete.

The delegates to the Constitutional Convention signed their names below the Constitution to show they approved of it.

12. "The power under the Constitution will always be in the people," wrote George Washington in 1787. Explain what you think he meant.

_____

_____

_____

_____

_____

_____

Section 3.

The Senators and Representatives before mentioned, and the Members of the several State legislatures, and all executive and judicial Officers, both of the United States and of the several States, shall be bound by Oath or Affirmation, to support this Constitution; but no religious Test shall ever be required as a Qualification to any Office or public Trust under the United States.

ARTICLE VII

The ratification of the Conventions of nine States, shall be sufficient for the Establishment of this Constitution between the States so ratifying the same.

Done in Convention by the Unanimous Consent of the States present the Seventeenth Day of September in the Year of our Lord one thousand seven hundred and Eighty-seven and of the Independence of the United States of America the twelfth. In witness whereof We have hereunto subscribed our Names.

Attest:
William Jackson,
Secretary
George Washington,
President and Deputy from Virginia

New Hampshire
John Langdon
Nicholas Gilman

Massachusetts
Nathaniel Gorham
Rufus King

Connecticut
William Samuel
   Johnson
Roger Sherman

New York
Alexander Hamilton

New Jersey
William Livingston
David Brearley
William Paterson
Jonathan Dayton

Pennsylvania
Benjamin Franklin
Thomas Mifflin
Robert Morris
George Clymer
Thomas FitzSimons
Jared Ingersoll
James Wilson
Gouverneur Morris

Delaware
George Read
Gunning Bedford, Jr.
John Dickinson
Richard Bassett
Jacob Broom

Maryland
James McHenry
Dan of St. Thomas
   Jenifer
Daniel Carroll

Virginia
John Blair
James Madison, Jr.

North Carolina
William Blount
Richard Dobbs
   Spaight
Hugh Williamson

South Carolina
John Rutledge
Charles
   Cotesworth Pinckney
Charles Pinckney
Pierce Butler

Georgia
William Few
Abraham Baldwin

AMENDMENTS
Amendment 1

Congress shall make no law respecting an establishment of religion, or prohibiting the free exercise thereof, or abridging the freedom of speech, or of the press; or the right of the people peaceably to assemble, and to petition the Government for a redress of grievances.

Amendment 2

A well-regulated Militia being necessary to the security of a free State, the right of the people to keep and bear Arms, shall not be infringed.

Amendment 3

No Soldier shall, in time of peace be quartered in any house, without the consent of the Owner, nor, in time of war, but in a manner to be prescribed by law.

Amendment 4

The right of the people to be secure in their persons, houses, papers, and effects, against unreasonable searches and seizures, shall not be violated, and no Warrants shall issue, but upon probable cause, supported by Oath or affirmation, and particularly describing the place to be searched, and the persons or things to be seized.

Amendment 5

No person shall be held to answer for a capital, or otherwise infamous crime, unless on a presentment or indictment of a Grand Jury, except in cases arising in the land or naval forces, or in the Militia, when in actual service in time of War, or public danger; nor shall any person be subject for the same offence to be twice put in jeopardy of life or limb; nor shall be compelled in any criminal case to be a witness against himself, nor be deprived of life, liberty, or property, without due process of law; nor shall private property be taken for public use, without just compensation.

The first ten amendments to the Constitution are called the Bill of Rights.

First Amendment—1791
Freedom of Religion and Speech
Congress cannot set up an official religion or stop people from practicing a religion. Congress cannot stop people or newspapers from saying what they want. People can gather peacefully to complain to the government.

Second Amendment—1791
Right to Have Firearms
People have the right to own and carry guns.

Third Amendment—1791
Right Not to House Soldiers
During peacetime, citizens do not have to house soldiers.

Fourth Amendment—1791
Search and Arrest Warrant
People or homes cannot be searched without reason. A search warrant is needed to search a house.

Fifth Amendment—1791
Rights of People Accused of Crimes
Only a grand jury can accuse people of a serious crime. No one can be tried twice for the same crime if found not guilty. People cannot be forced to testify against themselves.

13. Write the amendment number that protects each right.

_____ to speak freely

_____ to be protected against unreasonable searches

_____ to not be put on trial twice for the same crime

Sixth Amendment—1791
Right to a Jury Trial
People have the right to a fast trial by a jury and to hear the charges and evidence against them. They also have the right to a lawyer and to call witnesses in their own defense.

Seventh Amendment—1791
Right to a Jury Trial in a Civil Case
In a civil, or noncriminal case, a person also has the right to a trial by jury.

Eighth Amendment—1791
Protection From Unfair Punishment
A person accused of a crime cannot be forced to pay a very high bail. A person convicted of a crime cannot be asked to pay an unfairly high fine or be punished in a cruel or unusual way.

Ninth Amendment—1791
Other Rights
People have other rights that are not specifically mentioned in the Constitution.

Tenth Amendment—1791
Powers of the States and the People
Some powers are not given to the federal government or denied to states. These rights belong to the states or to the people.

Eleventh Amendment—1795
Limits on Rights to Sue States
People from another state or foreign country cannot sue a state.

Amendment 6
In all criminal prosecutions, the accused shall enjoy the right to a speedy and public trial, by an impartial jury of the State and district wherein the crime shall have been committed, which district shall have been previously ascertained by law, and to be informed of the nature and cause of the accusation; to be confronted with the witnesses against him; to have compulsory process for obtaining witnesses in his favor, and to have the Assistance of Counsel for his defense.

Amendment 7
In Suits at common law, where the value in controversy shall exceed twenty dollars, the right of trial by jury shall be preserved, and no fact tried by a jury, shall be otherwise re-examined in any Court of the United States, than according to the rules of the common law.

Amendment 8
Excessive bail shall not be required, nor excessive fines imposed, nor cruel and unusual punishment inflicted.

Amendment 9
The enumeration in the Constitution, of certain rights, shall not be construed to deny or disparage others retained by the people.

Amendment 10
The powers not delegated to the United States by the Constitution, nor prohibited by it to the States, are reserved to the States respectively, or to the people.

Amendment 11
The Judicial power of the United States shall not be construed to extend to any suit in law or equity, commenced or prosecuted against one of the United States by Citizens of another State, or by Citizens or Subjects of any Foreign State.

Amendment 12

The Electors shall meet in their respective States and vote by ballot for President and Vice President, one of whom, at least, shall not be an inhabitant of the same State with themselves; they shall name in their ballots the person voted for as President, and in distinct ballots the person voted for as Vice President, and they shall make distinct lists of all persons voted for as President, and of all persons voted for as Vice President, and of the number of votes for each, which lists they shall sign and certify, and transmit sealed to the seat of the government of the United States, directed to the President of the Senate;— The President of the Senate shall, in the presence of the Senate and the House of Representatives, open all the certificates and the votes shall then be counted;— the person having the greatest Number of votes for President shall be the President, if such number be a majority of the whole number of Electors appointed; and if no person have such a majority, then, from the persons having the highest numbers not exceeding three on the list of those voted for as President, the House of Representatives shall choose immediately, by ballot, the President. But in choosing the President, the votes shall be taken by States, the representation from each State having one vote; a quorum for this purpose shall consist of a member or members from two thirds of the States, and a majority of all the States shall be necessary to a choice. And if the House of Representatives shall not choose a President whenever the right of choice shall devolve upon them, before the fourth day of March next following, then the Vice President shall act as President, as in case of death or other constitutional disability of the President. The person having the greatest number of votes as Vice President, shall be the Vice President, if such number be a majority of the whole number of Electors appointed, and if no person have a majority, then from the two highest numbers on the list, the Senate shall choose the Vice President; a quorum for the purpose shall consist of two thirds of the whole number of Senators, a majority of the whole number shall be necessary to a choice. But no person constitutionally ineligible to the office of President shall be eligible to that of Vice-President of the United States.

Twelfth Amendment—1804 Election of President and Vice President

This amendment changed the way the Electoral College chooses the President and Vice President. Before this amendment, candidates for President and Vice President ran separately, and each elector had two votes—one for President and one for Vice President. The candidate receiving the most votes became President, and the runner-up became Vice President.

Under this amendment, a candidate for President and a candidate for Vice President must run together. Each elector has only one vote, and the pair of candidates that receives more than half the electoral votes become the President and Vice President. If no one receives a majority of the electoral votes, the House of Representatives votes for the President from a list of the top three vote getters. In this situation, each state has one vote, and the candidate must receive more than half of the votes to become President.

If the Representatives fail to elect a President by March 4 (later changed to January 20), the Vice President serves as President. If no candidate receives at least half the electoral votes for Vice President, the names of the two top vote getters are sent to the Senate. The Senators then vote on the names, and the person receiving more than half the votes becomes Vice President.

Thirteenth Amendment—1865
Abolition of Slavery

The United States outlaws slavery. Congress can pass any laws that are needed to carry out this amendment.

Fourteenth Amendment—1868
Rights of Citizens

People born in the United States are citizens of both the United States and of the state in which they live. States must treat their citizens equally. States cannot deny their citizens the rights outlined in the Bill of Rights.

This section of the amendment made former slaves citizens of both the United States and their home state.

Based on its population, each state has a certain number of Representatives in Congress. The number of Representatives from a state might be lowered, however, if the state does not let certain citizens vote.

This section tried to force states in the South to let former slaves vote.

14. Why would a state not want to have its number of Representatives in Congress cut?

_____

_____

_____

_____

_____

Amendment 13

Section 1. Neither slavery nor involuntary servitude, except as a punishment for crime whereof the party shall have been duly convicted, shall exist within the United States, or any place subject to their jurisdiction.

Section 2. Congress shall have power to enforce this article by appropriate legislation.

Amendment 14

Section 1. All persons born or naturalized in the United States and subject to the jurisdiction thereof, are citizens of the United States and of the State wherein they reside. No State shall make or enforce any law which shall abridge the privileges or immunities of citizens of the United States; nor shall any State deprive any person of life, liberty, or property, without due process of law; nor deny to any person within its jurisdiction the equal protection of the laws.

Section 2. Representatives shall be apportioned among the several States according to their respective numbers, counting the whole number of persons in each State, excluding Indians not taxed. But when the right to vote at any election for the choice of electors for President and Vice President of the United States, Representatives in Congress, the Executive and Judicial officers of a State, or the members of the Legislature thereof, is denied to any of the male inhabitants of such State, being twenty-one years of age and citizens of the United States, or in any way abridged, except for participation in rebellion, or other crime, the basis of representation therein shall be reduced in the proportion which the number of such male citizens shall bear to the whole number of male citizens twenty-one years of age in such State.

Section 3. No person shall be a Senator or Representative in Congress, or elector of President and Vice President, or hold any office, civil or military, under the United States, or under any State, who, having previously taken an oath, as a member of Congress, or as an officer of the United States, or as a member of any State legislature, or as an executive or judicial officer of any State, to support the Constitution of the United States, shall have engaged in insurrection or rebellion against the same, or given aid or comfort to the enemies thereof. But Congress may, by a vote of two thirds of each House, remove such disability.

Section 4. The validity of the public debt of the United States, authorized by law, including debts incurred for payment of pensions and bounties for services in suppressing insurrection or rebellion, shall not be questioned. But neither the United States nor any State shall assume or pay any debt or obligation incurred in aid of insurrection or rebellion against the United States, or any claim for the loss or emancipation of any slave; but all such debts, obligations and claims shall be held illegal and void.

Section 5. The Congress shall have power to enforce, by appropriate legislation, the provisions of this article.

Amendment 15

Section 1. The right of citizens of the United States to vote shall not be denied or abridged by the United States or by any State on account of race, color, or previous condition of servitude.

Section 2. The Congress shall have power to enforce this article by appropriate legislation.

Officials who took part in the Civil War against the United States cannot hold federal or state office. Congress can remove this provision by a two-thirds vote.

The United States will pay back the money it borrowed to fight the Civil War. The money that the South borrowed to fight the Civil War will not be paid back to lenders. The former owners of slaves will not be paid for the slaves that were set free. Congress can pass any necessary laws to enforce this article.

15. List two ways in which the Fourteenth Amendment tended to punish those who rebelled against the United States.

_____

_____

_____

_____

_____

_____

_____

_____

_____

Fifteenth Amendment—1870
Voting Rights
The federal and state government cannot stop people from voting based on race or color. Former slaves must be allowed to vote.

Sixteenth Amendment—1913
Income Tax

Congress has the power to collect an income tax regardless of the population of a state. (Originally, Section 9 of Article 1 had denied this power to Congress.)

Seventeenth Amendment—1913
Direct Election of Senators

The voters of each state will elect their Senators directly. (Originally, Article 1, Section 3 said state legislatures would elect Senators.)

A state can hold a special election to fill an empty Senate seat. Until then, the governor can appoint a Senator to fill an empty seat.

Eighteenth Amendment—1919
Prohibition

Making, importing, or selling alcoholic drinks is illegal in the United States. This was called Prohibition because the amendment prohibited, or outlawed, alcohol.

Congress and the states can make any laws to prohibit alcohol.

This amendment becomes part of the Constitution if it is approved within seven years.

This amendment was repealed, or cancelled, in 1933 by the Twenty-first Amendment.

16. Write the amendment number that did each of the following:

_____ let the Federal Government collect income tax

_____ guaranteed voting rights for African Americans

_____ outlawed the sale of alcohol

_____ abolished slavery

_____ let voters elect their Senators

Amendment 16

The Congress shall have power to lay and collect taxes on incomes, from whatever source derived, without apportionment among the several States, and without regard to any census or enumeration.

Amendment 17

The Senate of the United States shall be composed of two Senators from each State, elected by the people thereof, for six years; and each Senator shall have one vote. The electors in each State shall have the qualifications requisite for electors of the most numerous branch of the State legislatures.

When vacancies happen in the representation of any State in the Senate, the executive authority of such State shall issue writs of election to fill such vacancies: Provided, That the legislature of any State may empower the executive thereof to make temporary appointments until the people fill the vacancies by election as the legislature may direct.

This amendment shall not be so construed as to affect the election or term of any Senator chosen before it becomes valid as part of the Constitution.

Amendment 18

Section 1. After one year from the ratification of this article the manufacture, sale, or transportation of intoxicating liquors within, the importation thereof into, or the exportation thereof from the United States and all territory subject to the jurisdiction thereof for beverage purposes is hereby prohibited.

Section 2. The Congress and the several States shall have concurrent power to enforce this article by appropriate legislation.

Section 3. This article shall be inoperative unless it shall have been ratified as an amendment to the Constitution by the legislatures of the several States, as provided in the Constitution, within seven years of the date of the submission hereof to the States by Congress.

Amendment 19

The right of citizens of the United States to vote shall not be denied or abridged by the United States or by any State on account of sex.

Congress shall have power to enforce this article by appropriate legislation.

Amendment 20

Section 1. The terms of the President and Vice President shall end at noon on the 20th day of January, and the terms of Senators and Representatives at noon on the 3d day of January, of the years in which such terms would have ended if this article had not been ratified; and the terms of their successors shall then begin.

Section 2. The Congress shall assemble at least once in every year, and such meeting shall begin at noon on the 3d day of January, unless they shall by law appoint a different day.

Section 3. If, at the time fixed for the beginning of the term of the President, the President elect shall have died, the Vice President elect shall become President. If a President shall not have been chosen before the time fixed for the beginning of his term, or if the President-elect shall have failed to qualify, then the Vice President elect shall act as President until a President shall have qualified; and the Congress may by law provide for the case wherein neither a President elect nor a Vice President elect shall have qualified, declaring who shall then act as President, or the manner in which one who is to act shall be selected, and such person shall act accordingly until a President or Vice President shall have qualified.

Section 4. The Congress may by law provide for the case of the death of any of the persons from whom the House of Representatives may choose a President whenever the right of choice shall have devolved upon them, and for the case of the death of any of the persons from whom the Senate may choose a Vice President whenever the right of choice shall have devolved upon them.

Section 5. Sections 1 and 2 shall take effect on the 15th day of October following the ratification of this article.

Section 6. This article shall be inoperative unless it shall have been ratified as an amendment to the Constitution by the legislatures of three fourths of the several States within seven years from the date of its submission.

**Nineteenth Amendment—1920
Women's Right to Vote**

No government can stop people from voting because of their sex. Congress can pass necessary laws to carry out this amendment.

**Twentieth Amendment—1933
Terms of Office**

The term of a new President begins on January 20. This date is called Inauguration Day. Members of Congress take office on January 3. (Originally their terms began on March 4.)

Congress must meet at least once a year. They should first meet on January 3, unless they choose a different day.

If a candidate for President does not win a majority of votes in the Electoral College and dies while the election is being decided in the House, Congress has the power to pass laws to resolve the problem. Congress has similar power if a candidate for Vice President dies while the election is being decided in the Senate.

Sections 1 and 2 of this amendment take effect on the fifteenth day of October after the amendment becomes part of the Constitution. This amendment has to be approved by three fourths of the states within seven years.

Twenty-first Amendment—1933
Repeal of Prohibition
The Eighteenth Amendment, which outlawed alcohol, is no longer in effect.

Any state may pass laws to prohibit alcohol.

17. How long was the Eighteenth Amendment in effect in the United States?

_____

Twenty-second Amendment—1951
Limit on Terms of the President
A President can only be elected to the office for two terms (eight years). If a President serves more than two years of the last President's term, then the President may only be re-elected once.

18. Do you think a President should be limited to just two terms in office? Why or why not?

_____

_____

_____

_____

_____

_____

Amendment 21

Section 1. The eighteenth article of amendment to the Constitution of the United States is hereby repealed.

Section 2. The transportation or importation into any State, Territory, or possession of the United States for delivery or use therein of intoxicating liquors, in violation of the laws thereof, is hereby prohibited.

Section 3. This article shall be inoperative unless it shall have been ratified as an amendment to the Constitution by conventions in the several States, as provided in the Constitution, within seven years from the date of the submission hereof to the States by the Congress.

Amendment 22

Section 1. No person shall be elected to the office of the President more than twice, and no person who has held the office of President, or acted as President, for more than two years of a term to which some other person was elected President shall be elected to the office of the President more than once. But this Article shall not apply to any person holding the office of President, when this Article was proposed by the Congress, and shall not prevent any person who may be holding the office of President, or acting as President, during the term within which this Article becomes operative from holding the office of President or acting as President during the remainder of such term.

Section 2. This article shall be inoperative unless it shall have been ratified as an amendment to the Constitution by the legislatures of three fourths of the several states within seven years from the date of its submission to the States by the Congress.

Amendment 23

Section 1. The District constituting the seat of Government of the United States shall appoint in such manner as the Congress may direct:

A number of electors of President and Vice President equal to the whole number of Senators and Representatives in Congress to which the District would be entitled if it were a State, but in no event more than the least populous State; they shall be in addition to those appointed by the States, they shall be considered, for the purposes of the election of President and Vice President, to be electors appointed by a State; and they shall meet in the District and perform such duties as provided by the twelfth article of amendment.

Amendment 24

Section 1. The right of citizens of the United States to vote in any primary or other election for President or Vice President, for electors for President or Vice President, or for Senator or Representative in Congress, shall not be denied or abridged by the United States or any State by reason of failure to pay any poll tax or other tax.

Section 2. The Congress shall have power to enforce this article by appropriate legislation.

Amendment 25

Section 1. In case of the removal of the President from office or of his death or resignation, the Vice President shall become President.

Section 2. Whenever there is a vacancy in the office of the Vice President, the President shall nominate a Vice President who shall take office upon confirmation by a majority vote of both Houses of Congress.

Section 3. Whenever the President transmits to the President pro tempore of the Senate and the Speaker of the House of Representatives his written declaration that he is unable to discharge the powers and duties of his office, and until he transmits to them a written declaration to the contrary, such powers and duties shall be discharged by the Vice President as Acting President.

Twenty-third Amendment—1961 Presidential Elections for District of Columbia

People living in Washington, D.C., have the right to vote in presidential elections. Washington, D.C., can never have more electoral votes than the state with the smallest number of people.

Twenty-fourth Amendment—1964 Outlawing of Poll Tax

No one can be stopped from voting in a federal election because he or she has not paid a poll tax or any other kind of tax.

Congress can make laws to carry out this amendment.

Twenty-fifth Amendment—1967 Presidential Succession

If the President dies or resigns, the Vice President becomes President. If the office of Vice President is empty, the President appoints a new Vice President.

When the President is unable to carry out the duties of the office, Congress should be informed. The Vice President then serves as Acting President. The President may resume the duties of the office after informing Congress.

If the Vice President and half the President's top advisers, or Cabinet, inform Congress that the President cannot carry out his or her duties, the Vice President becomes Acting President. If the President informs Congress that he or she is able to carry out these duties, the President returns to office. However, after four days, if the Vice President and half the Cabinet again tell Congress that the President cannot carry out his or her duties, the President does not return to office. Instead, Congress must decide within 21 days whether the President is able to carry out his or her duties. If two thirds of Congress votes that the President cannot continue in office, the Vice President becomes Acting President. If two thirds do not vote in this way, the President remains in office.

People who are 18 years old have the right to vote in federal and state elections.

Congress can pass laws to carry out this amendment.

Over the years, amendments to the Constitution have improved our democracy by expanding voting rights to more and more citizens.

19. Write the number of the amendment that:

_____ gave votes to women

_____ gave votes to citizens in Washington, D.C.

_____ gave votes to 18-year-old people

_____ outlawed taxes that blocked voting

Twenty-seventh Amendment—1992
Limits on Congressional Salary Changes
Laws that increase the salaries of Senators and Representatives do not take effect immediately. They take effect after the next election of the House of Representatives.

Section 4. Whenever the Vice President and a majority of either the principal officers of the executive departments or of such other body as Congress may by law provide, transmit to the President pro tempore of the Senate and the Speaker of the House of Representatives their written declaration that the President is unable to discharge the powers and duties of his office, the Vice President shall immediately assume the powers and duties of the office as Acting President.

Thereafter, when the President transmits to the President pro tempore of the Senate and the Speaker of the House of Representatives his written declaration that no inability exists, he shall resume the powers and duties of his office unless the Vice President and a majority of either the principal officers of the executive department or of such other body as Congress may by law provide, transmit within four days to the President pro tempore of the Senate and the Speaker of the House of Representatives their written declaration that the President is unable to discharge the powers and duties of his office. Thereupon Congress shall decide the issue, assembling within forty-eight hours for that purpose if not in session. If the Congress, within twenty-one days after receipt of the latter written declaration, or, if Congress is not in session, within twenty-one days after Congress is required to assemble, determines by two-thirds vote of both Houses that the President is unable to discharge the powers and duties of his office, the Vice President shall continue to discharge the same as Acting President; otherwise, the President shall resume the powers and duties of his office.

Amendment 26

Section 1. The right of citizens of the United States, who are eighteen years of age or older, to vote shall not be denied or abridged by the United States or by any State on account of age.

Section 2. The Congress shall have the power to enforce this article by appropriate legislation.

Amendment 27

No law varying the compensation for the services of the Senators and Representatives, shall take effect, until an election of Representatives shall have intervened.

The United States of America, Political

Washington
★Olympia

★Salem

Oregon

Boise
★
Idaho

Montana
★Helena

North
Dakota
★Bismarck

Minne.

St. P

South Dakota
Pierre★

Sacramento
★

Carson
City
★

Salt Lake★
City

Wyoming

Cheyenne
★

Nebraska

Ia

Lincoln★

Nevada

Utah

Denver★

California

Colorado

Topeka★

Kansas

Arizona

Santa Fe★

Oklahoma

Phoenix
★

New
Mexico

Oklahoma
City★

Texas

Austin
★

Alaska

Juneau★

★Honolulu

Hawaii

New Hampshire

Vermont

Maine

Augusta ★

Montpelier ★

Concord ★

Massachusetts

Wisconsin

Madison ★

Michigan

Lansing ★

Albany ★

New York

Boston ★

Hartford ★

Providence

Rhode Island

Connecticut

New Jersey

Pennsylvania

Harrisburg ★

Trenton ★

Dover ★

Delaware

Maryland

Washington, D.C.

ta

aul ★

wa

Des Moines ★

Illinois

Indiana

Ohio

Columbus ★

West Virginia

Annapolis

Springfield ★

Indianapolis ★

Charleston ★

Virginia

Richmond ★

Jefferson City ★

Frankfort ★

Missouri

Kentucky

Nashville ★

Raleigh ★

North Carolina

Arkansas

Tennessee

Columbia

South Carolina

Little Rock ★

Alabama

Atlanta ★

Mississippi

Georgia

Louisiana

Jackson ★

Montgomery ★

Baton Rouge ★

Tallahassee ★

Florida

LEGEND

⊛ National capital

★ State capital

N
W E
S

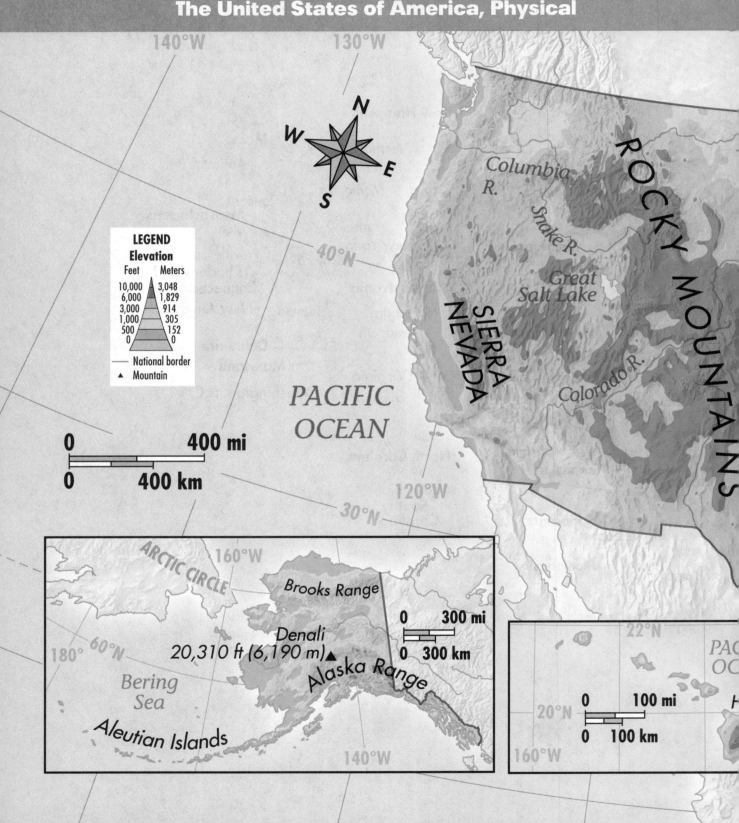

140°W

130°W

N
W   E
S

LEGEND
Elevation
Feet	Meters
10,000	3,048
6,000	1,829
3,000	914
1,000	305
500	152
0	0

— National border
▲ Mountain

40°N

Columbia R.

Snake R.

Great Salt Lake

SIERRA NEVADA

Colorado R.

ROCKY MOUNTAINS

PACIFIC OCEAN

0 ——— 400 mi
0 ——— 400 km

120°W

30°N

ARCTIC CIRCLE

160°W

Brooks Range

Denali
20,310 ft (6,190 m) ▲
Alaska Range

0 — 300 mi
0 — 300 km

180°

60°N

Bering Sea

Aleutian Islands

140°W

22°N

PAC
OC

20°N

0 — 100 mi
0 — 100 km

160°W

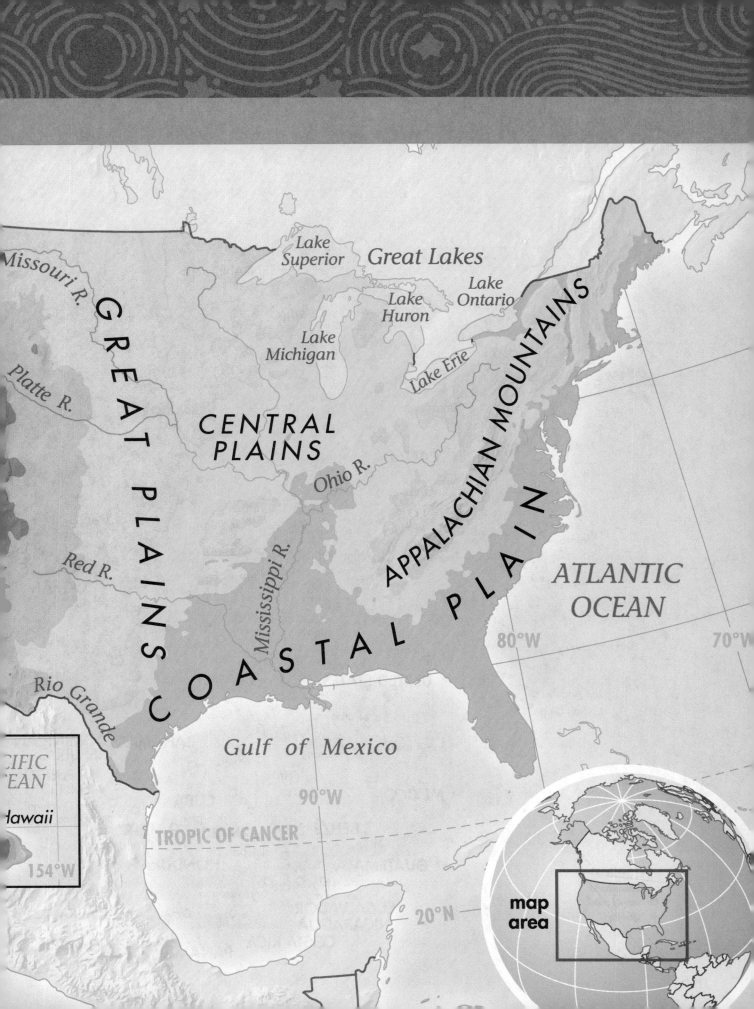

Missouri R.

Lake
Superior

Great Lakes

Lake
Ontario

GREAT PLAINS

Lake
Huron

Platte R.

Lake
Michigan

Lake Erie

CENTRAL
PLAINS

APPALACHIAN MOUNTAINS

Ohio R.

Red R.

COASTAL PLAIN

ATLANTIC
OCEAN

Mississippi R.

80°W

70°W

Rio Grande

CIFIC
CEAN

Gulf of Mexico

90°W

Hawaii

TROPIC OF CANCER

154°W

20°N

map
area

North America, Political

ARCTIC OCEAN

Bering Strait

Bering Sea

Beaufort Sea

Viscount Melville Sound

GREENLAND
(Denmark)

Baffin Bay

Davis Strait

ALASKA
(U.S.)

Fairbanks

Anchorage

Gulf of Alaska

Foxe Basin

Labrador Sea

Juneau

Great Bear Lake

Great Slave Lake

CANADA

Hudson Strait

Hudson Bay

Lake Athabasca

James Bay

Gulf of St. Lawrence

Edmonton

Calgary

Lake Winnipeg

Quebec

ATLANTIC OCEAN

Vancouver

Puget Sound

Seattle

Regina

Winnipeg

Ottawa

Montreal

Boston

Portland

Great Lakes

Toronto

New York City

Detroit

Philadelphia

Washington, D.C.

Great Salt Lake

Salt Lake City

Chicago

San Francisco

Denver

UNITED STATES

St. Louis

30° N

Las Vegas

Phoenix

Atlanta

Los Angeles

Savannah

San Diego

Dallas

TROPIC OF CANCER

New Orleans

BAHAMAS

DOMINICAN REPUBLIC

San Antonio

Houston

Miami

Nassau

PUERTO RICO (U.S.)

Gulf of Mexico

MEXICO

Havana

CUBA

Santo Domingo

PACIFIC OCEAN

BELIZE

JAMAICA

Kingston

HAITI

Port-au-Prince

Mexico City

Belmopan

Caribbean Sea

GUATEMALA

HONDURAS

Guatemala City

Tegucigalpa

San Salvador

Managua

EL SALVADOR

NICARAGUA

San José

Panama City

COSTA RICA

PANAMA

LEGEND
— National border
⊛ National capital
• Other city

60° N

0°

ARCTIC CIRCLE

180°

150° W

30° N

30° W

60° W

90° W

120° W

0° EQUATOR

North America, Physical

ARCTIC OCEAN

Bering Strait

Point Barrow
Viscount Melville Sound
Beaufort Sea
Banks Island
Queen Elizabeth Islands
Melville I.   Devon I.
Victoria Island

Ellesmere Island
Greenland

Baffin Bay
Baffin Island
Foxe Basin
Davis Strait
Cape Farewell

Bering Sea
Aleutian Islands
Alaska Peninsula

Denali 20,310 ft (6,190 m)
Brooks Range
Alaska Range
Yukon River
Mackenzie R.
Great Bear Lake

Kodiak Island
Gulf of Alaska
Mt. Logan 19,524 ft (5,951 m)
Yukon Plateau
Liard R.
Peace R.
Great Slave L.
Athabasca R.
Lake Athabasca

CANADIAN SHIELD

Hudson Strait
Labrador Sea

ATLANTIC OCEAN

Haida Qwaii (Queen Charlotte Islands)
Vancouver Island
Puget Sound

Coast Mountains
Cascade Range
Sierra Nevada
Great Salt Lake
GREAT BASIN

Saskatchewan R.
Lake Winnipeg

Hudson Bay

James Bay

Labrador
Newfoundland
Gulf of St. Lawrence
Nova Scotia

R O C K Y   M O U N T A I N S
G R E A T   P L A I N S

Snake R.
Missouri R.
Black Hills
Platte R.
Arkansas
Mississippi R.

Great Lakes
St. Lawrence R.
APPALACHIAN MOUNTAINS

Bay of Fundy
Cape Cod
Long Island

Mt. Whitney 14,495 ft (4,418 m)
Death Valley (lowest point in N.A.) −282 ft (−86 m)

Colorado R.
Ozark Plateau
INTERIOR PLAINS
Ohio R.

Cape Hatteras

Sonoran Desert
Baja California
Rio Grande
Sierra Madre Occidental
Sierra Madre Oriental

COASTAL PLAIN

Gulf of Mexico

Bahamas
Puerto Rico
Lesser Antilles
Cuba
G r e a t e r   A n t i l l e s
Hispaniola

Citlaltépetl ▲ 18,701 ft (5,700 m)

Yucatán Peninsula
Jamaica
Caribbean Sea

Lake Nicaragua
Isthmus of Panama

PACIFIC OCEAN

LEGEND
Elevation

Feet	Meters
10,000	3,048
6,000	1,829
3,000	914
1,000	305
500	152
0	0

▲ Peak
▼ Below sea level

60° N
180°
150° W
120° W
90° W
60° W
30° W
0°
30° N
TROPIC OF CANCER
EQUATOR
ARCTIC CIRCLE

The World, Political

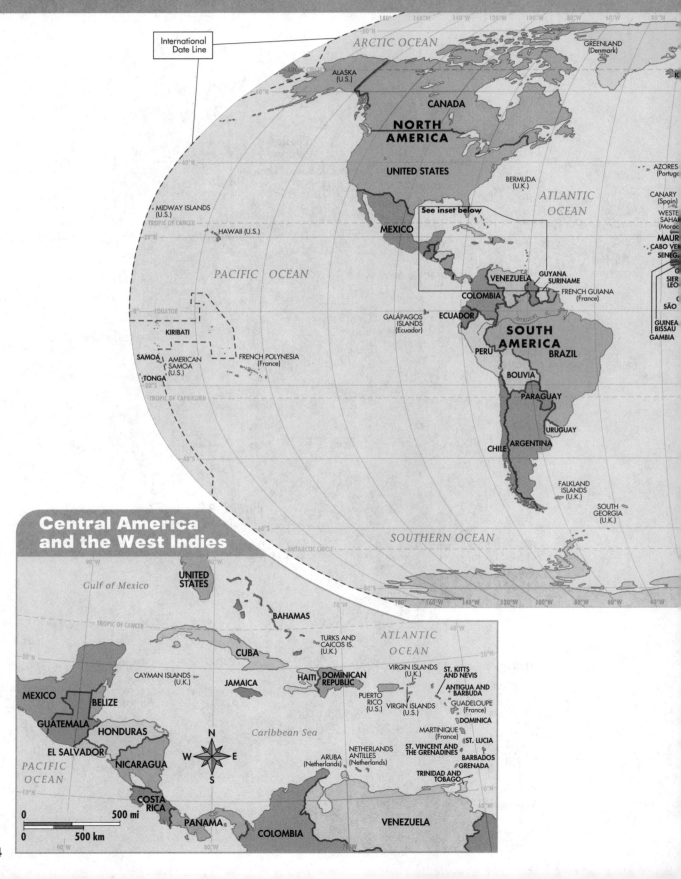

International Date Line

ARCTIC OCEAN

GREENLAND (Denmark)

ALASKA (U.S.)

CANADA

NORTH AMERICA

UNITED STATES

BERMUDA (U.K.)

ATLANTIC OCEAN

AZORES (Portuga...

See inset below

CANARY (Spain)

WESTE... SAHA... (Moroc...

MEXICO

MAUR...
CABO VE...
SENEG...

MIDWAY ISLANDS (U.S.)

TROPIC OF CANCER

HAWAII (U.S.)

VENEZUELA

GUYANA
SURINAME

FRENCH GUIANA (France)

COLOMBIA

SIER
LEO...

SÃO...

PACIFIC OCEAN

GALÁPAGOS ISLANDS (Ecuador)

ECUADOR

GUINEA BISSAU

GAMBIA

EQUATOR

KIRIBATI

PERU

SOUTH AMERICA

BRAZIL

SAMOA

AMERICAN SAMOA (U.S.)

FRENCH POLYNESIA (France)

BOLIVIA

TONGA

PARAGUAY

URUGUAY

TROPIC OF CAPRICORN

ARGENTINA

CHILE

FALKLAND ISLANDS (U.K.)

SOUTH GEORGIA (U.K.)

ANTARCTIC CIRCLE

SOUTHERN OCEAN

Central America and the West Indies

UNITED STATES

Gulf of Mexico

BAHAMAS

TROPIC OF CANCER

TURKS AND CAICOS IS. (U.K.)

ATLANTIC OCEAN

CUBA

CAYMAN ISLANDS (U.K.)

JAMAICA

HAITI

DOMINICAN REPUBLIC

VIRGIN ISLANDS (U.K.)

ST. KITTS AND NEVIS

ANTIGUA AND BARBUDA

MEXICO

BELIZE

PUERTO RICO (U.S.)

VIRGIN ISLANDS (U.S.)

GUADELOUPE (France)

DOMINICA

GUATEMALA

HONDURAS

Caribbean Sea

MARTINIQUE (France)

ST. LUCIA

EL SALVADOR

NICARAGUA

NETHERLANDS ANTILLES (Netherlands)

ST. VINCENT AND THE GRENADINES

BARBADOS

GRENADA

PACIFIC OCEAN

ARUBA (Netherlands)

TRINIDAD AND TOBAGO

N
W   E
S

0   500 mi
0   500 km

COSTA RICA

PANAMA

COLOMBIA

VENEZUELA

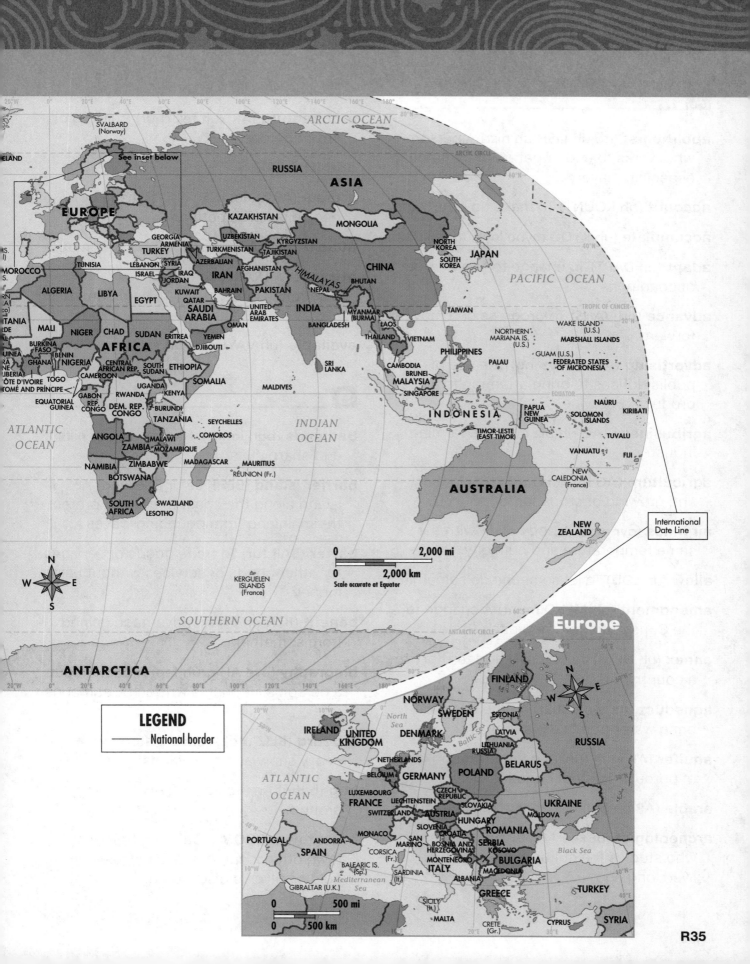

Glossary

A

abolitionist (ab uh LISH uh nist) A person who works to end or get rid of something, especially slavery.

account (uh KOUNT) To make up or provide.

accumulate (uh KYOO myoo layt) To build up.

adapt (uh DAPT) To change to fit a new set of conditions.

advance (ad VANS) To progress or a move forward.

advertising (AD vur tyz ing) The use of public notices to bring attention to a product or service.

agribusiness (AG rih biz nus) The farming industry.

agriculture (AG rih kul chur) The planting and growing of crops for food.

air mass (ayr mas) A body of air with the same temperature and humidity.

allow (uh LOU) To let someone do something.

amendment (uh MEND munt) A change to the Constitution of the United States.

annex (uh NEKS) To officially add territory to a country.

aqueduct (AK wuh dukt) A pipe used to bring water from a distance.

aquifer (AK wuh fuhr) An underground layer of porous rock that contains water.

arable (AR uh bul) Capable of growing crops.

archeologist (ar kee AHL uh jist) A scientist who studies the culture of people who lived long ago.

architecture (AR kuh tek chur) Building or structure design.

arid (EHR id) Dry.

artifact (AR tih fakt) An object made by people, such as pottery.

atlas (AT lus) A collection or book of maps.

attract (uh TRAKT) To pull or draw something or someone toward something else.

available (uh VAYL uh bul) Able to be used.

B

Badlands (bad lands) A region of dry hills and sharp cliffs.

barrier island (BEHR ee ur EYE lund) An island along the coast that helps protect the mainland from pounding waves.

barter (BAR tur) To trade goods or services for other goods or services without using money.

benefit (BEN uh fit) An advantage gained from something.

biography (bye AH gruh fee) A book about a person's life that is written by someone else.

blizzard (BLIZ urd) A severe storm with heavy snow and high winds.

bog (bahg) An area of soft, wet, spongy ground.

boomtown (BOOM toun) A fast-growing town often located near a place where gold or silver is discovered.

borrow (BAWR oh) To take and use something with the agreement of returning it at a later time.

boundary (BOUN dree) A line or natural feature that divides one area or state from another.

boycott (BOI kaht) A refusal to buy or use something.

C

camouflage (KAM uh flazh) Disguising or blending in with one's surroundings.

canal (kuh NAL) A waterway that has been dug across land to carry water for crops or for boats to travel through.

candidate (KAN dih dayt) A person who runs for a particular job or office.

canyon (KAN yun) A deep valley with steep rocky walls.

capital resource (KAP ut ul REE sors) Something people make in order to produce other products.

cardinal direction (KAR dih nul duh REK shun) One of the four main compass points of north, south, east, and west.

Central Plains (SEHN trul playnz) Plains that include the eastern Midwest.

Central Valley (SEHN trul VA lee) A large valley in central California.

checks and balances (cheks und BAL un sus) The separation of powers in a democracy that gives each branch of government–the legislative, executive, and judicial–some form of authority over the others.

citizen (SIH tih zun) A member of a city, state, or town who has legal rights and responsibilities.

civil rights (SIV ul ryts) The rights that all people should have.

claim (klaym) The official declaration of owning something, such as an area of land.

cliff dwelling (klif DWEL ing) A home in cliffs.

climate (KLY mut) The weather patterns in one place over a long period of time.

Cold War (kold wahr) The conflict between the United States and the Soviet Union over economic and political ideas.

colony (KAHL uh nee) A settlement ruled by another country.

combine (kum BYN) To join.

command economy (kuh MAND ih KAH nuh mee) An economy in which the government decides what goods and services can be sold.

commerce (KAH murs) The buying and selling of goods.

commodity (kuh MAH dih tee) An economic good such as oil, natural gas, or copper.

communism (KAHM yuh niz um) An economic and political system in which the government owns all the land and most industries in the name of the people.

compass rose (KUM pus ROHZ) A symbol on a map that shows directions.

compromise (KAHM pruh myz) An agreement.

confederation (kun feh duh RAY shun) A union of states that agree to cooperate.

congress (KAHNG grus) A group of people responsible for making a country's laws.

consequence (KAHN suh kwens) The effect or result of an event.

conserve (kun SURV) To limit the use of something.

considerable (kun SIH dur uh bul) Rather large or great.

constitution (kahn stuh TOO shun) A plan of government.

consumer (kun SOO mur) Someone who buys or uses goods and services.

contribute (kun TRIH byoot) To give to.

control (kun TROHL) Power or command over something or someone.

convince (kun VINS) To persuade.

cooperate (koh AH puh rayt) To work together toward the same end.

craft (kraft) An object made by hand.

create (kree AYT) To cause something to happen as a result of action.

critical (KRIH tih kul) Of major importance.

crop rotation (krahp roh TAY shun) The planting of different crops in different years.

crucial (KROO shul) Of great importance.

culture (KUL chur) A way of life for a group of people.

currency (KUR un see) A country's money.

D

define (dih FYN) To explain or describe in a specific way.

degree (dih GREE) A unit of measure; there are 360 degrees of latitude and longitude used to locate places on Earth.

delegate (DEL ih gut) Someone who represents a group of people.

demand (dih MAND) The amount of a particular good or service that consumers desire.

democracy (dih MAHK ruh see) A government in which citizens have the power to make political decisions.

depend (dih PEND) To rely on.

depression (dih PREH shun) A time when business activity is slow and many people are out of work.

desert (DEH zurt) An area that receives less than ten inches of rain in one year.

develop (dih VEL up) To grow.

diverse (duh VURS) Showing much variety.

division of labor (duh VIH zhun uv LAY bur) Dividing a job among skilled workers.

drought (drout) A long period with little or no rain.

E

economy (ih KAH nuh mee) The way a place uses its resources to produce goods and services.

elevation (el uh VAY shun) Height above sea level.

emancipation (ih man sih PAY shun) The act of setting someone or something free.

endangered species (en DAYN jurd SPEE sees) A kind of animal or plant that is in danger of becoming extinct.

enforce (en FORS) To compel people to follow a rule or law.

enslaved (en SLAYVD) To work without pay or freedom.

ensure (en SHUR) To make sure, or make certain.

entrepreneur (ahn truh pruh NOOR) A person who risks money and time to start a new business.

equator (ih KWAY tur) An imaginary line that runs around the center of Earth halfway between the North and South Poles.

erosion (ih ROH zhun) The process by which wind and water wear away rock.

essential (ih SEN shul) Absolutely necessary.

establish (ih STAH blish) To set up, to organize.

evacuation (ih vah kyuh WAY shun) The action of moving a person to safety.

executive branch (eg ZEK yoo tiv branch) The part of government that carries out the laws; the U.S. president and his or her administration.

export (EK sport) To sell or trade something to another country.

extensive (ik STEN siv) Far-reaching.

extinct (ek STINGT) No longer existing.

F

factor (FAK tur) A cause.

fall line (fawl lyn) A line of waterfalls such as where a piedmont meets a coastal plain.

fascism (FAH shih zum) A form of government that gives all power to the state, does away with individual freedoms, and uses the military to enforce the law.

favorable (FAY vur uh bul) Acceptable or fitting.

feature (FEE chur) A part or characteristic.

flood plain (flud PLAYN) A plain that is formed by flooding along a river.

folklore (FOHLK lohr) The traditions and beliefs of a group of people.

fossil fuel (FAH sul FYOO ul) A fuel formed in the earth from the remains of plants and animals.

free enterprise system (free EN tur pryz SIS tum) An economy in which people are free to start their own businesses or to produce whatever good or service they want.

G

generate (JEN uh rayt) To produce or create.

geography (jee AH gruh fee) The study of Earth.

geyser (GYE zur) A hot spring that erupts and sends hot water from underground into the air.

glacier (GLAY shur) A huge sheet of ice that covers land.

globe (glohb) A round model of Earth.

gold rush (gohld rush) The quick movement of people to a place where gold has been discovered.

gray water (gray WAW tur) Recycled water.

Great Plains (grayt playnz) A vast area of plains east of the Rocky Mountains.

grid (grid) A system of lines that cross each other forming a pattern of squares; on maps, grids are used to locate places.

growing season (GROH wing SEE zun) A period of time when the temperature is high enough for plants to grow.

guarantee (ger un TEE) To secure or ensure something.

Gullah (GUH luh) A group of people in the Southeast who have kept much of their African heritage.

gusher (GUH shur) An oil well that produces a large amount of oil.

H

hemisphere (heh muh SFEER) Half of Earth.

heritage (HER uh tij) The customs and traditions of a cultural group that have been passed down from parents to children.

high-tech (hye TEK) Using the newest or latest technology.

homestead (HOHM sted) Land given to settlers by the United States government if they lived and raised crops on it.

hub (hub) A center of activity.

human resource (HYOO mun REE sors) A person who makes products or provides services.

humidity (hyoo MIH duh tee) The amount of moisture in the air.

hunter-gatherer (hun tur GA thur ur) Someone who hunts animals and collects wild plants for food.

hurricane (hur uh KAYN) A strong, swirling storm with rain and winds blowing more than 74 miles per hour.

hydroelectric power (hye droh ih LEK trik POU ur) Power produced by capturing the energy of flowing water.

I

immigrant (IH muh grunt) A person who moves to one country from another.

import (im PORT) To bring something in from another country for sale or trade.

impress (im PRES) To amaze or have an impact on.

incentive (in SEN tiv) Something that encourages one to take an action or do something.

income (IN kum) The money a person or business earns for doing a job or providing a good or service.

indentured servant (in DEN churd SUR vunt) A person who agrees to work for a set period of time without pay in exchange for necessities.

independence (in duh PEN duns) Freedom from rule by others.

individual (in duh VIJ wul) A single human being.

industry (IN dus tree) The part of the economy in which machines are used to do the work.

inflation (in FLAY shun) A rise in the usual price of many goods and services.

influence (IN floo uns) To have an effect or impact.

initial (ih NIH shul) At first.

innovation (ih nuh VAY shun) New inventions or ideas.

intent (in TENT) Focused on a specific purpose.

interdependent (in tur dih PEN dunt) When nations rely on one another for goods, services, or resources.

interest (IN tuh rest) A small fee paid to bank customers in exchange for allowing the bank to use their money; a fee charged by banks for borrowing money.

intermediate direction (in tur MEE dee ut duh REK shun) Any of the four directions that are between the cardinal directions: northeast, northwest, southeast, and southwest.

international trade (in tur NA shuh nul trayd) Trade between different countries.

interstate highway (IN tur stayt HYE way) A highway that connects states.

involve (in VOLV) To take into account; include.

irrigation (ih ruh GAY shun) The process of bringing water to fields, usually by means of ditches and channels.

J

jazz (jaz) A type of music of African American origin.

judicial branch (joo DIH shul branch) The part of government that decides what laws mean and makes sure that laws are applied fairly.

junction (JUNK shun) A point where things such as rivers meet.

jury (JUR ee) A panel of ordinary citizens who make decisions in a court of law.

K

key (kee) A low island.

L

labor union (LAY bur YOON yuhn) A workers' group that tries to gain better pay and working conditions.

landform (LAND form) A natural feature of Earth's surface.

latitude (LA tuh tood) Lines that measure the distance north and south of the equator.

legislative branch (LEH juh slay tiv branch) The part of government that makes laws.

levee (LEH vee) A barrier of earth built to prevent flooding.

liberty (LIH bur tee) Freedom to govern oneself.

lighthouse (LYT hous) A tall tower with a very strong light used to guide ships at night.

limit (LIH mut) To control.

livestock (LYV stahk) Animals raised on farms and ranches for human use.

longitude (LAHN juh tood) Lines that measure the distances east and west of the prime meridian.

M

magma (MAG muh) Molten rock beneath Earth's surface.

maintain (mayn TAYN) To preserve; to continue.

manufacturing (man yuh FAK chur ing) Making goods by machines, usually in factories.

map legend (map LEH jund) A box that explains the symbols on the map.

map scale (map skayl) A symbol that shows the relationship between distance on the map and distance on Earth.

market economy (MAR kut ih KAH nuh mee) A free enterprise system in which supply and demand determines goods and services.

mastery (MA stuh ree) Great knowledge or skill in a particular field.

meat-packing (MEET pak ing) Something that processes meat from animals for food.

mesa (MAY suh) A flat-topped landform with slopes on all sides.

metropolitan area (meh troh PAH luh tun ER ee uh) A large city and its surrounding area.

mineral (MIN rul) Nonliving material that is found in the earth.

mission (MISH un) A settlement set up by a religious group to teach religion and help area people.

missionary (MIH shuh ner ee) A person sent to a new land to spread his or her religion.

monitor (MAH nuh tur) To control.

N

natural gas (NA chuh rul gas) A fossil fuel like oil.

natural resource (NA chuh rul REE sors) Something in the environment that people can use.

nocturnal (nahk TUR nul) Active at night.

nomad (NOH mad) A person who moves from place to place in order to survive.

nonrenewable (nahn rih NOO uh bul) A resource that cannot be replaced.

Northwest Ordinance (north west OR dun nuns) A law that determined how the Northwest Territory would become states.

notable (NOH tuh bul) Worthy of attention or notice.

nutrient (NOO tree unt) A substance that helps plants grow.

O

occupy (AHK yoo pye) To take up space.

opportunity cost (ah pur TOO nuh tee kawst) The value of something that must be given up to get the thing you want.

oppose (uh POHZ) To go against.

oral (AWR ul) Spoken.

organize (AWR guh nyz) To form a group.

outsourcing (OUT sor sing) When companies employ people to work outside of the company.

overfishing (OH vur fih shing) When people catch fish faster than natural processes can replace them.

P

pace (pays) The rate at which something moves or grows.

Pacific Rim (puh SIH fik rim) A geographic area made up of countries that border the Pacific Ocean.

participate (par TIH suh payt) To take part in an activity.

patent (PA tunt) A government document that gives an inventor the right to make and sell an invention.

patriotism (PAY tree uh tih zum) The pride and support a people feel for their country.

peninsula (puh NIN suh luh) A piece of land almost surrounded by water.

permit (pur MIT) To allow to do something.

perspective (pur SPEK tiv) Point of view; outlook.

petition (puh TIH shun) A formal request.

petrified (PEH truh fyd) Made into a fossil.

physical map (FIH zih kul map) A map that shows geographic information of a place, such as landforms and bodies of water.

piedmont (PEED mahnt) Foothills near mountains.

pioneer (pye uh NEER) A person from a group who is the first to settle in an area.

plantation (plan TAY shun) A large farm with many workers.

plateau (pla TOH) A large, flat, raised area of land.

plow (plou) A farm tool, pulled by a tractor or animal, used to turn the soil.

political map (puh LIH tih kul map) A map that shows information such as state or national borders, capitals, and important cities.

pollution (puh LOO shun) Chemical or physical waste that causes the air, water, and land to be dirty.

population density (pah pyuh LAY shun DEN suh tee) A measure of how many people, on average, live on each square mile of land in a certain area.

port (port) A place where people or goods can enter or leave a country.

prairie (PRER ee) An area in which grass grows well but trees are rare.

precipitation (prih sip uh TAY shun) The amount of moisture that falls as rain or snow.

prefer (prih FUR) To like something better than another.

primary source (PRY muh ree sors) A source that is made or written by a person who witnessed an event firsthand.

prime meridian (PRYM muh RIH dee un) The 0° line of longitude, drawn from the North Pole to the South Pole, that divides Earth into the Western Hemisphere and the Eastern Hemisphere.

private property (PRYE vut PRAH pur tee) The land or goods that people or companies own.

process (PRAH ses) To use a series of actions to make something.

produce (pruh DOOS) To make.

producer (pruh DOO sur) A person who makes goods or services to sell.

product (PRAH dukt) Something that people make or grow.

productive (pruh DUK tiv) Able to make large amounts of goods.

productivity (proh duk TIH vuh tee) The amount of goods or services company workers can make or provide.

profit (PRAH fit) The money a business earns after all its expenses are paid.

promote (pruh MOHT) To make widely known.

protect (pruh TEKT) To keep safe.

provide (pruh VYD) To give or make something available.

pueblo (PWEH bloh) A Spanish word that means "village," and which refers to some American Indian groups in the Southwest.

pulp (pulp) A mix of wood chips, water, and chemicals used to make paper.

purpose (PUR pus) The reason why something exists.

pursue (pur SOO) To chase.

Q

quarry (KWOR ee) A place where stone is dug, cut, or blasted out of the ground.

R

radiant (RAY dee unt) Glowing brightly.

rain shadow (rayn SHA doh) An area such as the side of a mountain chain that receives less precipitation than the other side.

ranch (ranch) A large farm where cattle or other animals are raised.

ratify (RAT uh fye) To approve officially.

recall (ree KAWL) To remember.

Reconstruction (ree kun STRUK shun) The period of rebuilding after the Civil War during which Southern states rejoined the Union.

refinery (rih FYE nuh ree) A factory that separates crude oil into different groups of chemicals.

reforest (ree FAWR ust) To plant young trees to replace ones that have been cut down.

region (REE jun) A large area in which places share similar characteristics.

renewable (rih NOO uh bul) A natural resource that can be replaced.

republic (rih PUB lik) A type of government in which people elect leaders to represent them.

require (rih KWYR) To need.

reservation (reh zur VAY shun) An area of land set aside for American Indians to live on.

reservoir (REH zur vwahr) A lake where water is stored.

restore (rih STOR) To bring back to health.

reveal (rih VEEL) To make known.

rivalry (RYE vul ree) A competition for superiority.

ruins (ROO inz) The remains of something that has been badly damaged or destroyed.

rural (ROOR ul) In small towns or farms.

S

sachem (SAY chum) A ruler or leader among some American Indian groups.

savanna (suh VA nuh) A grassy plain with few trees.

scarcity (SKAYR suh tee) A shortage.

secede (suh SEED) To officially separate from an organization.

secondary source (SEH kun dayr ee sors) A source that was written or created by someone who did not witness an event.

seek (seek) To try to get, find, or discover something.

segregation (seh grih GAY shun) A system under which people of different races are kept separate.

self-evident (self EH vuh dunt) Something that does not need explaining or proof, such as basic rights.

semiarid (seh mee AR id) Dry but receives some rain.

shortage (SHOR tij) A situation in which something that is needed cannot be obtained.

significant (sig NIH fih kunt) Very important.

silicon (SIL uh kahn) A material from rocks and sand used to manufacture computers.

situate (SIH chuh wayt) To set in a particular location.

sound (sound) A large area of seawater that separates a mainland and an island.

sovereignty (SAH vrun tee) The right to rule.

specialization (speh shuh luh ZAY shun) A process in which each worker performs a single step in production.

states' rights (stayts ryts) The idea that the power of the state must be protected from the power of the federal government and that each state should solve its own problems.

steamboat (steem BOHT) A boat powered by a steam engine.

storm surge (storm surj) A rising of the sea caused by a storm.

suffrage (SUF rij) The right to vote.

supply (suh PLY) The amount of goods or services available for a consumer to buy.

surround (suh ROUND) To be all around something.

survive (sur VYV) To continue to live.

sweatshop (SWET shahp) A factory where workers work long hours for little pay.

symbol (SIM bul) A thing that stands for or represents something else.

T

task (task) A piece of work to be done.

technology (tek NAHL uh jee) The use of scientific knowledge or tools to do work.

temperature (tem pur CHUR) A measurement telling how hot or cold something is.

territory (ter uh TAWR ee) A large area of land that is under the control of an outside government. In the United States, a territory does not have the same rights that a state does.

terrorist (TAYR ur ist) A person who uses great fear or terror for political reasons.

timber (TIM bur) Trees that are cut or grown for wood.

tornado (tawr NAY doh) A storm with very fast winds that can form a funnel-shaped cloud.

totem pole (TOH tum pohl) A tall post carved with images of people and animals to represent family history.

tourist (TOOR ist) Someone who travels for pleasure.

trading post (TRAY ding pohst) A store or small settlement set up in a distant place to allow trade to take place.

tradition (truh DISH un) A custom or belief that is passed on from one generation to the next.

transcontinental (trans kahn tih NEN tul) Across the continent.

transfer (TRANS fur) To move from one place to another; carry.

tsunami (soo NAH mee) A giant wave that can reach 50 feet high and cause great damage when it reaches land.

tundra (TUN druh) A cold area where trees cannot grow.

typical (TIH pih kul) Common or usual.

U

unalienable (un AYL yuh nuh bul) Unable to be taken away, such as unalienable rights.

urban (UR bun) In the city.

V

varied (VER eed) Different or changed.

vineyard (VIN yurd) A farm where grapes are grown.

volcano (vahl KAY noh) A vent in Earth's crust caused by molten rock forcing its way to the surface.

W

watershed (WAH tur shed) An area drained by a river or a group of rivers.

weather (WETH ur) The condition of the air at a certain time and place.

wetland (WET land) An area where water lies on or near the surface of the ground, as a swamp or marsh.

wetu (WEH too) An American Indian home made of wooden poles covered with tree bark or reed mats.

Glosario

A

abolitionist/abolicionista Persona que trabaja para poner fin a algo o terminar por completo con ello, en especial la esclavitud.

account/considerar Creer, estimar.

accumulate/acumular Juntar.

adapt/adaptarse Cambiar para ajustarse a una nueva serie de condiciones.

advance/avance Progresar o moverse hacia adelante.

advertising/publicidad Uso de avisos al público para atraer la atención hacia un producto o servicio.

agribusiness/agroindustria Industria de la agricultura.

agriculture/agricultura Siembra y cultivo de plantas para alimentarse.

air mass/masa de aire Porción de aire con la misma temperatura y humedad.

allow/permitir Dejar que alguien haga algo.

amendment/enmienda Modificación de la Constitución de los Estados Unidos.

annex/anexar Agregar un territorio a un país oficialmente.

aqueduct/acueducto Tubería que se usa para llevar agua a distancia.

aquifer/acuífero Capa subterránea de roca porosa que contiene agua.

arable/cultivable Referido a la tierra en la que se puede sembrar y obtener cosechas.

archeologist/arqueólogo Científico que estudia la cultura de personas que vivieron hace mucho tiempo.

architecture/arquitectura Diseño de edificios o estructuras.

arid/árido Clima seco, pero no como el del desierto.

artifact/artefacto Objeto hecho por los seres humanos, como un artículo de cerámica.

atlas/atlas Colección o libro de mapas.

attract/atraer Acercar algo o a alguien hacia otra cosa.

available/disponible Que se puede usar.

B

Badlands/Badlands Región con colinas secas y acantilados altos.

barrier island/isla barrera Isla que está frente a la costa y que ayuda a proteger la tierra firme de las olas.

barter/hacer un trueque Intercambiar un bien o un servicio por otro bien u otro servicio sin usar dinero.

benefit/beneficio Ventaja obtenida de algo.

biography/biografía Libro sobre la vida de una persona escrito por otra persona.

blizzard/ventisca Fuerte tormenta de nieve con vientos potentes.

bog/ciénaga Área con suelo blando y húmedo donde crece musgo.

boomtown/*boomtown* Pueblo que crece rápidamente, generalmente ubicado cerca de un lugar donde se descubre oro o plata.

borrow/pedir prestado Tomar y usar algo con el compromiso de devolverlo en otro momento.

boundary/límite Línea o formación natural que divide un área o un estado de otro.

boycott/boicot El hecho de negarse a comprar o usar algo.

C

camouflage/camuflaje Acción de ocultarse o mezclarse con los alrededores.

canal/canal Vía de navegación que se cava para transportar agua para los cultivos o para que lo transiten barcos.

candidate/candidato Persona que se postula para cierto trabajo o cargo.

canyon/cañón Valle con laderas empinadas y rocosas.

capital resource/recurso de capital Algo que las personas hacen para producir otros productos.

cardinal direction/punto cardinal Una de las cuatro direcciones principales de la rosa de los vientos: norte, sur, este y oeste.

Central Plains/Llanuras Centrales Llanuras que ocupan el este de la región del Medio Oeste.

Central Valley/valle Central Valle extenso ubicado en el centro de California.

checks and balances/sistema de controles y equilibrio División de poderes en una democracia que da a cada poder del gobierno (el ejecutivo, el legislativo y el judicial) alguna forma de autoridad sobre los otros.

citizen/ciudadano Miembro de una ciudad, un estado o un país que tiene derechos y responsabilidades por ley.

civil rights/derechos civiles Derechos que deben tener todas las personas.

claim/reclamación Declaración oficial de poseer algo, como un terreno.

cliff dwelling/vivienda en los acantilados Casa construida en acantilados.

climate/clima Patrón de tiempo de un área durante un período largo.

Cold War/Guerra Fría Conflicto entre los Estados Unidos y la Unión Soviética por sus ideas económicas y políticas.

colony/colonia Asentamiento gobernado por otro país.

combine/combinar Unir.

command economy/economía dirigida Economía en la que el gobierno decide qué bienes y servicios se pueden vender.

commerce/comercio Compra y venta de bienes.

commodity/bien de consumo Bien económico, como el petróleo, el gas natural o el cobre.

communism/comunismo Sistema político y económico en el que el gobierno posee toda la tierra y la mayor parte de las industrias en nombre del pueblo.

compass rose/rosa de los vientos Símbolo en un mapa que muestra las direcciones.

compromise/acuerdo Trato.

confederation/confederación Unión de estados que acuerdan cooperar.

congress/congreso Grupo de personas responsable de la creación de las leyes de un país.

consequence/consecuencia Efecto o resultado de un suceso.

conserve/conservar Limitar el uso de algo.

considerable/considerable Bastante grande o importante.

constitution/constitución Plan de gobierno.

consumer/consumidor Alguien que compra o usa bienes y servicios.

contribute/contribuir Dar.

control/control Poder, o mando sobre algo o alguien.

convince/convencer Persuadir.

cooperate/cooperar Trabajar en conjunto para lograr el mismo objetivo.

craft/manualidad Objeto hecho a mano.

create/crear Hacer que algo ocurra como resultado de una acción.

critical/crítico De gran importancia.

crop rotation/rotación de cultivos Plantación de diferentes cultivos en diferentes años.

crucial/crucial De gran importancia.

culture/cultura Forma de vida de un grupo de personas.

currency/moneda corriente Dinero que se usa en un país.

D

define/definir Explicar o describir de una manera específica.

degree/grado Unidad de medida. Hay 360 grados de latitud y longitud que se usan para localizar lugares en la Tierra.

delegate/delegado Alguien que representa a un grupo de personas.

demand/demanda Cantidad de cierto producto o servicio que los consumidores desean.

democracy/democracia Gobierno en el que los ciudadanos tienen el poder de tomar decisiones políticas.

depend/depender Confiar.

depression/depresión Época en la que la actividad comercial decae y mucha gente no tiene empleo.

desert/desierto Área que recibe menos de diez pulgadas de lluvia por año.

develop/desarrollar Crecer.

diverse/diverso Que muestra mucha variedad.

division of labor/división del trabajo Dividir un trabajo entre varios trabajadores especializados.

drought/sequía Largo período en el que hay poca lluvia o nada.

E

economy/economía Manera en que se usan los recursos de un lugar para producir bienes y servicios.

elevation/altitud Altura sobre el nivel del mar.

emancipation/emancipación Acción de liberar a alguien o liberar algo.

endangered species/especie en peligro de extinción Tipo de planta o animal que corre riesgo de desaparecer.

enforce/hacer cumplir Obligar a las personas a obedecer las leyes y reglas.

enslaved/esclavizado Que trabaja sin paga ni libertad.

ensure/garantizar Dar seguridad o certeza.

entrepreneur/empresario Persona que arriesga dinero y tiempo para crear una empresa nueva.

equator/ecuador Línea imaginaria que rodea la Tierra en un punto medio entre el Polo Norte y el Polo Sur.

erosion/erosión Proceso por el que el viento y el agua desgastan la roca.

essential/esencial Absolutamente necesario.

establish/fundar Crear, organizar.

evacuation/evacuación Acción de llevar a una persona a un lugar seguro.

executive branch/poder ejecutivo Parte del gobierno encargada de ejecutar las leyes; el o la presidente de los Estados Unidos y sus funcionarios.

export/exportar Vender algo a otro país.

extensive/amplio De gran alcance.

extinct/extinto Que ya no existe.

F

factor/factor Causa.

fall line/línea de cascadas Línea de cataratas, como el lugar donde un piedemonte se encuentra con una llanura costera.

fascism/fascismo Forma de gobierno que entrega todo el poder al estado, elimina las libertades individuales y usa el ejército para hacer cumplir la ley.

favorable/favorable Aceptable o adecuado.

feature/característica Parte o cualidad.

flood plain/terreno inundable Llanura que se forma debido a las inundaciones a la largo de un río.

folklore/folklore Tradiciones y creencias de un grupo de personas.

fossil fuel/combustible fósil Combustible formado en la tierra a partir de los restos de plantas y animales.

free enterprise system/sistema de libre empresa Economía en la que las personas son libres de crear sus propias empresas o producir el bien o el servicio que desean.

G

generate/generar Producir o crear.

geography/geografía Estudio de la Tierra.

geyser/géiser Fuente de agua caliente subterránea que lanza vapor y agua hirviendo al aire.

glacier/glaciar Enorme manto de hielo que cubre la tierra.

globe/globo terráqueo Modelo de la Tierra en forma de esfera.

gold rush/fiebre del oro Movimiento rápido de gente hacia un lugar en el que se ha descubierto oro.

gray water/aguas grises Agua reciclada.

Great Plains/Grandes Llanuras Extensa área de llanuras al oeste de las Montañas Rocosas.

grid/cuadrícula Sistema de líneas que se cruzan unas con otras y forman un patrón de cuadrados. En un mapa, las cuadrículas se usan para localizar lugares.

growing season/temporada de cultivo Período en el que la temperatura es lo suficientemente alta para que crezcan plantas.

guarantee/garantizar Asegurar algo.

Gullah/gullah Grupo de personas del Sureste que han conservado gran parte de su herencia africana.

gusher/pozo surtidor Pozo de petróleo que produce una gran cantidad de petróleo.

H

hemisphere/hemisferio Una mitad de la Tierra.

heritage/herencia Costumbres y tradiciones de un grupo cultural que se han pasado de padres a hijos.

high-tech/alta tecnología La tecnología más moderna.

homestead/finca Tierra que el gobierno de los Estados Unidos otorgaba a los colonos con la condición de que vivieran y cultivaran allí.

hub/eje Centro de actividad.

human resource/recurso humano Persona que hace productos o brinda servicios.

humidity/humedad Cantidad de agua en el aire.

hunter-gatherer/cazador-recolector Alguien que caza animales y recolecta plantas silvestres para obtener alimento.

hurricane/huracán Tormenta arremolinada muy fuerte con lluvias y vientos que soplan a más de 74 millas por hora.

hydroelectric power/energía hidroeléctrica Energía producida por la fuerza del agua que fluye.

I

immigrant/inmigrante Alguien que llega de un país a otro país.

import/importar Traer algo de otro país para venderlo.

impress/impresionar Asombrar o impactar.

incentive/incentivo Algo que nos anima a entrar en acción o hacer algo.

income/ingreso Dinero que una persona o una empresa gana por hacer un trabajo o proveer un bien o servicio.

indentured servant/siervo por contrato
Persona que acepta trabajar sin paga
durante un período determinado a cambio
de la satisfacción de sus necesidades.

independence/independencia Liberación
del dominio de otros.

individual/individuo Un único ser humano.

industry/industria Parte de la economía
que se relaciona con el uso de máquinas
para hacer las tareas.

inflation/inflación Aumento en el precio
usual de muchos bienes y servicios.

influence/influir Tener un efecto o impacto.

initial/inicial Al principio.

innovation/innovación Nuevos inventos o
nuevas ideas.

intent/decidido Concentrado en un objetivo
específico.

interdependent/interdependientes
Cuando las naciones dependen unas de
otras para obtener bienes, servicios o
recursos.

interest/interés Pequeña tarifa que se paga
a los clientes de los bancos a cambio
de usar su dinero; tarifa que los bancos
cobran por prestar dinero.

**intermediate direction/punto cardinal
intermedio** Cualquiera de las cuatro
direcciones que están entre los puntos
cardinales: noreste, noroeste, sureste y
suroeste.

**international trade/comercio
internacional** Comercio entre países.

interstate highway/carretera interestatal
Carretera que conecta estados.

involve/comprender Tener en cuenta;
incluir.

irrigation/irrigación Proceso de llevar agua a
las tierras, generalmente mediante acequias
y canales.

J

jazz/jazz Tipo de música de origen
afroamericano.

judicial branch/poder judicial Parte del
gobierno que decide lo que significan las
leyes y se asegura de que las leyes se
apliquen con justicia.

junction/confluencia (ríos) Punto donde
varias cosas, como los ríos, se unen.

jury/jurado Panel de ciudadanos comunes
que toman decisiones en una corte.

K

key/cayo Isla baja.

L

labor union/sindicato Grupo de
trabajadores que intentan obtener
mejores sueldos y condiciones de trabajo.

landform/accidente geográfico Formación
natural de la superficie de la Tierra.

latitude/latitud Líneas que miden la
distancia al norte y al sur del ecuador.

legislative branch/poder legislativo Parte
del gobierno que crea las leyes.

levee/dique Barrera de tierra que se
construye para evitar las inundaciones.

liberty/libertad Posibilidad de autogobernarse.

lighthouse/faro Torre alta con una luz muy brillante que se usa para guiar a los barcos durante la noche.

limit/limitar Controlar.

livestock/ganado Animales criados en granjas y ranchos para el uso humano.

longitude/longitud Líneas que miden la distancia al este y al oeste del primer meridiano.

M

magma/magma Roca derretida que está debajo de la superficie de la Tierra.

maintain/mantener Preservar; continuar.

manufacturing/manufacturación Proceso de elaborar bienes usando máquinas, por lo general en las fábricas.

map legend/leyenda del mapa Recuadro que explica lo que representan los símbolos del mapa.

map scale/escala del mapa Símbolo que muestra la relación entre la distancia que se ve en el mapa y la distancia en la Tierra.

market economy/economía de mercado Sistema de libre empresa en el que la oferta y la demanda determinan los bienes y los servicios.

mastery/maestría Gran conocimiento o destreza en un área particular.

meat-packing/empacadora de carne Algo que procesa la carne de los animales para poder comerla.

mesa/mesa Accidente geográfico con cima plana que tiene pendientes en todos sus lados.

metropolitan area/área metropolitana Ciudad grande y área que la rodea.

mineral/mineral Material sin vida que se encuentra en la tierra.

mission/misión Asentamiento establecido por un grupo religioso para enseñar religión y ayudar a la gente del lugar.

missionary/misionero Persona enviada a una nueva tierra para difundir su religión.

monitor/monitorear Controlar.

N

natural gas/gas natural Combustible fósil, como el petróleo.

natural resource/recurso natural Algo que existe en el medio ambiente y que las personas pueden usar.

nocturnal/nocturno Activo durante la noche.

nomad/nómada Persona que se traslada de un lugar a otro para sobrevivir.

nonrenewable/no renovable Recurso que no se puede reemplazar.

Northwest Ordinance/Decreto del Noroeste Ley que determinaba cómo el Territorio del Noroeste se dividiría en estados.

notable/notable Que llama la atención.

nutrient/nutriente Sustancias que ayudan a las plantas a crecer.

O

occupy/ocupar Llenar un espacio.

opportunity cost/costo de oportunidad Valor de algo que debes resignar para obtener lo que quieres.

oppose/oponerse Estar en contra de algo.

oral/oral Hablado.

organize/organizarse Formar un grupo.

outsourcing/subcontratación Cuando las compañías contratan gente para que trabaje fuera de la compañía.

overfishing/sobrepesca Cuando se capturan peces sin dar tiempo a que los procesos naturales puedan reemplazarlos.

P

pace/ritmo Velocidad a la que algo se mueve o crece.

Pacific Rim/Cuenca del Pacífico Área geográfica formada por los países que limitan con el océano Pacífico.

participate/participar Ser parte de una actividad.

patent/patente Documento del gobierno que le da a un inventor el derecho de producir y vender un invento.

patriotism/patriotismo Sentimiento de orgullo y apoyo que un pueblo siente por su país.

peninsula/península Porción de tierra rodeada de agua casi por completo.

permit/permitir Dejar hacer algo.

perspective/perspectiva Punto de vista; opinión.

petition/petición Solicitud formal.

petrified/petrificado Transformado en fósil.

physical map/mapa físico Mapa que muestra la información geográfica de un lugar, como accidentes geográficos y masas de agua.

piedmont/piedemonte Terreno alto que está cerca de las montañas.

pioneer/pionero Persona de un grupo que es la primera en establecerse en un área.

plantation/plantación Granja grande con muchos trabajadores.

plateau/meseta Área de tierra extensa, llana y elevada.

plow/arado Herramienta agrícola tirada por un tractor o un animal que se usa para remover el suelo.

political map/mapa político Mapa que muestra información como los límites estatales, las fronteras internacionales, las capitales y las ciudades importantes.

pollution/contaminación Desechos químicos o físicos que hacen que el aire, el agua y la tierra estén sucios.

population density/densidad demográfica Medida de cuántas personas, en promedio, viven en cada milla cuadrada de tierra en un área determinada.

port/puerto Lugar por donde pueden entrar o salir personas y bienes de un país.

prairie/pradera Área en la que el pasto crece bien, pero hay pocos árboles.

precipitation/precipitación Cantidad de humedad que cae en forma de lluvia o nieve.

prefer/preferir Elegir algo porque gusta más que otra cosa.

primary source/fuente primaria Fuente que fue creada o escrita por alguien que presenció un suceso.

prime meridian/primer meridiano La línea de longitud marcada como 0°, trazada desde el Polo Norte hasta el Polo Sur, que divide la Tierra en el hemisferio occidental y el hemisferio oriental.

private property/propiedad privada Tierra o bienes que poseen las personas y las compañías.

process/procesar Usar una serie de acciones para hacer algo.

produce/producir Hacer.

producer/productor Persona que fabrica un bien u ofrece un servicio para venderlo.

product/producto Artículo que las personas hacen o siembran.

productive/productivo Que puede producir grandes cantidades de bienes.

productivity/productividad Cantidad de bienes o servicios que los trabajadores de una compañía pueden producir u ofrecer.

profit/ganancia Dinero que le queda a una empresa una vez que se han pagado todos los gastos.

promote/promocionar Hacer ampliamente conocido.

protect/proteger Mantener a salvo.

provide/proporcionar Dar algo o hacer que esté disponible.

pueblo/pueblo Aldea; grupo indígena americano del Suroeste.

pulp/pulpa Mezcla de astillas molidas, agua y productos químicos que se usa para producir papel.

purpose/propósito La razón por la que algo existe.

pursue/seguir Perseguir.

Q

quarry/cantera Lugar donde la roca o el mármol se extrae de la tierra, ya sea desenterrándola, cortándola o por medio de explosiones.

R

radiant/radiante Brillante.

rain shadow/sombra orográfica Área, como el lado de una cordillera, que recibe menos precipitaciones que el otro lado.

ranch/rancho Granja de gran tamaño donde se cría ganado.

ratify/ratificar Aprobar oficialmente.

recall/rememorar Recordar.

Reconstruction/Reconstrucción Período de reorganización después de la Guerra Civil durante el que los estados del Sur volvieron a la Unión.

refinery/refinería Fábrica que separa el petróleo crudo en distintos grupos de sustancias químicas.

reforest/reforestar Plantar árboles nuevos para reemplazar los que se talaron.

region/región Área extensa en la que los lugares comparten características similares.

renewable/renovable Recurso natural que se puede reemplazar.

republic/república Tipo de gobierno en el que el pueblo elige a los líderes que lo representan.

require/requerir Necesitar.

reservation/reserva Territorio que se aparta para que los indígenas americanos vivan en él.

reservoir/embalse Lago donde se almacena agua.

restore/recuperarse Recobrar la salud.

reveal/revelar Hacer que algo se sepa.

rivalry/rivalidad Competencia por la superioridad.

ruins/ruinas Restos de algo muy dañado o destruido.

rural/rural Perteneciente a los pueblos pequeños o a las granjas.

S

sachem/sachem Jefe o líder entre algunos grupos indígenas americanos.

savanna/sabana Pastizal con pocos árboles.

scarcity/escasez Poca cantidad de algo.

secede/separarse Dejar o abandonar algo oficialmente.

secondary source/fuente secundaria Fuente que fue escrita o creada por alguien que no presenció un suceso.

seek/buscar Intentar conseguir, encontrar o descubrir algo.

segregation/segregación Sistema en el cual las personas de diferentes razas deben mantenerse separadas.

self-evident/evidente Algo que no hace falta explicar ni demostrar, como los derechos básicos.

semiarid/semiárido Clima seco con un poco de lluvias.

shortage/carencia Situación en la que no se puede obtener algo que se necesita.

significant/significativo Muy importante.

silicon/silicio Material que se obtiene de las rocas y la arena y que se usa para fabricar computadoras.

situate/situar Ubicar en un lugar particular.

sound/sonda Extenso canal de agua marina que separa una isla de tierra firme.

sovereignty/soberanía Derecho a gobernar.

specialization/especialización Proceso en el que cada trabajador realiza una sola tarea en el proceso de producción.

states' rights/poder de los estados Idea de que el poder de los estados debe protegerse del poder del gobierno federal y de que cada estado debe resolver sus propios problemas.

steamboat/barco de vapor Barco con un motor que funciona a vapor.

storm surge/marejada ciclónica Aumento del nivel del mar a causa de una tormenta.

suffrage/sufragio Derecho a votar.

supply/oferta Cantidad de bienes o servicios disponibles para que el consumidor compre o contrate.

surround/rodear Estar alrededor de algo.

survive/sobrevivir Seguir viviendo.

sweatshop/taller donde se explota al obrero Fábrica donde los obreros trabajan muchas horas por poco dinero.

symbol/símbolo Algo que significa o representa otra cosa.

T

task/tarea Trabajo que se debe hacer.

technology/tecnología Uso de herramientas y el conocimiento científico para hacer un trabajo.

temperature/temperatura Medida que indica qué tan caliente o frío está algo.

territory/territorio Área extensa de tierra que no contiene su propio gobierno, sino que tiene un gobierno externo. En los Estados Unidos, un territorio no tiene los mismos derechos que un estado.

terrorist/terrorista Persona que usa el miedo o el terror por motivos políticos.

timber/maderero Referido a los árboles y bosques que se plantan y cortan para obtener madera.

tornado/tornado Tormenta con vientos muy rápidos que pueden formar una nube con forma de embudo.

totem pole/poste totémico Poste alto tallado con imágenes de personas o animales para representar la historia familiar.

tourist/turista Persona que viaja por placer.

trading post/puesto de comercio Tienda o asentamiento pequeño que se instala en un lugar lejano para que se pueda comerciar.

tradition/tradición Creencia o costumbre que pasa de generación en generación.

transcontinental/transcontinental A través de un continente.

transfer/transferir Llevar de un lugar a otro; trasladar.

tsunami/maremoto Ola gigante que puede alcanzar unos 50 pies de altura y puede causar grandes daños cuando llega a la tierra.

tundra/tundra Área fría donde los árboles no crecen.

typical/típico Común o usual.

U

unalienable/inalienable Que nadie puede negarlo, como los derechos inalienables.

urban/urbano Perteneciente a la ciudad.

V

varied/alterado Diferente o cambiado.

vineyard/viñedo Granja donde se cultivan uvas.

volcano/volcán Apertura en la corteza de la Tierra causada cuando la roca derretida empuja hacia la superficie.

W

watershed/cuenca hidrológica Zona drenada por un río o un grupo de ríos.

weather/tiempo Condición del aire en un cierto momento y lugar.

wetland/humedal Zona donde el agua está sobre la superficie del suelo o cerca de ella; por ejemplo un pantano o una marisma.

wetu/wetu Casa de los indígenas americanos hecha con postes de madera y cubierta con cortezas de árboles o alfombras de junco.

Index

This index lists the pages on which topics appear in this book. Page numbers followed by *m* refer to maps. Page numbers followed by *p* refer to photographs. Page numbers followed by *c* refer to charts or graphs. Page numbers followed by *t* refer to timelines. Bold page numbers indicate vocabulary definitions. The terms **See** and **See also** direct the reader to alternate entries.

Credits

Text Acknowledgments

Rosa Parks
Quote from Rosa Parks. Copyright © Rosa Parks.

Marjorie Stoneman Douglas
Quote by Marjory Stoneman Douglas, The Everglades: River of Grass, 1947. Copyright © Marjorie Stoneman Douglas.

Robert Moffet
Quote by Robert Moffet. Copyright © Robert Moffet.

Bill Gates
Quote by Bill Gates. Copyright © Bill Gates.

Henry Ford
Quote by Henry Ford. From "My Life and Work" by Henry Ford. Copyright © Henry Ford.

Baylor University
Quote from Martha Roane Lacy Howe. From the Oral Memories of Martha Roane Lacy Howe. Copyright © Baylor University .

Candace Savage
Quote by Candice Savage. From James R. Page, Wild Prairie: A Photographer's Personal Journey (2005). Published by Greystone Books, Vancouver.

Samuel T. Jones III
They Dance for Rain and Rainbows Song Lyrics About Pueblo Indians. Copyright © Sam Jones. Reprinted by permission.

Howard Berkes
Quote by Howard Berkes about Mount St. Helens eruption. Copyright © Howard Berkes.

Ansel Adams
Quote by Ansel Adams. From "The Portfolios of Ansel Adams" Copyright © Ansel Adams.

Peratrovich, Elizabeth
Quote by Elizabeth Peratrovich From "Alaska Native Brotherhood". Copyright © Elizabeth Peratrovich.

The Bancroft Library
Interview with Harold Zellerbach, 1971 by Harriet Nathan of the Oral History Center of the Bancroft Library. Copyright © The Bancroft Library.

The New York Times
"A Farm-Bread Unionis"t from The New York Times, March 11, 1968. Copyright © The New York Times Company

Harper Collins Publishers
Dragon's Gate by Laurence Yep. Copyright © Harper Collins Publishers.

The Nation
Dubious Battle in California from The Nation, September 12, 1936 by John Steinbeck. Copyright © The Nation.

Ochoa, Ellen
Quote by Astronaut Ellen Ochoa. Copyright © Ellen Ochoa

Little, Brown and Company
By the Great Horn Spoon! by Sid Fleischmann. Copyright © Little, Brown and Company.

IMDb.com, Inc.
Quote by Louis B Mayer. Copyright © Louis Mayer.

Arthur C Clarke
Quote by Arthur C. Clark. From "Hazards of Prophecy: The Failure of Imagination", 1973. Copyright © Arthur C. Clarke.

John Lewis
Quote by John Lewis. From "Speech at the March on Washington", 28 August 1963 . Copyright © by John Lewis.

Images

Cover
CVR: Hill Street Studios/Eric Raptosh/Getty Images

Front Matter
SSH1TL: Daniel Dempster Photography/Alamy Stock Photo; SSH1TR: Marek Lipka-Kadaj/Alamy Stock Photo; SSH1BL: David trevor/Alamy Stock Photo; SSH1BR: jsouthby/Masterfile; SSH2T: Oleksiy Maksymenko/imageBROKER/Alamy Stock Photo; SSH2B: D. Hurst/Alamy Stock Photo; SSH13: LordRunar/iStock/Getty Images; SSH14: North Wind Picture Archives/Alamy Stock Photo; SSH16: Asiseeit/E+/Getty Images; SSH17: Glasshouse Images/Alamy Stock Photo; SSH19 Buddy Mays/Alamy Stock Photo; SSH21: Historical /Corbis Historical/Getty Images;

Chapter 01
001: Kevin Smith/Design Pics/First Light/Getty Images; 003TL: Jeff McGraw/Shutterstock; 003TR: Peter Unger/Lonely Planet Images/Getty Images; 003C: Ron_Thomas/E+/Getty Images; 003BL: Anton Foltin/Shutterstock; 003BR: Jay Yuan/Shutterstock; 012: Greg Vaughn/Alamy Stock Photo; 011: Jupiterimages/Stockbyte/Getty Images; 014R: Shironosov/iStock/Getty Images; 014L: Alistair Berg/DigitalVision/Getty Images; 019: Stephen Simpson/Taxi/Getty Images; 022: James L. Stanfield/National Geographic/Getty Images; 023: Rick Dalton/Passage/Getty Images; 024L: Mevans/E+/Getty Images; 024R: Hero Images/Getty Images; 025L: Bram van

Broekhoven/Shutterstock; 025R: Jeff Greenberg/UIG//
Getty Images; 026: Lori Adamski Peek/ The Image Bank/
Getty Images; 028: Divanov/Shutterstock; 029: Education
Images/Citizens of the Planet/UIG/Getty Images; 030:
Horsemen/Shutterstock; 031: Brenda Carson/Shutterstock;
032: Pierre Longnus/Photographer's Choice/Getty
Images; 035: Matt_Brown/iStock/Getty Images; 036T:
Kevin Fleming/Corbis Documentary/Getty Images; 036B:
Romrodphoto/Shutterstock; 037TL: Greg Vaughn/Alamy
Stock Photo; 037TR: Alistair Berg/DigitalVision/Getty
Images; 037BL: James L. Stanfield/National Geographic/
Getty Images; 037BR: Divanov/Shutterstock;

Chapter 02

042-043: Sean Pavone/Alamy Stock Photo; 044: Prisma
Archivo/Alamy Stock Photo; 045BL: Niday Picture Library/
Alamy Stock Photo; 045BR: William Philpott/Hulton Archive/
Getty Images; 045TL: World History Archive/Alamy Stock
Photo; 045TR: Archive Images/Alamy Stock Photo; 048: W.
Langdon Kihn/National Geographic Creative/Alamy Stock
Photo; 051: Lynn Seldon/Danita Delimont/Alamy Stock Photo;
056: World History Archive/Alamy Stock Photo; 058: North
Wind Picture Archives/Alamy Stock Photo; 059: World History
Archive/Alamy Stock Photo; 062: Harold R. Stinnette Photo
Stock/Alamy Stock Photo; 064: North Wind Picture Archives;
065: Pony Express Poster, 1861 (litho), American School, (19th
century)/Private Collection/Peter Newark American Pictures/
Bridgeman Images; 066T: North Wind Picture Archives/Alamy
Stock Photo; 066B: GL Archive/Alamy Stock Photo; 067:
Archive Images/Alamy Stock Photo; 068: Courtesy Everett
Collection/Everett Collection Inc/Alamy Stock Photo; 069:
Niday Picture Library/Alamy Stock Photo; 070: Stephen Saks
Photography/Alamy Stock Photo; 072: Granger, NYC; 074T:
American Photo Archive/Alamy Stock Photo; 074TC: Everett
Collection Inc/Alamy Stock Photo; 074BC: Everett Collection
Historical/Alamy Stock Photo; 074B: PF-(bygone1)/Alamy
Stock Photo; 075: Everett Collection Historical/Alamy Stock
Photo; 076: Myles Santiago/Shutterstock; 078: B Christopher/
Alamy Stock Photo; 080: Everett Collection Historical/Alamy
Stock Photo; 081L: Courtesy: CSU Archives/Everett Collection
Inc/Alamy Stock Photo; 081C: Peter Turnley/Corbis/VCG/Getty
Images; 081R: Evelyn Hofer/Masters/Getty Images; 082: US
Marines Photo/Alamy Stock Photo; 084T: Pictorial Press Ltd/
Alamy Stock Photo; 084B: PF-(usna)/Alamy Stock Photo;

Chapter 03

090-091: Lissandra Melo/Shutterstock; 092: Orhan Cam/
Shutterstock; 093TL: GL Archive/Alamy Stock Photo; 093BL:
WDC Photos/Alamy Stock Photo; 093BR: Jeff Hutchens/
Getty Images; 093TR: Sam Harrel/Fairbanks Daily News-Miner/
ZUMA Press Inc/Alamy Stock Photo; 095: Tony Freeman/
PhotoEdit; 096: Ariel Skelley/Blend Images/Alamy Images; 097:
DanielBendjy/E+/Getty Images; 098: Painting/Alamy Stock
Photo; 099: Susan Law Cain/Shutterstock; 100: Ian Dagnall/
Alamy Stock Photo; 102T: Ian Dagnall Computing/Alamy Stock
Photo; 102B: Art Reserve/Alamy Stock Photo; 104: Andrew
Harrer/Bloomberg/Getty Images; 107: Kristoffer Tripplaar/

Alamy Stock Photo; 115: Education Images/Universal Images
Group North America LLC/Alamy Stock Photo; 116: George
Nazlis/Alamy Stock Vector; 117: 123RF; 119: Eye35/Alamy
Stock Photo; 120T: Ron Sachs/dpa picture alliance archive/
Alamy Stock Photo; 120B: Blakeley/Alamy Stock Photo; 122:
RosaIreneBetancourt 14/Alamy Stock Photo;

Chapter 04

126-127: Fuse/Corbis/Getty Images; 129TL: FineArt/Alamy
Stock Photo; 129TR: Xinhua/Alamy Stock Photo; 129BL:
Chitose Suzuki/Boston Herald; 129BR: Hulton Archive/Getty
Images; 132: Iakov Filimonov/Shutterstock; 134: Jim West/
Alamy Stock Photo; 136T: FineArt/Alamy Stock Photo; 136BL:
Patti McConville/Alamy Stock Photo; 136BR: Jim Parkin/Alamy
Stock Photo; 140: MPI/Stringer/ Archive Photos/Getty Images;
141: Basque Country - Mark Baynes/Alamy Stock Photo; 142:
Zoonar/monticello/Alamy Stock Photo; 143: Chitose Suzuki/
Boston Herald; 144L: Cathyrose Melloan/Alamy Stock Photo;
144R: Rick Friedman/ Corbis News/Getty Images; 145: ZUMA
Press, Inc./Alamy Stock Photo; 146: Kate_sept2004/E+/Getty
Images; 150: Xinhua/Alamy Stock Photo; 152: Jay Paull/
Archive Photos/Getty Images; 154: Travel mania/Shutterstock;
157T: Hulton Archive/Getty Images; 157B: Ricardo Funari/
BrazilPhotos/Alamy Stock Photo; 160-161: Ewing Galloway/
Alamy Stock Photo; 162T: Dennis Brack/Danita Delimont/Alamy
Stock Photo; 162B: Randy Duchaine/Alamy Stock Photo;164:
Steve Skjold/Alamy Stock Photo;

Chapter 05

168-169: Sergey Borisov/Alamy Stock Photo; 171TL: Wim
Wiskerke/Alamy Stock Photo; 171TR: Paul Fearn/Alamy Stock
Photo; 171BL: Everett Collection Inc/Alamy Stock Photo;
171BR: Paul Fearn/Alamy Stock Photo; 174: Christian Goupi/
age Fotostock; 176: DOD Photo/Alamy Stock Photo; 178:
Images-USA/Alamy Stock Photo; 179: Clarence Holmes
Photography/Alamy Stock Photo; 180: age fotostock/Alamy
Stock Photo; 181: Ray Warren NYC/Alamy Stock Photo; 182:
Alan Gignoux/Alamy Stock Photo; 184: Jannis Werner/Alamy
Stock Photo; 185: Roman Tiraspolsky/Shutterstock; 186: David
Lyons/Alamy Stock Photo; 188L: IanDagnall Computing/Alamy
Stock Photo; 188C: Paul Fearn/Alamy Stock Photo; 188R: Paul
Fearn/Alamy Stock Photo; 189L: Niday Picture Library/Alamy
Stock Photo; 189C: Wim Wiskerke/Alamy Stock Photo; 189R:
Paul Fearn/Alamy Stock Photo; 190: Sarin Images/Granger,
NYC; 191: Pictorial Press Ltd/Alamy Stock Photo; 192: North
Wind Picture Archives/Alamy Stock Photo; 195: European
immigrants passing the Statue of Liberty in New York Harbour,
1892 (coloured engraving), American School, (19th century)/
Private Collection/Peter Newark American Pictures/Bridgeman
Images; 196: David Cole/Alamy Stock Photo; 198: North Wind
Picture Archives/Alamy Stock Photo; 199: North Wind Picture
Archives/Alamy Stock Photo; 200-201: Washington Imaging/
Alamy Stock Photo; 202-203: Tom Croke/Alamy Stock Photo;
204: Heath Oldham/Shutterstock; 205L: Ian Dagnall/Alamy
Stock Photo; 205R: Batchelder/Alamy Stock Photo; 206: Andre
Jenny/Alamy Stock Photo; 208: SpeedKingz/Shutterstock;
210T: Everett Collection Inc/Alamy Stock Photo; 210B: Jacob